SIXTH EDITION

Eight
Modern Essayists

SIXTH EDITION

Eight Modern Essayists

WILLIAM SMART

VIRGINIA CENTER
FOR THE CREATIVE ARTS

ST. MARTIN'S PRESS

New York

Editor: Nancy Lyman
Revisions editor: Edward Hutchinson
Development editor: Sam Potts
Manager, publishing services: Emily Berleth
Publishing services associate: Kalea Chapman
Project management: Omega Publishing Services, Inc.
Art director: Sheree Goodman
Text design: Anna George
Cover design: Nadia Furlan-Lorbek
Cover art: Nadia Furlan-Lorbek

For information, write:
St. Martin's Press, Inc.
175 Fifth Avene
New York, NY 10010

ISBN: 0-312-10125-2

ACKNOWLEDGMENTS

Acknowledgments and copyrights are continued at the back of the book on pages 344–346, which constitute an extension of the copyright page.

It is a violation of the law to reproduce these selections by any means whatsoever without the written permission of the copyright holder.

"The Death of a Moth" and "Professions for Women" from *The Death of a Moth and Other Essays* by Virginia Woolf, copyright 1942 by Harcourt Brace & Company and renewed 1970 by Marjorie T. Parsons, Executrix, reprinted by permission of the publisher.

For Paul Matthews

Preface

E*IGHT MODERN ESSAYISTS* CONTINUES, in its thirtieth year and sixth edition, with the intent of giving students the opportunity to become comfortably familiar with several essays by a select group of outstanding writers, in the belief that through such familiarity their own writing will greatly improve. Reading this collection, students come to realize that all writers have distinct, personal styles and interests and, consequently, that there is no one way of writing that is "correct." Any style that a writer pursues with intelligence and integrity is perfectly valid. Writers as different as Virginia Woolf and Cynthia Ozick, or James Baldwin and James McConkey, nevertheless form a coherent collection in this book due to the high quality of their writing and their personal yet rigorous approaches to the form. The stylistic variety of these essayists has the added benefit that students can develop an eclectic taste in writers, and their reading will also carry over into the other books these writers have produced.

It is my goal with each new edition that the quality of essays will remain high while new writers add fresh views and interesting styles to the collection. I am confident that this edition maintains the level of quality that instructors have come to expect in *Eight Modern Essayists,* a level against which many other books measure themselves. James Baldwin appears once again in this collection; the removal of his work in the fifth edition raised many voices asking for his reinstatement. New to this edition are Cynthia Ozick and James McConkey. Ozick brings a strong urban voice with a distinctly literary sensibility. Her essays in this collection should broaden students' view of the form while emphasizing the sort of personal connections to the world that are the hallmark of *Eight Modern Essayists.* James McConkey's essays are intensely personal and very finely crafted works. I am particularly excited about including McConkey's essays because, while he is less well-known than the other writers, I look forward to having other instructors and students share the pleasure I had in discovering this strong and unique writer.

This edition represents a somewhat greater revision than previous ones, as I have replaced three writers rather than the usual two. The unfortunate effect of each new edition is that some writers must be dropped in order to provide space for new writers. Lewis Thomas, Paul Fussell, and Carol Bly are all worthy writers and they continue to be represented in this edition in the sampler section. As in the fifth edition, "A Sampler of Essays from Previous Editions" contains one piece by each of the writers who have been replaced in previous editions.

The real pleasure of editing *Eight Modern Essayists* for me has been the opportunity to introduce wonderful writers and a wonderful form to students, in the hope that reading those writers will not only improve their writing, but also affect their lives in positive and important ways. Students who enjoy the writers included here, I believe, will work harder and more enthusiastically to become better writers themselves. Better than anyone else, writers—especially essayists—teach us the power of honesty, of telling the truth about things, and this should be the ultimate goal of learning to write.

Contents

Contents

Contents

A Note to Students

GOOD WRITING BEGINS WITH KNOW-ing what good writing is, and the only way to do that is by reading the best writers who have preceded you. There is a classic statement on the subject by the seventeenth-century playwright Ben Jonson:

> It is fit for the beginner and learner to study others and the best. For the mind and memory are more sharply exercised in comprehending another man's things than our own; and such as accustom themselves and are familiar with the best authors shall ever and anon find somewhat of them in themselves.

You learn several things when you read a number of pieces by the same author: first, that he or she has a point of view that is fairly consistent; second, that good writers have a personal style of writing—that is to say, they have distinct "voices." It won't be long before you'll be able to tell George Orwell from Virginia Woolf or E. B. White from Joan Didion just by reading a couple of sentences. By then you will have learned that no single way of writing is better than all others. Different writers write different ways.

This collection of essays should encourage you to be bold, to try to write as well as the writers you are reading. While you may not be able to, just trying will make you a better writer. Good writing is hard work. It doesn't come easily, even for the best—indeed, *especially* for the best. You must be intelligent and perceptive and honest—and care deeply—but that is not enough. I tell students that if the writers in this collection were students in the course, they would be spending the most time on their papers, not the least.

The best writers are often the slowest, most careful writers. Because good writing often reads quickly doesn't mean it was written quickly. Keep in mind that the time you spend writing is never wasted time; you just don't realize when you're making progress. It's so slow sometimes. But good teachers will always give you a chance to write well if you are sincere about wanting to.

This is a book of essays for people who want to write well.

SIXTH EDITION

Eight
Modern Essayists

VIRGINIA WOOLF

The Bettmann Archive, Inc.

PERHAPS NO ENGLISH WRITER EVER GREW UP as surrounded by books, writers, and the affluence that makes culture possible as Virginia Woolf. At the time of her birth (in London in 1882) her father, Leslie Stephen, was already distinguished as a philosopher, critic, and editor of the *Cornhill Magazine.* His first wife had been Thackeray's youngest daughter; his second, Virginia's mother, was descended from French nobility. Meredith, Hardy, and Henry James were his close friends, as was James Russell Lowell, who accepted the invitation to be Virginia's godfather by sending along some verses that expressed the wish that "the child would be/ A sample of heredity." Later that same year Leslie Stephen was named editor of the *Dictionary of National Biography,* and it was in the presence of that enormous undertaking that Virginia was educated. Instead of being sent to school, she was simply turned loose in her father's library, and the breadth of the knowledge she gained therein reveals itself in nearly all her essays.

Books, though, were not the whole of her education, and for the rest one must look to St. Ives in Cornwall, where the Stephen family went for its summer holidays. There, close by the sea, Virginia and the other Stephen children, Thoby, Vanessa, and Adrian—along with the children from their mother's first marriage—spent many happy days picnicking, boating, and playing games. In *To the Lighthouse* (1927) Virginia Woolf describes their summers in Cornwall with great fidelity.

When Sir Leslie died in 1904, the four Stephen children gave up the house at Hyde Park Gate and moved to 46 Gordon Square, Bloomsbury. Soon Thoby's friends, Lytton Strachey and Clive Bell, started coming around to carry on the discussions they had begun at Cambridge under the name of the "Midnight Society." And thus began what has since been known as the "Bloomsbury Group," by no means a formal organization, but merely a gathering of friends who believed (as their Cambridge mentor, G. E. Moore, had declared in his *Principia Ethica*) that the appreciation of beauty and the need for personal relationships were man's supreme endeavors.

After Thoby died of typhoid in Greece in 1906 and Vanessa married Clive Bell a year later, Virginia and Adrian moved to Fitzroy Square, a short distance away, and the Thursday night meetings followed them. New friends began coming—among them the art critic Roger Fry, the economist John Maynard Keynes, and E. M. Forster—until, by the late nineteen-twenties, the group was so famous that the word Bloomsbury had become synonymous with highbrow. Nor was it always used as a compliment; D. H. Lawrence called them "Blooms-berries," gilded youth, beetles that stung like scorpions.

In 1912 Virginia Stephen married Leonard Woolf, a socialist and political writer who had been one of Thoby's friends at Cambridge, and three years later she published her first novel, *The Voyage Out*. Then, in 1917, with no other intention than that of printing a few short works by themselves and their friends, purely for the fun of it, the Woolfs bought a hand printing press and set it up in the dining room of their house in Richmond. The first book they produced contained two stories, one by Virginia and the other by Leonard; a little later they published *Prelude* by Katherine Mansfield and *Poems 1919* by T. S. Eliot. What had started out as a lark suddenly became a successful business, and over the years that followed The Hogarth Press became famous as a publisher of new writers. Undoubtedly, the Woolfs made their greatest mistake as editors when they refused to publish Joyce's *Ulysses*.

In 1919 they bought the cottage Monks House in the village of Rodmell, near the River Ouse, in Sussex, and there they spent their weekends and hol-idays for the next twenty-two years. In March 1941, in a state of depression brought on both by the war and the fear that she might lose her mind and be a burden on her husband, Virginia Woolf committed suicide by drowning her-self in the Ouse. Later, her husband revealed that she had suffered several ner-vous breakdowns earlier in her life, going back as far as her mother's death in 1895.

Along with Joyce and Proust, Virginia Woolf is one of the great innovators of the modern novel, directing the reader's attention away from a sequence of outward actions and toward the complex inner lives of her characters. In her most successful novels—*Jacob's Room* (1922), *Mrs. Dalloway* (1925), *To the Lighthouse* (1927), *The Waves* (1931), and *Between the Acts* (published posthumously in 1941)—almost nothing happens on the surface of her charac-ters' lives. Instead, the action all takes place in their heads, in their responses both to each other and to the objects they are surrounded by. Time, also, changes: the chronological time of outward actions—in which morning is separated from night by a sequence of events or "actions"—is replaced by the *real* time of an alert consciousness; morning to night becomes a sequence of impressions, intuitions, memories, anticipations. In short, the conflicts between the characters all take place within their sensibilities and, because of that, the novels make large demands on the reader's perceptions.

However difficult her novels may sometimes be, as an essayist Virginia Woolf is always perfectly lucid. Seldom does she abandon her father's advice "to write in the fewest possible words, as clearly as possible, exactly what one meant." Moreover, she obviously benefited from the more than two hundred book reviews she wrote for the *Times Literary Supplement* from 1905 until a few years before her death. And yet she was never a formal, systematic critic, but rather a common reader, personal and subjective, who read "for his own pleasure rather than to impart knowledge or correct the opinions of others." And one notices that the books she loved the best and wrote the most engagingly about were not especially the classics, but all those memoirs, letters, biographies, and autobiographies of the obscure, all those "rubbish-heaps," as she put it, of "vanished moments and forgotten lives told in faltering and feeble accents. . . ." For Virginia Woolf was a novelist even when she was writing essays, and it made little difference to her if her characters came from real life or the pages of a book. All she wanted was to illuminate those lives, make them stand before us in all their vitality and confusion. Nothing else really mattered to her. "If one wishes to better the world," she once wrote, "one must, paradoxically enough, withdraw and spend more and more time fashioning one's sentences to perfection in solitude." ■

The Death of the Moth

Moths that fly by day are not properly to be called moths; they do not excite that pleasant sense of dark autumn nights and ivy-blossom which the commonest yellow-underwing asleep in the shadow of the curtain never fails to rouse in us. They are hybrid creatures, neither gay like butterflies nor sombre like their own species. Nevertheless the present specimen, with his narrow hay-coloured wings, fringed with a tassel of the same colour, seemed to be content with life. It was a pleasant morning, mid-September, mild, benignant, yet with a keener breath than that of the summer months. The plough was already scoring the field opposite the window, and where the share had been, the earth was pressed flat and gleamed with moisture. Such vigour came rolling in from the fields and the down beyond that it was difficult to keep the eyes strictly turned upon the book. The rooks too were keeping one of their annual festivities; soaring round the tree tops until it looked as if a vast net with thousands of black knots in it had been cast up into the air; which, after a few moments, sank slowly down upon the trees until every twig seemed to have a knot at the end of it. Then, suddenly, the net would be thrown into the air again in a wider circle this time, with the utmost clamour and vociferation, as though to be thrown into the air and settle slowly down upon the tree tops were a tremendously exciting experience.

The same energy which inspired the rooks, the ploughmen, the horses, and even, it seemed, the lean bare-backed downs, sent the moth fluttering from side to side of his square of the window-pane. One could not help watching him. One was, indeed, conscious of a queer feeling of pity for him. The possibilities of pleasure seemed that morning so enormous and so various that to have only a moth's part in life, and a day moth's at that, appeared a hard fate, and his zest in enjoying his meagre opportunities to the full, pathetic. He flew vigorously to one corner of his compartment, and, after waiting there a second, flew across to the other. What remained for him but to fly to a third corner and then to a fourth? That was all he could do, in spite of the size of the downs, the width of the sky, the far-off smoke of houses, and the romantic voice, now and then, of a steamer out at sea. What he could do he did. Watching him, it seemed as if a fibre, very thin but pure, of the enormous energy of the world had been thrust into his frail and diminutive body. As often as he crossed the pane, I could fancy that a thread of vital light became visible. He was little or nothing but life.

Yet, because he was so small, and so simple a form of the energy that was rolling in at the open window and driving its way through so many narrow and intricate corridors in my own brain and in those of other human beings, there was something marvelous as well as pathetic about him. It was as if someone had taken a tiny bead of pure life and decking it as lightly as possible with down and feathers, had set it dancing and zigzagging to show us the true nature of life. Thus displayed one could not get over the strangeness of it. One is apt to forget all about life, seeing it humped and bossed and garnished and cumbered so that it has to move with the greatest circumspection and dignity. Again, the thought of all that life might have been had he been born in any other shape caused one to view his simple activities with a kind of pity.

After a time, tired by his dancing apparently, he settled on the window ledge in the sun, and, the queer spectacle being at an end, I forgot about him. Then, looking up, my eye was caught by him. He was trying to resume his dancing, but seemed either so stiff or so awkward that he could only flutter to the bottom of the window-pane; and when he tried to fly across it he failed. Being intent on other matters I watched these futile attempts for a time without thinking, unconsciously waiting for him to resume his flight, as one waits for a machine, that has stopped momentarily, to start again without considering the reason of its failure. After perhaps a seventh attempt he slipped from the wooden ledge and fell, fluttering his wings, onto his back on the window sill. The helplessness of his attitude roused me. It flashed upon me he was in difficulties; he could no longer raise himself; his legs struggled vainly. But, as I stretched out a pencil, meaning to help him to right himself, it came over me that the failure and awkwardness were the approach of death. I laid the pencil down again.

The legs agitated themselves once more. I looked as if for the enemy against which he struggled. I looked out of doors. What had happened there? Presumably it was midday, and work in the fields had stopped. Stillness and quiet had replaced the previous animation. The birds had taken themselves off to feed in the brooks. The horses stood still. Yet the power was there all the same, massed outside indifferent, impersonal, not attending to anything in particular. Somehow it was opposed to the little hay-coloured moth. It was useless to try to do anything. One could only watch the extraordinary efforts made by those tiny legs against an on-coming doom which could, had it chosen, have submerged an entire city, not merely a city, but masses of human beings; nothing, I knew, had any chance against death. Nevertheless after a pause of exhaustion the legs fluttered again. It was superb this last protest, and so frantic that he succeeded at last in righting himself. One's sympathies, of course, were all on the side of life. Also, when there was nobody to care or to know, this gigantic effort on the part of an insignificant little moth, against a power of such magnitude, to retain what no one else valued or desired to keep, moved one strangely. Again, somehow, one saw life a pure bead. I lifted the pencil again, useless though I knew it to be. But even as I did so, the unmistakable tokens of death showed themselves. The body relaxed, and instantly grew stiff. The struggle was over. The insignificant little creature now knew death. As I looked at the dead moth, this minute wayside triumph of so great a force over so mean an antagonist filled me with wonder. Just as life had been strange a few minutes before, so death was now as strange. The moth having righted himself now lay most decently and uncomplainingly composed. O yes, he seemed to say, death is stronger than I am. [1942]

Shakespeare's Sister

IT WOULD HAVE BEEN IMPOSSIBLE, completely and entirely, for any woman to have written the plays of Shakespeare in the age of Shakespeare. Let me imagine, since facts are so hard to come by, what would have happened had Shakespeare had a wonderfully gifted sister, called Judith, let us say. Shakespeare himself went, very probably—his mother was an heiress—to the grammar school, where he may have learnt Latin—Ovid, Virgil and Horace—and the elements of grammar and logic. He was, it is well known, a wild boy who poached rabbits, perhaps shot a deer, and had, rather sooner than he should have done, to marry a woman in the neighbourhood, who bore him a child rather quicker than was right. That escapade sent him to seek his fortune in London. He had, it seemed, a taste for the theatre; he began by holding horses at the stage door. Very soon he got work in the theatre, became a successful actor, and lived at the hub of the universe, meeting everybody, knowing everybody, practising his art on the boards, exercising his wits in the streets, and even getting access to the palace of the queen. Meanwhile his extraordinarily gifted sister, let us suppose, remained at home. She was as adventurous, as imaginative, as agog to see the world as he was. But she was not sent to school. She had no chance of learning grammar and logic, let alone of reading Horace and Virgil. She picked up a book now and then, one of her brother's perhaps, and read a few pages. But then her parents came in and told her to mend the stockings or mind the stew and not moon about with books and papers. They would have spoken sharply but kindly, for they were substantial people who knew the conditions of life for a woman and loved their daughter—indeed, more likely than not she was the apple of her father's eye. Perhaps she scribbled some pages up in an apple loft on the sly, but was careful to hide them or set fire to them. Soon, however, before she was out of her teens, she was to be betrothed to the son of a neighbouring wool-stapler. She cried out that marriage was hateful to her, and for that she was severely beaten by her father. Then he ceased to scold her. He begged her instead not to hurt him, not to shame him in this matter of her marriage. He would give her a chain of beads or a fine petticoat, he said; and there were tears in his eyes. How could she disobey him? How could she break his heart? The force of her own gift alone drove her to it. She made up a small parcel of her belongings, let herself down by a rope one summer's night and took the road to London. She was not seventeen. The birds that sang in the hedge were not more musical than she was. She had the quickest fancy, a gift like her brother's, for the tune of words. Like him, she had a taste for the theatre. She stood at the stage door; she wanted to act, she said. Men laughed in her face. The manager—a fat, loose-lipped man—guffawed. He bellowed something about poodles dancing and women acting—no woman, he said, could possibly be an actress. He hinted—you can imagine what. She could get no training in her craft. Could she even seek her dinner in a tavern or roam the streets at midnight? Yet her genius was for fiction and lusted to feed abundantly upon the lives of men and women and the study of their ways. At last—for she was very young, oddly like Shakespeare the poet in her face, with the same grey eyes and rounded brows—at last Nick Greene the actor-manager took pity on her; she found herself with child by that gentleman and so—who shall measure the heat and violence of the poet's heart when caught and tangled in a woman's body?—killed herself one winter's night and lies buried at some cross-roads where the omnibuses now stop outside the Elephant and Castle.

That, more or less, is how the story would run, I think, if a woman in Shakespeare's day had had Shakespeare's genius. [1929]

■

The Shadow across the Page

Nᴇxᴛ ᴅᴀʏ ᴛʜᴇ ʟɪɢʜᴛ ᴏf ᴛʜᴇ ᴏᴄᴛᴏ-ber morning was falling in dusty shafts through the uncurtained windows, and the hum of traffic rose from the street. London then was winding itself up again; the factory was astir; the machines were beginning. It was tempting, after all this reading to look out of the window and see what London was doing on the morning of the twenty-sixth of October 1928. And what was London doing? Nobody, it seemed, was reading *Antony and Cleopatra*. London was wholly indifferent, it appeared, to Shakespeare's plays. Nobody cared a straw—and I do not blame them—for the future of fiction, the death of poetry or the development by the average woman of a prose style completely expressive of her mind. If opinions upon any of these matters had been chalked on the pavement, nobody would have stooped to read them. The nonchalance of the hurrying feet would have rubbed them out in half an hour. Here came an errand-boy; here a woman with a dog on a lead. The fascination of the London street is that no two people are ever alike; each seems bound on some private affair of his own. There were the businesslike, with their little bags; there were the drifters rattling sticks upon area railings; there were affable characters to whom the streets serve for clubroom, hailing men in carts and giving information without being asked for it. Also there were funerals to which men, thus suddenly reminded of the passing of their own bodies, lifted their hats. And then a very distinguished gentleman came slowly down a doorstep and paused to avoid collision with a bustling lady who had, by some means or other, acquired a splendid fur coat and a bunch of Parma violets. They all seemed separate, self-absorbed, on business of their own.

At this moment, as so often happens in London, there was a complete lull and suspension of traffic. Nothing came down the street; nobody passed. A single leaf detached itself from the plane tree at the end of the street, and in that pause and suspension fell. Somehow it was like a signal falling, a signal pointing to a force in things which one had overlooked. It seemed to point to a river, which flowed past, invisibly, round the corner, down the street, and took people and eddied them along, as the stream at Oxbridge had taken the undergraduate in his boat and the dead leaves. Now it was bringing from one side of the street to the other diagonally a girl in patent leather boots, and then a young man in a maroon overcoat; it was also bringing a taxi-cab; and it brought all three together at a point directly beneath my window; where the taxi stopped; and the girl and the young man stopped; and they got into the taxi; and then the cab glided off as if it were swept on by the current elsewhere.

The sight was ordinary enough; what was strange was the rhythmical order with which my imagination had invested it; and the fact that the ordinary sight of two people getting into a cab had the power to communicate something of their own seeming satisfaction. The sight of two people coming down the street and meeting at the corner seems to ease the mind of some strain, I thought, watching the taxi turn and make off. Perhaps to think, as I had been thinking these two days, of one sex as distinct from the other is an effort. It interferes with the unity of the mind. Now that effort had ceased and that unity had been restored by seeing two people come together and get into a taxi-cab. The mind is certainly a very mysterious organ, I reflected, drawing my head in from the window, about which nothing whatever is known, though we depend upon it so completely. Why do I feel that there are severances and oppositions in the mind, as there are strains from obvious causes on the body? What does one mean by "the unity of the mind," I pondered, for clearly the mind has so great a power of concentrating at any point at any moment that it seems to have no single state of being. It can separate itself from the people in the street, for example, and think of itself as apart from them, at an upper window looking down on them. Or it can think with other people spontaneously, as, for instance, in a crowd waiting to hear some piece of news read out. It can think back through its fathers or through its mothers, as I have said that a woman writing thinks back through her mothers. Again if one is a woman one is often surprised by a sudden splitting off of consciousness, say in walking down Whitehall, when from being the natural inheritor of that civilisation, she becomes, on the contrary, outside of it, alien and critical. Clearly the mind is always altering its focus, and bringing the world into different perspectives. But some of these states of mind seem, even if adopted spontaneously, to be less comfortable than others. In order to keep oneself continuing in them one is unconsciously holding something back, and gradually the repression becomes an effort. But there may be some state of mind in which one could continue without effort because nothing is required to be held back. And this perhaps, I thought, coming in from the window, is one of them. For certainly when I saw the couple get into the taxi-cab the mind felt as if, after being divided, it had come together again in a natural fusion. The obvious reason would be that it is natural for the sexes to co-operate. One has a profound, if irrational, instinct in favour of the theory that the union of man and woman makes for the greatest satisfaction, the most complete happiness. But the sight of the two people getting into the taxi and the satisfaction it gave me made me also ask whether there are two sexes in the mind corresponding to the two sexes in the body, and whether they also require to be united in order to get complete satisfaction and happiness. And I went on amateurishly to sketch a plan of the soul so that in each of us two powers preside, one male, one female; and in the man's brain, the man predominates over the woman, and in the woman's brain, the woman predominates over the man. The normal and comfortable state of being is that when the two live in harmony together, spiritually cooperating. If one is a man, still the woman part of the brain must have effect; and a woman also must have intercourse with the man in her. Coleridge perhaps meant this when he said that a great mind is androgynous. It is when this fusion takes place that the mind is fully fertilised and uses all its faculties. Perhaps a mind that is purely masculine cannot create, any more than a mind that is purely feminine, I thought. But it would be well to test what one meant by man-womanly, and conversely by woman-manly, by pausing and looking at a book or two.

Coleridge certainly did not mean, when he said that a great mind is androgynous, that it is a mind that has any special sympathy with women; a mind that takes up their cause or devotes itself to their interpretation. Perhaps the androgynous mind is less apt to make these distinctions than the single-sexed mind. He meant, perhaps, that the androgynous mind is resonant and porous; that it transmits emotion without impediment; that it is naturally creative, incandescent and undivided. In fact one goes back to Shakespeare's mind as the type of the androgynous, of the man-womanly mind, though it would be impossible to say what Shakespeare thought of women. And if it be true that it is one of the tokens of the fully developed mind that it does not think specially or separately of sex, how much harder it is to attain that condition now than ever before. Here I came to the books by living writers, and there paused and wondered if this fact were not at the root of something that had long puzzled me. No age can ever have been as stridently sex-conscious as our own; those innumerable books by men about women in the British Museum are a proof of it. The Suffrage campaign was no doubt to blame. It must have roused in men an extraordinary desire for self-assertion; it must have made them lay an emphasis upon their own sex and its characteristics which they would not have troubled to think about had they not been challenged. And when one is challenged, even by a few women in black bonnets, one retaliates, if one has never been challenged before, rather excessively. That perhaps accounts for some of the characteristics that I remember to have found here, I thought, taking down a new novel by Mr. A, who is in the prime of life and very well thought of, apparently, by the reviewers. I opened it. Indeed, it was delightful to read a man's writing again. It was so direct, so straightforward after the writing of women. It indicated such freedom of mind, such liberty of person, such confidence in himself. One had a sense of physical well-being in the presence of this well-nourished, well-educated, free mind, which had never been thwarted or opposed, but had had full liberty from birth to stretch itself in whatever way it liked. All this was admirable. But after reading a chapter or two a shadow seemed to lie across the page. It was a straight dark bar, a shadow shaped something like the letter "I." One began dodging this way and that to catch a glimpse of the landscape behind it. Whether that was indeed a tree or a woman walking I was not quite sure. Back one was always hailed to the letter "I." One began to be tired of "I." Not but what this "I" was a most respectable "I"; honest and logical; as hard as a nut, and polished for centuries by good teaching and good feeding. I respect and admire that "I" from the bottom of my heart. But— here I turned a page or two, looking for something or other—the worst of it is that in the shadow of the letter "I" all is shapeless as mist. Is that a tree? No, it is a woman. But . . . she has not a bone in her body, I thought, watching Phoebe, for that was her name, coming across the beach. Then Alan got up and the shadow of Alan at once obliterated Phoebe. For Alan had views and Phoebe was quenched in the flood of his views. And then Alan, I thought, has passions; and here I turned page after page very fast, feeling that the crisis was approaching, and so it was. It took place on the beach under the sun. It was done very openly. It was done very vigorously.

Nothing could have been more indecent. But . . . I had said "but" too often. One cannot go on saying "but." One must finish the sentence somehow, I rebuked myself. Shall I finish it, "But—I am bored!" But why was I bored? Partly because of the dominance of the letter "I" and the aridity, which, like the giant beech tree, it casts within its shade. Nothing will grow there. And partly for some more obscure reason. There seemed to be some obstacle, some impediment of Mr. A's mind which blocked the fountain of creative energy and shored it within narrow limits. And remembering the lunch party at Oxbridge, and the cigarette ash and the Manx cat and Tennyson and Christina Rossetti all in a bunch, it seemed possible that the impediment lay there. As he no longer hums under his breath, "There has fallen a splendid tear from the passion-flower at the gate," when Phoebe crosses the beach, and she no longer replies, "My heart is like a singing bird whose nest is in a water'd shoot," when Alan approaches what can he do? Being honest as the day and logical as the sun, there is only one thing he can do. And that he does, to do him justice, over and over (I said, turning the pages) and over again. And that, I added, aware of the awful nature of the confession, seems somehow dull. Shakespeare's indecency uproots a thousand other things in one's mind, and is far from being dull. But Shakespeare does it for pleasure; Mr. A, as the nurses say, does it on purpose. He does it in protest. He is protesting against the equality of the other sex by asserting his own superiority. He is therefore impeded and inhibited and self-conscious as Shakespeare might have been if he too had known Miss Clough and Miss Davies. Doubtless Elizabethan literature would have been very different from what it is if the woman's movement had begun in the sixteenth century and not in the nineteenth.

What, then, it amounts to, if this theory of the two sides of the mind holds good, is that virility has now become self-conscious—men, that is to say, are now writing only with the male side of their brains. It is a mistake for a woman to read them, for she will inevitably look for something that she will not find. It is the power of suggestion that one most misses, I thought, taking Mr. B the critic in my hand and reading, very carefully and very dutifully, his remarks upon the art of poetry. Very able they were, acute and full of learning; but the trouble was, that his feelings no longer communicated; his mind seemed separated into different chambers; not a sound carried from one to the other. Thus, when one takes a sentence of Mr. B into the mind it falls plump to the ground—dead; but when one takes a sentence of Coleridge into the mind, it explodes and gives birth to all kinds of other ideas, and that is the only sort of writing of which one can say that it has the secret of perpetual life.

But whatever the reason may be, it is a fact that one must deplore. For it means—here I had come to rows of books by Mr. Galsworthy and Mr. Kipling—that some of the finest works of our greatest living writers fall upon deaf ears. Do what she will a woman cannot find in them that fountain of perpetual life which the critics assure her is there. It is not only that they celebrate male virtues, enforce male values and describe the world of men; it is that the emotion with which these books are permeated is to a woman incomprehensible. It is coming, it is gathering, it is about to burst on one's head, one begins saying long before the end. That picture will fall on old Jolyon's head; he will die of the shock; the old clerk will speak over him two or three obituary words; and all the swans on the Thames will simultaneously burst out singing. But one will rush away before that happens and hide in the gooseberry bushes, for the emotion which is so deep, so subtle, so symbolical to a man moves a woman to wonder. So with Mr. Kipling's officers who turn their backs; and his Sowers who sow the Seed; and his Men who are alone with their Work; and the Flag—one blushes at all these capital letters as if one had been caught eavesdropping at some purely masculine orgy. The fact is that neither Mr. Galsworthy nor Mr. Kipling has a spark of the woman in him. Thus all their qualities seem to a woman, if one may generalise, crude and immature. They lack suggestive power. And when a book lacks suggestive power, however hard it hits the surface of the mind it cannot penetrate within.

And in that restless mood in which one takes books out and puts them back again without looking at them I began to envisage an age to come of pure, of self-assertive virility, such as the letters of professors (take Sir Walter Raleigh's letters, for instance) seem to forebode, and the rulers of Italy have already brought into being. For one can hardly fail to be impressed in Rome by the sense of unmitigated masculinity; and whatever the value of unmitigated masculinity upon the state, one may question the effect of it upon the art of poetry. At any rate, according to the newspapers, there is a certain anxiety about fiction in Italy. There has been a meeting of academicians whose object it is "to develop the Italian novel." "Men famous by birth, or in finance, industry or the Fascist corporations" came together the other day and discussed the matter, and a telegram was sent to the Duce expressing the hope "that the Fascist era would soon give birth to a poet worthy of it." We may all join in that pious hope, but it is doubtful whether poetry can come out of an incubator. Poetry ought to have a mother as well as a father. The Fascist poem, one may fear, will be a horrid little abortion such as one sees in a glass jar in the museum of some county town. Such monsters never live long, it is said; one has never seen a prodigy of that sort cropping grass in a field. Two heads on one body do not make for length of life.

However, the blame for all this, if one is anxious to lay blame, rests no more upon one sex than upon the other. All seducers and reformers are responsible, Lady Bessborough when she lied to Lord Granville; Miss Davies when she told the truth to Mr. Greg. All who have brought about a state of sex-consciousness are to blame, and it is they who drive me, when I want to stretch my faculties on a book, to seek it in that happy age, before Miss Davies and Miss Clough were born, when the writer used both sides of his mind equally. One must turn back to Shakespeare then, for Shakespeare was androgynous; and so was Keats and Sterne and Cowper and Lamb and Coleridge. Shelley perhaps was sexless. Milton and Ben Jonson had a dash too much of the male in them. So had Wordsworth and Tolstoi. In our time Proust was wholly androgynous, if not perhaps a little too much of a woman. But that failing is too rare for one to complain of it, since without some mixture of the kind the intellect seems to predominate and the other faculties of the mind harden and become barren. However, I consoled myself with the reflection that this is perhaps a passing phase; much of what I have said in obedience to my promise to give you the course of my thoughts will seem out of date; much of what flames in my eyes will seem dubious to you who have not yet come of age.

Even so, the very first sentence that I would write here, I said, crossing over to the writing-table and taking up the page headed Women and Fiction, is that it is fatal for any one who writes to think of their sex. It is fatal to be a man or woman pure and simple; one must be woman-manly or man-womanly. It is fatal for a woman to lay the least stress on any grievance; to plead even with justice any cause; in any way to speak consciously as a woman. And fatal is no figure of speech; for anything written with that conscious bias is doomed to death. It ceases to be fertilised. Brilliant and effective, powerful and masterly, as it may appear for a day or two, it must wither at nightfall; it cannot grow in the minds of others. Some collaboration has to take place in the mind between the woman and the man before the act of creation can be accomplished. Some marriage of opposites has to be consummated. The whole of the mind must lie wide open if we are to get the sense that the writer is communicating his experience with perfect fullness. There must be freedom and there must be peace. Not a wheel must grate, not a light glimmer. The curtains must be close drawn. The writer, I thought, once his experience is over, must lie back and let his mind celebrate its nuptials in darkness. He must not look or question what is being done. Rather, he must pluck the petals from a rose or watch the swans float calmly down the river. And I saw again the current which took the boat and the undergraduate and the dead leaves; and the taxi took the man and the woman, I thought, seeing them come together across the street, and the current swept them away, I thought, hearing far off the roar of London's traffic, into that tremendous stream. [1929]

■

*Professions for Women**

WHEN YOUR SECRETARY INVITED ME to come here, she told me that your Society is concerned with the employment of women and she suggested that I might tell you something about my own professional experiences. It is true I am a woman; it is true I am employed; but what professional experiences have I had? It is difficult to say. My profession is literature; and in that profession there are fewer experiences for women than in any other, with the exception of the stage— fewer, I mean, that are peculiar to women. For the road was cut many years ago—by Fanny Burney, by Aphra Behn, by Harriet Martineau, by Jane Austen, by George Eliot—many famous women, and many more unknown and forgotten, have been before me, making the path smooth, and regulating my steps. Thus, when I came to write, there were very few material obstacles in my way. Writing was a reputable and harmless occupation. The family peace was not broken by the scratching of a pen. No demand was made upon the family purse. For ten and sixpence one can buy paper enough to write all the plays of Shakespeare—if one has a mind that way. Pianos and models, Paris, Vienna and Berlin, masters and mistresses, are not needed by a writer. The cheapness of writing paper is, of

---

*A paper read to The Women's Service League.

course, the reason why women have succeeded as writers before they have succeeded in the other professions.

But to tell you my story—it is a simple one. You have only got to figure to yourselves a girl in a bedroom with a pen in her hand. She had only to move that pen from left to right—from ten o'clock to one. Then it occurred to her to do what is simple and cheap enough after all—to slip a few of those pages into an envelope, fix a penny stamp in the corner, and drop the envelope into the red box at the corner. It was thus that I became a journalist; and my effort was rewarded on the first day of the following month—a very glorious day it was for me—by a letter from an editor containing a cheque for one pound ten shillings and sixpence. But to show you how little I deserve to be called a professional woman, how little I know of the struggles and difficulties of such lives, I have to admit that instead of spending that sum upon bread and butter, rent, shoes and stockings, or butcher's bills, I went out and bought a cat—a beautiful cat, a Persian cat, which very soon involved me in bitter disputes with my neighbours.

What could be easier than to write articles and to buy Persian cats with the profits? But wait a moment. Articles have to be about something. Mine, I seem to remember, was about a novel by a famous man. And while I was writing this review, I discovered that if I were going to review books I should need to do battle with a certain phantom. And the phantom was a woman, and when I came to know her better I called her after the heroine of a famous poem, The Angel in the House. It was she who used to come between me and my paper when I was writing reviews. It was she who bothered me and wasted my time and so tormented me that at last I killed her. You who come of a younger and happier generation may not have heard of her—you may not know what I mean by the Angel in the House. I will describe her as shortly as I can. She was intensely sympathetic. She was immensely charming. She was utterly unselfish. She excelled in the difficult arts of family life. She sacrificed herself daily. If there was chicken, she took the leg; if there was a draught she sat in it—in short she was so constituted that she never had a mind or a wish of her own, but preferred to sympathize always with the minds and wishes of others. Above all—I need not say it—she was pure. Her purity was supposed to be her chief beauty—her blushes, her great grace. In those days—the last of Queen Victoria—every house had its Angel. And when I came to write I encountered her with the very first words. The shadow of her wings fell on my page; I heard the rustling of her skirts in the room. Directly, that is to say, I took my pen in hand to review that novel by a famous man, she slipped behind me and whispered: "My dear, you are a young woman. You are writing about a book that has been written by a man. Be sympathetic; be tender; flatter; deceive; use all the arts and wiles of our sex. Never let anybody guess that you have a mind of your own. Above all, be pure." And she made as if to guide my pen. I now record the one act for which I take some credit to myself, though the credit rightly belongs to some excellent ancestors of mine who left me a certain sum of money—shall we say five hundred pounds a year?—so that it was not necessary for me to depend solely on charm for my living. I turned upon her and caught her by the throat. I did my best to kill her. My excuse, if I were to be had up in a court of law, would be that I acted in self-defence. Had I not killed her she would have killed me. She would have plucked the heart out of my writing. For, as I found, directly I put pen to paper, you cannot review even a novel without having a mind of your own, without expressing what you think to be the truth about human relations, morality, sex. And all these questions, according to the Angel in the House, cannot be dealt with freely and openly by women; they must charm, they must conciliate, they must—to put it bluntly—tell lies if they are to succeed. Thus, whenever I felt the shadow of her wing or the radiance of her halo upon my page, I took up the inkpot and flung it at her. She died hard. Her fictitious nature was of great assistance to her. It is far harder to kill a phantom than a reality. She was always creeping back when I thought I had despatched her. Though I flatter myself that I killed her in the end, the struggle was severe; it took much time that had better have been spent upon learning Greek grammar; or in roaming the world in search of adventures. But it was a real experience; it was an experience that was bound to befall all women writers at that time. Killing the Angel in the House was part of the occupation of a woman writer.

But to continue my story. The Angel was dead; what then remained? You may say that what remained was a simple and common object—a young woman in a bedroom with an inkpot. In other words, now that she had rid herself of falsehood, that young woman had only to be herself. Ah, but what is "herself"? I mean, what is a woman? I assure you, I do not know. I do not believe that you know. I do not believe that anybody can know until she has expressed herself in all the arts and professions open to human skill. That indeed is one of the reasons why I have come here—out of respect for you, who are in process of showing us by your experiments what a woman is, who are in process of providing us, by your failures and successes, with that extremely important piece of information.

But to continue the story of my professional experiences. I made one pound ten and six by my first review; and I bought a Persian cat with the proceeds. Then I grew ambitious. A Persian cat is all very well, I said; but a Persian cat is not enough. I must have a motor car. And it was thus that I became a novelist—for it is a very strange thing that people will give you a motor car if you will tell them a story. It is a still stranger thing that there is nothing so delightful in the world as telling stories. It is far pleasanter than writing reviews of famous novels. And yet, if I am to obey your secretary and tell you my professional experiences as a novelist, I must tell you about a very strange experience that befell me as a novelist. And to understand it you must try to imagine a novelist's state of mind. I hope I am not giving away professional secrets if I say that a novelist's chief desire is to be as unconscious as possible. He has to induce in himself a state of perpetual lethargy. He wants life to proceed with the utmost quiet and regularity. He wants to see the same faces, to read the same books, to do the same things day after day, month after month, while he is writing, so that nothing may break the illusion in which he is living—so that nothing may disturb or disquiet the mysterious nosings about, feelings round, darts, dashes and sudden discoveries of that very shy and illusive spirit, the imagination. I suspect that this state is the same both for men and women. Be that as it may, I want you to imagine me writing a novel in a state of trance. I want you to figure to yourselves a girl sitting with a pen in her hand, which for minutes, and indeed for hours, she never dips into the inkpot. The image that comes to my mind when I think of this girl is the image of a fisherman lying sunk in dreams on the verge of a deep lake with a rod held out over the water. She was letting her imagination sweep unchecked round every rock and cranny of the world that lies submerged in the depths of our unconscious being. Now came the experience, the experience that I believe to be far commoner with women writers than with men. The line raced through the girl's fingers. Her imagination had rushed away. It had sought the pools, the depths, the dark places where the largest fish slumber. And then there was a smash. There was an explosion. There was foam and confusion. The imagination had dashed itself against something hard. The girl was roused from her dream. She was indeed in a state of the most acute and difficult distress. To speak without figure she had thought of something, something about the body, about the passions which it was unfitting for her as a woman to say. Men, her reason told her, would be shocked. The consciousness of what men will say of a woman who speaks the truth about her passions had roused her from her artist's state of unconsciousness. She could write no more. The trance was over. Her imagination could work no longer. This I believe to be a very common experience with women writers—they are impeded by the extreme conventionality of the other sex. For though men sensibly allow themselves great freedom in these respects, I doubt that they realize or can control the extreme severity with which they condemn such freedom in women.

These then were two very genuine experiences of my own. These were two of the adventures of my professional life. The first—killing the Angel in the House—I think I solved. She died. But the second, telling the truth about my own experiences as a body, I do not think I solved. I doubt that any woman has solved it yet. The obstacles against her are still immensely powerful—and yet they are very difficult to define. Outwardly, what is simpler than to write books? Outwardly, what obstacles are there for a woman rather than for a man? Inwardly, I think, the case is very different; she has still many ghosts to fight, many prejudices to overcome. Indeed it will be a long time still, I think, before a woman can sit down to write a book without finding a phantom to be slain, a rock to be dashed against. And if this is so in literature, the freest of all professions for women, how is it in the new professions which you are now for the first time entering?

Those are the questions that I should like, had I time, to ask you. And indeed, if I have laid stress upon these professional experiences of mine, it is because I believe that they are, though in different forms, yours also. Even when the path is nominally open—when there is nothing to prevent a woman from being a doctor, a lawyer, a civil servant—there are many phantoms and obstacles, as I believe, looming in her way. To discuss and define them is I think of great value and importance; for thus only can the labour be shared, the difficulties be solved. But besides this, it is necessary also to discuss the ends and the aims for which we are fighting, for which we are doing battle with these formidable obstacles. Those aims cannot be taken for granted; they must be perpetually questioned and examined. The whole position, as I see it—here in this hall surrounded by women practising for the first time in history I know not how many different professions—is one of extraordinary interest and importance. You have won rooms of your own in the house hitherto exclusively owned by men. You are able, though not without great labour and effort, to pay the rent. You are earning your five hundred pounds a year. But this freedom is only a beginning; the room is your own, but it is still bare. It has to be furnished; it has to be decorated; it has to be shared. How are you going to furnish it, how are you going to decorate it? With whom are you going to share it, and upon what terms? These, I think, are questions of the utmost importance and interest. For the first time in history you are able to ask them; for the first time you are able to decide for yourselves what the answers should be. Willingly would I stay and discuss those questions and answers—but not tonight. My time is up; and I must cease.   [1931]

■

A Sketch of the Past

TWO DAYS AGO—SUNDAY 16TH APRIL 1939 to be precise—Nessa said that if I did not start writing my memoirs I should soon be too old. I should be eighty-five, and should have forgotten—witness the unhappy case of Lady Strachey. As it happens that I am sick of writing Roger's life, perhaps I will spend two or three mornings making a sketch.* There are several difficulties. In the first place, the enormous number of things I can remember; in the second, the number of different ways in which memoirs can be written. As a great memoir reader, I know many different ways. But if I begin to go through them and to analyse them and their merits and faults, the mornings—I cannot take more than two or three at most—will be gone. So without stopping to choose my way, in the sure and certain knowledge that it will find itself—or if not it will not matter—I begin: the first memory.

This was of red and purple flowers on a black ground—my mother's dress; and she was sitting either in a train or in an omnibus, and I was on her lap. I therefore saw the flowers she was wearing very close; and can still see purple and red and blue, I think, against the black; they must have been anemones, I suppose. Perhaps we were going to St Ives; more probably, for from the light it must have been evening, we were coming back to London. But it is more convenient artistically to suppose that we were going to St

---

*VW was at work on *Roger Fry: A Biography*.

Ives, for that will lead to my other memory, which also seems to be my first memory, and in fact it is the most important of all my memories. If life has a base that it stands upon, if it is a bowl that one fills and fills and fills— then my bowl without a doubt stands upon this memory. It is of lying half asleep, half awake, in bed in the nursery at St Ives. It is of hearing the waves breaking, one, two, one, two, and sending a splash of water over the beach; and then breaking, one, two, one, two, behind a yellow blind. It is of hearing the blind draw its little acorn across the floor as the wind blew the blind out. It is of lying and hearing this splash and seeing this light, and feeling, it is almost impossible that I should be here; of feeling the purest ecstasy I can conceive.

I could spend hours trying to write that as it should be written, in order to give the feeling which is even at this moment very strong in me. But I should fail (unless I had some wonderful luck); I dare say I should only succeed in having the luck if I had begun by describing Virginia herself.

Here I come to one of the memoir writer's difficulties—one of the reasons why, though I read so many, so many are failures. They leave out the person to whom things happened. The reason is that it is so difficult to describe any human being. So they say: "This is what happened"; but they do not say what the person was like to whom it happened. And the events mean very little unless we know first to whom they happened. Who was I then? Adeline Virginia Stephen, the second daughter of Leslie and Julia Prinsep Stephen, born on 25th January 1882, descended from a great many people, some famous, others obscure; born into a large connection, born not of rich parents, but of well-to-do parents, born into a very communicative, literate, letter writing, visiting, articulate, late nineteenth century world; so that I could if I liked to take the trouble, write a great deal here not only about my mother and father but about uncles and aunts, cousins and friends. But I do not know how much of this, or what part of this, made me feel what I felt in the nursery at St Ives. I do not know how far I differ from other people. That is another memoir writer's difficulty. Yet to describe oneself truly one must have some standard of comparison; was I clever, stupid, good looking, ugly, passionate, cold—? Owing partly to the fact that I was never at school, never competed in any way with children of my own age, I have never been able to compare my gifts and defects with other people's. But of course there was one external reason for the intensity of this first impression: the impression of the waves and the acorn on the blind; the feeling, as I describe it sometimes to myself, of lying in a grape and seeing through a film of semi-transparent yellow—it was due partly to the many months we spent in London. The change of nursery was a great change. And there was the long train journey; and the excitement. I remember the dark; the lights; the stir of the going up to bed.

But to fix my mind upon the nursery—it had a balcony; there was a partition, but it joined the balcony of my father's and mother's bedroom. My mother would come out onto her balcony in a white dressing gown. There were passion flowers growing on the wall; they were great starry blossoms, with purple streaks, and large green buds, part empty, part full.

If I were a painter I should paint these first impressions in pale yellow, silver, and green. There was the pale yellow blind; the green sea; and the silver of the passion flowers. I should make a picture that was globular; semi-transparent. I should make a picture of curved petals; of shells; of things that were semi-transparent; I should make curved shapes, showing the light through, but not giving a clear outline. Everything would be large and dim; and what was seen would at the same time be heard; sounds would come through this petal or leaf—sounds indistinguishable from sights. Sound and sight seem to make equal parts of these first impressions. When I think of the early morning in bed I also hear the caw of rooks falling from a great height. The sound seems to fall through an elastic, gummy air; which holds it up; which prevents it from being sharp and distinct. The quality of the air above Talland House seemed to suspend sound, to let it sink down slowly, as if it were caught in a blue gummy veil. The rooks cawing is part of the waves breaking—one, two, one, two—and the splash as the wave drew back and then it gathered again, and I lay there half awake, half asleep, drawing in such ecstasy as I cannot describe.

The next memory—all these colour-and-sound memories hang together at St Ives—was much more robust; it was highly sensual. It was later. It still makes me feel warm; as if everything were ripe; humming; sunny; smelling so many smells at once; and all making a whole that even now makes me stop—as I stopped then going down to the beach; I stopped at the top to look down at the gardens. They were sunk beneath the road. The apples were on a level with one's head. The gardens gave off a murmur of bees; the apples were red and gold; there were also pink flowers; and grey and silver leaves. The buzz, the croon, the smell, all seemed to press voluptuously against some membrane; not to burst it; but to hum round one such a complete rapture of pleasure that I stopped, smelt; looked. But again I cannot describe that rapture. It was rapture rather than ecstasy.

The strength of these pictures—but sight was always then so much mixed with sound that picture is not the right word—the strength anyhow of these impressions makes me again digress. Those moments—in the nursery, on the road to the beach—can still be more real than the present moment. This I have just tested. For I got up and crossed the garden. Percy was digging the asparagus bed; Louie was shaking a mat in front of the bedroom door. But I was seeing them through the sight I saw here—the nursery and the road to the beach. At times I can go back to St Ives more completely than I can this morning. I can reach a state where I seem to be watching things happen as if I were there. That is, I suppose, that my memory supplies what I had forgotten, so that it seems as if it were happening independently, though I am really making it happen. In certain favourable moods, memories—what one has forgotten—come to the top. Now if this is so, is it not possible—I often wonder—that things we have felt with great intensity have an existence independent of our minds; are in fact still in existence? And if so, will it not be possible, in time, that some devices will be invented by which we can tap them? I see it—the past—as an avenue lying behind; a long ribbon of scenes, emotions. There at the end of the avenue still, are the garden and the nursery. Instead of re-membering here a scene and there a sound, I shall fit a plug into the wall; and listen in to the past. I shall turn up August 1890. I feel that strong emotion must leave its trace; and it is only a question of discovering how we can get ourselves again attached to it, so that we shall be able to live our lives through from the start.

But the peculiarity of these two strong memories is that each was very simple. I am hardly aware of myself, but only of the sensation. I am only the container of the feeling of ecstasy, of the feeling of rapture. Perhaps this is characteristic of all childhood memories; perhaps it accounts for their strength. Later we add to feelings much that makes them more complex; and therefore less strong; or if not less strong, less isolated, less complete. But instead of analysing this, here is an instance of what I mean—my feeling about the looking-glass in the hall.

There was a small looking-glass in the hall at Talland House. It had, I remember, a ledge with a brush on it. By standing on tiptoe I could see my face in the glass. When I was six or seven perhaps, I got into the habit of looking at my face in the glass. But I only did this if I was sure that I was alone. I was ashamed of it. A strong feeling of guilt seemed naturally attached to it. But why was this so? One obvious reason occurs to me—Vanessa and I were both what was called tomboys; that is, we played cricket, scrambled over rocks, climbed trees, were said not to care for clothes and so on. Perhaps therefore to have been found looking in the glass would have been against our tomboy code. But I think that my feeling of shame went a great deal deeper. I am almost inclined to drag in my grandfather—Sir James, who once smoked a cigar, liked it, and so threw away his cigar and never smoked another. I am almost inclined to think that I inherited a streak of the puritan, of the Clapham Sect. At any rate, the looking-glass shame has lasted all my life, long after the tomboy phase was over. I cannot now powder my nose in public. Everything to do with dress—to be fitted, to come into a room wearing a new dress—still frightens me; at least makes me shy, self-conscious, uncomfortable. "Oh to be able to run, like Julian Morrell, all over the garden in a new dress", I thought not many years ago at Garsington; when Julian undid a parcel and put on a new dress and scampered round and round like a hare. Yet femininity was very strong in our family. We were famous for our beauty—my mother's beauty, Stella's beauty, gave me as early as I can remember, pride and pleasure. What then gave me this feeling of shame, unless it were that I inherited some opposite instinct? My father was spartan, ascetic, puritanical. He had I think no feeling for pictures; no ear for music; no sense of the sound of words. This leads me to think that my—I would say "our" if I knew enough about Vanessa, Thoby and Adrian—but how little we know even about brothers and sisters—this leads me to think that my natural love for beauty was checked by some ancestral dread. Yet this did not prevent me from feeling ecstasies and raptures spontaneously and intensely and without any shame or the least sense of guilt, so long as they were disconnected with my own body. I thus detect another element in the shame which I had in being caught looking at myself in the glass in the hall. I must have been ashamed or afraid of my own body. Another memory, also of the hall, may help to explain this. There was a slab outside the dining room door for standing dishes upon. Once when I was very small Gerald Duckworth lifted me onto this, and as I sat there he began to explore my body. I can remember the feel of his hand going under my clothes; going firmly and steadily lower and lower. I remember how I hoped that he would stop; how I stiffened and wriggled as his hand approached my private parts. But it did not stop. His hand explored my private parts too. I remember resenting, disliking it—what is the word for so dumb and mixed a feeling? It must have been strong, since I still recall it. This seems to show that a feeling about certain parts of the body; how they must not be touched; how it is wrong to allow them to be touched; must be instinctive. It proves that Virginia Stephen was not born on the 25th January 1882, but was born many thousands of years ago; and had from the very first to encounter instincts already acquired by thousands of ancestresses in the past.

And this throws light not merely on my own case, but upon the problem that I touched on the first page; why it is so difficult to give any account of the person to whom things happen. The person is evidently immensely complicated. Witness the incident of the looking-glass. Though I have done my best to explain why I was ashamed of looking at my own face I have only been able to discover some possible reasons; there may be others; I do not suppose that I have got at the truth; yet this is a simple incident; and it happened to me personally; and I have no motive for lying about it. In spite of all this, people write what they call "lives" of other people; that is, they collect a number of events, and leave the person to whom it happened unknown. Let me add a dream; for it may refer to the incident of the looking-glass. I dreamt that I was looking in a glass when a horrible face—the face of an animal—suddenly showed over my shoulder. I cannot be sure if this was a dream, or if it happened. Was I looking in the glass one day when something in the background moved, and seemed to me alive? I cannot be sure. But I have always remembered the other face in the glass, whether it was a dream or a fact, and that it frightened me.

These then are some of my first memories. But of course as an account of my life they are misleading, because the things one does not remember are as important; perhaps they are more important. If I could remember one whole day I should be able to describe, superficially at least, what life was like as a child. Unfortunately, one only remembers what is exceptional. And there seems to be no reason why one thing is exceptional and another not. Why have I forgotten so many things that must have been, one would have thought, more memorable than what I do remember? Why remember the hum of bees in the garden going down to the beach, and forget completely being thrown naked by father into the sea? (Mrs Swanwick says she saw that happen.)

This leads to a digression, which perhaps may explain a little of my own psychology; even of other people's. Often when I have been writing one of my so-called novels I have been baffled by this same problem; that is, how to describe what I call in my private shorthand—"non-being". Every day includes much more non-being than being. Yesterday for example, Tuesday the 18th of April was [as] it happened a good day; above the average in "being". It was fine; I enjoyed writing these first pages; my head was re-lieved of the pressure of writing about Roger; I walked over Mount Misery and along the river; and save that the tide was out, the country, which I notice very closely always, was coloured and shaded as I like—there were the willows, I remember, all plumy and soft green and purple against the blue. I also read Chaucer with pleasure; and began a book—the memoirs of Madame de la Fayette—which interested me. These separate moments of being were however embedded in many more moments of non-being. I have already forgotten what Leonard and I talked about at lunch; and at tea; although it was a good day the goodness was embedded in a kind of nondescript cotton wool. This is always so. A great part of every day is not lived consciously. One walks, eats, sees things, deals with what has to be done; the broken vacuum cleaner; ordering dinner; writing orders to Mabel; washing; cooking dinner; bookbinding. When it is a bad day the proportion of non-being is much larger. I had a slight temperature last week; almost the whole day was non-being. The real novelist can somehow convey both sorts of being. I think Jane Austen can; and Trollope; perhaps Thackeray and Dickens and Tolstoy. I have never been able to do both. I tried—in *Night and Day*; and in *The Years*. But I will leave the literary side alone for the moment.

As a child then, my days, just as they do now, contained a large proportion of this cotton wool, this non-being. Week after week passed at St Ives and nothing made any dint upon me. Then, for no reason that I know about, there was a sudden violent shock; something happened so violently that I have remembered it all my life. I will give a few instances. The first: I was fighting with Thoby on the lawn. We were pommelling each other with our fists. Just as I raised my fist to hit him, I felt: why hurt another person? I dropped my hand instantly, and stood there, and let him beat me. I remember the feeling. It was a feeling of hopeless sadness. It was as if I became aware of something terrible; and of my own powerlessness. I slunk off alone, feeling horribly depressed. The second instance was also in the garden at St Ives. I was looking at the flower bed by the front door; "That is the whole", I said. I was looking at a plant with a spread of leaves; and it seemed suddenly plain that the flower itself was a part of the earth; that a ring enclosed what was the flower; and that was the real flower; part earth; part flower. It was a thought I put away as being likely to be very useful to me later. The third case was also at St Ives. Some people called Valpy had been staying at St Ives, and had left. We were waiting at dinner one night, when somehow I overheard my father or my mother say that Mr Valpy had killed himself. The next thing I remember is being in the garden at night and walking on the path by the apple tree. It seemed to me that the apple tree was connected with the horror of Mr Valpy's suicide. I could not pass it. I stood there looking at the grey-green creases of the bark—it was a moonlit night—in a trance of horror. I seemed to be dragged down, hopelessly, into some pit of absolute despair from which I could not escape. My body seemed paralysed.

These are three instances of exceptional moments. I often tell them over, or rather they come to the surface unexpectedly. But now that for the first time I have written them down, I realise something that I have never realised before. Two of these moments ended in a state of despair. The other ended, on the contrary, in a state of satisfaction. When I said about the flower, "That is the whole", I felt that I had made a discovery. I felt that I had put away in my mind something that I should go back [to], to turn over and explore. It strikes me now that this was a profound difference. It was the difference in the first place between despair and satisfaction. This difference I think arose from the fact that I was quite unable to deal with the pain of discovering that people hurt each other; that a man I had seen had killed himself. The sense of horror held me powerless. But in the case of the flower I found a reason; and was thus able to deal with the sensation. I was not powerless. I was conscious—if only at a distance—that I should in time explain it. I do not know if I was older when I saw the flower than I was when I had the other two experiences. I only know that many of these exceptional moments brought with them a peculiar horror and a physical collapse; they seemed dominant; myself passive. This suggests that as one gets older one has a greater power through reason to provide an expla- nation; and that this explanation blunts the sledge-hammer force of the blow. I think this is true, because though I still have the peculiarity that I receive these sudden shocks, they are now always welcome; after the first surprise, I always feel instantly that they are particularly valuable. And so I go on to suppose that the shock-receiving capacity is what makes me a writer. I hazard the explanation that a shock is at once in my case followed by the desire to explain it. I feel that I have had a blow; but it is not, as I thought as a child, simply a blow from an enemy hidden behind the cotton wool of daily life; it is or will become a revelation of some order; it is a token of some real thing behind appearances; and I make it real by putting it into words. It is only by putting it into words that I make it whole; this wholeness means that it has lost its power to hurt me; it gives me, perhaps because by doing so I take away the pain, a great delight to put the severed parts together. Perhaps this is the strongest pleasure known to me. It is the rapture I get when in writing I seem to be discovering what belongs to what; making a scene come right; making a character come together. From this I reach what I might call a philosophy; at any rate it is a constant idea of mine; that behind the cotton wool is hidden a pattern; that we—I mean all human beings—are connected with this; that the whole world is a work of art; that we are parts of the work of art. *Hamlet* or a Beethoven quartet is the truth about this vast mass that we call the world. But there is no Shakespeare, there is no Beethoven; certainly and emphatically there is no God; we are the words; we are the music; we are the thing itself. And I see this when I have a shock.

This intuition of mine—it is so instinctive that it seems given to me, not made by me—has certainly given its scale to my life ever since I saw the flower in the bed by the front door at St Ives. If I were painting myself I should have to find some—rod, shall I say—something that would stand for the conception. It proves that one's life is not confined to one's body and what one says and does; one is living all the time in relation to certain background rods or conceptions. Mine is that there is a pattern hid behind the cotton wool. And this conception affects me every day. I prove this, now, by spending the morning writing, when I might be walking, running a shop, or learning to do something that will be useful if war comes. I feel that by writing I am doing what is far more necessary than anything else.

All artists I suppose feel something like this. It is one of the obscure elements in life that has never been much discussed. It is left out in almost all biographies and autobiographies, even of artists. Why did Dickens spend his entire life writing stories? What was his conception? I bring in Dickens partly because I am reading *Nicholas Nickleby* at the moment; also partly because it struck me, on my walk yesterday, that these moments of being of mine were scaffolding in the background; were the invisible and silent part of my life as a child. But in the foreground there were of course people; and these people were very like characters in Dickens. They were caricatures; they were very simple; they were immensely alive. They could be made with three strokes of the pen, if I could do it. Dickens owes his astonishing power to make characters alive to the fact that he saw them as a child sees them; as I saw Mr Wolstenholme; C. B. Clarke, and Mr Gibbs.

I name these three people because they all died when I was a child. Therefore they have never been altered. I see them exactly as I saw them then. Mr Wolstenholme was a very old gentleman who came every summer to stay with us. He was brown; he had a beard and very small eyes in fat cheeks; and he fitted into a brown wicker beehive chair as if it had been his nest. He used to sit in this beehive chair smoking and reading. He had only one characteristic—that when he ate plum tart he spurted the juice through his nose so that it made a purple stain on his grey moustache. This seemed enough to cause us perpetual delight. We called him "The Wooly One". By way of shading him a little I remember that we had to be kind to him because he was not happy at home; that he was very poor, yet once gave Thoby half a crown; that he had a son who was drowned in Australia; and I know too that he was a great mathematician. He never said a word all the time I knew him. But he still seems to me a complete character; and whenever I think of him I begin to laugh.

Mr Gibbs was perhaps less simple. He wore a tie ring; had a bald, benevolent head; was dry; neat; precise; and had folds of skin under his chin. He made father groan—"why can't you go—why can't you go?" And he gave Vanessa and myself two ermine skins, with slits down the middle out of which poured endless wealth—streams of silver. I also remember him lying in bed, dying; husky; in a night shirt; and showing us drawings by Retzsch. The character of Mr Gibbs also seems to me complete and amuses me very much.

As for C. B. Clarke, he was an old botanist; and he said to my father, "All you young botanists like Osmunda." He had an aunt aged eighty who went for a walking tour in the New Forest. That is all—that is all I have to say about these three old gentlemen. But how real they were! How we laughed at them! What an immense part they played in our lives!

One more caricature comes into my mind; though pity entered into this one. I am thinking of Justine Nonon. She was immensely old. Little hairs sprouted on her long bony chin. She was a hunchback; and walked like a spider, feeling her way with her long dry fingers from one chair to another. Most of the time she sat in the arm-chair beside the fire. I used to sit on her knee; and her knee jogged up and down; and she sang in a hoarse cracked voice "Ron ron ron—et plon plon plon—" and then her knee gave and I was tumbled onto the floor. She was French; she had been with the Thackerays. She only came to us on visits. She lived by herself at Shepherd's Bush; and used to bring Adrian a glass jar of honey. I got the notion that she was extremely poor; and it made me uncomfortable that she brought this honey, because I felt she did it by way of making her visit acceptable. She said too: "I have come in my carriage and pair"—which meant the red omnibus. For this too I pitied her; also because she began to wheeze; and the nurses said she would not live much longer; and soon she died. That is all I know about her; but I remember her as if she were a completely real person, with nothing left out, like the three old men.   [1939]

GEORGE ORWELL

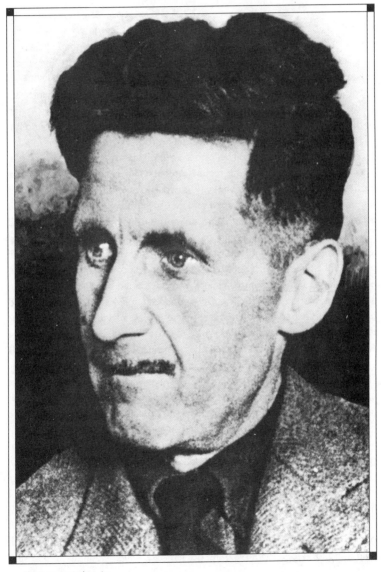

The Bettmann Archive, Inc.

$\blacksquare$

BORN AT MOTIHARI, BENGAL, IN 1903, THE son of a minor official in the Bengal Civil Service, George Orwell attended private schools in England on scholarships from the age of eight until he was graduated from Eton in 1921. But then, instead of going on to one of the universities as might have been expected, Orwell took the advice of a tutor who suggested that he "see something of the world" and joined the Indian Imperial Police. For five years he was a police officer in Burma, then resigned, as he said, "mainly because I could not go on any longer serving an imperialism which I had come to regard as very largely a racket."

For the next year and a half he lived in Paris on his savings and tried to write, but with little success. When his money ran out in the summer of 1929, he got his first taste of poverty as a *plongeur* (dishwasher) in a Paris restaurant, then as a tramp and day laborer in London and the south of England. Indeed, being a tramp, sleeping in doss-houses, and eating hand-me-out meals so stimulated Orwell's imagination (and perhaps the psychic needs of an acute class-consciousness from having been a scholarship boy in exclusive schools) that even after he became a schoolteacher, and later a clerk in a London book shop, he continued to dress up in old clothes and go "on the bum" on weekends. In 1933 he published his first book, *Down and Out in Paris and London*, a vivid account of his experiences during the summer of 1929, and used instead of his real name, Eric Blair, the pseudonym "George Orwell." As with most other writers who have taken pen names, the purpose was to keep a secret—in this case from his former Eton schoolmates: that he had once been "down and out." Though he published poetry and many book reviews during the next three years under his real name, he continued to use the name "Orwell" for his books (the novels *Burmese Days*, *A Clergyman's Daughter*, and *Keep the Aspidistra Flying*).

Between the summer of 1936 and the spring of 1937 Orwell underwent a great metamorphosis. Until then he had been a rather shabby, "serious"—but conventional—young poet on the fringes of the London literati, a very Gissing-like, unsuccessful writer, not at all interested in politics. But then a number of things happened. First, Victor Gollancz commissioned him to go to the north of England and observe the lives of the unemployed coal miners and to write a book about it, which the Left Book Club, a socialist organization, would publish (*The Road to Wigan Pier*). Next, he got married, which meant he had to start earning a bit more money. Then John Lehmann invited him to submit something for a new magazine he was editing, and Orwell wrote his first real *essay* (as opposed to book review or reportage): he called it "Shooting an Elephant." And finally, in December 1936, he left for the Spanish Civil War.

At the time that he arrived in Barcelona, Orwell was so naive about politics that he had only the vaguest notion which faction of the Left (the Republican, or Socialist, side) he wished to join. He was interested in the war mainly as a *war*, not as a battle of political ideologies. But his experiences over the next four months changed everything. To put it very simply, what Orwell discovered was that politics was all lies: that the Tory-dominated British press was distorting the truth about what was happening in Spain; and that the Soviets, who were presumably on the side of the workers, were in fact maneuvering to bring about a socialist defeat. As Orwell wrote many years later, "The Spanish war and other events in 1936–37 turned the scale and thereafter I knew where I stood. Every line of serious work that I have written since 1936 has been written, directly or indirectly, against totalitarianism and *for* democratic socialism, as I understand it." In April 1937, Orwell was severely wounded while fighting on the Aragon front and was lucky to get out of Spain alive. When he got back to England he wrote the first of his important books, *Homage to Catalonia* (1938).

If the political events he observed in Spain were the turning point of Orwell's intellectual life, his near death might be called its psychological equivalent, for after 1936 Eric Blair vanished: no more poetry, no more *belles lettres* book reviews, and only one more conventional novel, *Coming Up for Air* (1939). "George Orwell" became George Orwell, a fiercely dedicated political journalist. But even that doesn't describe the writer who emerged from Spain, for Orwell was more than a mere journalist; he became a devil's advocate of twentieth-century liberalism, an iconoclast in the temples of socialism and communism. His last two books, *Animal Farm* (1945) and *1984* (1949), must be read not as novels nor even strictly as satires—though of course *Animal Farm* is a satire—but as arguments in the service of truth and human freedom.

Orwell died of tuberculosis in 1950, a few months after finishing *1984*. Looking back over his work, the critic V. S. Pritchett declared that Orwell had been "the conscience of his generation," a claim one might examine by reading Orwell's *Collected Essays, Journalism and Letters*, published in 1968 in four volumes.

Orwell was never a member of any political organization. Though he approved of many aspects of socialism, he was never a socialist. Though he defended the rights of the poor and oppressed, and occasionally (as in *1984*) sentimentalized their virtues, he never thought that their limited consciousness was the desired goal of man. Orwell believed in only one thing: honesty—or as he said in one of his essays, the "power of facing unpleasant facts." What he had discovered in Spain in 1937 was that objective truth could cease to exist, that the people who controlled the means of communication could—and *did*—alter it at will, and therefore, as his friend Arthur Koestler had said, history was dead. This, then, was Orwell's great perception, and it was his fear that this sort of "thought-control" was happening not only in the "totalitarian" countries but the "democracies" as well that underlay everything he wrote during the last thirteen years of his life.

As a writer, Orwell's rules were very simple: be clear, be concrete, and avoid all frills and mannerisms. But even these rules, as fine as they are, go only part way in explaining the particular forcefulness of his writing. To understand the rest, one must recall Joseph Conrad's credo: "My task, which I am trying to achieve is, by the power of the written word, to make you hear, to make you feel—it is, above all, to make you *see*." Hearing, feeling, seeing—that is precisely what we are doing when we read George Orwell, and because of it we shall go on reading him for a long time to come. ∎

Shooting an Elephant

IN MOULMEIN, IN LOWER BURMA, I was hated by large numbers of people—the only time in my life that I have been important enough for this to happen to me. I was sub-divisional police officer of the town, and in an aimless, petty kind of way anti-European feeling was very bitter. No one had the guts to raise a riot, but if a European woman went through the bazaars alone somebody would probably spit betel juice over her dress. As a police officer I was an obvious target and was baited whenever it seemed safe to do so. When a nimble Burman tripped me up on the football field and the referee (another Burman) looked the other way, the crowd yelled with hideous laughter. This happened more than once. In the end the sneering yellow faces of young men that met me everywhere, the insults hooted after me when I was at a safe distance, got badly on my nerves. The young Buddhist priests were the worst of all. There were several thousands of them in the town and none of them seemed to have anything to do except stand on street corners and jeer at Europeans.

All this was perplexing and upsetting. For at that time I had already made up my mind that imperialism was an evil thing and the sooner I chucked up my job and got out of it the better. Theoretically—and secretly, of course—I was all for the Burmese and all against their oppressors, the British. As for the job I was doing, I hated it more bitterly than I can perhaps make clear. In a job like that you see the dirty work of Empire at close quarters. The wretched prisoners huddling in the stinking cages of the lock-ups, the gray, cowed faces of the long-term convicts, the scarred buttocks of the men who had been flogged with bamboos—all these oppressed me with an intolerable sense of guilt. But I could get nothing into perspective. I was young and ill educated and I had had to think out my problems in the utter silence that is imposed on every Englishman in the East. I did not even know that the British Empire is dying, still less did I know that it is a great deal better than the younger empires that are going to supplant it. All I knew was that I was stuck between my hatred of the empire I served and my rage against the evil-spirited little beasts who tried to make my job impossible. With one part of my mind I thought of the British Raj as an unbreakable tyranny, as something clamped down, in *saecula saeculorum,* upon the will of prostrate peoples; with another part I thought that the greatest joy in the world would be to drive a bayonet into a Buddhist priest's guts. Feelings like these are the normal by-products of imperialism; ask any Anglo-Indian official, if you can catch him off duty. One day something happened which in a roundabout way was en-lightening. It was a tiny incident in itself; but it gave me a better glimpse than I had had before of the real nature of imperialism—the real motives for which despotic governments act. Early one morning the sub-inspector at a police station the other end of the town rang me up on the 'phone and said that an elephant was ravaging the bazaar. Would I please come and do something about it? I did not know what I could do, but I wanted to see what was happening and I got on to a pony and started out. I took my rifle, an old .44 Winchester and much too small to kill an elephant, but I thought the noise might be useful *in terrorem*. Various Burmans stopped me on the way and told me about the elephant's doings. It was not, of course, a wild elephant, but a tame one which had gone "must." It had been chained up, as tame elephants always are when their attack of "must" is due, but on the previous night it had broken its chain and escaped. Its mahout, the only person who could manage it when it was in that state, had set out in pursuit, but had taken the wrong direction and was now twelve hours' journey away, and in the morning the elephant had suddenly reappeared in the town. The Burmese population had no weapons and were quite helpless against it. It had already destroyed somebody's bamboo hut, killed a cow and raided some fruit-stalls and devoured the stock; also it had met the municipal rubbish van and, when the driver jumped out and took to his heels, had turned the van over and inflicted violences upon it.

The Burmese sub-inspector and some Indian constables were waiting for me in the quarter where the elephant had been seen. It was a very poor quarter, a labyrinth of squalid bamboo huts, thatched with palm-leaf, winding all over a steep hillside. I remember that it was a cloudy, stuffy morning at the beginning of the rains. We began questioning the people as to where the elephant had gone and, as usual, failed to get any definite information. That is invariably the case in the East; a story always sounds clear enough at a distance, but the nearer you get to the scene of events the vaguer it becomes. Some of the people said that the elephant had gone in one direction, some said that he had gone in another, some professed not even to have heard of any elephant. I had almost made up my mind that the whole story was a pack of lies, when we heard yells a little distance away. There was a loud, scandalized cry of "Go away, child! Go away this instant!" and an old woman with a switch in her hand came round the corner of a hut, violently shooing away a crowd of naked children. Some more women followed, clicking their tongues and exclaiming; evidently there was something that the children ought not to have seen. I rounded the hut and saw a man's dead body sprawling in the mud. He was an Indian, a black Dravidian coolie, almost naked, and he could not have been dead many minutes. The people said that the elephant had come suddenly upon him round the corner of the hut, caught him with its trunk, put its foot on his back and ground him into the earth. This was the rainy season and the ground was soft, and his face had scored a trench a foot deep and a couple of yards long. He was lying on his belly with arms crucified and head sharply twisted to one side. His face was coated with mud, the eyes wide open, the teeth bared and grinning with an expression of unendurable agony. (Never tell me, by the way, that the dead look peaceful. Most of the corpses I have seen looked devilish.) The friction of the great beast's foot had stripped the skin from his back as neatly as one skins a rabbit. As soon as I saw the dead man I sent an orderly to a friend's house nearby to borrow an elephant rifle. I had already sent back the pony, not wanting it to go mad with fright and throw me if it smelt the elephant.

The orderly came back in a few minutes with a rifle and five cartridges, and meanwhile some Burmans had arrived and told us that the elephant was in the paddy fields below, only a few hundred yards away. As I started forward practically the whole population of the quarter flocked out of the houses and followed me. They had seen the rifle and were all shouting excitedly that I was going to shoot the elephant. They had not shown much interest in the elephant when he was merely ravaging their homes, but it was different now that he was going to be shot. It was a bit of fun to them, as it would be to an English crowd; besides they wanted the meat. It made me vaguely uneasy. I had no intention of shooting the elephant—I had merely sent for the rifle to defend myself if necessary—and it is always unnerving to have a crowd following you. I marched down the hill, looking and feeling a fool, with the rifle over my shoulder and an ever-growing army of people jostling at my heels. At the bottom, when you got away from the huts, there was a metalled road and beyond that a miry waste of paddy fields a thousand yards across, not yet ploughed but soggy from the first rains and dotted with coarse grass. The elephant was standing eight yards from the road, his left side toward us. He took not the slightest notice of the crowd's approach. He was tearing up bunches of grass, beating them against his knees to clean them, and stuffing them into his mouth.

I had halted on the road. As soon as I saw the elephant I knew with perfect certainty that I ought not to shoot him. It is a serious matter to shoot a working elephant—it is comparable to destroying a huge and costly piece of machinery—and obviously one ought not to do it if it can possibly be avoided. And at that distance, peacefully eating, the elephant looked no more dangerous than a cow. I thought then and I think now that his attack of "must" was already passing off; in which case he would merely wander harmlessly about until the mahout came back and caught him. Moreover, I did not in the least want to shoot him. I decided that I would watch him for a little while to make sure that he did not turn savage again, and then go home.

But at that moment I glanced round at the crowd that had followed me. It was an immense crowd, two thousand at the least and growing every minute. It blocked the road for a long distance on either side. I looked at the sea of yellow faces above the garish clothes—faces all happy and excited over this bit of fun, all certain that the elephant was going to be shot. They were watching me as they would watch a conjurer about to perform a trick. They did not like me, but with the magical rifle in my hands I was momentarily worth watching. And suddenly I realized that I should have to shoot the elephant after all. The people expected it of me and I had got to do it; I could feel their two thousand wills pressing me forward, irresistibly. And it was at this moment, as I stood there with the rifle in my hands, that I first grasped the hollowness, the futility of the white man's dominion in the East. Here was I, the white man with his gun, standing in front of the unarmed native crowd—seemingly the leading actor of the piece; but in reality I was only an absurd puppet pushed to and fro by the will of those yellow faces behind. I perceived in this moment that when the white man turns tyrant it is his own freedom that he destroys. He becomes a sort of hollow, posing dummy, the conventionalized figure of a sahib. For it is the condition of his rule that he shall spend his life in trying to impress the "natives," and so in every crisis he has got to do what the "natives" expect of him. He wears a mask, and his face grows to fit it. I had got to shoot the elephant. I had committed myself to doing it when I sent for the rifle. A sahib has got to act like a sahib; he has got to appear resolute, to know his own mind and do definite things. To come all that way, rifle in hand, with two thousand people marching at my heels, and then to trail feebly away, having done nothing—no, that was impossible. The crowd would laugh at me. And my whole life, every white man's life in the East, was one long struggle not to be laughed at.

But I did not want to shoot the elephant. I watched him beating his bunch of grass against his knees with that preoccupied grandmotherly air that elephants have. It seemed to me that it would be murder to shoot him. At that age I was not squeamish about killing animals, but I had never shot an elephant and never wanted to. (Somehow it always seems worse to kill a *large* animal.) Besides, there was the beast's owner to be considered. Alive, the elephant was worth at least a hundred pounds; dead, he would only be worth the value of his tusks, five pounds, possibly. But I had got to act quickly. I turned to some experienced-looking Burmans who had been there when we arrived, and asked them how the elephant had been behaving. They all said the same thing: he took no notice of you if you left him alone, but he might charge if you went too close to him.

It was perfectly clear to me what I ought to do. I ought to walk up to within, say, twenty-five yards of the elephant and test his behavior. If he charged, I could shoot; if he took no notice of me, it would be safe to leave him until the mahout came back. But also I knew that I was going to do no such thing. I was a poor shot with a rifle and the ground was soft mud into which one would sink at every step. If the elephant charged and I missed him, I should have about as much chance as a toad under a steam-roller. But even then I was not thinking particularly of my own skin, only of the watchful yellow faces behind. For at that moment, with the crowd watching me, I was not afraid in the ordinary sense, as I would have been if I had been alone. A white man mustn't be frightened in front of "natives"; and so, in general, he isn't frightened. The sole thought in my mind was that if anything went wrong those two thousand Burmans would see me pursued, caught, trampled on, and reduced to a grinning corpse like that Indian up the hill. And if that happened it was quite probable that some of them would laugh. That would never do. There was only one alternative. I shoved the cartridges into the magazine and lay down on the road to get a better aim.

The crowd grew very still, and a deep, low, happy sigh, as of people who see the theater curtain go up at last, breathed from innumerable throats. They were going to have their bit of fun after all. The rifle was a beautiful German thing with cross-hair sights. I did not then know that in shooting an elephant one would shoot to cut an imaginary bar running from ear-hole to ear-hole. I ought, therefore, as the elephant was sideways on, to have aimed straight at his ear-hole; actually I aimed several inches in front of this, thinking the brain would be further forward.

When I pulled the trigger I did not hear the bang or feel the kick—one never does when a shot goes home—but I heard the devilish roar of glee that went up from the crowd. In that instant, in too short a time, one would have thought, even for the bullet to get there, a mysterious, terrible change had come over the elephant. He neither stirred, nor fell, but every line of his body had altered. He looked suddenly stricken, shrunken, immensely old, as though the frightful impact of the bullet had paralyzed

him without knocking him down. At last, after what seemed a long time—
it might have been five seconds, I dare say—he sagged flabbily to his knees.
His mouth slobbered. An enormous senility seemed to have settled upon
him. One could have imagined him thousands of years old. I fired again
into the same spot. At the second shot he did not collapse but climbed with
desperate slowness to his feet and stood weakly upright, with legs sag-
ging and head drooping. I fired a third time. That was the shot that did for
him. You could see the agony of it jolt his whole body and knock the last
remnant of strength from his legs. But in falling he seemed for a moment
to rise, for as his hind legs collapsed beneath him he seemed to tower up-
ward like a huge rock toppling, his trunk reaching skyward like a tree.
He trumpeted, for the first and only time. And then down he came, his
belly toward me, with a crash that seemed to shake the ground even where
I lay.

I got up. The Burmans were already racing past me across the mud. It
was obvious that the elephant would never rise again, but he was not dead.
He was breathing very rhythmically with long rattling gasps, his great
mound of a side painfully rising and falling. His mouth was wide open—I
could see far down into caverns of pale pink throat. I waited a long time
for him to die, but his breathing did not weaken. Finally I fired my two remaining shots into the spot where I thought his heart must be. The thick
blood welled out of him like red velvet, but still he did not die. His body
did not even jerk when the shots hit him, the tortured breathing continued
without a pause. He was dying, very slowly and in great agony, but in some
world remote from me where not even a bullet could damage him further.
I felt that I had got to put an end to that dreadful noise. It seemed dreadful
to see the great beast lying there, powerless to move and yet powerless to
die, and not even to be able to finish him. I sent back for my small rifle and
poured shot after shot into his heart and down his throat. They seemed to
make no impression. The tortured gasps continued as steadily as the tick-
ing of a clock.

In the end I could not stand it any longer and went away. I heard later
that it took him half an hour to die. Burmans were bringing dahs and
baskets even before I left, and I was told they had stripped his body almost
to the bones by the afternoon.

Afterward, of course, there were endless discussions about the shooting of the elephant. The owner was furious, but he was only an Indian and
could do nothing. Besides, legally I had done the right thing, for a mad
elephant has to be killed, like a mad dog, if its owner fails to control it.
Among the Europeans opinion was divided. The older men said I was

right, the younger men said it was a damn shame to shoot an elephant for killing a coolie, because an elephant was worth more than any damn Coringhee coolie. And afterward I was very glad that the coolie had been killed; it put me legally in the right and it gave me a sufficient pretext for shooting the elephant. I often wondered whether any of the others grasped that I had done it solely to avoid looking a fool.   [1936]

■

A Hanging

It WAS IN BURMA, A SODDEN MORN-ing of the rains. A sickly light, like yellow tinfoil, was slanting over the high walls into the jail yard. We were waiting outside the condemned cells, a row of sheds fronted with double bars, like small animal cages. Each cell measured about ten feet by ten and was quite bare within except for a plank bed and a pot for drinking water. In some of them brown silent men were squatting at the inner bars, with their blankets draped round them. These were the condemned men, due to be hanged within the next week or two.

One prisoner had been brought out of his cell. He was a Hindu, a puny wisp of a man, with a shaven head and vague liquid eyes. He had a thick, sprouting moustache, absurdly too big for his body, rather like the moustache of a comic man on the films. Six tall Indian warders were guarding him and getting him ready for the gallows. Two of them stood by with rifles and fixed bayonets, while the others handcuffed him, passed a chain through his handcuffs and fixed it to their belts, and lashed his arms tight to his sides. They crowded very close about him, with their hands always on him in a careful, caressing grip, as though all the while feeling him to make sure he was there. It was like men handling a fish which is still alive and may jump back into the water. But he stood quite unresisting, yielding his arms limply to the ropes, as though he hardly noticed what was happening.

Eight o'clock struck and a bugle call, desolately thin in the wet air, floated from the distant barracks. The superintendent of the jail, who was standing apart from the rest of us, moodily prodding the gravel with his stick, raised his head at the sound. He was an army doctor, with a gray toothbrush moustache and a gruff voice. "For God's sake hurry up, Francis," he said irritably. "The man ought to have been dead by this time. Aren't you ready yet?"

Francis, the head jailer, a fat Dravidian in a white drill suit and gold spectacles, waved his black hand. "Yes sir, yes sir," he bubbled. "All iss satis-factorily prepared. The hangman iss waiting. We shall proceed."

"Well, quick march, then. The prisoners can't get their breakfast till this job's over."

We set out for the gallows. Two warders marched on either side of the prisoner, with their rifles at the slope; two others marched close against him, gripping him by arm and shoulder, as though at once pushing and supporting him. The rest of us, magistrates and the like, followed behind. Suddenly, when we had gone ten yards, the procession stopped short without any order or warning. A dreadful thing had happened—a dog, come goodness knows whence, had appeared in the yard. It came bounding among us with a loud volley of barks, and leapt round us wagging its whole body, wild with glee at finding so many human beings together. It was a large woolly dog, half Airedale, half pariah. For a moment it pranced round us, and then, before anyone could stop it, it had made a dash for the pris-oner and, jumping up, tried to lick his face. Everyone stood aghast, too taken aback even to grab at the dog.

"Who let that bloody brute in here?" said the superintendent angrily. "Catch it, someone!"

A warder, detached from the escort, charged clumsily after the dog, but it danced and gamboled just out of his reach, taking everything as part of the game. A young Eurasian jailer picked up a handful of gravel and tried to stone the dog away, but it dodged the stones and came after us again. Its yaps echoed from the jail walls. The prisoner, in the grasp of the two warders, looked on incuriously, as though this was another formality of the hanging. It was several minutes before someone managed to catch the dog. Then we put my handkerchief through its collar and moved off once more, with the dog still straining and whimpering.

It was about forty yards to the gallows. I watched the bare brown back of the prisoner marching in front of me. He walked clumsily with his bound arms, but quite steadily, with that bobbing gait of the Indian who never straightens his knees. At each step his muscles slid neatly into place, the lock of hair on his scalp danced up and down, his feet printed themselves on the wet gravel. And once, in spite of the men who gripped him by each shoulder, he stepped slightly aside to avoid a puddle on the path.

It is curious, but till that moment I had never realized what it means to destroy a healthy, conscious man. When I saw the prisoner step aside to avoid the puddle I saw the mystery, the unspeakable wrongness, of cutting a life short when it is in full tide. This man was not dying, he was alive just as we are alive. All the organs of his body were working—bowels digesting food, skin renewing itself, nails growing, tissues forming—all toiling away in solemn foolery. His nails would still be growing when he stood on the drop, when he was falling through the air with a tenth of a second to live. His eyes saw the yellow gravel and the gray walls, and his brain still remembered, foresaw, reasoned—reasoned even about puddles. He and we were a party of men walking together, seeing, hearing, feeling, understanding the same world; and in two minutes, with a sudden snap, one of us would be gone—one mind less, one world less.

The gallows stood in a small yard, separate from the main grounds of the prison, and overgrown with tall prickly weeds. It was a brick erection like three sides of a shed, with planking on top, and above that two beams and a crossbar with the rope dangling. The hangman, a gray-haired convict in the white uniform of the prison, was waiting beside his machine. He greeted us with a servile crouch as we entered. At a word from Francis the two warders, gripping the prisoner more closely than ever, half led half pushed him to the gallows and helped him clumsily up the ladder. Then the hangman climbed up and fixed the rope round the prisoner's neck.

We stood waiting, five yards away. The warders had formed in a rough circle round the gallows. And then, when the noose was fixed, the prisoner began crying out to his god. It was a high, reiterated cry of "Ram! Ram! Ram! Ram!" not urgent and fearful like a prayer or cry for help, but steady, rhythmical, almost like the tolling of a bell. The dog answered the sound with a whine. The hangman, still standing on the gallows, produced a small cotton bag like a flour bag and drew it down over the prisoner's face. But the sound, muffled by the cloth, still persisted, over and over again: "Ram! Ram! Ram! Ram! Ram!"

The hangman climbed down and stood ready, holding the lever. Minutes seemed to pass. The steady, muffled crying from the prisoner went on and on, "Ram! Ram! Ram!" never faltering for an instant. The superintendent, his head on his chest, was slowly poking the ground with his stick; perhaps he was counting the cries, allowing the prisoner a fixed number—fifty, perhaps, or a hundred. Everyone had changed color. The Indians had gone gray like bad coffee, and one or two of the bayonets were wavering. We looked at the lashed, hooded man on the drop, and listened to his cries—each cry another second of life; the same thought was in all our minds: oh, kill him quickly, get it over, stop that abominable noise!

Suddenly the superintendent made up his mind. Throwing up his head he made a swift motion with his stick. "Chalo!" he shouted almost fiercely.

There was a clanking noise, and then dead silence. The prisoner had vanished, and the rope was twisting on itself. I let go of the dog, and it galloped immediately to the back of the gallows; but when it got there it stopped short, barked, and then retreated into a corner of the yard, where it stood among the weeds, looking timorously out at us. We went round the gallows to inspect the prisoner's body. He was dangling with his toes pointed straight downward, very slowly revolving, as dead as a stone.

The superintendent reached out with his stick and poked the bare brown body; it oscillated slightly. "He's all right," said the superintendent. He backed out from under the gallows, and blew out a deep breath. The moody look had gone out of his face quite suddenly. He glanced at his wrist watch. "Eight minutes past eight. Well, that's all for this morning, thank God."

The warders unfixed bayonets and marched away. The dog, sobered and conscious of having misbehaved itself, slipped after them. We walked out of the gallows yard, past the condemned cells with their waiting prisoners, into the big central yard of the prison. The convicts, under the command of warders armed with lathis, were already receiving their breakfast. They squatted in long rows, each man holding a tin pannikin, while two warders with buckets marched round ladling out rice; it seemed quite a homely, jolly scene, after the hanging. An enormous relief had come upon us now that the job was done. One felt an impulse to sing, to break into a run, to snigger. All at once everyone began chattering gaily.

The Eurasian boy walking beside me nodded toward the way we had come, with a knowing smile: "Do you know, sir, our friend [he meant the dead man] when he heard his appeal had been dismissed, he pissed on the floor of his cell. From fright. Kindly take one of my cigarettes, sir. Do you not admire my new silver case, sir? From the boxwalah, two rupees eight annas. Classy European style."

Several people laughed—at what, nobody seemed certain.

Francis was walking by the superintendent, talking garrulously: "Well, sir, all hass passed off with the utmost satisfactoriness. It was all finished—flick! like that. It iss not always so—oah, no! I have known cases where the doctor wass obliged to go beneath the gallows and pull the prissoner's legs to ensure decease. Most disagreeable!"

"Wriggling about, eh? That's bad," said the superintendent.

"Ach, sir, it iss worse when they become refractory! One man, I recall, clung to the bars of hiss cage when we went to take him out. You will scarcely credit, sir, that it took six warders to dislodge him, three pulling at each leg. We reasoned with him. 'My dear fellow,' we said, 'think of all the pain and trouble you are causing to us!' But no, he would not listen! Ach, he wass very troublesome!"

I found that I was laughing quite loudly. Everyone was laughing. Even the superintendent grinned in a tolerant way. "You'd better all come out and have a drink," he said quite genially. "I've got a bottle of whisky in the car. We could do with it."

We went through the big double gates of the prison into the road. "Pulling at his legs!" exclaimed a Burmese magistrate suddenly, and burst into a loud chuckling. We all began laughing again. At that moment Francis' anecdote seemed extraordinarily funny. We all had a drink together, native and European alike, quite amicably. The dead man was a hundred yards away.   [1931]

■

Marrakech

As THE CORPSE WENT PAST THE FLIES left the restaurant table in a cloud and rushed after it, but they came back a few minutes later.

The little crowd of mourners—all men and boys, no women—threaded their way across the market-place between the piles of pomegranates and the taxis and the camels, wailing a short chant over and over again. What really appeals to the flies is that the corpses here are never put into coffins, they are merely wrapped in a piece of rag and carried on a rough wooden bier on the shoulders of four friends. When the friends get to the burying-ground they hack an oblong hole a foot or two deep, dump the body in it and fling over it a little of the dried-up, lumpy earth, which is like broken brick. No gravestone, no name, no identifying mark of any kind. The burying-ground is merely a huge waste of hummocky earth, like a derelict building-lot. After a month or two no one can even be certain where his own relatives are buried.

When you walk through a town like this—two hundred thousand inhabitants, of whom at least twenty thousand own literally nothing except the rags they stand up in—when you see how the people live, and still more how easily they die, it is always difficult to believe that you are walking among human beings. All colonial empires are in reality founded upon that fact. The people have brown faces—besides, there are so many of them! Are they really the same flesh as yourself? Do they even have names? Or are they merely a kind of undifferentiated brown stuff, about as individual as bees or coral insects? They rise out of the earth, they sweat and starve for a few years, and then they sink back into the nameless mounds of the graveyard and nobody notices that they are gone. And even the graves themselves soon fade back into the soil. Sometimes, out for a walk, as you break your way through the prickly pear, you notice that it is rather bumpy underfoot, and only a certain regularity in the bumps tells you that you are walking over skeletons.

I was feeding one of the gazelles in the public gardens.

Gazelles are almost the only animals that look good to eat when they are still alive, in fact, one can hardly look at their hindquarters without thinking of mint sauce. The gazelle I was feeding seemed to know that this thought was in my mind, for though it took the piece of bread I was holding out it obviously did not like me. It nibbled rapidly at the bread, then lowered its head and tried to butt me, then took another nibble and then butted again. Probably its idea was that if it could drive me away the bread would somehow remain hanging in mid-air.

An Arab navvy working on the path nearby lowered his heavy hoe and sidled towards us. He looked from the gazelle to the bread and from the bread to the gazelle, with a sort of quiet amazement, as though he had never seen anything quite like this before. Finally he said shyly in French:

"*I* could eat some of that bread."

I tore off a piece and he stowed it gratefully in some secret place under his rags. This man is an employee of the Municipality.

When you go through the Jewish quarters you gather some idea of what the medieval ghettoes were probably like. Under their Moorish rulers the Jews were only allowed to own land in certain restricted areas, and after centuries of this kind of treatment they have ceased to bother about over-crowding. Many of the streets are a good deal less than six feet wide, the houses are completely windowless, and sore-eyed children cluster everywhere in unbelievable numbers, like clouds of flies. Down the centre of the street there is generally running a little river of urine.

In the bazaar huge families of Jews, all dressed in the long black robe and little black skull-cap, are working in dark fly-infested booths that look like caves. A carpenter sits cross-legged at a prehistoric lathe, turning chairlegs at lightning speed. He works the lathe with a bow in his right hand and guides the chisel with his left foot, and thanks to a lifetime of sitting in this position his left leg is warped out of shape. At his side his grandson, aged six, is already starting on the simpler parts of the job.

I was just passing the coppersmiths' booths when somebody noticed that I was lighting a cigarette. Instantly, from the dark holes all round, there was a frenzied rush of Jews, many of them old grandfathers with flowing grey beards, all clamouring for a cigarette. Even a blind man somewhere at the back of one of the booths heard a rumour of cigarettes and came crawling out, groping in the air with his hand. In about a minute I had used up the whole packet. None of these people, I suppose, works less than twelve hours a day, and every one of them looks on a cigarette as a more or less impossible luxury.

As the Jews live in self-contained communities they follow the same trades as the Arabs, except for agriculture. Fruitsellers, potters, silversmiths, black-smiths, butchers, leatherworkers, tailors, water-carriers, beggars, porters—whichever way you look you see nothing but Jews. As a matter of fact there are thirteen thousand of them, all living in the space of a few acres. A good job Hitler isn't here. Perhaps he is on his way, however. You hear the usual dark rumours about the Jews, not only from the Arabs but from the poorer Europeans.

"Yes, *mon vieux,* they took my job away from me and gave it to a Jew. The Jews! They're the real rulers of this country, you know. They've got all the money. They control the banks, finance—everything."

"But," I said, "isn't it a fact that the average Jew is a labourer working for about a penny an hour?"

"Ah, that's only for show! They're all moneylenders really. They're cunning, the Jews."

In just the same way, a couple of hundred years ago, poor old women used to be burned for witchcraft when they could not even work enough magic to get themselves a square meal.

All people who work with their hands are partly invisible, and the more important the work they do, the less visible they are. Still, a white skin is always fairly conspicuous. In northern Europe, when you see a labourer ploughing a field, you probably give him a second glance. In a hot country, anywhere south of Gibraltar or east of Suez, the chances are that you don't even see him. I have noticed this again and again. In a tropical landscape one's eye takes in everything except the human beings. It takes in the dried-up soil, the prickly pear, the palm-tree and the distant mountain, but it always misses the peasant hoeing at his patch. He is the same colour as the earth, and a great deal less interesting to look at.

It is only because of this that the starved countries of Asia and Africa are accepted as tourist resorts. No one would think of running cheap trips to the Distressed Areas. But where the human beings have brown skins their poverty is simply not noticed. What does Morocco mean to a Frenchman? An orange-grove or a job in government service. Or to an Englishman? Camels, castles, palm-trees, Foreign Legionnaires, brass trays and bandits. One could probably live here for years without noticing that for nine-tenths of the people the reality of life is an endless, back-breaking struggle to wring a little food out of an eroded soil.

Most of Morocco is so desolate that no wild animal bigger than a hare can live on it. Huge areas which were once covered with forest have turned into a treeless waste where the soil is exactly like broken-up brick. Nevertheless a good deal of it is cultivated, with frightful labour. Everything is done by hand. Long lines of women, bent double like inverted capital Ls, work their way slowly across the field, tearing up the prickly weeds with their hands, and the peasant gathering lucerne for fodder pulls it up stalk by stalk instead of reaping it, thus saving an inch or two on each stalk. The plough is a wretched wooden thing, so frail that one can easily carry it on one's shoulder, and fitted underneath with a rough iron spike which stirs the soil to a depth of about four inches. This is as much as the strength of the animals is equal to. It is usual to plough with a cow and a donkey yoked together. Two donkeys would not be quite strong enough, but on the other hand two cows would cost a little more to feed. The peasants possess no harrows, they merely plough the soil several times over in different directions, finally leaving it in rough furrows, after which the whole field has to be shaped with hoes into small oblong patches, to conserve water. Except for a day or two after the rare rainstorms there is never enough water. Along the edges of the fields channels are hacked out to a depth of thirty or forty feet to get at the tiny trickles which run through the subsoil.

Every afternoon a file of very old women passes down the road outside my house, each carrying a load of firewood. All of them are mummified with age and the sun, and all of them are tiny. It seems to be generally the case in primitive communities that the women, when they get beyond a certain age, shrink to the size of children. One day a poor old creature who could not have been more than four feet tall crept past me under a vast load of wood. I stopped her and put a five-sou piece (a little more than a farthing) into her hand. She answered with a shrill wail, almost a scream, which was partly gratitude but mainly surprise. I suppose that from her point of view, by taking any notice of her, I seemed almost to be violating a law of nature. She accepted her status as an old woman, that is to say as a beast of burden. When a family is travelling it is quite usual to see a father and a grown-up son riding ahead on donkeys, and an old woman following on foot, carrying the baggage.

But what is strange about these people is their invisibility. For several weeks, always at about the same time of day, the file of old women had hobbled past the house with their firewood, and though they had registered themselves on my eyeballs I cannot truly say that I had seen them. Firewood was passing—that was how I saw it. It was only that one day I happened to be walking behind them, and the curious up-and-down motion of a load of wood drew my attention to the human being underneath it. Then for the first time I noticed the poor old earth-coloured bodies, bodies reduced to bones and leathery skin, bent double under the crushing weight. Yet I suppose I had not been five minutes on Moroccan soil before I noticed the overloading of the donkeys and was infuriated by it. There is no question that the donkeys are damnably treated. The Moroccan donkey is hardly bigger than a St. Bernard dog, it carries a load which in the British army would be considered too much for a fifteen-hands mule, and very often its pack-saddle is not taken off its back for weeks together. But what is peculiarly pitiful is that it is the most willing creature on earth, it follows its master like a dog and does not need either bridle or halter. After a dozen years of devoted work it suddenly drops dead, whereupon its master tips it into the ditch and the village dogs have torn its guts out before it is cold.

This kind of thing makes one's blood boil, whereas—on the whole—the plight of the human beings does not. I am not commenting, merely pointing to a fact. People with brown skins are next door to invisible. Anyone can be sorry for the donkey with its galled back, but it is generally owing to some kind of accident if one even notices the old woman under her load of sticks.

As the storks flew northward the Negroes were marching southward—a long, dusty column, infantry, screw-gun batteries and then more infantry, four or five thousand men in all, winding up the road with a clumping of boots and a clatter of iron wheels.

They were Senegalese, the blackest Negroes in Africa, so black that sometimes it is difficult to see whereabouts on their necks the hair begins. Their splendid bodies were hidden in reach-me-down khaki uniforms, their feet squashed into boots that looked like blocks of wood, and every tin hat seemed to be a couple of sizes too small. It was very hot and the men had marched a long way. They slumped under the weight of their packs and the curiously sensitive black faces were glistening with sweat.

As they went past a tall, very young Negro turned and caught my eye. But the look he gave me was not in the least the kind of look you might expect. Not hostile, not contemptuous, not sullen, not even inquisitive. It was the shy, wide-eyed Negro look, which actually is a look of profound respect. I saw how it was. This wretched boy, who is a French citizen and has therefore been dragged from the forest to scrub floors and catch syphilis in garrison towns, actually has feelings of reverence before a white skin. He has been taught that the white race are his masters, and he still believes it.

But there is one thought which every white man (and in this connection it doesn't matter twopence if he calls himself a Socialist) thinks when he sees a black army marching past. "How much longer can we go on kidding these people? How long before they turn their guns in the other direction?"

It was curious, really. Every white man there has this thought stowed somewhere or other in his mind. I had it, so had the other onlookers, so had the officers on their sweating chargers and the white NCOs marching in the ranks. It was a kind of secret which we all knew and were too clever to tell; only the Negroes didn't know it. And really it was almost like watching a flock of cattle to see the long column, a mile or two miles of armed men, flowing peacefully up the road, while the great white birds drifted over them in the opposite direction, glittering like scraps of paper.

[1939]

Politics and the English Language

Most people who bother with the matter at all would admit that the English language is in a bad way, but it is generally assumed that we cannot by conscious action do anything about it. Our civilization is decadent and our language—so the argument runs—must inevitably share in the general collapse. It follows that any struggle against the abuse of language is a sentimental archaism, like preferring candles to electric light or hansom cabs to aeroplanes. Underneath this lies the half-conscious belief that language is a natural growth and not an instrument which we shape for our own purposes.

Now, it is clear that the decline of a language must ultimately have political and economic causes: it is not due simply to the bad influence of this or that individual writer. But an effect can become a cause, reinforcing the original cause and producing the same effect in an intensified form, and so on indefinitely. A man may take to drink because he feels himself to be a failure, and then fail all the more completely because he drinks. It is rather the same thing that is happening to the English language. It becomes ugly and inaccurate because our thoughts are foolish, but the slovenliness of our language makes it easier for us to have foolish thoughts. The point is that the process is reversible. Modern English, especially written English, is full of bad habits which spread by imitation and which can be avoided if one is willing to take the necessary trouble. If one gets rid of these habits one can think more clearly, and to think clearly is a necessary first step toward political regeneration: so that the fight against bad English is not frivolous and is not the exclusive concern of professional writers. I will come back to this presently, and I hope that by that time the meaning of what I have said here will have become clearer. Meanwhile, here are five specimens of the English language as it is now habitually written.

These five passages have not been picked out because they are especially bad—I could have quoted far worse if I had chosen—but because they illustrate various of the mental vices from which we now suffer. They are a little below the average, but are fairly representative samples. I number them so that I can refer back to them when necessary:

(1) I am not, indeed, sure whether it is not true to say that the Milton who once seemed not unlike a seventeenth-century Shelley had not become, out

of an experience ever more bitter in each year, more alien [*sic*] to the founder
of that Jesuit sect which nothing could induce him to tolerate.

> – PROFESSOR HAROLD LASKI, Essay in
> *Freedom of Expression*

(2) Above all, we cannot play ducks and drakes with a native battery of
idioms which prescribes such egregious collocations of vocables as the Basic
put up with for *tolerate* or *put at a loss* for *bewilder.*

> – PROFESSOR LANCELOT HOGBEN, *Interglossa*

(3) On the one side we have the free personality: by definition it is not
neurotic, for it has neither conflict nor dream. Its desires, such as they are,
are transparent, for they are just what institutional approval keeps in the
forefront of consciousness; another institutional pattern would alter their
number and intensity; there is little in them that is natural, irreducible, or
culturally dangerous. But *on the other side,* the social bond itself is nothing
but the mutual reflection of these self-secure integrities. Recall the definition
of love. Is not this the very picture of a small academic? Where is there a
place in this hall of mirrors for either personality or fraternity?

> – Essay on psychology in *Politics* (New York)

(4) All the "best people" from the gentlemen's clubs, and all the frantic fascist
captains, united in common hatred of Socialism and bestial horror of the
rising tide of the mass revolutionary movement, have turned to acts of prov-
ocation, to foul incendiarism, to medieval legends of poisoned wells, to legal-
ize their own destruction of proletarian organizations, and rouse the agitated
petty-bourgeoisie to chauvinistic fervor on behalf of the fight against the revolutionary way out of the crisis.

> – Communist pamphlet

(5) If a new spirit *is* to be infused into this old country, there is one thorny
and contentious reform which must be tackled, and that is the humaniza-
tion and galvanization of the B.B.C. Timidity here will bespeak canker and
atrophy of the soul. The heart of Britain may be sound and of strong beat,
for instance, but the British lion's roar at present is like that of Bottom in
Shakespeare's *Midsummer Night's Dream*—as gentle as any sucking dove. A
virile new Britain cannot continue indefinitely to be traduced in the eyes, or
rather ears, of the world by the effete languors of Langham Place, brazenly
masquerading as "standard English." When the Voice of Britain is heard at
nine o'clock, better far and infinitely less ludicrous to hear aitches honestly
dropped than the present priggish, inflated, inhibited, school-ma'amish arch
braying of blameless bashful mewing maidens!

> – Letter in *Tribune*

Each of these passages has faults of its own, but, quite apart from avoidable ugliness, two qualities are common to all of them. The first is staleness

of imagery; the other is lack of precision. The writer either has a meaning and cannot express it, or he inadvertently says something else, or he is almost indifferent as to whether his words mean anything or not. This mixture of vagueness and sheer incompetence is the most marked characteristic of modern English prose, and especially of any kind of political writing. As soon as certain topics are raised, the concrete melts into the abstract and no one seems able to think of turns of speech that are not hackneyed: prose consists less and less of *words* chosen for the sake of their meaning, and more and more of *phrases* tacked together like the sections of a prefabricated henhouse. I list below, with notes and examples, various of the tricks by means of which the work of prose-construction is habitually dodged:

Dying metaphors.   A newly invented metaphor assists thought by evoking a visual image, while on the other hand a metaphor which is technically "dead" (e.g. *iron resolution*) has in effect reverted to being an ordinary word and can generally be used without loss of vividness. But in between these two classes there is a huge dump of worn-out metaphors which have lost all evocative power and are merely used because they save people the trouble of inventing phrases for themselves. Examples are: *Ring the changes on, take up the cudgels for, toe the line, ride roughshod over, stand shoulder to shoulder with, play into the hands of, no axe to grind, grist to the mill, fishing in troubled waters, on the order of the day, Achilles' heel, swan song, hotbed.* Many of these are used without knowledge of their meaning (what is a "rift," for instance?), and incompatible metaphors are frequently mixed, a sure sign that the writer is not interested in what he is saying. Some metaphors now current have been twisted out of their original meaning without those who use them ever being aware of the fact. For example, *toe the line* is sometimes written *tow the line.* Another example is *the hammer and the anvil,* now always used with the implication that the anvil gets the worst of it. In real life it is always the anvil that breaks the hammer, never the other way about: a writer who stopped to think what he was saying would be aware of this, and would avoid perverting the original phrase.

Operators or **verbal false limbs.**   These save the trouble of picking out appropriate verbs and nouns, and at the same time pad each sentence with extra syllables which give it an appearance of symmetry. Characteristic phrases are *render inoperative, militate against, make contact with, be subjected to, give rise to, give grounds for, have the effect of, play a leading part (role) in, make itself felt, take effect, exhibit a tendency to, serve the purpose of,* etc., etc. The key-note is the elimination of simple verbs. Instead of being a single word, such as *break, stop, spoil, mend, kill,* a verb becomes a *phrase,* made up of a noun or adjective tacked on to some general-purpose verb such as *prove, serve, form, play, render.* In addition, the passive voice is wherever possible used in preference to the active, and noun constructions are used instead of gerunds *(by examination of* instead of *by examining).* The range of verbs is further cut down by means of the *-ize* and *de-* formations, and the banal statements are given an appearance of profundity by means of the *not un-* formation. Simple conjunctions and prepositions are replaced by such phrases as *with respect to, having regard to, the fact that, by dint of, in view of, in the interests of, on the hypothesis that;* and the ends of sentences are saved from anticlimax by such resounding commonplaces as *greatly to be desired, cannot be left out of account, a development to be expected in the near future, deserving of serious consideration, brought to a satisfactory conclusion,* and so on and so forth.

Pretentious diction. Words like *phenomenon, element, individual* (as noun), *objective, categorical, effective, virtual, basic, primary, promote, constitute, exhibit, exploit, utilize, eliminate, liquidate,* are used to dress up simple statement and give an air of scientific impartiality to biased judgments. Adjectives like *epoch-making, epic, historic, unforgettable, triumphant, age-old, inevitable, inexorable, veritable,* are used to dignify the sordid processes of international politics, while writing that aims at glorifying war usually takes on an archaic color, its characteristic words being: *realm, throne, chariot, mailed fist, trident, sword, shield, buckler, banner, jackboot, clarion.* Foreign words and expressions such as *cul de sac, ancien régime, deus ex machina, mutatis mutandis, status quo, gleichschaltung, weltanschauung,* are used to give an air of culture and elegance. Except for the useful abbreviations *i.e., e.g.,* and *etc.,* there is no real need for any of the hundreds of foreign phrases now current in English. Bad writers, and especially scientific, political, and sociological writers, are nearly always haunted by the notion that Latin or Greek words are grander than Saxon ones, and unnecessary words like *expedite, ameliorate, predict, extraneous, deracinated, clandestine, subaqueous,* and hundreds of others constantly gain ground from their Anglo-Saxon opposite numbers.* The jargon peculiar to Marxist

---

*An interesting illustration of this is the way in which the English flower names which were in use till very recently are being ousted by Greek ones, *snapdragon* becoming *antirrhinum, forget-me-not* becoming *myosotis,* etc. It is hard to see any practical reason for this change of fashion: it is probably due to an instinctive turning away from the more homely word and a vague feeling that the Greek word is scientific.

writing (*hyena, hangman, cannibal, petty bourgeois, these gentry, lackey, flunkey, mad dog, White Guard,* etc.) consists largely of words and phrases translated from Russian, German, or French; but the normal way of coining a new word is to use a Latin or Greek root with the appropriate affix and, where necessary, the *-ize* formation. It is often easier to make up words of this kind (*deregionalize, impermissible, extra-marital, nonfragmentary* and so forth) than to think up the English words that will cover one's meaning. The result, in general, is an increase in slovenliness and vagueness.

Meaningless words. In certain kinds of writing, particularly in art criticism and literary criticism, it is normal to come across long passages which are almost completely lacking in meaning.* Words like *romantic, plastic, values, human, dead, sentimental, natural, vitality,* as used in art criticism, are strictly meaningless, in the sense that they not only do not point to any discoverable object, but are hardly ever expected to do so by the reader. When one critic writes, "The outstanding feature of Mr. X's work is its living quality," while another writes, "The immediately striking thing about Mr. X's work is its peculiar deadness," the reader accepts this as a simple difference of opinion. If words like *black* and *white* were involved, instead of the jargon words *dead* and *living,* he would see at once that language was being used in an improper way. Many political words are similarly abused. The word *Fascism* has now no meaning except in so far as it signifies "something not desirable." The words *democracy, socialism, freedom, patriotic, realistic, justice,* have each of them several different meanings which cannot be reconciled with one another. In the case of a word like *democracy,* not only is there no agreed definition, but the attempt to make one is resisted from all sides. It is almost universally felt that when we call a country democratic we are praising it: consequently the defenders of every kind of régime claim that it is a democracy, and fear that they might have to stop using the word if it were tied down to any one meaning. Words of this kind are often used in a consciously dishonest way. That is, the person who uses them has his own private definition, but allows his hearer to think he means something quite different. Statements like

---

*Example: "Comfort's catholicity of perception and image, strangely Whitmanesque in range, almost the exact opposite in aesthetic compulsion, continues to evoke that trembling atmospheric accumulative hinting at a cruel, an inexorably serene timelessness. . . . Wrey Gardiner scores by aiming at simple bull's-eyes with precision. Only they are not so simple, and through this contented sadness runs more than the surface bittersweet of resignation." *(Poetry Quarterly.)*

Marshal Pétain was a true patriot, The Soviet press is the freest in the world, The Catholic Church is opposed to persecution, are almost always made with intent to deceive. Other words used in variable meanings, in most cases more or less dishonestly, are: *class, totalitarian, science, progressive, reactionary, bourgeois, equality.*

Now that I have made this catalogue of swindles and perversions, let me give another example of the kind of writing that they lead to. This time it must of its nature be an imaginary one. I am going to translate a passage of good English into modern English of the worst sort. Here is a well-known verse from *Ecclesiastes:*

> I returned and saw under the sun, that the race is not to the swift, nor the battle to the strong, neither yet bread to the wise, nor yet riches to men of understanding, nor yet favor to men of skill; but time and chance happeneth to them all.

Here it is in modern English:

> Objective consideration of contemporary phenomena compels the conclusion that success or failure in competitive activities exhibits no tendency to be commensurate with innate capacity, but that a considerable element of the unpredictable must invariably be taken into account.

This is a parody, but not a very gross one. Exhibit (3), above, for instance, contains several patches of the same kind of English. It will be seen that I have not made a full translation. The beginning and ending of the sentence follow the original meaning fairly closely, but in the middle the concrete illustrations—race, battle, bread—dissolve into the vague phrase "success or failure in competitive activities." This had to be so, because no modern writer of the kind I am discussing—no one capable of using phrases like "objective consideration of contemporary phenomena"—would ever tabulate his thoughts in that precise and detailed way. The whole tendency of modern prose is away from concreteness. Now analyze these two sentences a little more closely. The first contains forty-nine words but only sixty syllables, and all its words are those of everyday life. The second contains thirty-eight words of ninety syllables: eighteen of its words are from Latin roots and one from Greek. The first sentence contains six vivid images, and only one phrase ("time and chance") that could be called vague. The second contains not a single fresh, arresting phrase, and in spite of its ninety syllables it gives only a shortened version of the meaning contained in the first. Yet without a doubt it is the second kind of sentence that is gaining ground in modern English. I do not want to exaggerate.

This kind of writing is not yet universal, and outcrops of simplicity will occur here and there in the worst-written page. Still, if you or I were told to write a few lines on the uncertainty of human fortunes, we should probably come much nearer to my imaginary sentence than to the one from *Ecclesiastes.*

As I have tried to show, modern writing at its worst does not consist in picking out words for the sake of their meaning and inventing images in order to make the meaning clearer. It consists in gumming together long strips of words which have already been set in order by someone else, and making the results presentable by sheer humbug. The attraction of this way of writing is that it is easy. It is easier—even quicker, once you have the habit—to say *In my opinion it is not an unjustifiable assumption that* than to say *I think.* If you use readymade phrases, you not only don't have to hunt about for words; you also don't have to bother with the rhythms of your sentences, since these phrases are generally so arranged as to be more or less euphonious. When you are composing in a hurry—when you are dictating to a stenographer, for instance, or making a public speech—it is natural to fall into a pretentious, Latinized style. Tags like *a consideration which we should do well to bear in mind* or *a conclusion to which all of us would readily assent* will save many a sentence from coming down with a bump. By using stale metaphors, similes, and idioms, you save much mental effort, at the cost of leaving your meaning vague, not only for your reader but for yourself. This is the significance of mixed metaphors. The sole aim of a metaphor is to call up a visual image. When these images clash—as in *The Fascist octopus has sung its swan song, the jackboot is thrown into the melting pot*—it can be taken as certain that the writer is not seeing a mental image of the objects he is naming; in other words he is not really thinking. Look again at the examples I gave at the beginning of this essay. Professor Laski (1) uses five negatives in fifty-three words. One of these is superfluous, making nonsense of the whole passage, and in addition there is the slip—*alien* for akin—making further nonsense, and several avoidable pieces of clumsiness which increase the general vagueness. Professor Hogben (2) plays ducks and drakes with a battery which is able to write prescriptions, and, while disapproving of the everyday phrase *put up with,* is unwilling to look *egregious* up in the dictionary and see what it means; (3), if one takes an uncharitable attitude towards it, is simply meaningless: probably one could work out its intended meaning by reading the whole of the article in which it occurs. In (4), the writer knows more or less what he wants to say, but an accumulation of stale phrases chokes him like tea leaves blocking a sink. In (5), words and meaning have almost parted company. People who write in this manner usually have a general emotional meaning—they dislike one thing and want to express solidarity with another—but they are not interested in the detail of what they are saying. A scrupulous writer, in every sentence that he writes, will ask himself at least four questions, thus: What am I trying to say? What words will express it? What image or idiom will make it clearer? Is this image fresh enough to have an effect? And he will probably ask himself two more: Could I put it more shortly? Have I said anything that is avoidably ugly? But you are not obliged to go to all this trouble. You can shirk it by simply throwing your mind open and letting the ready-made phrases come crowding in. They will construct your sentences for you—even think your thoughts for you, to a certain extent—and at need they will perform the important service of partially concealing your meaning even from yourself. It is at this point that the special connection between politics and the debasement of language becomes clear.

In our time it is broadly true that political writing is bad writing. Where it is not true, it will generally be found that the writer is some kind of rebel, expressing his private opinions and not a "party line." Orthodoxy, of whatever color, seems to demand a lifeless, imitative style. The political dialects to be found in pamphlets, leading articles, manifestoes, White Papers and the speeches of undersecretaries do, of course, vary from party to party, but they are all alike in that one almost never finds in them a fresh, vivid, home-made turn of speech. When one watches some tired hack on the platform mechanically repeating the familiar phrases—*bestial atrocities, iron heel, blood-stained tyranny, free peoples of the world, stand shoulder to shoulder*—one often has a curious feeling that one is not watching a live human being but some kind of dummy: a feeling which suddenly becomes stronger at moments when the light catches the speaker's spectacles and turns them into blank discs which seem to have no eyes behind them. And this is not altogether fanciful. A speaker who uses that kind of phraseology has gone some distance towards turning himself into a machine. The appropriate noises are coming out of his larynx, but his brain is not involved as it would be if he were choosing his words for himself. If the speech he is making is one that he is accustomed to make over and over again, he may be almost unconscious of what he is saying, as one is when one utters the responses in church. And this reduced state of consciousness, if not indispensable, is at any rate favorable to political conformity.

In our time, political speech and writing are largely the defense of the indefensible. Things like the continuance of British rule in India, the Russian purges and deportations, the dropping of the atom bombs on

Japan, can indeed be defended, but only by arguments which are too brutal for most people to face, and which do not square with the professed aims of political parties. Thus political language has to consist largely of euphemism, question-begging and sheer cloudy vagueness. Defenseless villages are bombarded from the air, the inhabitants driven out into the countryside, the cattle machine-gunned, the huts set on fire with incendiary bullets: this is called *pacification*. Millions of peasants are robbed of their farms and sent trudging along the roads with no more than they can carry: this is called *transfer of population* or *rectification of frontiers*. People are imprisoned for years without trial, or shot in the back of the neck or sent to die of scurvy in Arctic lumber camps: this is called *elimination of unreliable elements*. Such phraseology is needed if one wants to name things without calling up mental pictures of them. Consider for instance some comfortable English professor defending Russian totalitarianism. He cannot say outright, "I believe in killing off your opponents when you can get good results by doing so." Probably, therefore, he will say something like this:

"While freely conceding that the Soviet régime exhibits certain features which the humanitarian may be inclined to deplore, we must, I think, agree that a certain curtailment of the right to political opposition is an unavoidable concomitant of transitional periods, and that the rigors which the Russian people have been called upon to undergo have been amply justified in the sphere of concrete achievement."

The inflated style is itself a kind of euphemism. A mass of Latin words falls upon the facts like soft snow, blurring the outlines and covering up all the details. The great enemy of clear language is insincerity. When there is a gap between one's real and one's declared aims, one turns as it were instinctively to long words and exhausted idioms, like a cuttlefish squirting out ink. In our age there is no such thing as "keeping out of politics." All issues are political issues, and politics itself is a mass of lies, evasions, folly, hatred and schizophrenia. When the general atmosphere is bad, language must suffer. I should expect to find—this is a guess which I have not sufficient knowledge to verify—that the German, Russian and Italian languages have all deteriorated in the last ten or fifteen years, as a result of dictatorship.

But if thought corrupts language, language can also corrupt thought. A bad usage can spread by tradition and imitation, even among people who should and do know better. The debased language that I have been discussing is in some ways very convenient. Phrases like *a not unjustifiable assumption, leaves much to be desired, would serve no good purpose, a consideration which we should do well to bear in mind,* are a continuous temptation, a packet of aspirins always at one's elbow. Look back through this essay, and for certain you will find that I have again and again committed the very faults I am protesting against. By this morning's post I have received a pamphlet dealing with conditions in Germany. The author tells me that he "felt impelled" to write it. I open it at random, and here is almost the first sentence that I see: "[The Allies] have an opportunity not only of achieving a radical transformation of Germany's social and political structure in such a way as to avoid a nationalistic reaction in Germany itself, but at the same time of laying the foundations of a co-operative and unified Europe." You see, he "feels impelled" to write—feels, presumably, that he has something new to say—and yet his words, like cavalry horses answering the bugle, group themselves automatically into the familiar dreary pattern. This invasion of one's mind by readymade phrases *(lay the foundations, achieve a radical transformation)* can only be prevented if one is constantly on guard against them, and every such phrase anaesthetizes a portion of one's brain.

I said earlier that the decadence of our language is probably curable. Those who deny this would argue, if they produced an argument at all, that language merely reflects existing social conditions, and that we cannot influence its development by any direct tinkering with words and constructions. So far as the general tone or spirit of a language goes, this may be true, but it is not true in detail. Silly words and expressions have often disappeared, not through any evolutionary process but owing to the conscious action of a minority. Two recent examples were *explore every avenue* and *leave no stone unturned,* which were killed by the jeers of a few journalists. There is a long list of flyblown metaphors which could similarly be got rid of if enough people would interest themselves in the job; and it should also be possible to laugh the *not un-* formation out of existence,* to reduce the amount of Latin and Greek in the average sentence, to drive out foreign phrases and strayed scientific words, and, in general, to make pretentiousness unfashionable. But all these are minor points. The defense of the English language implies more than this, and perhaps it is best to start by saying what it does *not* imply.

To begin with it has nothing to do with archaism, with the salvaging of obsolete words and turns of speech, or with the setting up of a "standard English" which must never be departed from. On the contrary, it is

---

*One can cure oneself of the *not un-* formation by memorizing this sentence: *A not unblack dog was chasing a not unsmall rabbit across a not ungreen field.*

especially concerned with the scrapping of every word or idiom which has outworn its usefulness. It has nothing to do with correct grammar and syntax, which are of no importance so long as one makes one's meaning clear, or with the avoidance of Americanisms, or with having what is called a "good prose style." On the other hand it is not concerned with fake simplicity and the attempt to make written English colloquial. Nor does it even imply in every case preferring the Saxon word to the Latin one, though it does imply using the fewest and shortest words that will cover one's meaning. What is above all needed is to let the meaning choose the word, and not the other way about. In prose, the worst thing one can do with words is to surrender to them. When you think of a concrete object, you think wordlessly, and then, if you want to describe the thing you have been visualizing you probably hunt about till you find the exact words that seem to fit it. When you think of something abstract you are more inclined to use words from the start, and unless you make a conscious effort to prevent it, the existing dialect will come rushing in and do the job for you, at the expense of blurring or even changing your meaning. Probably it is better to put off using words as long as possible and get one's meaning as clear as one can through pictures or sensations. Afterward one can choose—not simply *accept*—the phrases that will best cover the meaning, and then switch round and decide what impression one's words are likely to make on another person. This last effort of the mind cuts out all stale or mixed images, all prefabricated phrases, needless repetitions, and humbug and vagueness generally. But one can often be in doubt about the effect of a word or a phrase, and one needs rules that one can rely on when instinct fails. I think the following rules will cover most cases:

(i)   Never use a metaphor, simile, or other figure of speech which you are used to seeing in print.
(ii) Never use a long word where a short one will do.
(iii) If it is possible to cut a word out, always cut it out.
(iv) Never use the passive where you can use the active.
(v)   Never use a foreign phrase, a scientific word, or a jargon word if you can think of an everyday English equivalent.
(vi) Break any of these rules sooner than say anything outright barbarous.

These rules sound elementary, and so they are, but they demand a deep change of attitude in anyone who has grown used to writing in the style now fashionable. One could keep all of them and still write bad English, but one could not write the kind of stuff that I quoted in those five specimens at the beginning of this article.

I have not here been considering the literary use of language, but merely language as an instrument for expressing and not for concealing or preventing thought. Stuart Chase and others have come near to claiming that all abstract words are meaningless, and have used this as a pretext for advocating a kind of political quietism. Since you don't know what Fascism is, how can you struggle against Fascism? One need not swallow such absurdities as this, but one ought to recognize that the present political chaos is connected with the decay of language, and that one can probably bring about some improvement by starting at the verbal end. If you simplify your English, you are freed from the worst follies of orthodoxy. You cannot speak any of the necessary dialects, and when you make a stupid remark its stupidity will be obvious, even to yourself. Political language—and with variations this is true of all political parties, from Conservatives to Anarchists—is designed to make lies sound truthful and murder respectable, and to give an appearance of solidity to pure wind. One cannot change this all in a moment, but one can at least change one's own habits, and from time to time one can even, if one jeers loudly enough, send some worn-out and useless phrase—some *jackboot, Achilles' heel, hotbed, melting pot, acid test, veritable inferno,* or other lump of verbal refuse—into the dustbin where it belongs.   [1946]

Why I Write

FROM A VERY EARLY AGE, PERHAPS the age of five or six, I knew that when I grew up I should be a writer. Between the ages of about seventeen and twenty-four I tried to abandon this idea, but I did so with the consciousness that I was outraging my true nature and that sooner or later I should have to settle down and write books.

I was the middle child of three, but there was a gap of five years on either side, and I barely saw my father before I was eight. For this and other reasons I was somewhat lonely, and I soon developed disagreeable mannerisms which made me unpopular throughout my schooldays. I had the lonely child's habit of making up stories and holding conversations with imaginary persons, and I think from the very start my literary ambitions were mixed up with the feeling of being isolated and undervalued. I knew that I had a facility with words and a power of facing unpleasant facts, and I felt that this created a sort of private world in which I could get my own back for my failure in everyday life. Nevertheless the volume of serious—i.e. seriously intended—writing which I produced all through my childhood and boyhood would not amount to half a dozen pages. I wrote my first poem at the age of four or five, my mother taking it down to dictation. I cannot remember anything about it except that it was about a tiger and the tiger had "chair-like teeth"—a good enough phrase, but I fancy the poem was a plagiarism of Blake's "Tiger, Tiger". At eleven, when the war of 1914–18 broke out, I wrote a patriotic poem which was printed in the local newspaper, as was another, two years later, on the death of Kitchener. From time to time, when I was a bit older, I wrote bad and usually unfinished "nature poems" in the Georgian style. I also, about twice, attempted a short story which was a ghastly failure. That was the total of the would-be serious work that I actually set down on paper during all those years.

However, throughout this time I did in a sense engage in literary activities. To begin with there was the made-to-order stuff which I produced quickly, easily and without much pleasure to myself. Apart from school work, I wrote *vers d'occasion,* semicomic poems which I could turn out at what now seems to me astonishing speed—at fourteen I wrote a whole rhyming play, in imitation of Aristophanes, in about a week—and helped to edit school magazines, both printed and in manuscript. These magazines were the most pitiful burlesque stuff that you could imagine, and I took far less trouble with them than I now would with the cheapest journalism. But side by side with all this, for fifteen years or more, I was carrying out a literary exercise of a quite different kind: this was the making up of a continuous "story" about myself, a sort of diary existing only in the mind. I believe this is a common habit of children and adolescents. As a very small child I used to imagine that I was, say, Robin Hood, and picture myself as the hero of thrilling adventures, but quite soon my "story" ceased to be narcissistic in a crude way and became more and more a mere description of what I was doing and the things I saw. For minutes at a time this kind of thing would be running through my head: "He pushed the door open and entered the room. A yellow beam of sunlight, filtering through the muslin curtains, slanted on to the table, where a matchbox, half open, lay beside the inkpot. With his right hand in his pocket he moved across to the window. Down in the street a tortoiseshell cat was chasing a dead leaf," etc etc. This habit continued till I was about twenty-five, right through my non-literary years. Although I had to search, and did search, for the right words, I seemed to be making this descriptive effort almost against my will, under a kind of compulsion from outside. The "story" must, I suppose, have reflected the styles of the various writers I admired at different ages, but as far as I remember it always had the same meticulous descriptive quality.

When I was about sixteen I suddenly discovered the joy of mere words, i.e. the sounds and associations of words. The lines from *Paradise Lost,*

> So hee with difficulty and labour hard
> Moved on: with difficulty and labour hee,

which do not now seem to me so very wonderful, sent shivers down my backbone; and the spelling "hee" for "he" was an added pleasure. As for the need to describe things, I knew all about it already. So it is clear what kind of books I wanted to write, in so far as I could be said to want to write books at that time. I wanted to write enormous naturalistic novels with unhappy endings, full of detailed descriptions and arresting similes, and also full of purple passages in which words were used partly for the sake of their sound. And in fact my first completed novel, *Burmese Days,* which I wrote when I was thirty but projected much earlier, is rather that kind of book.

I give all this background information because I do not think one can assess a writer's motives without knowing something of his early development. His subject matter will be determined by the age he lives in—at least this is true in tumultuous, revolutionary ages like our own—but before he ever begins to write he will have acquired an emotional attitude from which he will never completely escape. It is his job, no doubt, to discipline his temperament and avoid getting stuck at some immature stage, or in some perverse mood: but if he escapes from his early influences altogether, he will have killed his impulse to write. Putting aside the need to earn a living, I think there are four great motives for writing, at any rate for writing prose. They exist in different degrees in every writer, and in any one writer the proportions will vary from time to time, according to the atmosphere in which he is living. They are:

1. *Sheer egoism.* Desire to seem clever, to be talked about, to be remembered after death, to get your own back on grown-ups who snubbed you in childhood, etc. etc. It is humbug to pretend that this is not a motive, and a strong one. Writers share this characteristic with scientists, artists, politicians, lawyers, soldiers, successful businessmen—in short, with the whole top crust of humanity. The great mass of human beings are not acutely selfish. After the age of about thirty they abandon individual ambition—in many cases, indeed, they almost abandon the sense of being individuals at all—and live chiefly for others, or are simply smothered under drudgery. But there is also the minority of gifted, wilful people who are determined to live their own lives to the end, and writers belong in this class. Serious writers, I should say, are on the whole more vain and self-centered than journalists, though less interested in money.

2. *Aesthetic enthusiasm.* Perception of beauty in the external world, or, on the other hand, in words and their right arrangement. Pleasure in the impact of one sound on another, in the firmness of good prose or the rhythm of a good story. Desire to share an experience which one feels is valuable and ought not to be missed. The aesthetic motive is very feeble in a lot of writers, but even a pamphleteer or a writer of textbooks will have pet words and phrases which appeal to him for non-utilitarian reasons; or he may feel strongly about typography, width of margins, etc. Above the level of a railway guide, no book is quite free from aesthetic considerations.

3. *Historical impulse.* Desire to see things as they are, to find out true facts and store them up for the use of posterity.

4. *Political purpose*—using the word "political" in the widest possible sense. Desire to push the world in a certain direction, to alter other people's idea of the kind of society that they should strive after. Once again, no book is genuinely free from political bias. The opinion that art should have nothing to do with politics is itself a political attitude.

It can be seen how these various impulses must war against one another, and how they must fluctuate from person to person and from time to time. By nature—taking your "nature" to be the state you have attained when you are first adult—I am a person in whom the first three motives would outweigh the fourth. In a peaceful age I might have written ornate or merely descriptive books, and might have remained almost unaware of my political loyalties. As it is I have been forced into becoming a sort of pamphleteer. First I spent five years in an unsuitable profession (the Indian Imperial Police, in Burma), and then I underwent poverty and the sense of failure. This increased my natural hatred of authority and made me for the first time fully aware of the existence of the working classes, and the job in Burma had given me some understanding of the nature of imperialism: but these experiences were not enough to give me an accurate political orientation. Then came Hitler, the Spanish civil war, etc. By the end of 1935 I had still failed to reach a firm decision. I remember a little poem that I wrote at that date, expressing my dilemma:

> A happy vicar I might have been
> Two hundred years ago,
> To preach upon eternal doom
> And watch my walnuts grow;

> But born, alas, in an evil time,
> I missed that pleasant haven,
> For the hair has grown on my upper lip
> And the clergy are all clean-shaven.

> And later still the times were good,
> We were so easy to please,
> We rocked our troubled thoughts to sleep
> On the bosoms of the trees.

> All ignorant we dared to own
> The joys we now dissemble;
> The greenfinch on the apple bough
> Could make my enemies tremble.

> But girls' bellies and apricots,
> Roach in a shaded stream,
> Horses, ducks in flight at dawn,
> All these are a dream.

> It is forbidden to dream again;
> We maim our joys or hide them;
> Horses are made of chromium steel
> And little fat men shall ride them.

> I am the worm who never turned,
> The eunuch without a harem;
> Between the priest and the commissar
> I walk like Eugene Aram;

> And the commissar is telling my fortune
> While the radio plays,
> But the priest has promised an Austin Seven,
> For Duggie always pays.

> I dreamed I dwelt in marble halls,
> And woke to find it true;
> I wasn't born for an age like this;
> Was Smith? Was Jones? Were you?

The Spanish war and other events in 1936–37 turned the scale and thereafter I knew where I stood. Every line of serious work that I have written since 1936 has been written, directly or indirectly, *against* totalitarianism and *for* democratic Socialism, as I understand it. It seems to me nonsense, in a period like our own, to think that one can avoid writing of such subjects. Everyone writes of them in one guise or another. It is simply a question of which side one takes and what approach one follows. And the more one is conscious of one's political bias, the more chance one has of acting politically without sacrificing one's aesthetic and intellectual integrity.

What I have most wanted to do throughout the past ten years is to make political writing into an art. My starting point is always a feeling of partisanship, a sense of injustice. When I sit down to write a book, I do not say to myself, "I am going to produce a work of art." I write it because there is some lie that I want to expose, some fact to which I want to draw attention, and my initial concern is to get a hearing. But I could not do the work of writing a book, or even a long magazine article, if it were not also an aesthetic experience. Anyone who cares to examine my work will see that even when it is downright propaganda it contains much that a full-time politician would consider irrelevant. I am not able, and I do not want, completely to abandon the world-view that I acquired in childhood. So long as I remain alive and well I shall continue to feel strongly about prose style, to love the surface of the earth, and to take pleasure in solid objects and scraps of useless information. It is no use trying to suppress that side of myself. The job is to reconcile my ingrained likes and dislikes with the essentially public, non-individual activities that this age forces on all of us.

It is not easy. It raises problems of construction and of language, and it raises in a new way the problem of truthfulness. Let me give just one example of the cruder kind of difficulty that arises. My book about the Spanish civil war, *Homage to Catalonia,* is, of course, a frankly political book, but in the main it is written with a certain detachment and regard for form. I did try very hard in it to tell the whole truth without violating my literary instincts. But among other things it contains a long chapter, full of newspaper quotations and the like, defending the Trotskyists who were accused of plotting with Franco. Clearly such a chapter, which after a year or two would lose its interest for any ordinary reader, must ruin the book. A critic whom I respect read me a lecture about it. "Why did you put in all that stuff?" he said. "You've turned what might have been a good book into journalism." What he said was true, but I could not have done otherwise. I happened to know, what very few people in England had been allowed to know, that innocent men were being falsely accused. If I had not been angry about that I should never have written the book.

In one form or another this problem comes up again. The problem of language is subtler and would take too long to discuss. I will only say that of late years I have tried to write less picturesquely and more exactly. In any case I find that by the time you have perfected any style of writing, you have always outgrown it. *Animal Farm* was the first book in which I tried, with full consciousness of what I was doing, to fuse political purpose and artistic purpose into one whole. I have not written a novel for seven years, but I hope to write another fairly soon. It is bound to be a failure, every book is a failure, but I know with some clarity what kind of book I want to write.

Looking back through the last page or two, I see that I have made it appear as though my motives in writing were wholly public-spirited. I don't want to leave that as the final impression. All writers are vain, selfish and lazy, and at the very bottom of their motives there lies a mystery. Writing a book is a horrible, exhausting struggle, like a long bout of some painful illness. One would never undertake such a thing if one were not driven on by some demon whom one can neither resist nor understand. For all one knows that demon is simply the same instinct that makes a baby squall for attention. And yet it is also true that one can write nothing readable unless one constantly struggles to efface one's own personality. Good prose is like a window pane. I cannot say with certainty which of my motives are the strongest, but I know which of them deserve to be followed. And looking back through my work, I see that it is invariably where I lacked a *political* purpose that I wrote lifeless books and was betrayed into purple passages, sentences without meaning, decorative adjectives and humbug generally.

[1946]

E. B. WHITE

Jim Kalett

THE YOUNGEST OF SIX CHILDREN, E. B. WHITE was born in Mt. Vernon, New York, on July 11, 1899. At the time, Mt. Vernon was still a small town—certainly not the beginning of suburbia that it is today—and White's father, who was prospering as a piano manufacturer, had moved his family up from Brooklyn because he thought Mt. Vernon would be a better place to raise children. As it turned out, it was almost perfect. Their house was large, the streets were shady, and the town was as peaceful as an upper-middle-class suburb could be at the turn of the century. "There was," White has written, describing their house, "an iron vase on the lawn and a copy of *Wet Days at Edgewood* on the library table." Years later, he recalled the things he did: "I rode my bicycle sitting backward on the handle bars, I made up poems, I played selections from *Aïda* on the piano. In winter, I tended goal in the hockey games on the frozen pond in the dell." To such idyllic pastimes was added, in 1905, a camp on one of the Belgrade lakes in Maine, and each August for many years thereafter the family went there for its summer vacation. Indeed, one gathers from his writings that there were few catastrophes in White's childhood more serious than hay fever, which recurred throughout his life. In 1917 he graduated from Mt. Vernon High School, and the following fall he entered Cornell University.

Unlike their cousins, the novelists, the American humorists of this century seem more or less to have taken to college, and White was no exception. He joined a fraternity, got gentlemanly marks in his courses, rode a motorcycle, and spent two months during his sophomore year as a private in the U.S. Army. (Enlisting only a few weeks before the Armistice, he got no farther than the campus drill field and faced no enemy worse than a flu epidemic, "which I met stoically with a bag of licorice drops.") His real interest, however, was writing, and in his senior year he was editor-in-chief of the *Cornell Daily Sun*.

After his graduation in 1921, White tried his hand for a while at various jobs in New York City, but was dissatisfied and restless. Then, in March 1922, he and a friend decided to head west in White's Model T Ford. It was a leisurely trip, and when they arrived in Seattle six months later, White took a job as a reporter with the Seattle *Times*. But poetry, not journalism, was the thing he had his eye on in those days, and when the job fell through the following summer, it was with relief that he began looking around for something to do. What turned up was a steamer on its way to Alaska and Siberia, and White determined to go with it. With the last of his money he bought a one-way ticket as far as Skagway, and trusted that once on board he could get a job that would take him the full round trip. Luckily, he did, and that fall he returned to New York City.

For the next two years he worked in an advertising agency and tried to write poetry, but without much success. Then, in 1925, *The New Yorker* was founded, and very soon White was submitting poems and sketches. Harold Ross, the editor, was so impressed that he asked White to come to work, which he did, and for the next eleven years his wit and good sense did much to make the magazine the success that it was. He not only wrote many of the "Notes and Comments" that appeared in the "Talk of the Town," but also thought up the witty captions and taglines that turned normal space-fillers into capsule editorials on the absurdities of both man and the press. Even though most of his work during those years was unsigned, the recurrent style was unmistakable to anyone who read *The New Yorker* regularly. In 1929 White published his first two books: *The Lady Is Cold,* a collection of light verse, and *Is Sex Necessary?*, a spoof on scientific sex literature written in collaboration with his office mate, James Thurber.

In 1937, "desiring," he said, "to simplify my life," E. B. White left New York and moved his family to a saltwater farm in North Brooklin, Maine. The following summer he began a regular monthly column for *Harper's Magazine* entitled "One Man's Meat," and it was soon apparent that an aspect of his character that had hitherto remained largely hidden was beginning to emerge. The essays that he sent down from Maine revealed a depth one wouldn't have expected from his earlier *New Yorker* pieces. The wit and clear sight into the nature of things were still there, but with a difference. No longer were they being exercised for the sake of cleverness alone—the thing one regrets about much of the work of Benchley, Sullivan, and even Thurber at times—but more seriously, as a means of revealing not merely man's absurdities, but his virtues as well. White, it turned out, could be as serious as he could be clever. Although *Quo Vadimus? or The Case for the Bicycle,* a collection of sketches that had appeared in *The New Yorker,* was published in 1939, the sort of humor that it contained was already a thing of the past. In 1943 he wrote the last of his columns for *Harper's* and returned to New York City, where he resumed the writing of *The New Yorker's* editorial page. The magazine's staff had been depleted by the war, and Ross had asked him to help. A few years later he moved back to Maine and began writing his "Letters from the East" (and other points of the compass) for *The New Yorker*.

Altogether White wrote fifteen books and either edited or collaborated on four others. Two of the most charming are children's stories that take their place alongside such modern classics as *The Wind in the Willows* and the Pooh books: *Stuart Little* (1945) and *Charlotte's Web* (1952). In 1941 he and his wife, Katharine S. White, edited *A Subtreasury of American Humor*, and in 1959 he revised, introduced, and wrote a chapter on style for a grammar handbook he had used as a student at Cornell. To everyone's surprise, *The Elements of Style*, by William Strunk, Jr., and E. B. White, became a national best-seller. White's best essays appear in three collections: *One Man's Meat* (1944), *The Second Tree from the Corner* (1954), and *The Points of My Compass* (1962). In 1970 White published a third children's book, *The Trumpet of the Swan*, and in 1977 he was awarded a Pulitzer Prize Special Citation in Letters for his lifetime's work. In 1985 he died, on his farm in Maine, at the age of eighty-six.

The themes that White came back to in essay after essay are, first, that the natural is preferable to the artificial or mechanical, and, secondly, that even though time moves on apace and things constantly change, the larger patterns of Nature are recurrent. The first idea is generally presented as a lament for the past, and thus the imperceptive reader often comes away with the impression that White is a nostalgic reactionary. Read closely, however, the essays are quite clear in their scorn for sentimentality, and whatever homage is paid the past proves to be not a love for the simple and uncomplicated, but just the opposite, a love of the excitement and adventure that is inseparable from physical hardships. As our material goods and comforts increase, White would say, we lose touch with reality; we are dehumanized; we become no better than the machine we created; indeed, worse (see "The Hour of Letdown" in *The Second Tree from the Corner*). Fortunately, however, there is always Nature, and no matter how furiously we hack away at her, in the end she is victorious. These beliefs, and the proof of his life, place White directly in the tradition of his fellow New Englanders, Thoreau and Frost.

"With some writers," White wrote in *The Elements of Style*, "style not only reveals the spirit of the man, it reveals his identity, as surely as would his fingerprints." Then he added, a little later, "The approach to style is by way of plainness, simplicity, orderliness, sincerity." Taken together, the two statements—however simple they appear on the surface—imply an extremely subtle attitude toward style. "How," one might ask, "am I to do both at the same time—be plain, simple, orderly, and sincere, and yet reveal the complexities of my identity?" No easy, practicable answer is given, for White knew that it is a problem that can be solved only by each solitary writer in his own unending struggle to make the words he sets down on paper approach the temper of his thought. But he does tell us two important things. The first is a belief: "The whole duty of a writer is to please and satisfy himself, and the true writer always plays to an audience of one." And the second is a method: "I write by ear, always with difficulty and seldom with any exact notion of what is taking place under the hood." In short, style, E. B. White would say, is a matter of character, intuition, faith, mystery . . . and hard work.   ■

Once More to the Lake

ONE SUMMER, ALONG ABOUT 1904, my father rented a camp on a lake in Maine and took us all there for the month of August. We all got ringworm from some kittens and had to rub Pond's Extract on our arms and legs night and morning, and my father rolled over in a canoe with all his clothes on; but outside of that the vacation was a success and from then on none of us ever thought there was any place in the world like that lake in Maine. We returned summer after summer—always on August 1st for one month. I have since become a salt-water man, but sometimes in summer there are days when the restlessness of the tides and the fearful cold of the sea water and the incessant wind which blows across the afternoon and into the evening makes me wish for the placidity of a lake in the woods. A few weeks ago this feeling got so strong I bought myself a couple of bass hooks and a spinner and returned to the lake where we used to go, for a week's fishing and to revisit old haunts.

I took along my son, who had never had any fresh water up his nose and who had seen lily pads only from train windows. On the journey over to the lake I began to wonder what it would be like. I wondered how time would have marred this unique, this holy spot—the coves and streams, the hills that the sun set behind, the camps and the paths behind the camps. I was sure that the tarred road would have found it out and I wondered in what other ways it would be desolated. It is strange how much you can remember about places like that once you allow your mind to return into the grooves which lead back. You remember one thing, and that suddenly reminds you of another thing. I guess I remembered clearest of all the early mornings, when the lake was cool and motionless, remembered how the bedroom smelled of the lumber it was made of and of the wet woods whose scent entered through the screen. The partitions in the camp were thin and did not extend clear to the top of the rooms, and as I was always the first up I would dress softly so as not to wake the others, and sneak out into the sweet outdoors and start out in the canoe, keeping close along the shore in the long shadows of the pines. I remembered being very careful never to rub my paddle against the gunwale for fear of disturbing the stillness of the cathedral.

The lake had never been what you would call a wild lake. There were cottages sprinkled around the shores, and it was in farming country although the shores of the lake were quite heavily wooded. Some of the cottages were owned by nearby farmers, and you would live at the shore and eat your meals at the farmhouse. That's what our family did. But although it wasn't wild, it was a fairly large and undisturbed lake and there were places in it which, to a child at least, seemed infinitely remote and primeval.

I was right about the tar: it led to within half a mile of the shore. But when I got back there, with my boy, and we settled into a camp near a farmhouse and into the kind of summertime I had known, I could tell that it was going to be pretty much the same as it had been before—I knew it, lying in bed the first morning, smelling the bedroom, and hearing the boy sneak quietly out and go off along the shore in a boat. I began to sustain the illusion that he was I, and therefore, by simple transposition, that I was my father. This sensation persisted, kept cropping up all the time we were there. It was not an entirely new feeling, but in this setting it grew much stronger. I seemed to be living a dual existence. I would be in the middle of some simple act, I would be picking up a bait box or laying down a table fork, or I would be saying something, and suddenly it would be not I but my father who was saying the words or making the gestures. It gave me a creepy sensation.

We went fishing the first morning. I felt the same damp moss covering the worms in the bait can, and saw the dragonfly alight on the tip of my rod as it hovered a few inches from the surface of the water. It was the arrival of this fly that convinced me beyond any doubt that everything was as it always had been, that the years were a mirage and there had been no years. The small waves were the same, chucking the rowboat under the chin as we fished at anchor, and the boat was the same boat, the same color green and the ribs broken in the same places, and under the floor-boards the same fresh-water leavings and debris—the dead helgramite, the wisps of moss, the rusty discarded fishhook, the dried blood from yesterday's catch. We stared silently at the tips of our rods, at the dragonflies that came and went. I lowered the top of mine into the water, tentatively, pensively dislodging the fly, which darted two feet away, poised, darted two feet back, and came to rest again a little farther up the rod. There had been no years between the ducking of this dragonfly and the other one—the one that was part of memory. I looked at the boy, who was silently watching his fly, and it was my hands that held his rod, my eyes watching. I felt dizzy and didn't know which rod I was at the end of.

We caught two bass, hauling them in briskly as though they were mackerel, pulling them over the side of the boat in a business-like manner without any landing net, and stunning them with a blow on the back of the head. When we got back for a swim before lunch, the lake was exactly where we had left it, the same number of inches from the dock, and there was only the merest suggestion of a breeze. This seemed an utterly enchanted sea, this lake you could leave to its own devices for a few hours and come back to, and find that it had not stirred, this constant and trustworthy body of water. In the shallows, the dark, water-soaked sticks and twigs, smooth and old, were undulating in clusters on the bottom against the clean ribbed sand, and the track of the mussel was plain. A school of minnows swam by, each minnow with its small individual shadow, doubling the attendance, so clear and sharp in the sunlight. Some of the other campers were in swimming, along the shore, one of them with a cake of soap, and the water felt thin and clear and unsubstantial. Over the years there had been this person with the cake of soap, this cultist, and here he was. There had been no years.

Up to the farmhouse to dinner through the teeming, dusty field, the road under our sneakers was only a two-track road. The middle track was missing, the one with the marks of the hooves and the splotches of dried, flaky manure. There had always been three tracks to choose from in choosing which track to walk in; now the choice was narrowed down to two. For a moment I missed terribly the middle alternative. But the way led past the tennis court, and something about the way it lay there in the sun reassured me; the tape had loosened along the backline, the alleys were green with plantains and other weeds, and the net (installed in June and removed in September) sagged in the dry noon, and the whole place steamed with midday heat and hunger and emptiness. There was a choice of pie for dessert, and one was blueberry and one was apple, and the waitresses were the same country girls, there having been no passage of time, only the illusion of it as in a dropped curtain—the waitresses were still fifteen; their hair had been washed, that was the only difference—they had been to the movies and seen the pretty girls with the clean hair.

Summertime, oh summertime, pattern of life indelible, the fadeproof lake, the woods unshatterable, the pasture with the sweetfern and the juniper forever and ever, summer without end; this was the background, and the life along the shore was the design, the cottages with their innocent and tranquil design, their tiny docks with the flagpole and the American flag floating against the white clouds in the blue sky, the little paths over the roots of the trees leading from camp to camp and the paths leading back to the outhouses and the can of lime for sprinkling, and at the souvenir counters at the store the miniature birchbark canoes and the post cards that showed things looking a little better than they looked. This was the Ameri-can family at play, escaping the city heat, wondering whether the new-comers in the camp at the head of the cove were "common" or "nice," wondering whether it was true that the people who drove up for Sunday dinner at the farmhouse were turned away because there wasn't enough chicken.

It seemed to me, as I kept remembering all this, that those times and those summers had been infinitely precious and worth saving. There had been jollity and peace and goodness. The arriving (at the beginning of August) had been so big a business in itself, at the railway station the farm wagon drawn up, the first smell of the pine-laden air, the first glimpse of the smiling farmer, and the great importance of the trunks and your father's enormous authority in such matters, and the feel of the wagon under you for the long ten-mile haul, and at the top of the last long hill catching the first view of the lake after eleven months of not seeing this cherished body of water. The shouts and cries of the other campers when they saw you, and the trunks to be unpacked, to give up their rich burden. (Arriving was less exciting nowadays, when you sneaked up in your car and parked it under a tree near the camp and took out the bags and in five minutes it was all over, no fuss, no loud wonderful fuss about trunks.)

Peace and goodness and jollity. The only thing that was wrong now, really, was the sound of the place, an unfamiliar nervous sound of the outboard motors. This was the note that jarred, the one thing that would sometimes break the illusion and set the years moving. In those other summertimes all motors were inboard; and when they were at a little dis-tance, the noise they made was a sedative, an ingredient of summer sleep. They were one-cylinder and two-cylinder engines, and some were make-and-break and some were jump-spark, but they all made a sleepy sound across the lake. The one-lungers throbbed and fluttered, and the twin-cylinder ones purred and purred, and that was a quiet sound too. But now the campers all had outboards. In the daytime, in the hot mornings, these motors made a petulant, irritable sound; at night, in the still evening when the afterglow lit the water, they whined about one's ears like mosquitoes. My boy loved our rented outboard, and his great desire was to achieve singlehanded mastery over it, and authority, and he soon learned the trick of choking it a little (but not too much), and the adjustment of the needle valve. Watching him I would remember the things you could do with the old one-cylinder engine with the heavy flywheel, how you could have it eating out of your hand if you got really close to it spiritually. Motor boats in those days didn't have clutches, and you would make a landing by shutting off the motor at the proper time and coasting in with a dead rudder. But there was a way of reversing them, if you learned the trick, by cutting the switch and putting it on again exactly on the final dying revolution of the flywheel, so that it would kick back against compression and begin reversing. Approaching a dock in a strong following breeze, it was difficult to slow up sufficiently by the ordinary coasting method, and if a boy felt he had complete mastery over his motor, he was tempted to keep it running beyond its time and then reverse it a few feet from the dock. It took a cool nerve, because if you threw the switch a twentieth of a second too soon you would catch the flywheel when it still had speed enough to go up past center, and the boat would leap ahead, charging bull-fashion at the dock.

We had a good week at the camp. The bass were biting well and the sun shone endlessly, day after day. We would be tired at night and lie down in the accumulated heat of the little bedrooms after the long hot day and the breeze would stir almost imperceptibly outside and the smell of the swamp drift in through the rusty screens. Sleep would come easily and in the morning the red squirrel would be on the roof, tapping out his gay routine. I kept remembering everything, lying in bed in the mornings—the small steamboat that had a long rounded stern like the lip of a Ubangi, and how quietly she ran on the moonlight sails, when the older boys played their mandolins and the girls sang and we ate doughnuts dipped in sugar, and how sweet the music was on the water in the shining night, and what it had felt like to think about girls then. After breakfast we would go up to the store and the things were in the same place—the minnows in a bottle, the plugs and spinners disarranged and pawed over by the youngsters from the boys' camp, the fig newtons and the Beeman's gum. Outside, the road was tarred and cars stood in front of the store. Inside, all was just as it had always been, except there was more Coca-Cola and not so much Moxie and root beer and birch beer and sarsaparilla. We would walk out with a bottle of pop apiece and sometimes the pop would backfire up our noses and hurt. We explored the streams, quietly, where the turtles slid off the sunny logs and dug their way into the soft bottom; and we lay on the town wharf and fed worms to the tame bass. Everywhere we went I had trouble making out which was I, the one walking at my side, the one walking in my pants.

One afternoon while we were there at that lake a thunderstorm came up. It was like the revival of an old melodrama that I had seen long ago with childish awe. The second-act climax of the drama of the electrical disturbance over a lake in America had not changed in any important respect. This was the big scene, still the big scene. The whole thing was so familiar, the first feeling of oppression and heat and a general air around camp of not wanting to go very far away. In midafternoon (it was all the same) a curious darkening of the sky, and a lull in everything that had made life tick; and then the way the boats suddenly swung the other way at their moorings with the coming of a breeze out of the new quarter, and the premonitory rumble. Then the kettle drums, then the snare, then the bass drum and cymbals, then crackling light against the dark, and the gods grinning and licking their chops in the hills. Afterward the calm, the rain steadily rustling in the calm lake, the return of light and hope and spirits, and the campers running out in joy and relief to go swimming in the rain, their bright cries perpetuating the deathless joke about how they were getting simply drenched, and the children screaming with delight at the new sensation of bathing in the rain, and the joke about getting drenched linking the generations in a strong indestructible chain. And the comedian who waded in carrying an umbrella.

When the others went swimming my son said he was going in too. He pulled his dripping trunks from the line where they had hung all through the shower, and wrung them out. Languidly, and with no thought of going in, I watched him, his hard little body, skinny and bare, saw him wince slightly as he pulled up around his vitals the small, soggy, icy garment. As he buckled the swollen belt suddenly my groin felt the chill of death.

[1941]

Death of a Pig

I SPENT SEVERAL DAYS AND NIGHTS IN mid-September with an ailing pig and I feel driven to account for this stretch of time, more particularly since the pig died at last, and I lived, and things might easily have gone the other way round and none left to do the accounting. Even now, so close to the event, I cannot recall the hours sharply and am not ready to say whether death came on the third night or the fourth night. This uncertainty afflicts me with a sense of personal deterioration; if I were in decent health I would know how many nights I had sat up with a pig.

The scheme of buying a spring pig in blossomtime, feeding it through summer and fall, and butchering it when the solid cold weather arrives, is a familiar scheme to me and follows an antique pattern. It is a tragedy enacted on most farms with perfect fidelity to the original script. The murder, being premeditated, is in the first degree but is quick and skillful, and the smoked bacon and ham provide a ceremonial ending whose fitness is seldom questioned.

Once in a while something slips—one of the actors goes up in his lines and the whole performance stumbles and halts. My pig simply failed to show up for a meal. The alarm spread rapidly. The classic outline of the tragedy was lost. I found myself cast suddenly in the role of pig's friend and physician—a farcical character with an enema bag for a prop. I had a presentiment, the very first afternoon, that the play would never regain its balance and that my sympathies were now wholly with the pig. This was slapstick—the sort of dramatic treatment that instantly appealed to my old dachshund, Fred, who joined the vigil, held the bag, and, when all was over, presided at the interment. When we slid the body into the grave, we both were shaken to the core. The loss we felt was not the loss of ham but the loss of pig. He had evidently become precious to me, not that he represented a distant nourishment in a hungry time, but that he had suffered in a suffering world. But I'm running ahead of my story and shall have to go back.

My pigpen is at the bottom of an old orchard below the house. The pigs I have raised have lived in a faded building that once was an icehouse. There is a pleasant yard to move about in, shaded by an apple tree that overhangs the low rail fence. A pig couldn't ask for anything better—or none has, at any rate. The sawdust in the icehouse makes a comfortable bottom in which to root, and a warm bed. This sawdust, however, came under suspicion when the pig took sick. One of my neighbors said he thought the pig would have done better on new ground—the same principle that applies in planting potatoes. He said there might be something unhealthy about that sawdust, that he never thought well of sawdust.

It was about four o'clock in the afternoon when I first noticed that there was something wrong with the pig. He failed to appear at the trough for his supper, and when a pig (or a child) refuses supper a chill wave of fear runs through any household, or ice-household. After examining my pig, who was stretched out in the sawdust inside the building, I went to the phone and cranked it four times. Mr. Dameron answered. "What's good for a sick pig?" I asked. (There is never any identification needed on a country phone; the person on the other end knows who is talking by the sound of the voice and by the character of the question.)

"I don't know, I never had a sick pig," said Mr. Dameron, "but I can find out quick enough. You hang up and I'll call Henry."

Mr. Dameron was back on the line again in five minutes. "Henry says roll him over on his back and give him two ounces of castor oil or sweet oil, and if that doesn't do the trick give him an injection of soapy water. He says he's almost sure the pig's plugged up, and even if he's wrong, it can't do any harm."

I thanked Mr. Dameron. I didn't go right down to the pig, though. I sank into a chair and sat still for a few minutes to think about my troubles, and then I got up and went to the barn, catching up on some odds and ends that needed tending to. Unconsciously I held off, for an hour, the deed by which I would officially recognize the collapse of the performance of raising a pig; I wanted no interruption in the regularity of feeding, the steadiness of growth, the even succession of days. I wanted no interruption, wanted no oil, no deviation. I just wanted to keep on raising a pig, full meal after full meal, spring into summer into fall. I didn't even know whether there were two ounces of castor oil on the place.

Shortly after five o'clock I remembered that we had been invited out to dinner that night and realized that if I were to dose a pig there was no time to lose. The dinner date seemed a familiar conflict: I move in a desultory society and often a week or two will roll by without my going to anybody's house to dinner or anyone's coming to mine, but when an occasion does arise, and I am summoned, something usually turns up (an hour or two in advance) to make all human intercourse seem vastly inappropriate. I have come to believe that there is in hostesses a special power of divination, and that they deliberately arrange dinners to coincide with pig failure or some other sort of failure. At any rate, it was after five o'clock and I knew I could put off no longer the evil hour.

When my son and I arrived at the pigyard, armed with a small bottle of castor oil and a length of clothesline, the pig had emerged from his house and was standing in the middle of his yard, listlessly. He gave us a slim greeting. I could see that he felt uncomfortable and uncertain. I had brought the clothesline thinking I'd have to tie him (the pig weighed more than a hundred pounds) but we never used it. My son reached down, grabbed both front legs, upset him quickly, and when he opened his mouth to scream I turned the oil into his throat—a pink, corrugated area I had never seen before. I had just time to read the label while the neck of the bottle was in his mouth. It said Puretest. The screams, slightly muffled by oil, were pitched in the hysterically high range of pigsound, as though torture were being carried out, but they didn't last long: it was all over rather suddenly, and, his legs released, the pig righted himself.

In the upset position the corners of his mouth had been turned down, giving him a frowning expression. Back on his feet again, he regained the set smile that a pig wears even in sickness. He stood his ground, sucking slightly at the residue of oil; a few drops leaked out of his lips while his wicked eyes, shaded by their coy little lashes, turned on me in disgust and hatred. I scratched him gently with oily fingers and he remained quiet, as though trying to recall the satisfaction of being scratched when in health, and seeming to rehearse in his mind the indignity to which he had just been subjected. I noticed, as I stood there, four or five small dark spots on his back near the tail end, reddish brown in color, each about the size of a housefly. I could not make out what they were. They did not look troublesome but at the same time they did not look like mere surface bruises or chafe marks. Rather they seemed blemishes of internal origin. His stiff white bristles almost completely hid them and I had to part the bristles with my fingers to get a good look.

Several hours later, a few minutes before midnight, having dined well and at someone else's expense, I returned to the pighouse with a flashlight. The patient was asleep. Kneeling, I felt his ears (as you might put your hand on the forehead of a child) and they seemed cool, and then with the light made a careful examination of the yard and the house for a sign that the oil had worked. I found none and went to bed.

We had been having an unseasonable spell of weather—hot, close days, with the fog shutting in every night, scaling for a few hours in midday, then creeping back again at dark, drifting in first over the trees on the point, then suddenly blowing across the fields, blotting out the world and taking possession of houses, men, and animals. Everyone kept hoping for a break, but the break failed to come. Next day was another hot one. I visited the pig before breakfast and tried to tempt him with a little milk in his trough. He just stared at it, while I make a sucking sound through my teeth to remind him of past pleasures of the feast. With very small, timid pigs, weanlings, this ruse is often quite successful and will encourage them to eat; but with a large, sick pig the ruse is senseless and the sound I made must have made him feel, if anything, more miserable. He not only did not crave food, he felt a positive revulsion to it. I found a place under the apple tree where he had vomited in the night.

At this point, although a depression had settled over me, I didn't suppose that I was going to lose my pig. From the lustiness of a healthy pig a man derives a feeling of personal lustiness; the stuff that goes into the trough and is received with such enthusiasm is an earnest of some later feast of his own, and when this suddenly comes to an end and the food lies stale and untouched, souring in the sun, the pig's imbalance becomes the man's vicariously, and life seems insecure, displaced, transitory.

As my own spirits declined, along with the pig's, the spirits of my vile old dachshund rose. The frequency of our trips down the footpath through the orchard to the pigyard delighted him, although he suffers greatly from arthritis, moves with difficulty, and would be bedridden if he could find anyone willing to serve him meals on a tray.

He never missed a chance to visit the pig with me, and he made many professional calls on his own. You could see him down there at all hours, his white face parting the grass along the fence as he wobbled and stumbled about, his stethoscope dangling—a happy quack, writing his villainous prescriptions and grinning his corrosive grin. When the enema bag appeared, and the bucket of warm suds, his happiness was complete, and he managed to squeeze his enormous body between the two lowest rails of the yard and then assumed full charge of the irrigation. Once, when I lowered the bag to check the flow, he reached in and hurriedly drank a few mouthfuls of the suds to test their potency. I have noticed that Fred will feverishly consume any substance that is associated with trouble—the bitter flavor is to his liking. When the bag was above reach, he concentrated on the pig and was everywhere at once, a tower of strength and inconvenience. The pig, curiously enough, stood rather quietly through this colonic carnival, and the enema, though ineffective, was not as difficult as I had anticipated.

I discovered, though, that once having given a pig an enema there is no turning back, no chance of resuming one of life's more stereotyped roles. The pig's lot and mine were inextricably bound now, as though the rubber tube were the silver cord. From then until the time of his death I held the pig steadily in the bowl of my mind; the task of trying to deliver him from his misery became a strong obsession. His suffering soon became the embodiment of all earthly wretchedness. Along toward the end of the afternoon, defeated in physicking, I phoned the veterinary twenty miles away and placed the case formally in his hands. He was full of questions, and when I casually mentioned the dark spots on the pig's back, his voice changed its tone.

"I don't want to scare you," he said, "but when there are spots, erysipelas has to be considered."

Together we considered erysipelas, with frequent interruptions from the telephone operator, who wasn't sure the connection had been established.

"If a pig has erysipelas can he give it to a person?" I asked.

"Yes, he can," replied the vet.

"Have they answered?" asked the operator.

"Yes, they have," I said. Then I addressed the vet again. "You better come over here and examine this pig right away."

"I can't come myself," said the vet, "but McFarland can come this evening if that's all right. Mac knows more about pigs than I do anyway. You needn't worry too much about the spots. To indicate erysipelas they would have to be deep hemorrhagic infarcts."

"Deep hemorrhagic what?" I asked.

"Infarcts," said the vet.

"Have they answered?" asked the operator.

"Well," I said, "I don't know what you'd call these spots, except they're about the size of a housefly. If the pig has erysipelas I guess I have it, too, by this time, because we've been very close lately."

"McFarland will be over," said the vet.

I hung up. My throat felt dry and I went to the cupboard and got a bottle of whiskey. Deep hemorrhagic infarcts—the phrase began fastening its hooks in my head. I had assumed that there could be nothing much wrong with a pig during the months it was being groomed for murder; my confidence in the essential health and endurance of pigs had been strong and deep, particularly in the health of pigs that belonged to me and that were part of my proud scheme. The awakening had been violent and I minded it all the more because I knew that what could be true of my pig could be true also of the rest of my tidy world. I tried to put this distasteful idea from me, but it kept recurring. I took a short drink of the whiskey and then, although I wanted to go down to the yard and look for fresh signs, I was scared to. I was certain I had erysipelas.

It was long after dark and the supper dishes had been put away when a car drove in and McFarland got out. He had a girl with him. I could just make her out in the darkness—she seemed young and pretty. "This is Miss Owen," he said. "We've been having a picnic supper on the shore, that's why I'm late."

McFarland stood in the driveway and stripped off his jacket, then his shirt. His stocky arms and capable hands showed up in my flashlight's gleam as I helped him find his coverall and get zipped up. The rear seat of his car contained an astonishing amount of paraphernalia, which he soon overhauled, selecting a chain, a syringe, a bottle of oil, a rubber tube, and some other things I couldn't identify. Miss Owen said she'd go along with us and see the pig. I led the way down the warm slope of the orchard, my light picking out the path for them, and we all three climbed the fence, entered the pighouse, and squatted by the pig while McFarland took a rectal reading. My flashlight picked up the glitter of an engagement ring on the girl's hand.

"No elevation," said McFarland, twisting the thermometer in the light. "You needn't worry about erysipelas." He ran his hand slowly over the pig's stomach and at one point the pig cried out in pain.

"Poor piggledy-wiggledy!" said Miss Owen.

The treatment I had been giving the pig for two days was then repeated, somewhat more expertly, by the doctor, Miss Owen and I handing him things as he needed them—holding the chain that he had looped around the pig's upper jaw, holding the syringe, holding the bottle stopper, the end of the tube, all of us working in darkness and in comfort, working with the instinctive teamwork induced by emergency conditions, the pig unprotesting, the house shadowy, protecting, intimate. I went to bed tired but with a feeling of relief that I had turned over part of the responsibility of the case to a licensed doctor. I was beginning to think, though, that the pig was not going to live.

He died twenty-four hours later, or it might have been forty-eight—there is a blur in time here, and I may have lost or picked up a day in the telling and the pig one in the dying. At intervals during the last day I took cool fresh water down to him and at such times as he found the strength to get to his feet he would stand with head in the pail and snuffle his snout around. He drank a few sips but no more; yet it seemed to comfort him to dip his nose in water and bobble it about, sucking in and blowing out through his teeth. Much of the time, now, he lay indoors half buried in sawdust. Once, near the last, while I was attending him I saw him try to make a bed for himself but he lacked the strength, and when he set his snout into the dust he was unable to plow even the little furrow he needed to lie down in.

He came out of the house to die. When I went down, before going to bed, he lay stretched in the yard a few feet from the door. I knelt, saw that he was dead, and left him there: his face had a mild look, expressive neither of deep peace nor of deep suffering, although I think he had suffered a good deal. I went back up to the house and to bed, and cried internally— deep hemorrhagic intears. I didn't wake till nearly eight the next morning, and when I looked out the open window the grave was already being dug, down beyond the dump under a wild apple. I could hear the spade strike against the small rocks that blocked the way. Never send to know for whom the grave is dug, I said to myself, it's dug for thee. Fred, I well knew, was supervising the work of digging, so I ate breakfast slowly.

It was a Saturday morning. The thicket in which I found the grave-diggers at work was dark and warm, the sky overcast. Here, among alders and young hackmatacks, at the foot of the apple tree, Lennie had dug a beautiful hole, five feet long, three feet wide, three feet deep. He was standing in it, removing the last spadefuls of earth while Fred patrolled the brink in simple but impressive circles, disturbing the loose earth of the mound so that it trickled back in. There had been no rain in weeks and the soil, even three feet down, was dry and powdery. As I stood and stared, an enormous earthworm which had been partially exposed by the spade at the bottom dug itself deeper and made a slow withdrawal, seeking even remoter moistures at even lonelier depths. And just as Lennie stepped out and rested his spade against the tree and lit a cigarette, a small green apple separated itself from a branch overhead and fell into the hole. Everything about this last scene seemed over-written—the dismal sky, the shabby woods, the imminence of rain, the worm (legendary bedfellow of the dead), the apple (conventional garnish of a pig).

But even so, there was a directness and dispatch about animal burial, I thought, that made it a more decent affair than human burial: there was no stopover in the undertaker's foul parlor, no wreath nor spray; and when we hitched a line to the pig's hind legs and dragged him swiftly from his yard, throwing our weight into the harness and leaving a wake of crushed grass and smoothed rubble over the dump, ours was a businesslike procession, with Fred, the dishonorable pallbearer, staggering along in the rear, his perverse bereavement showing in every seam in his face; and the post mortem performed handily and swiftly right at the edge of the grave, so that the innards that had caused the pig's death preceded him into the ground and he lay at last resting squarely on the cause of his own undoing.

I threw in the first shovelful, and then we worked rapidly and without talk, until the job was complete. I picked up the rope, made it fast to Fred's collar (he is a notorious ghoul), and we all three filed back up the path to the house, Fred bringing up the rear and holding back every inch of the way, feigning unusual stiffness. I noticed that although he weighed far less than the pig, he was harder to drag, being possessed of the vital spark.

The news of the death of my pig traveled fast and far, and I received many expressions of sympathy from friends and neighbors, for no one took the event lightly and the premature expiration of a pig is, I soon discovered, a departure which the community marks solemnly on its calendar, a sorrow in which it feels fully involved. I have written this account in penitence and in grief, as a man who failed to raise his pig, and to explain my deviation from the classic course of so many raised pigs. The grave in the woods is unmarked, but Fred can direct the mourner to it unerringly and with immense good will, and I know he and I shall often revisit it, singly and together, in seasons of reflection and despair, on flagless memorial days of our own choosing. [1948]

■

On a Florida Key

I AM WRITING THIS IN A BEACH COT-tage on a Florida key. It is raining to beat the cars. The rollers from a westerly storm are creaming along the shore, making a steady boiling noise instead of the usual intermittent slap. The Chamber of Commerce has drawn the friendly blind against this ugliness and is busy getting out some advance notices of the style parade which is to be held next Wednesday at the pavilion. The paper says cooler tomorrow.

The walls of my room are of matched boarding, applied horizontally and painted green. On the floor is a straw mat. Under the mat is a layer of sand that has been tracked into the cottage and has sifted through the straw. I have thought some of taking the mat up and sweeping the sand into a pile and removing it, but have decided against it. This is the way keys form, apparently, and I have no particular reason to interfere. On a small wooden base in one corner of the room is a gas heater, supplied from a tank on the premises. This device can raise the temperature of the room with great rapidity by converting the oxygen of the air into heat. In deciding whether to light the heater or leave it alone, one has only to choose whether he wants to congeal in a well-ventilated room or suffocate in comfort. After a little practice, a nice balance can be established—enough oxygen left to sustain life, yet enough heat generated to prevent death from exposure.

On the west wall hangs an Indian rug, and to one edge of the rug is pinned a button which carries the legend: Junior Programs Joop Club. Built into the north wall is a cabinet made of pecky cypress. On the top shelf are three large pine cones, two of them painted emerald-green, the third painted brick-red. Also a gilded candlestick in the shape of a Roman chariot. Another shelf holds some shells which, at the expenditure of considerable effort on somebody's part, have been made to look like birds. On the bottom shelf is a tiny toy collie, made of rabbit fur, with a tongue of red flannel.

In the kitchenette just beyond where I sit is a gas stove and a small electric refrigerator of an ancient vintage. The ice trays show deep claw marks, where people have tried to pry them free, using can openers and knives and screwdrivers and petulance. When the refrigerator snaps on it makes a noise which can be heard all through the cottage and the lights everywhere go dim for a second and then return to their normal brilliancy. This refrigerator contains the milk, the butter, and the eggs for tomorrow's breakfast. More milk will arrive in the morning, but I will save it for use on the morrow, so that every day I shall use the milk of the previous day, never taking advantage of the opportunity to enjoy perfectly fresh milk. This is a situation which could be avoided if I had the guts to throw away a whole bottle of milk, but nobody has that much courage in the world today. It is a sin to throw away milk and we know it.

The water that flows from the faucets in the kitchen sink and in the bathroom contains sulphur and is not good to drink. It leaves deep-brown stains around the drains. Applied to the face with a shaving brush, it feels as though fine sandpaper were being drawn across your jowls. It is so hard and sulphurous that ordinary soap will not yield to it, and the breakfast dishes have to be washed with a washing powder known as Dreft.

On the porch of the cottage, each in a special stand, are two carboys of spring water—for drinking, making coffee, and brushing teeth. There is a deposit of two dollars on bottle and stand, and the water itself costs fifty cents. Two rival companies furnish water to the community, and I happened to get mixed up with both of them. Every couple of days a man from one or the other of the companies shows up and hangs around for a while, whining about the presence on my porch of the rival's carboy. I have made an attempt to dismiss one company and retain the other, but to accomplish it would require a dominant personality and I haven't one. I have been surprised to see how long it takes a man to drink up ten gallons of water. I should have thought I could have done it in half the time it has taken me.

This morning I read in the paper of an old Negro, one hundred-and-one years old, and he was boasting of the quantity of whiskey he had drunk in his life. He said he had once worked in a distillery and they used to give him half a gallon of whiskey a day to take home, which kept him going all right during the week, but on weekends, he said, he would have to buy a gallon extry, to tide him over till Monday.

In the kitchen cabinet is a bag of oranges for morning juice. Each orange is stamped "Color Added." The dyeing of an orange, to make it orange, is man's most impudent gesture to date. It is really an appalling piece of effrontery, carrying the clear implication that Nature doesn't know what she is up to. I think an orange, dyed orange, is as repulsive as a pine cone painted green. I think it is about as ugly a thing as I have ever seen, and it seems hard to believe that here, within ten miles, probably, of the trees that bore the fruit, I can't buy an orange that somebody hasn't smeared with paint. But I doubt that there are many who feel that way about it, because fraudulence has become a national virtue and is well thought of in many circles. In the last twenty-four hours, I see by this morning's paper, 136 cars of oranges have been shipped. There are probably millions of children today who have never seen a natural orange—only an artificially colored one. If they should see a natural orange they might think something had gone wrong with it.

There are two moving picture theaters in the town to which my key is attached by a bridge. In one of them colored people are allowed in the balcony. In the other, colored people are not allowed at all. I saw a patriotic newsreel there the other day which ended with a picture of the American flag blowing in the breeze, and the words: one nation indivisible, with liberty and justice for all. Everyone clapped, but I decided I could not clap for liberty and justice (for all) while I was in a theater from which Negroes had been barred. And I felt there were too many people in the world who think liberty and justice for all means liberty and justice for themselves and their friends. I sat there wondering what would happen to me if I were to jump up and say in a loud voice: "If you folks like liberty and justice so much, why do you keep Negroes from this theater?" I am sure it would have surprised everybody very much and it is the kind of thing I dream about doing but never do. If I had done it I suppose the management would have taken me by the arm and marched me out of the theater, on the grounds that it is disturbing the peace to speak up for liberty just as the feature is coming on. When a man is in the South he must do as the Southerners do; but although I am willing to call my wife "sugar" I am not willing to call a colored person a nigger.

Northerners are quite likely to feel that Southerners are bigoted on the race question, and Southerners almost invariably figure that Northerners are without any practical experience and therefore their opinions aren't worth much. The Jim Crow philosophy of color is unsatisfying to a Northerner, but is regarded as sensible and expedient to residents of towns where the Negro population is as large as or larger than the white. Whether one makes a practical answer or an idealistic answer to a question depends partly on whether one is talking in terms of one year, or ten years, or a hundred years. It is, in other words, conceivable that the Negroes of a hundred years from now will enjoy a greater degree of liberty if the present restrictions on today's Negroes are not relaxed too fast. But that doesn't get today's Negroes in to see Hedy Lamarr.

I have to laugh when I think about the sheer inconsistency of the Southern attitude about color: the Negro barred from the movie house because of color, the orange with "color added" for its ultimate triumph. Some of the cities in this part of the State have fête days to commemorate the past and advertise the future, and in my mind I have been designing a float that I would like to enter in the parades. It would contain a beautiful Negro woman riding with the other bathing beauties and stamped with the magical words, Color Added.

In the cottage next door is a lady who is an ardent isolationist and who keeps running in and out with pamphlets, books, and marked-up newspapers, hoping to convince me that America should mind its own business. She tracks sand in, as well as ideas, and I have to sweep up after her two or three times a day.

Floridians are complaining this year that business is below par. They tell you that the boom in industry causes this unwholesome situation. When tycoons are busy in the North they have no time for sunning themselves, or even for sitting in a semitropical cottage in the rain. Miami is appropriating a few extra thousand dollars for its advertising campaign, hoping to lure executives away from the defense program for a few golden moments.

Although I am no archeologist, I love Florida as much for the remains of her unfinished cities as for the bright cabanas on her beaches. I love to prowl the dead sidewalks that run off into the live jungle, under the broiling sun of noon, where the cabbage palms throw their spiny shade across the stillborn streets and the creepers bind old curbstones in a fierce sensual embrace and the mocking birds dwell in song upon the remembered grandeur of real estate's purple hour. A boulevard which has been reclaimed by Nature is an exciting avenue; it breathes a strange prophetic perfume, as of some century still to come, when the birds will remember, and the spiders, and the little quick lizards that toast themselves on the smooth hard surfaces that once held the impossible dreams of men. Here along these bristling walks is a decayed symmetry in a living forest—straight lines softened by a kindly and haphazard Nature, pavements nourishing life with the beginnings of topsoil, the cracks in the walks possessed by root structures, the brilliant blossoms of the domesticated vine run wild, and overhead the turkey buzzard in the clear sky, on quiet wings, awaiting new mammalian death among the hibiscus, the yucca, the Spanish bayonet, and the palm. I remember the wonderful days and the tall dream of rainbow's end; the offices with the wall charts, the pins in the charts, the orchestras playing gently to prepare the soul of the wanderer for the mysteries of subdivision, the free bus service to the rainbow's beginning, the luncheon served on the little tables under the trees, the warm sweet air so full of the deadly contagion, the dotted line, the signature, and the premonitory qualms and the shadow of the buzzard in the wild wide Florida sky.

I love these rudimentary cities that were conceived in haste and greed and never rose to suffer the scarifying effects of human habitation, cities of not quite forgotten hopes, untouched by neon and by filth. And I love the beaches too, out beyond the cottage colony, where they are wild and free still, visited by the sandpipers that retreat before each wave, like children, and by an occasional hipsprung farmwife hunting shells, or sometimes by a veteran digging for *Donax variabilis* to take back to his hungry mate in the trailer camp.

The sound of the sea is the most time-effacing sound there is. The centuries reroll in a cloud and the earth becomes green again when you listen, with eyes shut, to the sea—a young green time when the water and the land were just getting acquainted and had known each other for only a few billion years and the mollusks were just beginning to dip and creep in the shallows; and now man the invertebrate, under his ribbed umbrella, anoints himself with oil and pulls on his Polaroid glasses to stop the glare and stretches out his long brown body at ease upon a towel on the warm sand and listens.

The sea answers all questions, and always in the same way; for when you read in the papers the interminable discussions and the bickering and the

prognostications and the turmoil, the disagreements and the fateful deci-
sions and agreements and the plans and the programs and the threats and
the counter threats, then you close your eyes and the sea dispatches one
more big roller in the unbroken line since the beginning of the world and
it combs and breaks and returns foaming and saying: "So soon?" [1941]

■

The Ring of Time

AFTER THE LIONS HAD RETURNED TO
their cages, creeping angrily through the chutes, a little bunch of us drifted
away and into an open doorway nearby, where we stood for a while in semi-
darkness, watching a big brown circus horse go harumphing around the
practice ring. His trainer was a woman of about forty, and the two of them,
horse and woman, seemed caught up in one of those desultory treadmills
of afternoon from which there is no apparent escape. The day was hot, and
we kibitzers were grateful to be briefly out of the sun's glare. The long rein,
or tape, by which the woman guided her charge counterclockwise in his
dull career formed the radius of their private circle, of which she was the
revolving center; and she, too, stepped a tiny circumference of her own, in
order to accommodate the horse and allow him his maximum scope. She
had on a short-skirted costume and a conical straw hat. Her legs were bare
and she wore high heels, which probed deep into the loose tanbark and
kept her ankles in a state of constant turmoil. The great size and meekness
of the horse, the repetitious exercise, the heat of the afternoon, all exerted
a hypnotic charm that invited boredom; we spectators were experiencing a
languor—we neither expected relief nor felt entitled to any. We had paid a
dollar to get into the grounds, to be sure, but we had got our dollar's worth
a few minutes before, when the lion trainer's whiplash had got caught
around a toe of one of the lions. What more did we want for a dollar?

Behind me I heard someone say, "Excuse me, please," in a low voice. She was halfway into the building when I turned and saw her—a girl of sixteen or seventeen, politely threading her way through us onlookers who blocked the entrance. As she emerged in front of us, I saw that she was barefoot, her dirty little feet fighting the uneven ground. In most respects she was like any of two or three dozen showgirls you encounter if you wander about in the winter quarters of Mr. John Ringling North's circus, in Sarasota—cleverly proportioned, deeply browned by the sun, dusty, eager, and almost naked. But her grave face and the naturalness of her manner gave her a sort of quick distinction and brought a new note into the gloomy octagonal building where we had all cast our lot for a few moments. As soon as she had squeezed through the crowd, she spoke a word or two to the older woman, whom I took to be her mother, stepped to the ring, and waited while the horse coasted to a stop in front of her. She gave the animal a couple of affectionate swipes on his enormous neck and then swung herself aboard. The horse immediately resumed his rocking canter, the woman goading him on, chanting something that sounded like "Hop! Hop!"

In attempting to recapture this mild spectacle, I am merely acting as recording secretary for one of the oldest of societies—the society of those who, at one time or another, have surrendered, without even a show of resistance, to the bedazzlement of a circus rider. As a writing man, or secretary, I have always felt charged with the safekeeping of all unexpected items of worldly or unworldly enchantment, as though I might be held personally responsible if even a small one were to be lost. But it is not easy to communicate anything of this nature. The circus comes as close to being the world in microcosm as anything I know; in a way, it puts all the rest of show business in the shade. Its magic is universal and complex. Out of its wild disorder comes order; from its rank smell rises the good aroma of courage and daring; out of its preliminary shabbiness comes the final splendor. And buried in the familiar boasts of its advance agents lies the modesty of most of its people. For me the circus is at its best before it has been put together. It is at its best at certain moments when it comes to a point, as through a burning glass, in the activity and destiny of a single performer out of so many. One ring is always bigger than three. One rider, one aerialist, is always greater than six. In short, a man has to catch the circus unawares to experience its full impact and share its gaudy dream.

The ten-minute ride the girl took achieved—as far as I was concerned, who wasn't looking for it, and quite unbeknownst to her, who wasn't even striving for it—the thing that is sought by performers everywhere, on whatever stage, whether struggling in the tidal currents of Shakespeare or bucking the difficult motion of a horse. I somewhat got the idea she was just cadging a ride, improving a shining ten minutes in the diligent way all serious artists seize free moments to hone the blade of their talent and keep themselves in trim. Her brief tour included only elementary postures and tricks, perhaps because her warmup at this hour was unscheduled and the ring was not rigged for a real practice session. She swung herself off and on the horse several times, gripping his mane. She did a few knee-stands—or whatever they are called—dropping to her knees and quickly bouncing back up on her feet again. Most of the time she simply rode in a standing position, well aft on the beast, her hands hanging easily at her sides, her head erect, her straw-colored ponytail lightly brushing her shoulders, the blood of exertion showing faintly through the tan of her skin. Twice she managed a one-foot stance—a sort of ballet pose, with arms out-stretched. At one point the neck strap of her bathing suit broke and she went twice around the ring in the classic attitude of a woman making minor repairs to a garment. The fact that she was standing on the back of a moving horse while doing this invested the matter with a clownish significance that per-fectly fitted the spirit of the circus—jocund, yet charming. She just rolled the strap into a neat ball and stowed it inside her bodice while the horse rocked and rolled beneath her in dutiful innocence. The bathing suit proved as self-reliant as its owner and stood up well enough without benefit of strap.

The richness of the scene was in its plainness, its natural condition—of horse, of ring, of girl, even to the girl's bare feet that gripped the bare back of her proud and ridiculous mount. The enchantment grew not out of any-thing that happened or was performed but out of something that seemed to go round and around and around with the girl, attending her, a steady gleam in the shape of a circle—a ring of ambition, of happiness, of youth. (And the positive pleasures of equilibrium under difficulties.) In a week or two, all would be changed, all (or almost all) lost: the girl would wear makeup, the horse would wear gold, the ring would be painted, the bark would be clean for the feet of the horse, the girl's feet would be clean for the slippers that she'd wear. All, all would be lost.

As I watched with the others, our jaws adroop, our eyes alight, I became painfully conscious of the element of time. Everything in the hideous old building seemed to take the shape of a circle, conforming to the course of the horse. The rider's gaze, as she peered straight ahead, seemed to be cir-cular, as though bent by force of circumstance; then time itself began running in circles, and so the beginning was where the end was, and the two were the same, and one thing ran into the next and time went round and around and got nowhere. The girl wasn't so young that she did not know the delicious satisfaction of having a perfectly behaved body and the fun of using it to do a trick most people can't do, but she was too young to know that time does not really move in a circle at all. I thought: "She will never be as beautiful as this again"—a thought that made me acutely unhappy—and in a flash my mind (which is too much of a busybody to suit me) had projected her twenty-five years ahead, and she was now in the center of the ring, on foot, wearing a conical hat and high-heeled shoes, the image of the older woman, holding the long rein, caught in the treadmill of an afternoon long in the future. "She is at that enviable moment in life [I thought] when she believes she can go once around the ring, make one complete circuit, and at the end be exactly the same age as at the start." Everything in her movements, her expression, told you that for her the ring of time was perfectly formed, changeless, predictable, without beginning or end, like the ring in which she was travelling at this moment with the horse that wallowed under her. And then I slipped back into my trance, and time was circular again—time, pausing quietly with the rest of us, so as not to disturb the balance of a performer.

Her ride ended as casually as it had begun. The older woman stopped the horse, and the girl slid to the ground. As she walked toward us to leave, there was a quick, small burst of applause. She smiled broadly, in surprise and pleasure; then her face suddenly regained its gravity and she disappeared through the door.

It has been ambitious and plucky of me to attempt to describe what is indescribable, and I have failed, as I knew I would. But I have discharged my duty to my society; and besides, a writer, like an acrobat, must occasionally try a stunt that is too much for him. At any rate, it is worth reporting that long before the circus comes to town, its most notable performances have already been given. Under the bright lights of the finished show, a performer need only reflect the electric candle power that is directed upon him; but in the dark and dirty old training rings and in the makeshift cages, whatever light is generated, whatever excitement, whatever beauty, must come from original sources—from internal fires of professional hunger and delight, from the exuberance and gravity of youth. It is the difference between planetary light and the combustion of stars.

[1956]

Walden

Miss Nims, take a letter to Henry David Thoreau. Dear Henry: I thought of you the other afternoon as I was approaching Concord doing fifty on Route 62. That is a high speed at which to hold a philosopher in one's mind, but in this century we are a nimble bunch.

On one of the lawns in the outskirts of the village a woman was cutting the grass with a motorized lawn mower. What made me think of you was that the machine had rather got away from her, although she was game enough, and in the brief glimpse I had of the scene it appeared to me that the lawn was mowing the lady. She kept a tight grip on the handles, which throbbed violently with every explosion of the one-cylinder motor, and as she sheered around bushes and lurched along at a reluctant trot behind her impetuous servant, she looked like a puppy who had grabbed something that was too much for him. Concord hasn't changed much, Henry; the farm implements and the animals still have the upper hand.

I may as well admit that I was journeying to Concord with the deliberate intention of visiting your woods; for although I have never knelt at the grave of a philosopher nor placed wreaths on moldy poets, and have often gone a mile out of my way to avoid some place of historical interest, I have always wanted to see Walden Pond. The account which you left of your sojourn there is, you will be amused to learn, a document of increasing pertinence; each year it seems to gain a little headway, as the world loses ground. We may all be transcendental yet, whether we like it or not. As our common complexities increase, any tale of individual simplicity (and yours is the best written and the cockiest) acquires a new fascination; as our goods accumulate, but not our well-being, your report of an existence without material adornment takes on a certain awkward credibility.

My purpose in going to Walden Pond, like yours, was not to live cheaply or to live dearly there, but to transact some private business with the fewest obstacles. Approaching Concord, doing forty, doing forty-five, doing fifty, the steering wheel held snug in my palms, the highway held grimly in my vision, the crown of the road now serving me (on the righthand curves), now defeating me (on the lefthand curves), I began to rouse myself from the stupefaction which a day's motor journey induces. It was a delicious evening, Henry, when the whole body is one sense, and imbibes delight through every pore, if I may coin a phrase. Fields were richly brown where the harrow, drawn by the stripped Ford, had lately sunk its teeth; pastures were green; and overhead the sky had that same everlasting great look which you will find on Page 144 of the Oxford pocket edition. I could feel the road entering me, through tire, wheel, spring, and cushion; shall I not have intelligence with earth too? Am I not partly leaves and vegetable mold myself?—a man of infinite horsepower, yet partly leaves.

Stay with me on 62 and it will take you into Concord. As I say, it was a delicious evening. The snake had come forth to die in a bloody S on the highway, the wheel upon its head, its bowels flat now and exposed. The turtle had come up too to cross the road and die in the attempt, its hard shell smashed under the rubber blow, its intestinal yearning (for the other side of the road) forever squashed. There was a sign by the wayside which announced that the road had a "cotton surface." You wouldn't know what that is, but neither, for that matter, did I. There is a cryptic ingredient in many of our modern improvements—we are awed and pleased without knowing quite what we are enjoying. It is something to be traveling on a road with a cotton surface.

The civilization round Concord today is an odd distillation of city, village, farm, and manor. The houses, yards, fields look not quite suburban, not quite rural. Under the bronze beech and the blue spruce of the departed baron grazes the milch goat of the heirs. Under the porte-cochère stands the reconditioned station wagon; under the grape arbor sit the puppies for sale. (But why do men degenerate ever? What makes families run out?)

It was June and everywhere June was publishing her immemorial stanza; in the lilacs, in the syringa, in the freshly edged paths and the sweetness of moist beloved gardens, and the little wire wickets that preserve the tulips' front. Farmers were already moving the fruits of their toil into their yards, arranging the rhubarb, the asparagus, the strictly fresh eggs on the painted stands under the little shed roofs with the patent shingles. And though it was almost a hundred years since you had taken your ax and started cutting out your home on Walden Pond, I was interested to observe that the philosophical spirit was still alive in Massachusetts: in the center of a vacant lot some boys were assembling the framework of the rude shelter, their whole mind and skill concentrated in the rather inauspicious helter-skelton of studs and rafters. They too were escaping from town, to live naturally, in a rich blend of savagery and philosophy.

That evening, after supper at the inn, I strolled out into the twilight to dream my shapeless transcendental dreams and see that the car was locked up for the night (first open the right front door, then reach over, straining, and pull up the handles of the left rear and the left front till you hear the click, then the handle of the right rear, then shut the right front but open it again remembering that the key is still in the ignition switch, remove the key, shut the right front again with a bang, push the tiny keyhole cover to one side, insert key, turn, and withdraw). It is what we all do, Henry. It is called locking the car. It is said to confuse thieves and keep them from making off with the laprobe. Four doors to lock behind one robe. The driver himself never uses a laprobe, the free movement of his legs being vital to the operation of the vehicle; so that when he locks the car it is a pure and unselfish act. I have in my life gained very little essential heat from laprobes, yet I have ever been at pains to lock them up.

The evening was full of sounds, some of which would have stirred your memory. The robins still love the elms of New England villages at sundown. There is enough of the thrush in them to make song inevitable at the end of the day, and enough of the tramp to make them hang round the dwellings of men. A robin, like many another American, dearly loves a white house with green blinds. Concord is still full of them.

Your fellow-townsmen were stirring abroad—not many afoot, most of them in their cars; and the sound which they made in Concord at evening was a rustling and a whispering. The sound lacks steadfastness and is wholly unlike that of a train. A train, as you know who lived so near the Fitchburg line, whistles once or twice sadly and is gone, trailing a memory in smoke, soothing to ear and mind. Automobiles, skirting a village green, are like flies that have gained the inner ear—they buzz, cease, pause, start, shift, stop, halt, brake, and the whole effect is a nervous polytone curiously disturbing.

As I wandered along, the toc toc of ping pong balls drifted from an attic window. In front of the Reuben Brown house a Buick was drawn up. At the wheel, motionless, his hat upon his head, a man sat, listening to Amos and Andy on the radio (it is a drama of many scenes and without an end). The deep voice of Andrew Brown, emerging from the car, although it originated more than two hundred miles away, was unstrained by distance. When you used to sit on the shore of your pond on Sunday morning, listening to the church bells of Acton and Concord, you were aware of the excellent filter of the intervening atmosphere. Science has attended to that, and sound now maintains its intensity without regard for distance. Properly sponsored, it goes on forever.

A fire engine, out for a trial spin, roared past Emerson's house, hot with readiness for public duty. Over the barn roofs the martins dipped and chittered. A swarthy daughter of an asparagus grower, in culottes, shirt, and bandanna, pedalled past on her bicycle. It was indeed a delicious evening, and I returned to the inn (I believe it was your house once) to rock with the old ladies on the concrete veranda.

Next morning early I started afoot for Walden, out Main Street and down Thoreau, past the depot and the Minuteman Chevrolet Company. The morning was fresh, and in a bean field along the way I flushed an agriculturalist, quietly studying his beans. Thoreau Street soon joined Number 126, an artery of the State. We number our highways nowadays, our speed being so great we can remember little of their quality or character and are lucky to remember their number. (Men have an indistinct notion that if they keep up this activity long enough all will at length ride somewhere, in next to no time.) Your pond is on 126.

I knew I must be nearing your woodland retreat when the Golden Pheasant lunchroom came into view—Sealtest ice cream, toasted sandwiches, hot frankfurters, waffles, tonics, and lunches. Were I the proprietor, I should add rice, Indian meal, and molasses—just for old time's sake. The Pheasant, incidentally, is for sale: a chance for some nature lover who wishes to set himself up beside a pond in the Concord atmosphere and live deliberately, fronting only the essential facts of life on Number 126. Beyond the Pheasant was a place called Walden Breezes, an oasis whose porch pillars were made of old green shutters sawed into lengths. On the porch was a distorting mirror, to give the traveler a comical image of himself, who had miraculously learned to gaze in an ordinary glass without smiling. Behind the Breezes, in a sun-parched clearing, dwelt your philosophical descendants in their trailers, each trailer the size of your hut, but all grouped together for the sake of congeniality. Trailer people leave the city, as you did, to discover solitude and in any weather, at any hour of the day or night, to improve the nick of time; but they soon collect in villages and get bogged deeper in the mud than ever. The camp behind Walden Breezes was just rousing itself to the morning. The ground was packed hard under the heel, and the sun came through the clearing to bake the soil and enlarge the wry smell of cramped housekeeping. Cushman's bakery truck had stopped to deliver an early basket of rolls. A camp dog, seeing me in the road, barked petulantly. A man emerged from one of the trailers and set forth with a bucket to draw water from some forest tap.

Leaving the highway I turned off into the woods toward the pond, which was apparent through the foliage. The floor of the forest was strewn with dried old oak leaves and *Transcripts*. From beneath the flattened popcorn wrapper (*granum explosum*) peeped the frail violet. I followed a footpath and descended to the water's edge. The pond lay clear and blue in the morning light, as you have seen it so many times. In the shallows a man's waterlogged shirt undulated gently. A few flies came out to greet me and convoy me to your cove, past the No Bathing signs on which the fellows and the girls had scrawled their names. I felt strangely excited suddenly to be snooping around your premises, tiptoeing along watchfully, as though not to tread by mistake upon the intervening century. Before I got to the cove I heard something which seemed to me quite wonderful: I heard your frog, a full, clear *troonk,* guiding me, still hoarse and solemn, bridging the years as the robins had bridged them in the sweetness of the village evening. But he soon quit, and I came on a couple of young boys throwing stones at him.

Your front yard is marked by a bronze tablet set in a stone. Four small granite posts, a few feet away, show where the house was. On top of the tablet was a pair of faded blue bathing trunks with a white stripe. Back of it is a pile of stones, a sort of cairn, left by your visitors as a tribute I suppose. It is a rather ugly little heap of stones, Henry. In fact the hillside itself seems faded, browbeaten; a few tall skinny pines, bare of lower limbs, a smattering of young maples in suitable green, some birches and oaks, and a number of trees felled by the last big wind. It was from the bole of one of these fallen pines, torn up by the roots, that I extracted the stone which I added to the cairn—a sentimental act in which I was interrupted by a small terrier from a nearby picnic group, who confronted me and wanted to know about the stone.

I sat down for a while on one of the posts of your house to listen to the bluebottles and the dragonflies. The invaded glade sprawled shabby and mean at my feet, but the flies were tuned to the old vibration. There were the remains of a fire in your ruins, but I doubt that it was yours; also two beer bottles trodden into the soil and become part of earth. A young oak had taken root in your house, and two or three ferns, unrolling like the ticklers at a banquet. The only other furnishings were a DuBarry pattern sheet, a page torn from a picture magazine, and some crusts in wax paper.

Before I quit I walked clear round the pond and found the place where you used to sit on the northeast side to get the sun in the fall, and the beach where you got sand for scrubbing your floor. On the eastern side of the pond, where the highway borders it, the State has built dressing rooms for swimmers, a float with diving towers, drinking fountains of porcelain, and rowboats for hire. The pond is in fact a State Preserve, and carries a twenty-dollar fine for picking wild flowers, a decree signed in all solemnity by your fellow-citizens Walter C. Wardwell, Erson B. Barlow, and Nathaniel I. Bowditch. There was a smell of creosote where they had been building a wide wooden stairway to the road and the parking area. Swimmers and boaters were arriving; bodies plunged vigorously into the water and emerged wet and beautiful in the bright air. As I left, a boatload of town boys were splashing about in mid-pond, kidding and fooling, the young fellows singing at the tops of their lungs in a wild chorus:

> *Amer-ica, Amer-ica, God shed his grace on thee,*
> *And crown thy good with brotherhood*
> *From sea to shi-ning sea!*

I walked back to town along the railroad, following your custom. The rails were expanding noisily in the hot sun, and on the slope of the roadbed the wild grape and the blackberry sent up their creepers to the track.

The expense of my brief sojourn in Concord was:

Canvas shoes $1.95		
Baseball bat .... .25	gifts to take back
Left-handed fielder's glove 1.25	to a boy
Hotel and meals 4.25	
In all $7.70	

As you see, this amount was almost what you spent for food for eight months. I cannot defend the shoes or the expenditure for shelter and food: they reveal a meanness and grossness in my nature which you would find contemptible. The baseball equipment, however, is the kind of impediment with which you were never on even terms. You must remember that the house where you practiced the sort of economy which I respect was haunted only by mice and squirrels. You never had to cope with a shortstop.   [1939]

JAMES BALDWIN

UPI/Bettmann Newsphotos

$\blacksquare$

JAMES BALDWIN WAS BORN IN THE HARLEM section of New York City on August 2, 1924. The eldest of nine children, his childhood was, in his own words, a "bleak fantasy" of poverty, hopelessness, the violence of Harlem's streets, and—overshadowing it all—the grim religious fanaticism of his father, a lay preacher in an evangelical church. By the time he was fourteen Baldwin saw that only two possible ways lay open to him: either he would sink into the abyss of liquor, sex, drugs, and crime that was already beginning to claim many of his friends; or he would find himself a "gimmick," some role or position that would make him less susceptible to the frustrations of Harlem. The gimmick he found was religion, and for the next three years Baldwin was a young minister in a storefront church. He finally abandoned religion as a result of the books he was reading, especially Dostoevsky, and his growing confidence that what he most wanted to do was write.

Following his graduation from DeWitt Clinton High School in 1942, Baldwin began that succession of odd jobs that characterizes the modern, moneyless writer learning his craft. Then, in 1945, he received his first grant, a Saxton Fellowship for an unfinished novel, and since that time he has had to do very little nonliterary work. (Baldwin is a good example of the twentieth-century artist who is supported by foundations: between the years 1948 and 1959 he received grants or fellowships from the *Partisan Review*, the National Institute of Arts and Letters, and the Rosenwald, Guggenheim, and Ford Foundations.)

In 1948 he left America for Europe, and for the next nine years lived mainly in Paris on the fringe of a colony of black artists that included Richard Wright and Chester Himes. Gradually he began to publish essays in magazines such as *Commentary, Harper's,* and *Partisan Review,* and in 1953 his first novel, *Go Tell It on the Mountain,* was published. Largely autobiographical, it describes a climactic day in the life of a Harlem family, during which each of the principal characters reviews his life at the same time that the oldest son of the family is experiencing his soul's salvation. In 1955 Baldwin published *Notes of a Native Son,* a collection of essays, and, in the following year, a second novel, *Giovanni's Room.* The latter is interesting primarily for the way in which it reveals Baldwin's attempt to follow Ralph Ellison's advice that he not confine himself to writing about Negroes (there are none in the book), and in the fact that it deals with homosexuality without capitalizing on its more sensational aspects.

Upon returning to the United States in 1958, Baldwin took up residence in Greenwich Village (where he had lived before going to Europe), and published another collection of essays, *Nobody Knows My Name* (1961), a novel, *Another Country* (1962), and a long essay prophesying racial conflict in America, *The Fire Next Time* (1963). In 1964 his play *Blues for Mister Charlie* was produced by the Actor's Studio in New York, and a year later an earlier play, *The Amen Corner* (written in 1953), was produced on Broadway. Although Baldwin published a number of books in the 1960s and 1970s—among them his first collection of short stories, *Going to Meet the Man* (1965); another novel, *Tell Me How Long the Train's Been Gone* (1968); and a long, autobiographical essay on his involvement in black militancy, *No Name in the Street* (1972); and the novels *If Beale Street Could Talk* (1974) and *Just Above My Head* (1979)—none of it was as good as his early essays.

It is impossible to know what readers one or two generations from now will think of James Baldwin, whether he will still be read or simply dismissed as a minor novelist and interesting polemicist during a special period of our history, for nothing is more transitory than sociopolitical issues. At the same time, *all* works of art reflect the age in which they are written, and everything, in a sense, is political. Those which survive do so because they manage to transcend the purely temporal aspects of their subjects: they reveal problems—relationships between people—that exist from generation to generation and from nation to nation. Thus, if an essay such as "Notes of a Native Son" lasts beyond our own time, it will most likely be not solely because of what it tells us about Black–White relations, but rather, for what it says about the relationship between fathers and sons. And surely this is what Baldwin had in mind when he said that he did not wish to become "merely a Negro writer." He added, "I wanted to find out in what way the *specialness* of my experience could be made to connect me with other people instead of dividing me from them."

Fortunately, as an essayist Baldwin developed a style that is both clear and forceful, that draws its strength not from eccentricities but from its combination of candor and a strict adherence to logic. Baldwin recognized both its strengths and weaknesses when he described his style as being a mixture of "the King James Bible, the rhetoric of the store-front church, something ironic and violent and perpetually understated in Negro speech—and something of Dickens' love of bravura." It seems perfectly suited to the things he wrote about: bitterness, self-pity, rage, and—above all—the struggle to be a man. ■

Notes of a Native Son

O<small>N THE 29TH OF JULY, IN 1943, MY</small> father died. On the same day, a few hours later, his last child was born. Over a month before this, while all our energies were concentrated in waiting for these events, there had been, in Detroit, one of the bloodiest race riots of the century. A few hours after my father's funeral, while he lay in state in the undertaker's chapel, a race riot broke out in Harlem. On the morning of the 3rd of August, we drove my father to the graveyard through a wilderness of smashed plate glass.

The day of my father's funeral had also been my nineteenth birthday. As we drove him to the graveyard, the spoils of injustice, anarchy, discontent, and hatred were all around us. It seemed to me that God himself had devised, to mark my father's end, the most sustained and brutally dissonant of codas. And it seemed to me, too, that the violence which rose all about us as my father left the world had been devised as a corrective for the pride of his eldest son. I had declined to believe in that apocalypse which had been central to my father's vision; very well, life seemed to be saying, here is something that will certainly pass for an apocalypse until the real thing comes along. I had inclined to be contemptuous of my father for the conditions of his life, for the conditions of our lives. When his life had ended I began to wonder about that life and also, in a new way, to be apprehensive about my own.

I had not known my father very well. We had got on badly, partly because we shared, in our different fashions, the vice of stubborn pride. When he was dead I realized that I had hardly ever spoken to him. When he had been dead a long time I began to wish I had. It seems to be typical of life in America, where opportunities, real and fancied, are thicker than anywhere else on the globe, that the second generation has no time to talk to the first. No one, including my father, seems to have known exactly how old he was, but his mother had been born during slavery. He was of the first generation of free men. He, along with thousands of other Negroes, came North after 1919 and I was part of that generation which had never seen the landscape of what Negroes sometimes call the Old Country.

He had been born in New Orleans and had been a quite young man there during the time that Louis Armstrong, a boy, was running errands for the dives and honky-tonks of what was always presented to me as one of the most wicked of cities—to this day, whenever I think of New Orleans,

I also helplessly think of Sodom and Gomorrah. My father never mentioned Louis Armstrong, except to forbid us to play his records; but there was a picture of him on our wall for a long time. One of my father's strong-willed female relatives had placed it there and forbade my father to take it down. He never did, but he eventually maneuvered her out of the house and when, some years later, she was in trouble and near death, he refused to do anything to help her.

He was, I think, very handsome. I gather this from photographs and from my own memories of him, dressed in his Sunday best and on his way to preach a sermon somewhere, when I was little. Handsome, proud, and ingrown, "like a toe-nail," somebody said. But he looked to me, as I grew older, like pictures I had seen of African tribal chieftains: he really should have been naked, with war-paint on and barbaric mementos, standing among spears. He could be chilling in the pulpit and indescribably cruel in his personal life and he was certainly the most bitter man I have ever met; yet it must be said that there was something else in him, buried in him, which lent him his tremendous power and, even, a rather crushing charm. It had something to do with his blackness, I think—he was very black— with his blackness and his beauty, and with the fact that he knew that he was black but did not know that he was beautiful. He claimed to be proud of his blackness but it had also been the cause of much humiliation and it had fixed bleak boundaries to his life. He was not a young man when we were growing up and he had already suffered many kinds of ruin; in his outrageously demanding and protective way he loved his children, who were black like him and menaced, like him; and all these things sometimes showed in his face when he tried, never to my knowledge with any success, to establish contact with any of us. When he took one of his children on his knee to play, the child always became fretful and began to cry; when he tried to help one of us with our homework the absolutely unabating tension which emanated from him caused our minds and our tongues to become paralyzed, so that he, scarcely knowing why, flew into a rage and the child, not knowing why, was punished. If it ever entered his head to bring a surprise home for his children, it was, almost unfailingly, the wrong surprise and even the big watermelons he often brought home on his back in the summertime led to the most appalling scenes. I do not remember, in all those years, that one of his children was ever glad to see him come home. From what I was able to gather of his early life, it seemed that this inability to establish contact with other people had always marked him and had been one of the things which had driven him out of New Orleans. There was something in him, therefore, groping and tentative, which was never expressed and which was buried with him. One saw it most clearly when he was facing new people and hoping to impress them. But he never did, not for long. We went from church to smaller and more improbable church, he found himself in less and less demand as a minister, and by the time he died none of his friends had come to see him for a long time. He had lived and died in an intolerable bitterness of spirit and it frightened me, as we drove him to the graveyard through those unquiet, ruined streets, to see how powerful and overflowing this bitterness could be and to realize that this bitterness now was mine.

When he died I had been away from home for a little over a year. In that year I had had time to become aware of the meaning of all my father's bitter warnings, had discovered the secret of his proudly pursed lips and rigid carriage: I had discovered the weight of white people in the world. I saw that this had been for my ancestors and now would be for me an awful thing to live with and that the bitterness which had helped to kill my father could also kill me.

He had been ill a long time—in the mind, as we now realized, reliving instances of his fantastic intransigence in the new light of his affliction and endeavoring to feel a sorrow for him which never, quite, came true. We had not known that he was being eaten up by paranoia, and the discovery that his cruelty, to our bodies and our minds, had been one of the symptoms of his illness was not, then, enough to enable us to forgive him. The younger children felt, quite simply, relief that he would not be coming home anymore. My mother's observation that it was he, after all, who had kept them alive all these years meant nothing because the problems of keeping children alive are not real for children. The older children felt, with my father gone, that they could invite their friends to the house without fear that their friends would be insulted or, as had sometimes happened with me, being told that their friends were in league with the devil and intended to rob our family of everything we owned. (I didn't fail to wonder, and it made me hate him, what on earth we owned that anybody else would want.)

His illness was beyond all hope of healing before anyone realized that he was ill. He had always been so strange and had lived, like a prophet, in such unimaginably close communion with the Lord that his long silences which were punctuated by moans and hallelujahs and snatches of old songs while he sat at the living room window never seemed odd to us. It was not until he refused to eat because, he said, his family was trying to poison him that my mother was forced to accept as a fact what had, until then, been only an unwilling suspicion. When he was committed, it was discovered that he had tuberculosis and, as it turned out, the disease of his mind allowed the disease of his body to destroy him. For the doctors could not force him to eat, either, and, though he was fed intravenously, it was clear from the beginning that there was no hope for him.

In my mind's eye I could see him, sitting at the window, locked up in his terrors; hating and fearing every living soul including his children who had betrayed him, too, by reaching towards the world which had despised him. There were nine of us. I began to wonder what it could have felt like for such a man to have had nine children whom he could barely feed. He used to make little jokes about our poverty, which never, of course, seemed very funny to us; they could not have seemed very funny to him, either, or else our all too feeble response to them would never have caused such rages. He spent great energy and achieved, to our chagrin, no small amount of success in keeping us away from the people who surrounded us, people who had all-night rent parties to which we listened when we should have been sleeping, people who cursed and drank and flashed razor blades on Lenox Avenue. He could not understand why, if they had so much energy to spare, they could not use it to make their lives better. He treated almost everybody on our block with a most uncharitable asperity and neither they, nor, of course, their children were slow to reciprocate.

The only white people who came to our house were welfare workers and bill collectors. It was almost always my mother who dealt with them, for my father's temper, which was at the mercy of his pride, was never to be trusted. It was clear that he felt their very presence in his home to be a violation: this was conveyed by his carriage, almost ludicrously stiff, and by his voice, harsh and vindictively polite. When I was around nine or ten I wrote a play which was directed by a young, white schoolteacher, a woman, who then took an interest in me, and gave me books to read and, in order to corroborate my theatrical bent, decided to take me to see what she somewhat tactlessly referred to as "real" plays. Theater-going was forbidden in our house, but, with the really cruel intuitiveness of a child, I suspected that the color of this woman's skin would carry the day for me. When, at school, she suggested taking me to the theater, I did not, as I might have done if she had been a Negro, find a way of discouraging her, but agreed that she should pick me up at my house one evening. I then, very cleverly, left all the rest to my mother, who suggested to my father, as I knew she would, that it would not be very nice to let such a kind woman make the trip for nothing. Also, since it was a schoolteacher, I imagine that my mother countered the idea of sin with the idea of "education," which word, even with my father, carried a kind of bitter weight.

Before the teacher came my father took me aside to ask *why* she was coming, what *interest* she could possibly have in our house, in a boy like me. I said I didn't know but I, too, suggested that it had something to do with education. And I understood that my father was waiting for me to say something—I didn't quite know what; perhaps that I wanted his protection against this teacher and her "education." I said none of these things and the teacher came and we went out. It was clear, during the brief interview in our living room, that my father was agreeing very much against his will and that he would have refused permission if he had dared. The fact that he did not dare caused me to despise him: I had no way of knowing that he was facing in that living room a wholly unprecedented and frightening situation.

Later, when my father had been laid off from his job, this woman became very important to us. She was really a very sweet and generous woman and went to a great deal of trouble to be of help to us, particularly during one awful winter. My mother called her by the highest name she knew: she said she was a "christian." My father could scarcely disagree but during the four or five years of our relatively close association he never trusted her and was always trying to surprise in her open, Midwestern face the genuine, cunningly hidden, and hideous motivation. In later years, particularly when it began to be clear that this "education" of mine was going to lead me to perdition, he became more explicit and warned me that my white friends in high school were not really my friends and that I would see, when I was older, how white people would do anything to keep a Negro down. Some of them could be nice, he admitted, but none of them were to be trusted and most of them were not even nice. The best thing was to have as little to do with them as possible. I did not feel this way and I was certain, in my innocence, that I never would.

But the year which preceded my father's death had made a great change in my life. I had been living in New Jersey, working in defense plants, working and living among southerners, white and black. I knew about the south, of course, and about how southerners treated Negroes and how they expected them to behave, but it had never entered my mind that anyone would look at me and expect *me* to behave that way. I learned in New Jersey that to be a Negro meant, precisely, that one was never looked at but was simply at the mercy of the reflexes the color of one's skin caused in other people. I acted in New Jersey as I had always acted, that is as though I thought a great deal of myself—I had to *act* that way—with results that were, simply, unbelievable. I had scarcely arrived before I had earned the enmity, which was extraordinarily ingenious, of all my superiors and nearly all my co-workers. In the beginning, to make matters worse, I simply did not know what was happening. I did not know what I had done, and I shortly began to wonder what *anyone* could possibly do, to bring about such unanimous, active, and unbearably vocal hostility. I knew about jim-crow but I had never experienced it. I went to the same self-service restaurant three times and stood with all the Princeton boys before the counter, waiting for a hamburger and coffee; it was always an extraordinarily long time before anything was set before me; but it was not until the fourth visit that I learned that, in fact, nothing had ever been set before me: I had simply picked something up. Negroes were not served there, I was told, and they had been waiting for me to realize that I was always the only Negro present. Once I was told this, I determined to go there all the time. But now they were ready for me and, though some dreadful scenes were subsequently enacted in that restaurant, I never ate there again.

It was the same story all over New Jersey, in bars, bowling alleys, diners, places to live. I was always being forced to leave, silently, or with mutual imprecations. I very shortly became notorious and children giggled behind me when I passed and their elders whispered or shouted—they really believed that I was mad. And it did begin to work on my mind, of course; I began to be afraid to go anywhere and to compensate for this I went places to which I really should not have gone and where, God knows, I had no desire to be. My reputation in town naturally enhanced my reputation at work and my working day became one long series of acrobatics designed to keep me out of trouble. I cannot say that these acrobatics succeeded. It began to seem that the machinery of the organization I worked for was turning over, day and night, with but one aim: to eject me. I was fired once, and contrived, with the aid of a friend from New York, to get back on the payroll; was fired again, and bounced back again. It took a while to fire me for the third time, but the third time took. There were no loopholes anywhere. There was not even any way of getting back inside the gates.

That year in New Jersey lives in my mind as though it were the year during which, having an unsuspected predilection for it, I first contracted some dread, chronic disease, the unfailing symptom of which is a kind of blind fever, a pounding in the skull and fire in the bowels. Once this disease is contracted, one can never be really carefree again, for the fever, without an instant's warning, can recur at any moment. It can wreck more important things than race relations. There is not a Negro alive who does not have this rage in his blood—one has the choice, merely, of living with it consciously or surrendering to it. As for me, this fever has recurred in me, and does, and will until the day I die.

My last night in New Jersey, a white friend from New York took me to the nearest big town, Trenton, to go to the movies and have a few drinks. As it turned out, he also saved me from, at the very least, a violent whipping. Almost every detail of that night stands out very clearly in my memory. I even remember the name of the movie we saw because its title impressed me as being so patly ironical. It was a movie about the German occupation of France, starring Maureen O'Hara and Charles Laughton and called *This Land Is Mine*. I remember the name of the diner we walked into when the movie ended: it was the "American Diner." When we walked in the counterman asked what we wanted and I remember answering with the casual sharpness which had become my habit: "We want a hamburger and a cup of coffee, what do you think we want?" I do not know why, after a year of such rebuffs, I so completely failed to anticipate his answer, which was, of course, "We don't serve Negroes here." This reply failed to discompose me, at least for the moment. I made some sardonic comment about the name of the diner and we walked out into the streets.

This was the time of what was called the "brown-out," when the lights in all American cities were very dim. When we reentered the streets something happened to me which had the force of an optical illusion, or a nightmare. The streets were very crowded and I was facing north. People were moving in every direction but it seemed to me, in that instant, that all of the people I could see, and many more than that, were moving toward me, against me, and that everyone was white. I remember how their faces gleamed. And I felt, like a physical sensation, a *click* at the nape of my neck as though some interior string connecting my head to my body had been cut. I began to walk. I heard my friend call after me, but I ignored him. Heaven only knows what was going on in his mind, but he had the good sense not to touch me—I don't know what would have happened if he had—and to keep me in sight. I don't know what was going on in my mind, either; I certainly had no conscious plan. I wanted to do something to crush these white faces, which were crushing me. I walked for perhaps a block or two until I came to an enormous, glittering, and fashionable restaurant in which I knew not even the intercession of the Virgin would cause me to be served. I pushed through the doors and took the first vacant seat I saw, at a table for two, and waited.

I do not know how long I waited and I rather wonder, until today, what I could possibly have looked like. Whatever I looked like, I frightened the waitress who shortly appeared, and the moment she appeared all my fury flowed towards her. I hated her for her white face, and for her great, astounded, frightened eyes. I felt that if she found a black man so frightening I would make her fright worth-while.

She did not ask me what I wanted, but repeated, as though she had learned it somewhere, "We don't serve Negroes here." She did not say it with the blunt, derisive hostility to which I had grown so accustomed, but, rather, with a note of apology in her voice, and fear. This made me colder and more murderous than ever. I felt I had to do something with my hands. I wanted her to come close enough for me to get her neck between my hands.

So I pretended not to have understood her, hoping to draw her closer. And she did step a very short step closer, with her pencil poised incongruously over her pad, and repeated the formula: ". . . don't serve Negroes here."

Somehow, with the repetition of that phrase, which was already ringing in my head like a thousand bells of a nightmare, I realized that she would never come any closer and that I would have to strike from a distance. There was nothing on the table but an ordinary water-mug half full of water, and I picked this up and hurled it with all my strength at her. She ducked and it missed her and shattered against the mirror behind the bar. And, with that sound, my frozen blood abruptly thawed, I returned from wherever I had been, I *saw*, for the first time, the restaurant, the people with their mouths open, already, as it seemed to me, rising as one man, and I realized what I had done, and where I was, and I was frightened. I rose and began running for the door. A round, pot-bellied man grabbed me by the nape of the neck just as I reached the doors and began to beat me about the face. I kicked him and got loose and ran into the streets. My friend whispered, *"Run!"* and I ran.

My friend stayed outside the restaurant long enough to misdirect my pursuers and the police, who arrived, he told me, at once. I do not know what I said to him when he came to my room that night. I could not have said much. I felt, in the oddest, most awful way, that I had somehow betrayed him. I lived it over and over and over again, the way one relives an automobile accident after it has happened and one finds oneself alone and safe. I could not get over two facts, both equally difficult for the imagination to grasp, and one was that I could have been murdered. But the other was that I had been ready to commit murder. I saw nothing very clearly but I did see this: that my life, my *real* life, was in danger, and not from anything other people might do but from the hatred I carried in my own heart.

[2]

I had returned home around the second week in June—in great haste because it seemed that my father's death and my mother's confinement were both but a matter of hours. In the case of my mother, it soon became clear that she had simply made a miscalculation. This had always been her tendency and I don't believe that a single one of us arrived in the world, or has since arrived anywhere else, on time. But none of us dawdled so intolerably about the business of being born as did my baby sister. We sometimes amused ourselves, during those endless, stifling weeks, by picturing the baby sitting within in the safe, warm dark, bitterly regretting the necessity of becoming a part of our chaos and stubbornly putting it off as long as possible. I understood her perfectly and congratulated her on showing such good sense so soon. Death, however, sat as purposefully at my father's bedside as life stirred within my mother's womb and it was harder to understand why he so lingered in that long shadow. It seemed that he had bent, and for a long time, too, all of his energies towards dying. Now death was ready for him but my father held back.

All of Harlem, indeed, seemed to be infected by waiting. I had never before known it to be so violently still. Racial tensions throughout this country were exacerbated during the early years of the war, partly because the labor market brought together hundreds of thousands of ill-prepared people and partly because Negro soldiers, regardless of where they were born, received their military training in the south. What happened in defense plants and army camps had repercussions, naturally, in every Negro ghetto. The situation in Harlem had grown bad enough for clergymen, policemen, educators, politicians, and social workers to assert in one breath that there was no "crime wave" and to offer, in the very next breath, suggestions as to how to combat it. These suggestions always seemed to involve playgrounds, despite the fact that racial skirmishes were occurring in the playgrounds, too. Playground or not, crime wave or not, the Harlem police force had been augmented in March, and the unrest grew—perhaps, in fact, partly as a result of the ghetto's instinctive hatred of policemen. Perhaps the most revealing news item, out of the steady parade of reports of muggings, stabbings, shootings, assaults, gang wars, and accusations of police brutality, is the item concerning six Negro girls who set upon a white girl in the subway because, as they all too accurately put it, she was stepping on their toes. Indeed she was, all over the nation.

I had never before been so aware of policemen, on foot, on horseback, on corners, everywhere, always two by two. Nor had I ever been so aware of small knots of people. They were on stoops and on corners and in doorways, and what was striking about them, I think, was that they did not seem to be talking. Never, when I passed these groups, did the usual sound of a curse or a laugh ring out and neither did there seem to be any hum of gossip. There was certainly, on the other hand, occurring between them communication extraordinarily intense. Another thing that was striking was the unexpected diversity of the people who made up these groups. Usually, for example, one would see a group of sharpies standing on the street corner, jiving the passing chicks; or a group of older men, usually, for some reason, in the vicinity of a barber shop, discussing baseball scores, or the numbers, or making rather chilling observations about women they had known. Women, in a general way, tended to be seen less often together— unless they were church women, or very young girls, or prostitutes met together for an unprofessional instant. But that summer I saw the strangest combinations: large, respectable, churchly matrons standing on the stoops or the corners with their hair tied up, together with a girl in sleazy satin whose face bore the marks of gin and the razor, or heavy-set, abrupt, no-nonsense older men, in company with the most disreputable and fanatical "race" men, or these same "race" men with the sharpies, or these sharpies with the churchly women. Seventh Day Adventists and Methodists and Spiritualists seemed to be hobnobbing with Holyrollers and they were all, alike, entangled with the most flagrant disbelievers; something heavy in their stance seemed to indicate that they had all, incredibly, seen a common vision, and on each face there seemed to be the same strange, bitter shadow.

The churchly women and the matter-of-fact, no-nonsense men had children in the Army. The sleazy girls they talked to had lovers there, the sharpies and the "race" men had friends and brothers there. It would have demanded an unquestioning patriotism, happily as uncommon in this country as it is undesirable, for these people not to have been disturbed by the bitter letters they received, by the newspaper stories they read, not to have been enraged by the posters, then to be found all over New York, which described the Japanese as "yellow-bellied Japs." It was only the "race" men, to be sure, who spoke ceaselessly of being revenged—how this vengeance was to be exacted was not clear—for the indignities and dangers suffered by Negro boys in uniform; but everybody felt a directionless, hopeless bitterness, as well as that panic which can scarcely be suppressed when one knows that a human being one loves is beyond one's reach, and in danger. This helplessness and this gnawing uneasiness does something, at length, to even the toughest mind. Perhaps the best way to sum all this up is to say that the people I knew felt, mainly, a peculiar kind of relief when they knew that their boys were being shipped out of the south, to do battle overseas. It was, perhaps, like feeling that the most dangerous part of a dangerous journey had been passed and that now, even if death should come, it would come with honor and without the complicity of their countrymen. Such a death would be, in short, a fact with which one could hope to live.

It was on the 28th of July, which I believe was a Wednesday, that I visited my father for the first time during his illness and for the last time in his life. The moment I saw him I knew why I had put off this visit so long. I had told my mother that I did not want to see him because I hated him. But this was not true. It was only that I *had* hated him and I wanted to hold on to this hatred. I did not want to look on him as a ruin: it was not a ruin I had hated. I imagine that one of the reasons people cling to their hates so stubbornly is because they sense, once hate is gone, that they will be forced to deal with pain.

We traveled out to him, his older sister and myself, to what seemed to be the very end of a very Long Island. It was hot and dusty and we wrangled, my aunt and I, all the way out, over the fact that I had recently begun to smoke and, as she said, to give myself airs. But I knew that she wrangled with me because she could not bear to face the fact of her brother's dying. Neither could I endure the reality of her despair, her unstated bafflement as to what had happened to her brother's life, and her own. So we wrangled and I smoked and from time to time she fell into a heavy reverie. Covertly, I watched her face, which was the face of an old woman; it had fallen in, the eyes were sunken and lightless; soon she would be dying, too.

In my childhood—it had not been so long ago—I had thought her beautiful. She had been quick-witted and quick-moving and very generous with all the children and each of her visits had been an event. At one time one of my brothers and myself had thought of running away to live with her. Now she could no longer produce out of her handbag some unexpected and yet familiar delight. She made me feel pity and revulsion and fear. It was awful to realize that she no longer caused me to feel affection. The closer we came to the hospital the more querulous she became and at the same time, naturally, grew more dependent on me. Between pity and guilt and fear I began to feel that there was another me trapped in my skull like a jack-in-the-box who might escape my control at any moment and fill the air with screaming.

She began to cry the moment we entered the room and she saw him lying there, all shriveled and still, like a little black monkey. The great, gleaming apparatus which fed him and would have compelled him to be still even if he had been able to move brought to mind, not beneficence, but torture; the tubes entering his arm made me think of pictures I had seen, when a child, of Gulliver, tied down by the pygmies on that island. My aunt wept and wept, there was a whistling sound in my father's throat; nothing was said; he could not speak. I wanted to take his hand, to say something. But I do not know what I could have said, even if he could have heard me. He was not really in that room with us, he had at last really embarked on his journey; and though my aunt told me that he said he was going to meet Jesus, I did not hear anything except that whistling in his throat. The doctor came back and we left, into that unbearable train again, and home. In the morning came the telegram saying that he was dead. Then the house was suddenly full of relatives, friends, hysteria, and confusion and I quickly left my mother and the children to the care of those impressive women, who, in Negro communities at least, automatically appear at times of bereavement armed with lotions, proverbs, and patience, and an ability to cook. I went downtown. By the time I returned, later the same day, my mother had been carried to the hospital and the baby had been born.

[3]

For my father's funeral I had nothing black to wear and this posed a nagging problem all day long. It was one of those problems, simple, or impossible of solution, to which the mind insanely clings in order to avoid the mind's real trouble. I spent most of that day at the downtown apartment of a girl I knew, celebrating my birthday with whiskey and wondering what to wear that night. When planning a birthday celebration one naturally does not expect that it will be up against competition from a funeral and this girl had anticipated taking me out that night, for a big dinner and a night club afterwards. Sometime during the course of that long day we decided that we would go out anyway, when my father's funeral service was over. I imagine *I* decided it, since, as the funeral hour approached, it became clearer and clearer to me that I would not know what to do with myself when it was over. The girl, stifling her very lively concern as to the possible effects of the whiskey on one of my father's chief mourners, concentrated on being conciliatory and practically helpful. She found a black shirt for me somewhere and ironed it and, dressed in the darkest pants and jacket I owned, and slightly drunk, I made my way to my father's funeral.

The chapel was full, but not packed, and very quiet. There were, mainly, my father's relatives, and his children, and here and there I saw faces I had not seen since childhood, the faces of my father's one-time friends. They were very dark and solemn now, seeming somehow to suggest that they had known all along that something like this would happen. Chief among the mourners was my aunt, who had quarreled with my father all his life; by which I do not mean to suggest that her mourning was insincere or that she had not loved him. I suppose that she was one of the few people in the world who had, and their incessant quarreling proved precisely the strength of the tie that bound them. The only other person in the world, as far as I knew, whose relationship to my father rivaled my aunt's in depth was my mother, who was not there.

It seemed to me, of course, that it was a very long funeral. But it was, if anything, a rather shorter funeral than most, nor, since there were no overwhelming uncontrollable expressions of grief, could it be called—if I dare to use the word—successful. The minister who preached my father's funeral sermon was one of the few my father had still been seeing as he neared his end. He presented to us in his sermon a man whom none of us had ever seen—a man thoughtful, patient, and forbearing, a Christian inspiration to all who knew him, and a model for his children. And no doubt the children, in their disturbed and guilty state, were almost ready to believe this; he had been remote enough to be anything and, anyway, the shock of the incontrovertible, that it was really our father lying up there in that casket, prepared the mind for anything. His sister moaned and this grief-stricken moaning was taken as corroboration. The other faces held a dark, noncommittal thoughtfulness. This was not the man they had known, but they had scarcely expected to be confronted with *him;* this was, in a sense deeper than questions of fact, the man they had not known, and the man they had not known may have been the real one. The real man, whoever he had been, had suffered and now he was dead: this was all that was sure and all that mattered now. Every man in the chapel hoped that when his hour came he, too, would be eulogized, which is to say forgiven, and that all of his lapses, greeds, errors, and strayings from the truth would be invested with coherence and looked upon with charity. This was perhaps the last thing human beings could give each other and it was what they demanded, after all, of the Lord. Only the Lord saw the midnight tears, only He was present when one of His children, moaning and wringing hands, paced up and down the room. When one slapped one's child in anger the recoil in the heart reverberated through heaven and became part of the pain of the universe. And when the children were hungry and sullen and distrustful and one watched them, daily, growing wilder, and further away, and running headlong into danger, it was the Lord who knew what the charged heart endured as the strap was laid to the backside; the Lord alone who knew what one *would* have said if one had had, like the Lord, the gift of the living word. It was the Lord who knew of the impossibility every parent in that room faced: how to prepare the child for the day when the child would be despised and how to *create* in the child—by what means?—a stronger antidote to this poison than one had found for oneself. The avenues, side streets, bars, billiard halls, hospitals, police stations, and even the playgrounds of Harlem—not to mention the houses of correction, the jails, and the morgue—testified to the potency of the poison while remaining silent as to the efficacy of whatever antidote, irresistibly raising the question of whether or not such an antidote existed; raising, which was worse, the question of whether or not an antidote was desirable; perhaps poison should be fought with poison. With these several schisms in the mind and with more terrors in the heart than could be named, it was better not to judge the man who had gone down under an impossible burden. It was better to remember: *Thou knowest this man's fall; but thou knowest not his wrassling.*

While the preacher talked and I watched the children—years of changing their diapers, scrubbing them, slapping them, taking them to school, and scolding them had had the perhaps inevitable result of making me love them, though I am not sure I knew this then—my mind was busily breaking out with a rash of disconnected impressions. Snatches of popular songs, indecent jokes, bits of books I had read, movie sequences, faces, voices, political issues—I thought I was going mad; all these impressions suspended, as it were, in the solution of the faint nausea produced in me by the heat and liquor. For a moment I had the impression that my alcoholic breath, inefficiently disguised with chewing gum, filled the entire chapel. Then someone began singing one of my father's favorite songs and, abruptly, I was with him, sitting on his knee, in the hot, enormous, crowded church which was the first church we attended. It was the Abyssinia Baptist Church on 138th Street. We had not gone there long. With this image, a host of others came. I had forgotten, in the rage of my growing up, how proud my father had been of me when I was little. Apparently, I had had a voice and my father had liked to show me off before the members of the church. I had forgotten what he had looked like when he was pleased but now I remembered that he had always been grinning with pleasure when my solos ended. I even remembered certain expressions on his face when he teased my mother—had he loved her? I would never know. And when had it all begun to change? For now it seemed that he had not always been cruel. I remembered being taken for a haircut and scraping my knee on the footrest of the barber's chair and I remembered my father's face as he soothed my crying and applied the stinging iodine. Then I remembered our fights, fights which had been of the worst possible kind because my technique had been silence.

I remembered the one time in all our life together when we had really spoken to each other.

It was on a Sunday and it must have been shortly before I left home. We were walking, just the two of us, in our usual silence, to or from church. I was in high school and had been doing a lot of writing and I was, at about this time, the editor of the high school magazine. But I had also been a Young Minister and had been preaching from the pulpit. Lately, I had been taking fewer engagements and preached as rarely as possible. It was said in the church, quite truthfully, that I was "cooling off."

My father asked me abruptly. "You'd rather write than preach, wouldn't you?"

I was astonished at his question—because it was a real question. I answered, "Yes."

That was all we said. It was awful to remember that that was all we had *ever* said.

The casket now was opened and the mourners were being led up the aisle to look for the last time on the deceased. The assumption was that the family was too overcome with grief to be allowed to make this journey alone and I watched while my aunt was led to the casket and, muffled in black, and shaking, led back to her seat. I disapproved of forcing the children to look on their dead father, considering that the shock of his death, or, more truthfully, the shock of death as a reality, was already a little more than a child could bear, but my judgment in this matter had been overruled and there they were, bewildered and frightened and very small, being led, one by one, to the casket. But there is also something very gallant about children at such moments. It has something to do with their silence and gravity and with the fact that one cannot help them. Their legs, somehow, seem *exposed,* so that it is at once incredible and terribly clear that their legs are all they have to hold them up.

I had not wanted to go to the casket myself and I certainly had not wished to be led there, but there was no way of avoiding either of these forms. One of the deacons led me up and I looked on my father's face. I cannot say that it looked like him at all. His blackness had been equivocated by powder and there was no suggestion in that casket of what his power had or could have been. He was simply an old man dead, and it was hard to believe that he had ever given anyone either joy or pain. Yet, his life filled that room. Further up the avenue his wife was holding his newborn child. Life and death so close together, and love and hatred, and right and wrong, said something to me which I did not want to hear concerning man, concerning the life of man.

After the funeral, while I was downtown desperately celebrating my birthday, a Negro soldier, in the lobby of the Hotel Braddock, got into a fight with a white policeman over a Negro girl. Negro girls, white police-men, in or out of uniform, and Negro males—in or out of uniform—were part of the furniture of the lobby of the Hotel Braddock and this was certainly not the first time such an incident had occurred. It was destined, however, to receive an unprecedented publicity, for the fight between the policeman and the soldier ended with the shooting of the soldier. Rumor, flowing immediately to the streets outside, stated that the soldier had been shot in the back, an instantaneous and revealing invention, and that the soldier had died protecting a Negro woman. The facts were somewhat different—for example, the soldier had not been shot in the back, and was not dead, and the girl seems to have been as dubious a symbol of woman-hood as her white counterpart in Georgia usually is, but no one was in-terested in the facts. They preferred the invention because this invention expressed and corroborated their hates and fears so perfectly. It is just as well to remember that people are always doing this. Perhaps many of those legends, including Christianity, to which the world clings began their con-quest of the world with just some such concerted surrender to distortion. The effect, in Harlem, of this particular legend was like the effect of a lit match in a tin of gasoline. The mob gathered before the doors of the Hotel Braddock simply began to swell and to spread in every direction, and Harlem exploded.

The mob did not cross the ghetto lines. It would have been easy, for example, to have gone over to Morningside Park on the west side or to have crossed the Grand Central railroad tracks at 125th Street on the east side, to wreak havoc in white neighborhoods. The mob seems to have been mainly interested in something more potent and real than the white face, that is, in white power, and the principal damage done during the riot of the summer of 1943 was to white business establishments in Harlem. It might have been a far bloodier story, of course, if, at the hour the riot began, these establishments had still been open. From the Hotel Braddock the mob fanned out, east and west along 125th Street, and for the entire length of Lenox, Seventh, and Eighth avenues. Along each of these avenues, and along each major side street—116th, 125th, 135th, and so on—bars, stores, pawnshops, restaurants, even little luncheonettes had been smashed open and entered and looted—looted, it might be added, with more haste than efficiency. The shelves really looked as though a bomb had struck them. Cans of beans and soup and dog food, along with toilet paper, corn flakes, sardines, and milk tumbled every which way, and abandoned cash registers and cases of beer leaned crazily out of the splintered windows and were strewn along the avenues. Sheets, blankets, and clothing of every description formed a kind of path, as though people had dropped them while running. I truly had not realized that Harlem *had* so many stores until I saw them all smashed open; the first time the word *wealth* ever entered my mind in relation to Harlem was when I saw it scattered in the streets. But one's first, incongruous impression of plenty was countered immediately by an impression of waste. None of this was doing anybody any good. It would have been better to have left the plate glass as it had been and the goods lying in the stores.

It would have been better, but it would also have been intolerable, for Harlem had needed something to smash. To smash something is the ghetto's chronic need. Most of the time it is the members of the ghetto who smash each other, and themselves. But as long as the ghetto walls are standing there will always come a moment when these outlets do not work. That summer, for example, it was not enough to get into a fight on Lenox Avenue, or curse out one's cronies in the barber shops. If ever, indeed, the violence which fills Harlem's churches, pool halls, and bars erupts outward in a more direct fashion, Harlem and its citizens are likely to vanish in an apocalyptic flood. That this is not likely to happen is due to a great many reasons, most hidden and powerful among them the Negro's real relation to the white American. This relation prohibits, simply, anything as uncomplicated and satisfactory as pure hatred. In order really to hate white people, one has to blot so much out of the mind—and the heart—that this hatred itself becomes an exhausting and self-destructive pose. But this does not mean, on the other hand, that love comes easily: the white world is too powerful, too complacent, too ready with gratuitous humiliation, and, above all, too ignorant and too innocent for that. One is absolutely forced to make perpetual qualifications and one's own reactions are always canceling each other out. It is this, really, which has driven so many people mad, both white and black. One is always in the position of having to decide between amputation and gangrene. Amputation is swift but time may prove that the amputation was not necessary—or one may delay the amputation too long. Gangrene is slow, but it is impossible to be sure that one is reading one's symptoms right. The idea of going through life as a cripple is more than one can bear, and equally unbearable is the risk of swelling up slowly, in agony, with poison. And the trouble, finally, is that the risks are real even if the choices do not exist.

"But as for me and my house," my father had said, "we will serve the Lord." I wondered, as we drove him to his resting place, what this line had meant for him. I had heard him preach it many times. I had preached it once myself, proudly giving it an interpretation different from my father's. Now the whole thing came back to me, as though my father and I were on our way to Sunday school and I were memorizing the golden text: *And if it seem evil unto you to serve the Lord, choose you this day whom you will serve; whether the gods which your fathers served that were on the other side of the flood, or the gods of the Amorites, in whose land ye dwell: but as for me and my house, we will serve the Lord.* I suspected in these familiar lines a meaning which had never been there for me before. All of my father's texts and songs, which I had decided were meaningless, were arranged before me at his death like empty bottles, waiting to hold the meaning which life would give them for me. This was his legacy: nothing is ever escaped. That bleakly memorable morning I hated the unbelievable streets and the Negroes and whites who had, equally, made them that way. But I knew that it was folly, as my father would have said, this bitterness was folly. It was necessary to hold on to the things that mattered. The dead man mattered, the new life mattered; blackness and whiteness did not matter; to believe that they did was to acquiesce in one's own destruction. Hatred, which could destroy so much, never failed to destroy the man who hated and this was an immutable law.

It began to seem that one would have to hold in the mind forever two ideas which seemed to be in opposition. The first idea was acceptance, the acceptance, totally without rancor, of life as it is, and men as they are: in the light of this idea, it goes without saying that injustice is a commonplace. But this did not mean that one could be complacent, for the second idea was of equal power: that one must never, in one's own life, accept these injustices as commonplace but must fight them with all one's strength. This fight begins, however, in the heart and it now had been laid to my charge to keep my own heart free of hatred and despair. This intimation made my heart heavy and, now that my father was irrecoverable. I wished that he had been beside me so that I could have searched his face for the answers which only the future would give me now.   [1955]

Stranger in the Village

FROM ALL AVAILABLE EVIDENCE NO black man had ever set foot in this tiny Swiss village before I came. I was told before arriving that I would probably be a "sight" for the village; I took this to mean that people of my complexion were rarely seen in Switzerland, and also that city people are always something of a "sight" outside of the city. It did not occur to me—possibly because I am an American—that there could be people anywhere who had never seen a Negro.

It is a fact that cannot be explained on the basis of the inaccessibility of the village. The village is very high, but it is only four hours from Milan and three hours from Lausanne. It is true that it is virtually unknown. Few people making plans for a holiday would elect to come here. On the other hand, the villagers are able, presumably, to come and go as they please— which they do: to another town at the foot of the mountain, with a population of approximately five thousand, the nearest place to see a movie or go to the bank. In the village there is no movie house, no bank, no library, no theater; very few radios, one jeep, one station wagon; and, at the moment, one typewriter, mine, an invention which the woman next door to me here had never seen. There are about six hundred people living here, all Catholic—I conclude this from the fact that the Catholic church is open all year round, whereas the Protestant chapel, set off on a hill a little removed from the village, is open only in the summertime when the tourists arrive. There are four or five hotels, all closed now, and four or five *bistros,* of which, however, only two do any business during the winter. These two do not do a great deal, for life in the village seems to end around nine or ten o'clock. There are a few stores, butcher, baker, *épicerie,* a hardware store, and a money-changer—who cannot change travelers' checks, but must send them down to the bank, an operation which takes two or three days. There is something called the *Ballet Haus,* closed in the winter and used for God knows what, certainly not ballet, during the summer. There seems to be only one schoolhouse in the village, and this for the quite young children; I suppose this to mean that their older brothers and sisters at some point descend from these mountains in order to complete their education—possibly, again, to the town just below. The landscape is absolutely forbidding, mountains towering on all four sides, ice and snow as far as the eye can reach. In this white wilderness, men and women and children move all day, carrying washing, wood, buckets of milk or water, sometimes skiing on Sunday afternoons. All week long boys and young men are to be seen shoveling snow off the rooftops, or dragging wood down from the forest in sleds.

The village's only real attraction, which explains the tourist season, is the hot spring water. A disquietingly high proportion of these tourists are cripples, or semi-cripples, who come year after year—from other parts of Switzerland, usually—to take the waters. This lends the village, at the height of the season, a rather terrifying air of sanctity, as though it were a lesser Lourdes. There is often something beautiful, there is always something awful, in the spectacle of a person who has lost one of his faculties, a faculty he never questioned until it was gone, and who struggles to recover it. Yet people remain people, on crutches or indeed on deathbeds; and wherever I passed, the first summer I was here, among the native villagers or among the lame, a wind passed with me—of astonishment, curiosity, amusement, and outrage. That first summer I stayed two weeks and never intended to return. But I did return in the winter, to work; the village offers, obviously, no distractions whatever and has the further advantage of being extremely cheap. Now it is winter again, a year later, and I am here again. Everyone in the village knows my name, though they scarcely ever use it, knows that I come from America—though, this, apparently, they will never really believe: black men come from Africa—and everyone knows that I am the friend of the son of a woman who was born here, and that I am staying in their chalet. But I remain as much a stranger today as I was the first day I arrived, and the children shout *Neger! Neger!* as I walk along the streets.

It must be admitted that in the beginning I was far too shocked to have any real reaction. In so far as I reacted at all, I reacted by trying to be pleasant—it being a great part of the American Negro's education (long before he goes to school) that he must make people "like" him. This smile-and-the-world-smiles-with-you routine worked about as well in this situation as it had in the situation for which it was designed, which is to say that it did not work at all. No one, after all, can be liked whose human weight and complexity cannot be, or has not been, admitted. My smile was simply another unheard-of phenomenon which allowed them to see my teeth—they did not, really, see my smile and I began to think that, should I take to snarling, no one would notice any difference. All of the physical characteristics of the Negro which had caused me, in America, a very different and almost forgotten pain were nothing less than miraculous—or infernal—in the eyes of the village people. Some thought my hair was the color of tar, that it had the texture of wire, or the texture of cotton. It was jocularly suggested that I might let it all grow long and make myself a winter coat. If I sat in the sun for more than five minutes some daring creature was certain to come along and gingerly put his fingers on my hair, as though he were afraid of an electric shock, or put his hand on my hand, astonished that the color did not rub off. In all of this, in which it must be conceded there was the charm of genuine wonder and in which there was certainly no element of intentional unkindness, there was yet no suggestion that I was human: I was simply a living wonder.

I knew that they did not mean to be unkind, and I know it now; it is necessary, nevertheless, for me to repeat this to myself each time that I walk out of the chalet. The children who shout *Neger!* have no way of knowing the echoes this sound raises in me. They are brimming with good humor and the more daring swell with pride when I stop to speak with them. Just the same, there are days when I cannot pause and smile, when I have no heart to play with them; when, indeed, I mutter sourly to myself, exactly as I muttered on the streets of a city these children have never seen, when I was no bigger than these children are now: *Your* mother *was a nigger.* Joyce is right about history being a nightmare—but it may be the nightmare from which no one *can* awaken. People are trapped in history and history is trapped in them.

There is a custom in the village—I am told it is repeated in many villages—of "buying" African natives for the purpose of converting them to Christianity. There stands in the church all year round a small box with a slot for money, decorated with a black figurine, and into this box the villagers drop their francs. During the *carnaval* which precedes Lent, two village children have their faces blackened—out of which bloodless darkness their blue eyes shine like ice—and fantastic horsehair wigs are placed on their blond heads; thus disguised, they solicit among the villagers for money for the missionaries in Africa. Between the box in the church and the blackened children, the village "bought" last year six or eight African natives. This was reported to me with pride by the wife of one of the *bistro* owners and I was careful to express astonishment and pleasure at the solicitude shown by the village for the souls of black folk. The *bistro* owner's wife beamed with a pleasure far more genuine than my own and seemed to feel that I might now breathe more easily concerning the souls of at least six of my kinsmen.

I tried not to think of these so lately baptized kinsmen, of the price paid for them, or the peculiar price they themselves would pay, and said nothing about my father, who having taken his own conversion too literally never, at bottom, forgave the white world (which he described as heathen) for having saddled him with a Christ in whom, to judge at least from their treatment of him, they themselves no longer believed. I thought of white men arriving for the first time in an African village, strangers there, as I am a stranger here, and tried to imagine the astounded populace touching their hair and marveling at the color of their skin. But there is a great difference between being the first white man to be seen by Africans and being the first black man to be seen by whites. The white man takes the astonishment as tribute, for he arrives to conquer and to convert the natives, whose inferiority in relation to himself is not even to be questioned; whereas I, without a thought of conquest, find myself among a people whose culture controls me, has even, in a sense, created me, people who have cost me more in anguish and rage than they will ever know, who yet do not even know of my existence. The astonishment with which I might have greeted them, should they have stumbled into my African village a few hundred years ago, might have rejoiced their hearts. But the astonishment with which they greet me today can only poison mine.

And this is so despite everything I may do to feel differently, despite my friendly conversations with the *bistro* owner's wife, despite their three-year-old son who has at last become my friend, despite the *saluts* and *bonsoirs* which I exchange with people as I walk, despite the fact that I know that no individual can be taken to task for what history is doing, or has done. I say that the culture of these people controls me—but they can scarcely be held responsible for European culture. America comes out of Europe, but these people have never seen America, nor have most of them seen more of Europe than the hamlet at the foot of their mountain. Yet they move with an authority which I shall never have; and they regard me, quite rightly, not only as a stranger in their village but as a suspect latecomer, bearing no credentials, to everything they have—however unconsciously—inherited.

For this village, even were it incomparably more remote and incredibly more primitive, is the West, the West onto which I have been so strangely grafted. These people cannot be, from the point of view of power, strangers anywhere in the world; they have made the modern world, in effect, even if they do not know it. The most illiterate among them is related, in a way that I am not, to Dante, Shakespeare, Michelangelo, Aeschylus, Da Vinci, Rembrandt, and Racine; the cathedral at Chartres says something to them which it cannot say to me, as indeed would New York's Empire State Building, should anyone here ever see it. Out of their hymns and dances come Beethoven and Bach. Go back a few centuries and they are in their full glory—but I am in Africa, watching the conquerors arrive.

The rage of the disesteemed is personally fruitless, but it is also absolutely inevitable; this rage, so generally discounted, so little understood even among the people whose daily bread it is, is one of the things that makes history. Rage can only with difficulty, and never entirely, be brought under the domination of the intelligence and is therefore not susceptible to any arguments whatever. This is a fact which ordinary representatives of the *Herrenvolk,* having never felt this rage and being unable to imagine it, quite fail to understand. Also, rage cannot be hidden, it can only be dissembled. This dissembling deludes the thoughtless, and strengthens rage and adds, to rage, contempt. There are, no doubt, as many ways of coping with the resulting complex of tensions as there are black men in the world, but no black man can hope ever to be entirely liberated from this internal warfare—rage, dissembling, and contempt having inevitably accompanied his first realization of the power of white men. What is crucial here is that, since white men represent in the black man's world so heavy a weight, white men have for black men a reality which is far from being reciprocal; and hence all black men have toward all white men an attitude which is designed, really, either to rob the white man of the jewel of his naïveté, or else to make it cost him dear.

The black man insists, by whatever means he finds at his disposal, that the white man cease to regard him as an exotic rarity and recognize him as a human being. This is a very charged and difficult moment, for there is a great deal of will power involved in the white man's naïveté. Most people are not naturally reflective any more than they are naturally malicious, and the white man prefers to keep the black man at a certain human remove because it is easier for him thus to preserve his simplicity and avoid being called to account for crimes committed by his forefathers, or his neighbors. He is inescapably aware, nevertheless, that he is in a better position in the world than black men are, nor can he quite put to death the suspicion that he is hated by black men therefore. He does not wish to be hated, neither does he wish to change places, and at this point in his uneasiness he can scarcely avoid having recourse to those legends which white men have created about black men, the most usual effect of which is that the white man finds himself enmeshed, so to speak, in his own language which describes hell, as well as the attributes which lead one to hell, as being as black as night.

Every legend, moreover, contains its residuum of truth, and the root function of language is to control the universe by describing it. It is of quite considerable significance that black men remain, in the imagination, and in overwhelming numbers in fact, beyond the disciplines of salvation; and this despite the fact that the West has been "buying" African natives for centuries. There is, I should hazard, an instantaneous necessity to be divorced from this so visibly unsaved stranger, in whose heart, moreover, one cannot guess what dreams of vengeance are being nourished; and, at the same time, there are few things on earth more attractive than the idea of the unspeakable liberty which is allowed the unredeemed. When, beneath the black mask, a human being begins to make himself felt one cannot escape a certain awful wonder as to what kind of human being it is. What one's imagination makes of other people is dictated, of course, by the laws of one's own personality and it is one of the ironies of black-white relations that, by means of what the white man imagines the black man to be, the black man is enabled to know who the white man is.

I have said, for example, that I am as much a stranger in this village today as I was the first summer I arrived, but this is not quite true. The villagers wonder less about the texture of my hair than they did then, and wonder rather more about me. And the fact that their wonder now exists on another level is reflected in their attitudes and in their eyes. There are the children who make those delightful, hilarious, sometimes astonishingly grave overtures of friendship in the unpredictable fashion of children; other children, having been taught that the devil is a black man, scream in genuine anguish as I approach. Some of the older women never pass without a friendly greeting, never pass, indeed, if it seems that they will be able to engage me in conversation; other women look down or look away or rather contemptuously smirk. Some of the men drink with me and suggest that I learn how to ski—partly, I gather, because they cannot imagine what I would look like on skis—and want to know if I am married, and ask questions about my *métier*. But some of the men have accused *le sale nègre*— behind my back—of stealing wood and there is already in the eyes of some of them that peculiar, intent, paranoiac malevolence which one sometimes surprises in the eyes of American white men when, out walking with their Sunday girl, they see a Negro male approach.

There is a dreadful abyss between the streets of this village and the streets of the city in which I was born, between the children who shout *Neger!* today and those who shouted *Nigger!* yesterday—the abyss is experience, the American experience. The syllable hurled behind me today expresses, above all, wonder: I am a stranger here. But I am not a stranger in America and the same syllable riding on the American air expresses the war my presence has occasioned in the American soul.

For this village brings home to me this fact: that there was a day, and not really a very distant day, when Americans were scarcely Americans at all but discontented Europeans, facing a great unconquered continent and strolling, say, into a marketplace and seeing black men for the first time. The shock this spectacle afforded is suggested, surely, by the promptness with which they decided that these black men were not really men but cattle. It is true that the necessity on the part of the settlers of the New World of reconciling their moral assumptions with the fact—and the necessity—of slavery enhanced immensely the charm of this idea, and it is also true that this idea expresses, with a truly American bluntness, the attitude which to varying extents all masters have had toward all slaves.

But between all former slaves and slave-owners and the drama which begins for Americans over three hundred years ago at Jamestown, there are at least two differences to be observed. The American Negro slave could not suppose, for one thing, as slaves in past epochs had supposed and often done, that he would ever be able to wrest the power from his master's hands. This was a supposition which the modern era, which was to bring about such vast changes in the aims and dimensions of power, put to death; it only begins, in unprecedented fashion, and with dreadful implications, to be resurrected today. But even had this supposition persisted with undiminished force, the American Negro slave could not have used it to lend his condition dignity, for the reason that this supposition rests on another: that the slave in exile yet remains related to his past, has some means—if only in memory—of revering and sustaining the forms of his former life, is able, in short, to maintain his identity.

This was not the case with the American Negro slave. He is unique among the black men of the world in that his past was taken from him, almost literally, at one blow. One wonders what on earth the first slave found to say to the first dark child he bore. I am told that there are Haitians able to trace their ancestry back to African kings, but any American Negro wishing to go back so far will find his journey through time abruptly arrested by the signature on the bill of sale which served as the entrance paper for his ancestor. At the time—to say nothing of the circumstances— of the enslavement of the captive black man who was to become the American Negro, there was not the remotest possibility that he would ever take power from his master's hands. There was no reason to suppose that his situation would ever change, nor was there, shortly, anything to indicate that his situation had ever been different. It was his necessity, in the words of E. Franklin Frazier, to find a "motive for living under American culture or die." The identity of the American Negro comes out of this extreme situation, and the evolution of this identity was a source of the most intolerable anxiety in the minds and the lives of his masters.

For the history of the American Negro is unique also in this: that the question of his humanity, and of his rights therefore as a human being, became a burning one for several generations of Americans, so burning a question that it ultimately became one of those used to divide the nation. It is out of this argument that the venom of the epithet *Nigger!* is derived. It is an argument which Europe has never had, and hence Europe quite sincerely fails to understand how or why the argument arose in the first place, why its effects are so frequently disastrous and always so unpredictable, why it refuses until today to be entirely settled. Europe's black possessions remained—and do remain—in Europe's colonies, at which remove they represented no threat whatever to European identity. If they posed any problem at all for the European conscience, it was a problem which remained comfortingly abstract: in effect, the black man, *as a man,* did not exist for Europe. But in America, even as a slave, he was an inescapable part of the general social fabric and no American could escape having an attitude toward him. Americans attempt until today to make an abstraction of the Negro, but the very nature of these abstractions reveals the tremendous effects the presence of the Negro has had on the American character.

When one considers the history of the Negro in America it is of the greatest importance to recognize that the moral beliefs of a person, or a people, are never really as tenuous as life—which is not moral—very often causes them to appear; these create for them a frame of reference and a necessary hope, the hope being that when life has done its worst they will be enabled to rise above themselves and to triumph over life. Life would scarcely be bearable if this hope did not exist. Again, even when the worst has been said, to betray a belief is not by any means to have put oneself beyond its power; the betrayal of a belief is not the same thing as ceasing to believe. If this were not so there would be no moral standards in the world at all. Yet one must also recognize that morality is based on ideas and that all ideas are dangerous—dangerous because ideas can only lead to action and where the action leads no man can say. And dangerous in this respect: that confronted with the impossibility of remaining faithful to one's beliefs, and the equal impossibility of becoming free of them, one can be driven to the most inhuman excesses. The ideas on which American beliefs are based are not, though Americans often seem to think so, ideas which originated in America. They came out of Europe. And the establishment of democracy on the American continent was scarcely as radical a break with the past as was the necessity, which Americans faced, of broadening this concept to include black men.

This was, literally, a hard necessity. It was impossible, for one thing, for Americans to abandon their beliefs, not only because these beliefs alone seemed able to justify the sacrifices they had endured and the blood that they had spilled, but also because these beliefs afforded them their only bulwark against a moral chaos as absolute as the physical chaos of the continent it was their destiny to conquer. But in the situation in which Americans found themselves, these beliefs threatened an idea which, whether or not one likes to think so, is the very warp and woof of the heritage of the West, the idea of white supremacy.

Americans have made themselves notorious by the shrillness and the brutality with which they have insisted on this idea, but they did not invent it; and it has escaped the world's notice that those very excesses of which Americans have been guilty imply a certain, unprecedented uneasiness over the idea's life and power, if not, indeed, the idea's validity. The idea of white supremacy rests simply on the fact that white men are the creators of civilization (the present civilization, which is the only one that matters; all previous civilizations are simply "contributions" to our own) and are therefore civilization's guardians and defenders. Thus it was impossible for Americans to accept the black man as one of themselves, for to do so was to jeopardize their status as white men. But not so to accept him was to deny his human reality, his human weight and complexity, and the strain of denying the overwhelmingly undeniable forced Americans into rationalizations so fantastic that they approached the pathological.

At the root of the American Negro problem is the necessity of the American white man to find a way of living with the Negro in order to be able to live with himself. And the history of this problem can be reduced to the means used by Americans—lynch law and law, segregation and legal acceptance, terrorization and concession—either to come to terms with this necessity, or to find a way around it, or (most usually) to find a way of doing both these things at once. The resulting spectacle, at once foolish and dreadful, led someone to make the quite accurate observation that "the Negro-in-America is a form of insanity which overtakes white men."

In this long battle, a battle by no means finished, the unforeseeable effects of which will be felt by many future generations, the white man's motive was the protection of his identity; the black man was motivated by the need to establish an identity. And despite the terrorization which the Negro in America endured and endures sporadically until today, despite the cruel and totally inescapable ambivalence of his status in his country, the battle for his identity has long ago been won. He is not a visitor to the West, but a citizen there, an American; as American as the Americans who despise him, the Americans who fear him, the Americans who love him— the Americans who became less than themselves, or rose to be greater than themselves by virtue of the fact that the challenge he represented was inescapable. He is perhaps the only black man in the world whose relationship to white men is more terrible, more subtle, and more meaningful than the relationship of bitter possessed to uncertain possessor. His survival depended, and his development depends, on his ability to turn his peculiar status in the Western world to his own advantage and, it may be, to the very great advantage of that world. It remains for him to fashion out of his experience that which will give him sustenance, and a voice.

The cathedral at Chartres, I have said, says something to the people of this village which it cannot say to me; but it is important to understand that this cathedral says something to me which it cannot say to them. Perhaps they are struck by the power of the spires, the glory of the windows; but they have known God, after all, longer than I have known him, and in a different way, and I am terrified by the slippery bottomless well to be found in the crypt, down which heretics were hurled to death, and by the obscene, inescapable gargoyles jutting out of the stone and seeming to say that God and the devil can never be divorced. I doubt that the villagers think of the devil when they face a cathedral because they have never been identified with the devil. But I must accept the status which myth, if nothing else, gives me in the West before I can hope to change the myth.

Yet, if the American Negro has arrived at his identity by virtue of the absoluteness of his estrangement from his past, American white men still nourish the illusion that there is some means of recovering the European innocence, of returning to a state in which black men do not exist. This is one of the greatest errors Americans can make. The identity they fought so hard to protect has, by virtue of that battle, undergone a change: Americans are as unlike any other white people in the world as it is possible to be. I do not think, for example, that it is too much to suggest that the American vision of the world—which allows so little reality, generally speaking, for any of the darker forces in human life, which tends until today to paint moral issues in glaring black and white—owes a great deal to the battle waged by Americans to maintain between themselves and black men a human separation which could not be bridged. It is only now beginning to be borne in on us—very faintly, it must be admitted, very slowly, and very much against our will—that this vision of the world is dangerously inaccurate, and perfectly useless. For it protects our moral high-mindedness at the terrible expense of weakening our grasp of reality. People who shut their eyes to reality simply invite their own destruction, and anyone who insists on remaining in a state of innocence long after that innocence is dead turns himself into a monster.

The time has come to realize that the interracial drama acted out on the American continent has not only created a new black man, it has created a new white man, too. No road whatever will lead Americans back to the simplicity of this European village where white men still have the luxury of looking on me as a stranger. I am not, really, a stranger any longer for any American alive. One of the things that distinguishes Americans from other people is that no other people has ever been so deeply involved in the lives of black men, and vice versa. This fact faced, with all its implications, it can be seen that the history of the American Negro problem is not merely shameful, it is also something of an achievement. For even when the worst has been said, it must also be added that the perpetual challenge posed by this problem was always, somehow, perpetually met. It is precisely this black-white experience which may prove of indispensable value to us in the world we face today. This world is white no longer, and it will never be white again.   [1953]

Equal in Paris

ON THE 19TH OF DECEMBER, IN 1949, when I had been living in Paris for a little over a year, I was arrested as a receiver of stolen goods and spent eight days in prison. My arrest came about through an American tourist whom I had met twice in New York, who had been given my name and address and told to look me up. I was then living on the top floor of a ludicrously grim hotel on the rue du Bac, one of those enormous dark, cold, and hideous establishments in which Paris abounds that seem to breathe forth, in their airless, humid, stone-cold halls, the weak light, scurrying chambermaids, and creaking stairs, an odor of gentility long long dead. The place was run by an ancient Frenchman dressed in an elegant black suit which was green with age, who cannot properly be described as bewildered or even as being in a state of shock, since he had really stopped breathing around 1910. There he sat at his desk in the weirdly lit, fantastically furnished lobby, day in and day out, greeting each one of his extremely impoverished and *louche* lodgers with a stately inclination of the head that he had no doubt been taught in some impossibly remote time was the proper way for a *propriétaire* to greet his guests. If it had not been for his daughter, an extremely hardheaded *tricoteuse*—the inclination of *her* head was chilling and abrupt, like the downbeat of an ax—the hotel would certainly have gone bankrupt long before. It was said that this old man had not gone farther than the door of his hotel for thirty years, which was not at all difficult to believe. He looked as though the daylight would have killed him.

I did not, of course, spend much of my time in this palace. The moment I began living in French hotels I understood the necessity of French cafés. This made it rather difficult to look me up, for as soon as I was out of bed I hopefully took notebook and fountain pen off to the upstairs room of the Flore, where I consumed rather a lot of coffee and, as evening approached, rather a lot of alcohol, but did not get much writing done. But one night, in one of the cafés of St. Germain des Près, I was discovered by this New Yorker and only because we found ourselves in Paris we immediately established the illusion that we had been fast friends back in the good old U.S.A. This illusion proved itself too thin to support an evening's drinking, but by that time it was too late. I had committed myself to getting him a room in my hotel the next day, for he was living in one of the nest of hotels near the Gare St. Lazare, where, he said, the *propriétaire* was a thief, his wife a repressed nymphomaniac, the chambermaids "pigs," and the rent a crime. Americans are always talking this way about the French and so it did not occur to me that he meant what he said or that he would take into his own hands the means of avenging himself on the French Republic. It did not occur to me, either, that the means which he *did* take could possibly have brought about such dire results, results which were not less dire for being also comic-opera.

It came as the last of a series of disasters which had perhaps been made inevitable by the fact that I had come to Paris originally with a little over forty dollars in my pockets, nothing in the bank, and no grasp whatever of the French language. It developed, shortly, that I had no grasp of the French character either. I considered the French an ancient, intelligent, and cultured race, which indeed they are. I did not know, however, that ancient glories imply, at least in the middle of the present century, present fatigue and, quite probably, paranoia; that there is a limit to the role of the intel-

ligence in human affairs; and that no people come into possession of a
culture without having paid a heavy price for it. This price they cannot, of
course, assess, but it is revealed in their personalities and in their institutions. The very word "institutions," from my side of the ocean, where,
it seemed to me, we suffered no cruelly from the lack of them, had a
pleasant ring, as of safety and order and common sense; one had to come
into contact with these institutions in order to understand that they were
also outmoded, exasperating, completely impersonal, and very often cruel.
Similarly, the personality which had seemed from a distance to be so large
and free had to be dealt with before one could see that, if it was large, it
was also inflexible and, for the foreigner, full of strange, high, dusty rooms
which could not be inhabited. One had, in short, to come into contact
with an alien culture in order to understand that a culture was not a community basket-weaving project, nor yet an act of God; was something
neither desirable nor undesirable in itself, being inevitable, being nothing
more or less than the recorded and visible effects on a body of people of
the vicissitudes with which they had been forced to deal. And their great
men are revealed as simply another of these vicissitudes, even if, quite
against their will, the brief battle of their great men with them has left them
richer.

When my American friend left his hotel to move to mine, he took with
him, out of pique, a bedsheet belonging to the hotel and put it in his suit-
case. When he arrived at my hotel I borrowed the sheet, since my own were
filthy and the chambermaid showed no sign of bringing me any clean ones,
and put it on my bed. The sheets belonging to *my* hotel I put out in the
hall, congratulating myself on having thus forced on the attention of the
Grand Hôtel du Bac the unpleasant state of its linen. Thereafter, since, as
it turned out, we kept very different hours—I got up at noon, when, as I
gathered by meeting him on the stairs one day, he was only just getting
in—my new-found friend and I saw very little of each other.

On the evening of the 19th I was sitting thinking melancholy thoughts
about Christmas and staring at the walls of my room. I imagine that I had
sold something or that someone had sent me a Christmas present, for I
remember that I had a little money. In those days in Paris, though I floated,
so to speak, on a sea of acquaintances, I knew almost no one. Many people
were eliminated from my orbit by virtue of the fact that they had more
money than I did, which placed me, in my own eyes, in the humiliating
role of a free-loader; and other people were eliminated by virtue of the fact
that they enjoyed their poverty, shrilly insisting that this wretched round of
hotel rooms, bad food, humiliating concierges, and unpaid bills was the

Great Adventure. It couldn't, however, for me, end soon enough, this Great Adventure; there was a real question in my mind as to which would end soonest, the Great Adventure or me. This meant, however, that there were many evenings when I sat in my room, knowing that I couldn't work there, and not knowing what to do, or whom to see. On this particular evening I went down and knocked on the American's door.

There were two Frenchmen standing in the room, who immediately introduced themselves to me as policemen; which did not worry me. I had got used to policemen in Paris bobbing up at the most improbable times and places, asking to see one's *carte d'identité.* These policemen, however, showed very little interest in my papers. They were looking for something else. I could not imagine what this would be and, since I knew I certainly didn't have it, I scarcely followed the conversation they were having with my friend. I gathered that they were looking for some kind of gangster and since I wasn't a gangster and knew that gangsterism was not, insofar as he had one, my friend's style, I was sure that the two policemen would presently bow and say *Merci, messieurs,* and leave. For by this time, I remember very clearly, I was dying to have a drink and go to dinner.

I did not have a drink or go to dinner for many days after this, and when I did my outraged stomach promptly heaved everything up again. For now one of the policemen began to exhibit the most vivid interest in me and asked, very politely, if he might see my room. To which we mounted, making, I remember, the most civilized small talk on the way and even continuing it for some moments after we were in the room in which there was certainly nothing to be seen but the familiar poverty and disorder of that precarious group of people of whatever age, race, country, calling, or intention which Paris recognizes as *les étudiants* and sometimes, more ironically and precisely, as *les nonconformistes.* Then he moved to my bed, and in a terrible flash, not quite an instant before he lifted the bedspread, I understood what he was looking for. We looked at the sheet, on which I read, for the first time, lettered in the most brilliant scarlet I have ever seen, the name of the hotel from which it had been stolen. It was the first time the word *stolen* entered my mind. I had certainly seen the hotel monogram the day I put the sheet on the bed. It had simply meant nothing to me. In New York I had seen hotel monograms on everything from silver to soap and towels. Taking things from New York hotels was practically a custom, though, I suddenly realized, I had never known anyone to take a *sheet.* Sadly, and without a word to me, the inspector took the sheet from the bed, folded it under his arm, and we started back downstairs. I understood that I was under arrest.

And so we passed through the lobby, four of us, two of us very clearly criminal, under the eyes of the old man and his daughter, neither of whom said a word, into the streets where a light rain was falling. And I asked, in French, "But is this very serious?"

For I was thinking, it is, after all, only a sheet, not even new.

"No," said one of them. "It's not serious."

"It's nothing at all," said the other.

I took this to mean that we would receive a reprimand at the police station and be allowed to go to dinner. Later on I concluded that they were not being hypocritical or even trying to comfort us. They meant exactly what they said. It was only that they spoke another language.

In Paris everything is very slow. Also, when dealing with the bureaucracy, the man you are talking to is never the man you have to see. The man you have to see has just gone off to Belgium, or is busy with his family, or has just discovered that he is a cuckold; he will be in next Tuesday at three o'clock, or sometime in the course of the afternoon, or possibly tomorrow, or, possibly, in the next five minutes. But if he is coming in the next five minutes he will be far too busy to be able to see you today. So that I suppose I was not really astonished to learn at the commissariat that nothing could possibly be done about us before The Man arrived in the morning. But no, we could not go off and have dinner and come back in the morning. Of course he knew that we *would* come back—that was not the question. Indeed, there was no question: we would simply have to stay there for the night. We were placed in a cell which rather resembled a chicken coop. It was now about seven in the evening and I relinquished the thought of dinner and began to think of lunch.

I discouraged the chatter of my New York friend and this left me alone with my thoughts. I was beginning to be frightened and I bent all my energies, therefore, to keeping my panic under control. I began to realize that I was in a country I knew nothing about, in the hands of a people I did not understand at all. In a similar situation in New York I would have had some idea of what to do because I would have had some idea of what to expect. I am not speaking now of legality which, like most of the poor, I had never for an instant trusted, but of the temperament of the people with whom I had to deal. I had become very accomplished in New York at guessing and, therefore, to a limited extent manipulating to my advantage the reactions of the white world. But this was not New York. None of my old weapons could serve me here. I did not know what they saw when they looked at me. I knew very well what Americans saw when they looked at me and this allowed me to play endless and sinister variations on the role which they had assigned me; since I knew that it was, for them, of the utmost importance that they never be confronted with what, in their own personalities, made this role so necessary and gratifying to them, I knew that they could never call my hand or, indeed, afford to know what I was doing; so that I moved into every crucial situation with the deadly and rather desperate advantages of bitterly accumulated perception, of pride and contempt. This is an awful sword and shield to carry through the world, and the discovery that, in the game I was playing, I did myself a violence of which the world, at its most ferocious, would scarcely have been capable, was what had driven me out of New York. It was a strange feeling, in this situation, after a year in Paris, to discover that my weapons would never again serve me as they had.

It was quite clear to me that the Frenchmen in whose hands I found myself were no better or worse than their American counterparts. Certainly their uniforms frightened me quite as much, and their impersonality, and the threat, always very keenly felt by the poor, of violence, was as present in that commissariat as it had ever been for me in any police station. And I had seen, for example, what Paris policemen could do to Arab peanut vendors. The only difference here was that I did not understand these people, did not know what techniques their cruelty took, did not know enough about their personalities to see danger coming, to ward it off, did not know on what ground to meet it. That evening in the commissariat I was not a despised black man. They would simply have laughed at me if I had behaved like one. For them, I was an American. And here it was they who had the advantage, for that word, *Américain,* gave them some idea, far from inaccurate, of what to expect from me. In order to corroborate none of their ironical expectations I said nothing and did nothing—which was not the way any Frenchman, white or black, would have reacted. The question thrusting up from the bottom of my mind was not *what* I was, but *who.* And this question, since a *what* can get by with skill but a *who* demands resources, was my first real intimation of what humility must mean.

In the morning it was still raining. Between nine and ten o'clock a black Citroën took us off to the Ile de la Cité, to the great, gray Préfecture. I realize now that the questions I put to the various policemen who escorted us were always answered in such a way as to corroborate what I wished to hear. This was not out of politeness, but simply out of indifference—or, possibly, an ironical pity—since each of the policemen knew very well that nothing would speed or halt the machine in which I had become entangled. They knew I did not know this and there was certainly no point in their telling me. In one way or another I would certainly come out at the other side—for they also knew that being found with a stolen bedsheet in one's possession was not a crime punishable by the guillotine. (They had the advantage over me there, too, for there were certainly moments later on when I was not so sure.) If I did *not* come out at the other side—well, that was just too bad. So, to my question, put while we were in the Citroën— "Will it be over today?"—I received a *"Oui, bien sûr."* He was not lying. As it turned out, the *procès-verbal* was over that day. Trying to be realistic, I dismissed, in the Citroën, all thoughts of lunch and pushed my mind ahead to dinner.

At the Préfecture we were first placed in a tiny cell, in which it was almost impossible either to sit or to lie down. After a couple of hours of this we were taken down to an office, where, for the first time, I encountered the owner of the bedsheet and where the *procès-verbal* took place. This was simply an interrogation, quite chillingly clipped and efficient (so that there was, shortly, no doubt in one's own mind that one *should* be treated as a criminal), which was recorded by a secretary. When it was over, this report was given to us to sign. One had, of course, no choice but to sign it, even though my mastery of written French was very far from certain. We were being held, according to the law in France, incommunicado, and all my angry demands to be allowed to speak to my embassy or to see a lawyer met with a stony *"Oui, oui. Plus tard."* The *procès-verbal* over, we were taken back to the cell, before which, shortly, passed the owner of the bed-sheet. He said he hoped we had slept well, gave a vindictive wink, and disappeared.

By this time there was only one thing clear: that we had no way of controlling the sequence of events and could not possibly guess what this sequence would be. It seemed to me, since what I regarded as the high point—the *procès-verbal*—had been passed and since the hotelkeeper was once again in possession of his sheet, that we might reasonably expect to be released from police custody in a matter of hours. We had been detained now for what would soon be twenty-four hours, during which time I had learned only that the official charge against me was *receleur.* My mental shifting, between lunch and dinner, to say nothing of the physical lack of either of these delights, was beginning to make me dizzy. The steady chatter of my friend from New York, who was determined to keep my spirits up, made me feel murderous; I was praying that some power would release us from this freezing pile of stone before the impulse became the act. And I was beginning to wonder what was happening in that beautiful city, Paris, which lived outside these walls. I wondered how long it would take before anyone casually asked, "But where's Jimmy? He hasn't been around"—and realized, knowing the people I knew, that it would take several days.

Quite late in the afternoon we were taken from our cells; handcuffed, each to a separate officer; led through a maze of steps and corridors to the top of the building; fingerprinted; photographed. As in movies I had seen, I was placed against a wall, facing an old-fashioned camera, behind which stood one of the most completely cruel and indifferent faces I had ever seen, while someone next to me and, therefore, just outside my line of vision, read off in a voice from which all human feeling, even feeling of the most base description, had long since fled, what must be called my public characteristics—which, at that time and in that place, seemed anything but that. He might have been roaring to the hostile world secrets which I could barely, in the privacy of midnight, utter to myself. But he was only reading off my height, my features, my approximate weight, my color—that color which, in the United States, had often, odd as it may sound, been my salvation—the color of my hair, my age, my nationality. A light then flashed, the photographer and I staring at each other as though there was murder in our hearts, and then it was over. Handcuffed again, I was led downstairs to the bottom of the building, into a great enclosed shed in which had been gathered the very scrapings off the Paris streets. Old, old men, so ruined and old that life in them seemed really to prove the miracle of the quickening power of the Holy Ghost—for clearly their life was no longer their affair, it was no longer even their burden, they were simply the clay which had once been touched. And men not so old, with faces the color of lead and the consistency of oatmeal, eyes that made me think of stale *café-au-lait* spiked with arsenic, bodies which could take in food and water—any food and water—and pass it out, but which could not do anything more, except possibly, at midnight, along the riverbank where rats scurried, rape. And young men, harder and crueler than the Paris stones, older by far than I, their chronological senior by some five to seven years. And North Africans, old and young, who seemed the only living people in this place because they yet retained the grace to be bewildered. But they were not bewildered by being in this shed: they were simply bewildered because they were no longer in North Africa. There was a great hole in the center of this shed, which was the common toilet. Near it, though it was impossible to get very far from it, stood an old man with white hair, eating a piece of camembert. It was at this point, probably, that thought, for me, stopped, that physiology, if one may say so, took over. I found myself incapable of saying a word, not because I was afraid I would cry but because

I was afraid I would vomit. And I did not think any longer of the city of Paris but my mind flew back to that home from which I had fled. I was sure that I would never see it any more. And it must have seemed to me that my flight from home was the cruelest trick I had ever played on myself, since it had led me here, down to a lower point than any I could ever in my life have imagined—lower, far, than anything I had seen in that Harlem which I had so hated and so loved, the escape from which had soon become the greatest direction of my life. After we had been here an hour or so a functionary came and opened the door and called out our names. And I was sure that *this* was my release. But I was handcuffed again and led out of the Préfecture into the streets—it was dark now, it was still raining—and before the steps of the Préfecture stood the great police wagon, doors facing me, wide open. The handcuffs were taken off, I entered the wagon, which was peculiarly constructed. It was divided by a narrow aisle, and on each side of the aisle was a series of narrow doors. These doors opened on a narrow cubicle, beyond which was a door which opened onto another narrow cubicle: three or four cubicles, each private, with a locking door. I was placed in one of them; I remember there was a small vent just above my head which let in a little light. The door of my cubicle was locked from the outside. I had no idea where this wagon was taking me and, as it began to move, I began to cry. I suppose I cried all the way to prison, the prison called Fresnes, which is twelve kilometers outside of Paris.

For reasons I have no way at all of understanding, prisoners whose last initial is A, B, or C are always sent to Fresnes; everybody else is sent to a prison called, rather cynically it seems to me, La Santé. I will, obviously, never be allowed to enter La Santé, but I was told by people who certainly seemed to know that it was infinitely more unbearable than Fresnes. This arouses in me, until today, a positive storm of curiosity concerning what I promptly began to think of as The Other Prison. My colleague in crime, occurring lower in the alphabet, had been sent there and I confess that the minute he was gone I missed him. I missed him because he was not French and because he was the only person in the world who knew that the story I told was true.

For, once locked in, divested of shoelaces, belt, watch, money, papers, nailfile, in a freezing cell in which both the window and the toilet were broken, with six other adventurers, the story I told of *l'affaire du drap de lit* elicited only the wildest amusement or the most suspicious disbelief. Among the people who shared my cell the first three days no one, it is true, had been arrested for anything much more serious—or, at least, not serious in my eyes. I remember that there was a boy who had stolen a knitted sweater from a *monoprix,* who would probably, it was agreed, receive a six-month sentence. There was an older man there who had been arrested for some kind of petty larceny. There were two North Africans, vivid, brutish, and beautiful, who alternated between gaiety and fury, not at the fact of their arrest but at the state of the cell. None poured as much emotional energy into the fact of their arrest as I did; they took it, as I would have liked to take it, as simply another unlucky happening in a very dirty world. For, though I had grown accustomed to thinking of myself as looking upon the world with a hard, penetrating eye, the truth was that they were far more realistic about the world than I, and more nearly right about it. The gap between us, which only a gesture I made could have bridged, grew steadily, during thirty-six hours, wider. I could not make any gesture simply because they frightened me. I was unable to accept my imprisonment as a fact, even as a temporary fact. I could not, even for a moment, accept my present companions as *my* companions. And they, of course, felt this and put it down, with perfect justice, to the fact that I was an American.

There was nothing to do all day long. It appeared that we would one day come to trial but no one knew when. We were awakened at seven-thirty by a rapping on what I believe is called the Judas, that small opening in the door of the cell which allows the guards to survey the prisoners. At this rapping we rose from the floor—we slept on straw pallets and each of us was covered with one thin blanket—and moved to the door of the cell. We peered through the opening into the center of the prison, which was, as I remember, three tiers high, all gray stone and gunmetal steel, precisely that prison I had seen in movies, except that, in the movies, I had not known that it was cold in prison. I had not known that when one's shoelaces and belt have been removed one is, in the strangest way, demoralized. The necessity of shuffling and the necessity of holding up one's trousers with one hand turn one into a rag doll. And the movies fail, of course, to give one any idea of what prison food is like. Along the corridor, at seven-thirty, came three men, each pushing before him a great garbage can, mounted on wheels. In the garbage can of the first was the bread—this was passed to one through the small opening in the door. In the can of the second was the coffee. In the can of the third was what was always called *la soupe,* a pallid paste of potatoes which had certainly been bubbling on the back of the prison stove long before that first, so momentous revolution. Naturally, it was cold by this time and, starving as I was, I could not eat it. I drank the coffee—which was not coffee—because it was hot, and spent the rest of the day, huddled in my blanket, munching on the bread. It was not the

French bread one bought in bakeries. In the evening the same procession returned. At ten-thirty the lights went out. I had a recurring dream, each night, a nightmare which always involved my mother's fried chicken. At the moment I was about to eat it came the rapping at the door. Silence is really all I remember of those first three days, silence and the color gray.

I am not sure now whether it was on the third or the fourth day that I was taken to trial for the first time. The days had nothing, obviously, to distinguish them from one another. I remember that I was very much aware that Christmas Day was approaching and I wondered if I was really going to spend Christmas Day in prison. And I remember that the first trial came the day before Christmas Eve.

On the morning of the first trial I was awakened by hearing my name called. I was told, hanging in a kind of void between my mother's fried chicken and the cold prison floor, "*Vous préparez. Vous êtes extrait*"—which simply terrified me, since I did not know what interpretation to put on the word "*extrait*," and since my cellmates had been amusing themselves with me by telling terrible stories about the inefficiency of French prisons, an inefficiency so extreme that it had often happened that someone who was supposed to be taken out and tried found himself on the wrong line and was guillotined instead. The best way of putting my reaction to this is to say that, though I knew they were teasing me, it was simply not possible for me to totally *dis*believe them. As far as I was concerned, once in the hands of the law in France, anything could happen. I shuffled along with the others who were *extrait* to the center of the prison, trying, rather, to linger in the office, which seemed the only warm spot in the whole world, and found myself again in that dreadful wagon, and was carried again to the Ile de la Cité, this time to the Palais de Justice. The entire day, except for ten minutes, was spent in one of the cells, first waiting to be tried, then waiting to be taken back to prison.

For I was *not* tried that day. By and by I was handcuffed and led through the halls, upstairs to the courtroom where I found my New York friend. We were placed together, both stage-whisperingly certain that this was the end of our ordeal. Nevertheless, while I waited for our case to be called, my eyes searched the courtroom, looking for a face I knew, hoping, anyway, that there was someone there who knew *me*, who would carry to someone outside the news that I was in trouble. But there was no one I knew there and I had had time to realize that there was probably only one man in Paris who could help me, an American patent attorney for whom I had worked as an office boy. He could have helped me because he had a quite solid position and some prestige and would have testified that, while working for him, I had handled large sums of money regularly, which made it rather unlikely that I would stoop to trafficking in bedsheets. However, he was somewhere in Paris, probably at this very moment enjoying a snack and a glass of wine and as far as the possibility of reaching him was concerned, he might as well have been on Mars. I tried to watch the proceedings and to make my mind a blank. But the proceedings were not reassuring. The boy, for example, who had stolen the sweater *did* receive a six-month sentence. It seemed to me that all the sentences meted out that day were excessive; though, again, it seemed that all the people who were sentenced that day had made, or clearly were going to make, crime their career. This seemed to be the opinion of the judge, who scarcely looked at the prisoners or listened to them; it seemed to be the opinion of the prisoners, who scarcely bothered to speak in their own behalf; it seemed to be the opinion of the lawyers, state lawyers for the most part, who were defending them. The great impulse of the courtroom seemed to be to put these people where they could not be seen—and not because they were offended at the crimes, unless, indeed, they were offended that the crimes were so petty, but because they did not wish to know that their society could be counted on to produce, probably in greater and greater numbers, a whole body of people for whom crime was the only possible career. Any society inevitably produces its criminals, but a society at once rigid and unstable can do nothing whatever to alleviate the poverty of its lowest members, cannot present to the hypothetical young man at the crucial moment that so-well-advertised right path. And the fact, perhaps, that the French are the earth's least sentimental people and must also be numbered among the most proud aggravates the plight of their lowest, youngest, and unluckiest members, for it means that the idea of rehabilitation is scarcely real to them. I confess that this attitude on their part raises in me sentiments of exasperation, admiration, and despair, revealing as it does, in both the best and the worst sense, their renowned and spectacular hard-headedness.

Finally our case was called and we rose. We gave our names. At the point that it developed that we were American the proceedings ceased, a hurried consultation took place between the judge and what I took to be several lawyers. Someone called out for an interpreter. The arresting officer had forgotten to mention our nationalities and there was, therefore, no interpreter in the court. Even if our French had been better than it was we would not have been allowed to stand trial without an interpreter. Before I clearly understood what was happening, I was handcuffed again and led out of the courtroom. The trial had been set back for the 27th of December.

I have sometimes wondered if I would *ever* have got out of prison if it had not been for the older man who had been arrested for the mysterious petty larceny. He was acquitted that day and when he returned to the cell—for he could not be released until morning—he found me sitting numbly on the floor, having just been prevented, by the sight of a man, all blood, being carried back to *his* cell on a stretcher, from seizing the bars and screaming until they let me out. The sight of the man on the stretcher proved, however, that screaming would not do much for me. The petty-larceny man went around asking if he could do anything in the world outside for those he was leaving behind. When he came to me I, at first, responded, "No, nothing"—for I suppose I had by now retreated into the attitude, the earliest I remember, that of my father, which was simply (since I had lost his God) that nothing could help me. And I suppose I will remember with gratitude until I die the fact that the man now insisted: *"Mais, êtes-vous sûr?"* Then it swept over me that he was going *outside* and he instantly became my first contact since the Lord alone knew how long with the outside world. At the same time, I remember, I did not really believe that he would help me. There was no reason why he should. But I gave him the phone number of my attorney friend and my own name.

So, in the middle of the next day, Christmas Eve, I shuffled downstairs again, to meet my visitor. He looked extremely well fed and sane and clean. He told me I had nothing to worry about any more. Only not even he could do anything to make the mill of justice grind any faster. He would, however, send me a lawyer of his acquaintance who would defend me on the 27th, and he would himself, along with several other people, appear as a character witness. He gave me a package of Lucky Strikes (which the turnkey took from me on the way upstairs) and said that, though it was doubtful that there would be any celebration in the prison, he would see to it that I got a fine Christmas dinner when I got out. And this, somehow, seemed very funny. I remember being astonished at the discovery that I was actually laughing. I was, too, I imagine, also rather disappointed that my hair had not turned white, that my face was clearly not going to bear any marks of tragedy, disappointed at bottom, no doubt, to realize, facing him in that room, that far worse things had happened to most people and that, indeed, to paraphrase my mother, if this was the worst thing that ever happened to me I could consider myself among the luckiest people ever to be born. He injected—my visitor—into my solitary nightmare common sense, the world, and the hint of blacker things to come.

The next day, Christmas, unable to endure my cell, and feeling that, after all, the day demanded a gesture, I asked to be allowed to go to Mass, hoping to hear some music. But I found myself, for a freezing hour and a half, locked in exactly the same kind of cubicle as in the wagon which had first brought me to prison, peering through a slot placed at the level of the eye at an old Frenchman, hatted, overcoated, muffled, and gloved, preaching in this language which I did not understand, to this row of wooden boxes, the story of Jesus Christ's love for men.

The next day, the 26th, I spent learning a peculiar kind of game, played with match-sticks, with my cellmates. For, since I no longer felt that I would stay in this cell forever, I was beginning to be able to make peace with it for a time. On the 27th I went again to trial and, as had been predicted, the case against us was dismissed. The story of the *drap de lit,* finally told, caused great merriment in the courtroom, whereupon my friend decided that the French were "great." I was chilled by their merriment, even though it was meant to warm me. It could only remind me of the laughter I had often heard at home, laughter which I had sometimes deliberately elicited. This laughter is the laughter of those who consider themselves to be at a safe remove from all the wretched, for whom the pain of the living is not real. I had heard it so often in my native land that I had resolved to find a place where I would never hear it any more. In some deep, black, stony, and liberating way, my life, in my own eyes, began during that first year in Paris, when it was borne in on me that this laughter is universal and never can be stilled. [1955]

Here Be Dragons

To be androgynous, *webster's* informs us, is to have both male and female characteristics. This means that there is a man in every woman and a woman in every man. Sometimes this is recognized only when the chips are, brutally, down—when there is no longer any way to avoid this recognition. But love between a man and a woman, or love between any two human beings, would not be possible did we not have available to us the spiritual resources of both sexes.

To be androgynous does not imply both male and female sexual equipment, which is the state, uncommon, of the hermaphrodite. However, the existence of the hermaphrodite reveals, in intimidating exaggeration, the truth concerning every human being—which is why the hermaphrodite is called a freak. The human being does not, in general, enjoy being intimidated by what he/she finds in the mirror.

The hermaphrodite, therefore, may make his/her living in side shows or brothels, whereas the merely androgynous are running banks or filling stations or maternity wards, churches, armies or countries.

The last time you had a drink, whether you were alone or with another, you were having a drink with an androgynous human being; and this is true for the last time you broke bread or, as I have tried to suggest, the last time you made love.

There seems to be a vast amount of confusion in the Western world concerning these matters, but love and sexual activity are not synonymous: only by becoming inhuman can the human being pretend that they are. The mare is not obliged to love the stallion, nor is the bull required to love the cow. They are doing what comes naturally.

But this by no means sums up the state or the possibilities of the human being in whom the awakening of desire fuels imagination and in whom imagination fuels desire. In other words, it is not possible for the human being to be as simple as a stallion or a mare, because the human imagination is perpetually required to examine, control, and redefine reality, of which we must assume ourselves to be the center and the key. Nature and revelation are perpetually challenging each other; this relentless tension is one of the keys to human history and to what is known as the human condition.

Now, I can speak only of the Western world and must rely on my own experience, but the simple truth of this universal duality, this perpetual possibility of communion and completion, seems so alarming that I have watched it lead to addiction, despair, death, and madness. Nowhere have I seen this panic more vividly than in my country and in my generation.

The American idea of sexuality appears to be rooted in the American idea of masculinity. Idea may not be the precise word, for the idea of one's sexuality can only with great violence be divorced or distanced from the idea of the self. Yet something resembling this rupture has certainly occurred (and is occurring) in American life, and violence has been the

American daily bread since we have heard of America. This violence, furthermore, is not merely literal and actual but appears to be admired and lusted after, and the key to the American imagination.

All countries or groups make of their trials a legend or, as in the case of Europe, a dubious romance called "history." But no other country has ever made so successful and glamorous a romance out of genocide and slavery; therefore, perhaps the word I am searching for is not idea but ideal.

The American *ideal,* then, of sexuality appears to be rooted in the American ideal of masculinity. This ideal has created cowboys and Indians, good guys and bad guys, punks and studs, tough guys and softies, butch and faggot, black and white. It is an ideal so paralytically infantile that it is virtually forbidden—as an unpatriotic act—that the American boy evolve into the complexity of manhood.

The exigencies created by the triumph of the Industrial Revolution—or, in other terms, the rise of Europe to global dominance—had, among many mighty effects, that of commercializing the roles of men and women. Men became the propagators, or perpetrators, of property, and women became the means by which that property was protected and handed down. One may say that this was nothing more than the ancient and universal division of labor—women nurtured the tribe, men battled for it—but the concept of property had undergone a change. This change was vast and deep and sinister.

For the first time in human history, a man was reduced not merely to a thing but to a thing the value of which was determined, absolutely, by that thing's commercial value. That this pragmatic principle dictated the slaughter of the native American, the enslavement of the black and the monumental rape of Africa—to say nothing of creating the wealth of the Western world—no one, I suppose, will now attempt to deny.

But this principle also raped and starved Ireland, for example, as well as Latin America, and it controlled the pens of the men who signed the Declaration of Independence—a document more clearly commercial than moral. This is how, and why, the American Constitution was able to define the slave as three-fifths of a man, from which legal and commercial definition it legally followed that a black man "had no rights a white man was bound to respect."

Ancient maps of the world—when the world was flat—inform us, concerning that void where America was waiting to be discovered, HERE BE DRAGONS. Dragons may not have been here then, but they are certainly here now, breathing fire, belching smoke; or, to be less literary and biblical about it, attempting to intimidate the mores, morals, and morality of this particular and peculiar time and place. Nor, since this country is the issue of the entire globe and is also the most powerful nation currently to be found on it, are we speaking only of this time and place. And it can be said that the monumental struggles being waged in our time and not only in this place resemble, in awesome ways, the ancient struggle between those who insisted that the world was flat and those who apprehended that it was round.

Of course, I cannot possibly imagine what it can be like to have both male and female sexual equipment. That's a load of family jewels to be hauling about, and it seems to me that it must make choice incessant or impossible—or, in terms unavailable to me, unnecessary. Yet, not to be frivolous concerning what I know I cannot—or, more probably, dare not— imagine, I hazard that the physically androgynous state must create an all-but-intolerable loneliness, since we all exist, after all, and crucially, in the eye of the beholder. We all react to and, to whatever extent, become what that eye sees. This judgment begins in the eyes of one's parents (the crucial, the definitive, the all-but-everlasting judgment), and so we move, in the vast and claustrophobic gallery of Others, on up or down the line, to the eye of one's enemy or one's friend or one's lover.

It is virtually impossible to trust one's human value without the col- laboration or corroboration of that eye—which is to say that no one can live without it. One can, of course, instruct that eye as to what to see, but this effort, which is nothing less than ruthless intimidation, is wounding and exhausting: while it can keep humiliation at bay, it confirms the fact that humiliation is the central danger of one's life. And since one cannot risk love without risking humiliation, love becomes impossible.

I hit the streets when I was about six or seven, like most black kids of my generation, running errands, doing odd jobs. This was in the black world—my turf—which means that I felt protected. I think that I really was, though poverty is poverty and we were, if I may say so, among the truly needy, in spite of the tins of corned beef we got from home relief every week, along with prunes. (Catsup had not yet become a vegetable; indeed, I don't think we had ever heard of it.) My mother fried corned beef, she boiled it, she baked it, she put potatoes in it, she put rice in it, she disguised it in corn bread, she boiled it in soup(!), she wrapped it in cloth, she beat it with a hammer, she banged it against the wall, she threw it onto the ceiling. Finally, she gave up, for nothing could make us eat it anymore, and the tins reproachfully piled up on the shelf above the bathtub—along with the prunes, which we also couldn't eat anymore. While I won't speak for my brothers and sisters, I can't bear corned-beef hash or prunes even today.

Poverty. I remember one afternoon when someone dropped a dime in front of the subway station at 125th Street and Lenox Avenue and I and a man of about forty both scrambled for it. The man won, giving me a cheerful goodbye as he sauntered down the subway steps. I was bitterly disappointed, a dime being a dime, but I laughed, too.

The truly needy. Once, my father gave me a dime—the last dime in the house, though I didn't know that—to go to the store for kerosene for the stove, and I fell on the icy streets and dropped the dime and lost it. My father beat me with an iron cord from the kitchen to the back room and back again, until I lay, half-conscious, on my belly on the floor.

Yet—strange though it is to realize this, looking back—I never felt threatened in those years, when I was growing up in Harlem, my home town. I think this may be because it was familiar; the white people who lived there then were as poor as we, and there was no TV setting our teeth on edge with exhortations to buy what we could never hope to afford.

On the other hand, I was certainly unbelievably unhappy and pathologically shy, but that, I felt, was nobody's fault but mine. My father kept me in short pants longer than he should have, and I had been told, and I believed, that I was ugly. This meant that the idea of myself as a sexual possibility, or target, as a creature capable of desire, had never entered my mind. And it entered my mind, finally, by means of the rent made in my short boy-scout pants by a man who had lured me into a hallway, saying that he wanted to send me to the store. That was the very last time I agreed to run an errand for any stranger.

Yet I was, in peculiar truth, a very lucky boy. Shortly after I turned sixteen, a Harlem racketeer, a man of about thirty-eight, fell in love with me, and I will be grateful to that man until the day I die. I showed him all my poetry, because I had no one else in Harlem to show it to, and even now, I sometimes wonder what on earth his friends could have been thinking, confronted with stingy-brimmed, mustachioed, razor-toting Poppa and skinny, popeyed Me when he walked me (rarely) into various shady joints, I drinking ginger ale, he drinking brandy. I think I was supposed to be his nephew, some nonsense like that, though he was Spanish and Irish, with curly black hair. But I knew that he was showing me off and wanted his friends to be happy for him—which, indeed, if the way they treated me can be taken as a barometer, they were. They seemed to feel that this was his business—that he would be in trouble if it became *their* business.

And though I loved him, too—in my way, a boy's way—I was mightily tormented, for I was still a child evangelist, which everybody knew, Lord. My soul looks back and wonders.

For what this really means is that all of the American categories of male and female, straight or not, black or white, were shattered, thank heaven, very early in my life. Not without anguish, certainly; but once you have discerned the meaning of a label, it may seem to define you for others, but it does not have the power to define you to yourself.

This prepared me for my life downtown, where I quickly discovered that my existence was the punch line of a dirty joke.

The condition that is now called gay was then called queer. The operative word was *faggot* and, later, pussy, but those epithets really had nothing to do with the question of sexual preference: you were being told simply that you had no balls.

I certainly had no desire to harm anyone, nor did I understand how anyone could look at me and suppose me physically capable of *causing* any harm. But boys and men chased me, saying I was a danger to their sisters. I was thrown out of cafeterias and rooming houses because I was "bad" for the neighborhood.

The cops watched all this with a smile, never making the faintest motion to protect me or to disperse my attackers; in fact, I was even more afraid of the cops than I was of the populace.

By the time I was nineteen, I was working in the Garment Center. I was getting on very badly at home and delayed going home after work as long as possible. At the end of the workday, I would wander east, to the Forty-second Street Library. Sometimes, I would sit in Bryant Park—but I discovered that I could not sit there long. I fled, to the movies, and so discovered Forty-second Street. Today that street is exactly what it was when I was an adolescent: it has simply become more blatant.

There were no X-rated movies then, but there were, so to speak, X-rated audiences. For example, I went in complete innocence to the Apollo, on Forty-second Street, because foreign films were shown there—*The Lower Depths, Childhood of Maxim Gorky, La Bête Humaine*—and I walked out as untouched (by human hands) as I had been when I walked in. There were the stores, mainly on Sixth Avenue, that sold "girlie" magazines. These magazines were usually to be found at the back of the store, and I don't so much remember them as I remember the silent men who stood there. They stood, it seemed, for hours, with the magazines in their hands and a kind of miasma in their eyes. There were all kinds of men, mostly young and, in those days, almost exclusively white. Also, for what it's worth, they were heterosexual, since the images they studied, at crotch level, were those of women.

Actually, I guess I hit Forty-second Street twice and have very nearly blotted the first time out. I was not at the mercy of the street the first time, for, though I may have dreaded *going* home, I hadn't *left* home yet. Then, I spent a lot of time in the library, and I stole odds and ends out of Woolworth's—with no compunction at all, due to the way they treated us in Harlem. When I went to the movies, I imagine that a combination of innocence and terror prevented me from too clearly apprehending the action taking place in the darkness of the Apollo—though I understood it well enough to remain standing a great deal of the time. This cunning stratagem failed when, one afternoon, the young boy I was standing behind put his hand behind him and grabbed my cock at the very same moment that a young boy came up behind me and put his cock against my hand: ignobly enough, I fled, though I doubt that I was missed. The men in the men's room frightened me, so I moved in and out as quickly as possible, and I also dimly felt, I remember, that I didn't want to "fool around" and so risk hurting the feelings of my uptown friend.

But if I was paralyzed by guilt and terror, I cannot be judged or judge myself too harshly, for I remember the faces of the men. These men, so far from being or resembling faggots, looked and sounded like the vigilantes who banded together on weekends to beat faggots up. (And I was around long enough, suffered enough, and learned enough to be forced to realize that this was very often true. I might not have learned this if I had been a white boy; but sometimes a white man will tell a black boy anything, everything, weeping briny tears. He knows that the black boy can never betray him, for no one will believe his testimony.)

These men looked like cops, football players, soldiers, sailors, Marines or bank presidents, admen, boxers, construction workers; they had wives, mistresses, and children. I sometimes saw them in other settings—in, as it were, the daytime. Sometimes they spoke to me, sometimes not, for anguish has many days and styles. But I had first seen them in the men's room, sometimes on their knees, peering up into the stalls, or standing at the urinal stroking themselves, staring at another man, stroking, and with this miasma in their eyes. Sometimes, eventually, inevitably, I would find myself in bed with one of these men, a despairing and dreadful conjunction, since their need was as relentless as quicksand and as impersonal, and sexual rumor concerning blacks had preceded me. As for sexual roles, these were created by the imagination and limited only by one's stamina.

At bottom, what I had learned was that the male desire for a male roams everywhere, avid, desperate, unimaginably lonely, culminating often in drugs, piety, madness or death. It was also dreadfully like watching myself at the end of a long, slow-moving line: soon I would be next. All of this was very frightening. It was lonely and impersonal and demeaning. I could not believe—after all, I was only nineteen—that I could have been driven to the lonesome place where these men and I met each other so soon, to stay.

The American idea of masculinity: There are few things under heaven more difficult to understand or, when I was younger, to forgive.

During the Second World War (the first one having failed to make the world safe for democracy) and some time after the Civil War (which had failed, unaccountably, to liberate the slave), life for niggers was fairly rough in Greenwich Village. There were only about three of us, if I remember correctly, when I first hit those streets, and I was the youngest, the most visible, and the most vulnerable.

On every street corner, I was called a faggot. This meant that I was despised, and, however horrible this is, it is clear. What was *not* clear at that time of my life was what motivated the men and boys who mocked and chased me; for, if they found me when they were alone, they spoke to me very differently—frightening me, I must say, into a stunned and speechless paralysis. For when they were alone, they spoke very gently and wanted me to take them home and make love. (They could not take *me* home; they lived with their families.) The bafflement and the pain this caused in me remain beyond description. I was far too terrified to be able to accept their propositions, which could only result, it seemed to me, in making myself a candidate for gang rape. At the same time, I was moved by their loneliness, their halting, nearly speechless need. But I did not understand it.

One evening, for example, I was standing at the bottom of the steps to the Waverly Place subway station, saying goodbye to some friends who were about to take the subway. A gang of boys stood at the top of the steps and cried, in high, feminine voices, "Is this where the fags meet?"

Well. This meant that I certainly could not go back upstairs but would have to take the subway with my friends and get off at another station and maneuver my way home. But one of the gang saw me and, without missing a beat or saying a word to his friends, called my name and came down the steps, throwing one arm around me and asking where I'd been. He had let me know, some time before, that he wanted me to take him home—but I was surprised that he could be so open before his friends, who for their part seemed to find nothing astonishing in this encounter and disappeared, probably in search of other faggots.

The boys who are left of that time and place are all my age or older. But many of them are dead, and I remember how some of them died—some in the streets, some in the Army, some on the needle, some in jail. Many years later, we managed, without ever becoming friends—it was too late for that—to be friendly with one another. One of these men and I had a very brief, intense affair shortly before he died. He was on drugs and knew that he could not live long. "What a waste," he said, and he was right.

One of them said, "My God, Jimmy, you were moving so fast in those years, you never stopped to talk to me."

I said, "That's right, baby; I didn't stop because I didn't want you to think that I was trying to seduce you."

"Man," he said, indescribably, "why didn't you?"

But the queer—not yet gay—world was an even more intimidating area of this hall of mirrors. I knew that I was in the hall and present at this company—but the mirrors threw back only brief and distorted fragments of myself.

In the first place, as I have said, there were very few black people in the Village in those years, and of that handful, I was decidedly the most improbable. Perhaps, as they say in the theater, I was a hard type to cast; yet I was eager, vulnerable, and lonely. I was terribly shy, but boys *are* shy. I am saying that I don't think I felt absolutely, irredeemably grotesque—nothing that a friendly wave of the wand couldn't alter—but I was miserable. I moved through that world very quickly; I have described it as "my season in hell," for I was never able to make my peace with it.

It wasn't only that I didn't wish to seem or sound like a woman, for it was this detail that most harshly first struck my eye and ear. I am sure that I was afraid that I already seemed and sounded too much like a woman. In my childhood, at least until my adolescence, my playmates had called me a sissy. It seemed to me that many of the people I met were making fun of women, and I didn't see why. *I* certainly needed all the friends I could get, male *or* female, and women had nothing to do with whatever my trouble might prove to be.

At the same time, I had already been sexually involved with a couple of white women in the Village. There were virtually no black women there when I hit those streets, and none who needed or could have afforded to risk herself with an odd, raggedy-assed black boy who clearly had no future. (The first black girl I met who dug me I fell in love with, lived with and almost married. But I met her, though I was only twenty-two, many light-years too late.)

The white girls I had known or been involved with—different categories—had paralyzed me, because I simply did not know what, apart from my sex, they wanted. Sometimes it was great, sometimes it was just moaning and groaning, but, ultimately, I found myself at the mercy of a double fear. The fear of the world was bearable until it entered the bedroom. But it sometimes entered the bedroom by means of the motives of the girl, who intended to civilize you into becoming an appendage or who had found a black boy to sleep with because she wanted to humiliate her parents. Not an easy scene to play, in any case, since it can bring out the worst in both parties, and more than one white girl had already made me know that her color was more powerful than my dick.

Which had nothing to do with how I found myself in the gay world. I would have found myself there anyway, but perhaps the very last thing this black boy needed were clouds of imitation white women and speculations concerning the size of his organ; speculations sometimes accompanied by an attempt at the laying on of hands. *"Ooo!* Look at him! He's cute—he doesn't like you to touch him there!"

In short, I was black in that world, and I was used that way, and by people who truly meant me no harm.

And they could *not* have meant me any harm, because they did not see me. There were exceptions, of course, for I also met some beautiful people. Yet even today, it seems to me (possibly because I am black) very dangerous to model one's opposition to the arbitrary definition, the imposed ordeal, merely on the example supplied by one's oppressor.

The object of one's hatred is never, alas, conveniently outside but is seated in one's lap, stirring in one's bowels and dictating the beat of one's heart. And if one does not know this, one risks becoming an imitation—and, therefore, a continuation—of principles one imagines oneself to despise.

I, in any case, had endured far too much debasement willingly to debase myself. I had absolutely no fantasies about making love to the last cop or hoodlum who had beaten the shit out of me. I did not find it amusing, in any way whatever, to act out the role of the darky.

So I moved on out of there.

In fact, I found a friend—more accurately, a friend found *me*—an Italian, about five years older than I, who helped my morale greatly in those years. I was told that he had threatened to kill anyone who touched me. I don't know about that, but people stopped beating me up. Our relationship never seemed to worry him or his friends or his women.

My situation in the Village stabilized itself to the extent that I began working as a waiter in a black West Indian restaurant, The Calypso, on MacDougal Street. This led, by no means incidentally, to the desegregation of the San Remo, an Italian bar and restaurant on the corner of MacDougal and Bleecker. Every time I entered the San Remo, they threw me out. I had to pass it all the time on my way to and from work, which is, no doubt, why the insult rankled.

I had won the Saxton Fellowship, which was administered by Harper & Brothers, and I knew Frank S. MacGregor, the president of Harper's. One night, when he asked me where we should have dinner, I suggested, spontaneously, the San Remo.

We entered, and they seated us and we were served. I went back to MacGregor's house for a drink and then went straight back to the San Remo, sitting on a bar stool in the window. The San Remo thus began to attract a varied clientele, indeed—so much so that Allen Ginsberg and company arrived there the year I left New York for Paris.

As for the people who ran and worked at the San Remo, they never bothered me again. Indeed, the Italian community never bothered me again—or rarely and, as it were, by accident. But the Village was full of white tourists, and one night, when a mob gathered before the San Remo, demanding that I come out, the owners closed the joint and turned the lights out and we sat in the back room, in the dark, for a couple of hours, until they judged it safe to drive me home.

This was a strange, great and bewildering time in my life. Once I was in the San Remo, for example, I was *in,* and anybody who messed with me was *out*—that was all there was to it, and it happened more than once. And no one seemed to remember a time when I had not been there.

I could not quite get it together, but it seemed to me that I was no longer black for them and they had ceased to be white for me, for they sometimes introduced me to their families with every appearance of affection and pride and exhibited not the remotest interest in whatever my sexual proclivities chanced to be.

They had fought me very hard to prevent this moment, but perhaps we were all much relieved to have got beyond the obscenity of color.

Matters were equally bewildering, though in a different way, at The Calypso. All kinds of people came into our joint—I am now referring to white people—and one of their most vivid aspects, for me, was the cruelty of their alienation. They appeared to have no antecedents nor any real connections.

"Do you really *like* your mother?" someone asked me, seeming to be astounded, totally disbelieving the possibility.

I was astounded by the question. Certainly, my mother and I did not agree about everything, and I knew that she was very worried about the dangers of the life I lived, but that was normal, since I was a boy and she was a woman. Of course she was worried about me: she was my *mother.* But she knew I wasn't crazy and that I would certainly never do anything, deliberately, to hurt her. Or my tribe, my brothers and sisters, who were probably worried about me, too.

My family was a part of my life. I could not imagine life without them, might never have been able to reconcile myself to life without them. And certainly one of the reasons I was breaking my ass in the Village had to do with my need to try to move us out of our dangerous situation. I was perfectly aware of the odds—my father had made that very clear—but he had also given me my assignment. "Do you really *like* your mother?" did not cause me to wonder about my mother or myself but about the person asking the question.

And perhaps because of such questions, I was not even remotely tempted by the possibilities of psychiatry or psychoanalysis. For one thing, there were too many schools—Freud, Horney, Jung, Reich (to suggest merely the tip of that iceberg)—and, for another, it seemed to me that anyone who thought seriously that I had any desire to be "adjusted" to this society had to be ill; too ill, certainly, as time was to prove, to be trusted.

I sensed, then—without being able to articulate it—that this dependence on a formula for safety, for that is what it was, signaled a desperate moral abdiction. People went to the shrink in order to find justification for the empty lives they led and the meaningless work they did. Many turned, helplessly, hopefully, to Wilhelm Reich and perished in orgone boxes.

I seem to have strayed a long way from our subject, but our subject is social and historical—and continuous. The people who leaped into orgone boxes in search of the perfect orgasm were later to turn to acid. The people so dependent on psychiatric formulas were unable to give their children any sense of right or wrong—indeed, this sense was in themselves so fragile that during the McCarthy era, more than one shrink made a lot of money by convincing his patients, or clients, that their psychic health demanded that they inform on their friends. (Some of these people, after their surrender, attempted to absolve themselves in the civil rights movement.)

What happened to the children, therefore, is not even remotely astonishing. The flower children—who became the Weather Underground, the

Symbionese Liberation Army, the Manson Family—are creatures from this howling inner space.

I am not certain, therefore, that the present sexual revolution is either sexual or a revolution. It strikes me as a reaction to the spiritual famine of American life. The present androgynous "craze"—to underestimate it— strikes me as an attempt to be honest concerning one's nature, and it is instructive, I think, to note that there is virtually no emphasis on overt sexual activity. There is nothing more boring, anyway, than sexual activity as an end in itself, and a great many people who came out of the closet should reconsider.

Such figures as Boy George do not disturb me nearly so much as do those relentlessly hetero (sexual?) keepers of the keys and seals, those who know what the world needs in the way of order and who are ready and willing to supply that order.

This rage for order can result in chaos, and in this country, chaos connects with color. During the height of my involvement in the civil rights movement, for example, I was subjected to hate mail of a terrifying precision. Volumes concerning what my sisters, to say nothing of my mother, were capable of doing; to say nothing of my brothers; to say nothing of the monumental size of *my* organ and what I did with it. Someone described, in utterly riveting detail, a scene he swore he had witnessed (I *think* it was a *he*—such mail is rarely signed) on the steps of houses in Baltimore of niggers fucking their dogs.

At the same time, I was also on the mailing list of one of the more elegant of the KKK societies, and I still have some of that mail in my files. Someone, of course, eventually realized that the organization should not be sending that mail to this particular citizen, and it stopped coming—but not before I had had time to be struck by the similarity of tone between the hate mail and the mail of the society, and not before the society had informed me, by means of a parody of an Audubon Society postcard, what it felt and expected me to feel concerning a certain "Red-breasted" Martin Luther King, Jr.

The Michael Jackson cacophony is fascinating in that it is not about Jackson at all. I hope he has the good sense to know it and the good fortune to snatch his life out of the jaws of a carnivorous success. He will not swiftly be forgiven for having turned so many tables, for he damn sure grabbed the brass ring, and the man who broke the bank at Monte Carlo has nothing on Michael. All that noise is about America, as the dishonest custodian of black life and wealth; the blacks, especially males, in America; and the burning, buried American guilt; and sex and sexual roles and sexual panic;

money, success and despair—to all of which may now be added the bitter
need to find a head on which to place the crown of Miss America.

Freaks are called freaks and are treated as they are treated—in the main,
abominably—because they are human beings who cause to echo, deep
within us, our most profound terrors and desires.

Most of us, however, do not appear to be freaks—though we are rarely
what we appear to be. We are, for the most part, visibly male or female, our
social roles defined by our sexual equipment.

But we are all androgynous, not only because we are all born of a
woman impregnated by the seed of a man but because each of us, helplessly
and forever, contains the other—male in female, female in male, white
in black and black in white. We are a part of each other. Many of my
countrymen appear to find this fact exceedingly inconvenient and even
unfair, and so, very often, do I. But none of us can do anything about it.

[1985]

JOAN DIDION

UPI/Bettmann

JOAN DIDION WAS BORN IN SACRAMENTO, California, on December 5, 1934, a fifth-generation descendant of pioneers who had helped settle the Sacramento Valley in the 1840s. In her autobiographical essays she frequently points out how different Sacramento is from the California most people think of—Hollywood, freeways, a rootless population. Sacramento has always been farming country, and Didion's ancestors were landowners, their politics conservative, their religion Episcopal. She grew up in a world where the middle-class values of character, morality, and economy were firmly established.

During World War II her family was temporarily uprooted as they followed her father, an officer in the air corps, to air bases around the country, celebrating "makeshift Christmases in rented rooms." With the end of the war they returned to Sacramento and a settled life again, where there were "teacups hand-painted with cabbage roses" and they visited "the great-aunts on Sundays." After graduating from the local high school, Didion went to the University of California at Berkeley (A.B., 1956) and from there to New York, where she was an associate feature editor at *Vogue* for seven years. (As a senior at Berkeley she had won *Vogue's Prix de Paris.*) In 1964 she married John Gregory Dunne, a writer for *Time*, and a few months later they left New York for Los Angeles, intending to stay only six months; it was one of those leaves of absence from frustrating security that writers often take in order to see if they can make it on their own, just writing.

Fortunately, within a year Didion and Dunne had both established freelance associations with *The Saturday Evening Post*, and by the end of 1966 they shared a regular *Post* column entitled "Points West." (They have also collaborated on the screenplays for *The Panic in Needle Park, A Star Is Born*, and *True Confessions.*) In 1968 Didion published *Slouching Towards Bethlehem*, a collection of her essays from the *Post* and other magazines, and she began receiving serious attention from literary critics. (An earlier novel, *Run River*, 1963, written while she was at *Vogue*, had gone largely unnoticed.) What critics admired in *Slouching Towards Bethlehem* were Didion's economical style, her candidness, and the intense clarity with which she reported some of the most grotesque aspects of life in America in the late sixties.

In 1970 Joan Didion published *Play It as It Lays*, a novel of apocalyptic vision reminiscent of Nathanael West's *The Day of the Locust.* A depressing tale of abortion, divorce, and suicide in Hollywood and Las Vegas, *Play It as It Lays* is also, in the end, a story of survival: despite all that happens to her, the central character, Maria Wyeth, does not give up. As she says at the end, "I know what 'nothing' means, and keep on playing." *Play It as It Lays* was nominated for the 1970 National Book Award in Fiction.

In her third novel, *A Book of Common Prayer* (1977), Didion again portrays a woman who attempts to survive a catastrophic life. Charlotte Douglas, like Maria Wyeth, lacks heroic qualities; she is shallow, foolish, weak. Coming out of a protected, monied background, she is not prepared to deal with a world that is deceptively evil. And yet again, in the novel's moral complexity, Charlotte Douglas ends up being a deeply sympathetic character and a hero of sorts: she survives.

In 1979 a second collection of essays, *The White Album,* was published. Again creating vivid images of personal and cultural breakdown, Didion writes with painful honesty about the difficulty of maintaining a sense of meaningful purpose in a fragmented world. In an essay entitled "On the Morning After the Sixties" she explains the difference between the private values of her own generation and the collective beliefs of young people in the late sixties and early seventies: "If I could believe that going to a barricade would affect man's fate in the slightest I would go to that barricade, and often wish that I could, but I would be less than honest to say that I expect to happen on such a happy ending."

In the essay "Why I Write" Didion says she "can bring . . . no reports from any other front" than the very private one of the writer in "the act of writing." Yet in 1982 she went to the "front" (as it is) in El Salvador and brought back the most harrowing account of the troubles occurring there. Three long essays appeared in *The New York Review of Books* in October 1982 and later formed the bulk of her book *Salvador* (1983). In 1984 she published her fourth novel, *Democracy* (borrowing the title of a political satire written by Henry Adams in 1880). An exploration of the "dislocations" that have occurred in American life during the last twenty years, *Democracy* examines the relationships between money, political life, and the mass media as experienced by a woman, Inez Christian Victor, whose husband is a United States Senator who aspires to be President. Didion's most recent collection of essays, *After Henry,* was published in 1993.

Joan Didion's style is one of ellipses and vivid images, often put into para-doxical juxtapositions. She is simultaneously candid in her revelations of her personal life, and private. Her effects are often achieved as much by what she leaves out as what she includes. In an interview in *The Paris Review,* she re-vealed that the two writers who have had the greatest influence on her are Ernest Hemingway and Henry James—a stylistic paradox if ever there was one. It is perhaps easier to think of her style as *cinematic*—that is, deriving its power largely from a rapid "cutting" between vivid images. It is a style to which many readers today can respond more easily than the rhetorical cadences of the past. ■

Goodbye to All That

How many miles to Babylon?
Three score miles and ten—
Can I get there by candlelight?
Yes, and back again—
If your feet are nimble and light
You can get there by candlelight.

IT IS EASY TO SEE THE BEGINNINGS OF things, and harder to see the ends. I can remember now, with a clarity that makes the nerves in the back of my neck constrict, when New York began for me, but I cannot lay my finger upon the moment it ended, can never cut through the ambiguities and second starts and broken resolves to the exact place on the page where the heroine is no longer as optimistic as she once was. When I first saw New York I was twenty, and it was summertime, and I got off a DC-7 at the old Idlewild temporary terminal in a new dress which had seemed very smart in Sacramento but seemed less smart already, even in the old Idlewild temporary terminal, and the warm air smelled of mildew and some instinct, programmed by all the movies I had ever seen and all the songs I had ever heard sung and all the stories I had ever read about New York, informed me that it would never be quite the same again. In fact it never was. Some time later there was a song on all the jukeboxes on the upper East Side that went "but where is the schoolgirl who used to be me," and if it was late enough at night I used to wonder that. I know now that almost everyone wonders something like that, sooner or later and no matter what he or she is doing, but one of the mixed blessings of being twenty and twenty-one and even twenty-three is the conviction that nothing like this, all evidence to the contrary notwithstanding, has ever happened to anyone before.

Of course it might have been some other city, had circumstances been different and the time been different and had I been different, might have been Paris or Chicago or even San Francisco, but because I am talking about myself I am talking here about New York. That first night I opened my window on the bus into town and watched for the skyline, but all I could see were the wastes of Queens and the big signs that said MIDTOWN TUNNEL THIS LANE and then a flood of summer rain (even that seemed remarkable and exotic, for I had come out of the West where there was no summer rain), and for the next three days I sat wrapped in blankets in a hotel room air-conditioned to 35° and tried to get over a bad cold and a high fever. It did not occur to me to call a doctor, because I knew none, and although it did occur to me to call the desk and ask that the air conditioner be turned off, I never called, because I did not know how much to tip whoever might come—was anyone ever so young? I am here to tell you that someone was. All I could do during those three days was talk long-distance to the boy I already knew I would never marry in the spring. I would stay in New York, I told him, just six months, and I could see the Brooklyn Bridge from my window. As it turned out the bridge was the Triborough, and I stayed eight years.

In retrospect it seems to me that those days before I knew the names of all the bridges were happier than the ones that came later, but perhaps you will see that as we go along. Part of what I want to tell you is what it is like to be young in New York, how six months can become eight years with the deceptive ease of a film dissolve, for that is how those years appear to me now, in a long sequence of sentimental dissolves and old-fashioned trick shots—the Seagram Building fountains dissolve into snowflakes, I enter a revolving door at twenty and come out a good deal older, and on a different street. But most particularly I want to explain to you, and in the process perhaps to myself, why I no longer live in New York. It is often said that New York is a city for only the very rich and the very poor. It is less often said that New York is also, at least for those of us who came there from somewhere else, a city for only the very young.

I remember once, one cold bright December evening in New York, suggesting to a friend who complained of having been around too long that he come with me to a party where there would be, I assured him with the bright resourcefulness of twenty-three, "new faces." He laughed literally until he choked, and I had to roll down the taxi window and hit him on the back. "New faces," he said finally, "don't tell me about *new faces.*" It seemed that the last time he had gone to a party where he had been promised "new faces," there had been fifteen people in the room, and he had already slept with five of the women and owed money to all but two of the men. I laughed with him, but the first snow had just begun to fall and the big Christmas trees glittered yellow and white as far as I could see up Park Avenue and I had a new dress and it would be a long while before I would come to understand the particular moral of the story.

It would be a long while because, quite simply, I was in love with New York. I do not mean "love" in any colloquial way, I mean that I was in love with the city, the way you love the first person who ever touches you and never love anyone quite that way again. I remember walking across Sixty-second Street one twilight that first spring, or the second spring, they were all alike for a while. I was late to meet someone but I stopped at Lexington Avenue and bought a peach and stood on the corner eating it and knew that I had come out of the West and reached the mirage. I could taste the peach and feel the soft air blowing from a subway grating on my legs and I could smell lilac and garbage and expensive perfume and I knew that it would cost something sooner or later—because I did not belong there, did not come from there—but when you are twenty-two or twenty-three, you figure that later you will have a high emotional balance, and be able to pay whatever it costs. I still believed in possibilities then, still had the sense, so peculiar to New York, that something extraordinary would happen any minute, any day, any month. I was making only $65 or $70 a week then ("Put yourself in Hattie Carnegie's hands," I was advised without the slightest trace of irony by an editor of the magazine for which I worked), so little money that some weeks I had to charge food at Bloomingdale's gourmet shop in order to eat, a fact which went unmentioned in the letters I wrote to California. I never told my father that I needed money because then he would have sent it, and I would never know if I could do it by myself. At that time making a living seemed a game to me, with arbitrary but quite inflexible rules. And except on a certain kind of winter evening—six-thirty in the Seventies, say, already dark and bitter with a wind off the river, when I would be walking very fast toward a bus and would look in the bright windows of brownstones and see cooks working in clean kitchens and imagine women lighting candles on the floor above and beautiful children being bathed on the floor above that—except on nights like those, I never felt poor; I had the feeling that if I needed money I could always get it. I could write a syndicated column for teenagers under the name "Debbi Lynn" or I could smuggle gold into India or I could become a $100 call girl, and none of it would matter.

Nothing was irrevocable; everything was within reach. Just around every corner lay something curious and interesting, something I had never before seen or done or known about. I could go to a party and meet someone who called himself Mr. Emotional Appeal and ran The Emotional Appeal Institute or Tina Onassis Blandford or a Florida cracker who was then a regular on what he called "the Big C," the Southampton–El Morocco circuit ("I'm well-connected on the Big C, honey," he would tell me over collard greens on his vast borrowed terrace), or the widow of the celery king of the Harlem market or a piano salesman from Bonne Terre, Missouri, or someone who had already made and lost two fortunes in Midland, Texas. I could make promises to myself and to other people and there would be all the time in the world to keep them. I could stay up all night and make mistakes, and none of it would count.

You see I was in a curious position in New York: it never occurred to me that I was living a real life there. In my imagination I was always there for just another few months, just until Christmas or Easter or the first warm day in May. For that reason I was most comfortable in the company of Southerners. They seemed to be in New York as I was, on some indefinitely extended leave from wherever they belonged, disinclined to consider the future, temporary exiles who always knew when the flights left for New Orleans or Memphis or Richmond or, in my case, California. Someone who lives always with a plane schedule in the drawer lives on a slightly different calendar. Christmas, for example, was a difficult season. Other people could take it in stride, going to Stowe or going abroad or going for the day to their mothers' places in Connecticut; those of us who believed that we lived somewhere else would spend it making and canceling airline reservations, waiting for weatherbound flights as if for the last plane out of Lisbon in 1940, and finally comforting one another, those of us who were left, with the oranges and mementos and smoked-oyster stuffings of childhood, gathering close, colonials in a far country.

Which is precisely what we were. I am not sure that it is possible for anyone brought up in the East to appreciate entirely what New York, the idea of New York, means to those of us who came out of the West and the South. To an Eastern child, particularly a child who has always had an uncle on Wall Street and who has spent several hundred Saturdays first at F. A. O. Schwarz and being fitted for shoes at Best's and then waiting under the Biltmore clock and dancing to Lester Lanin, New York is just a city, albeit *the* city, a plausible place for people to live. But to those of us who came from places where no one had heard of Lester Lanin and Grand Central Station was a Saturday radio program, where Wall Street and Fifth Avenue and Madison Avenue were not places at all but abstractions ("Money," and "High Fashion," and "The Hucksters"), New York was no mere city. It was instead an infinitely romantic notion, the mysterious nexus of all love and money and power, the shining and perishable dream itself. To think of "living" there was to reduce the miraculous to the mundane; one does not "live" at Xanadu.

In fact it was difficult in the extreme for me to understand those young women for whom New York was not simply an ephemeral Estoril but a real place, girls who bought toasters and installed new cabinets in their apartments and committed themselves to some reasonable future. I never bought any furniture in New York. For a year or so I lived in other people's apartments; after that I lived in the Nineties in an apartment furnished entirely with things taken from storage by a friend whose wife had moved away. And when I left the apartment in the Nineties (that was when I was leaving everything, when it was all breaking up) I left everything in it, even my winter clothes and the map of Sacramento County I had hung on the bedroom wall to remind me who I was, and I moved into a monastic four-room floor-through on Seventy-fifth Street. "Monastic" is perhaps misleading here, implying some chic severity; until after I was married and my husband moved some furniture in, there was nothing at all in those four rooms except a cheap double mattress and box springs, ordered by telephone the day I decided to move, and two French garden chairs lent me by a friend who imported them. (It strikes me now that the people I knew in New York all had curious and self-defeating sidelines. They imported garden chairs which did not sell very well at Hammacher Schlemmer or they tried to market hair straighteners in Harlem or they ghosted exposés of Murder Incorporated for Sunday supplements. I think that perhaps none of us was very serious, *engagé* only about our most private lives.)

All I ever did to that apartment was hang fifty yards of yellow theatrical silk across the bedroom windows, because I had some idea that the gold light would make me feel better, but I did not bother to weight the curtains correctly and all that summer the long panels of transparent golden silk would blow out the windows and get tangled and drenched in the afternoon thunderstorms. That was the year, my twenty-eighth, when I was discovering that not all of the promises would be kept, that some things are in fact irrevocable and that it had counted after all, every evasion and every procrastination, every mistake, every word, all of it.

That is what it was all about, wasn't it? Promises? Now when New York comes back to me it comes in hallucinatory flashes, so clinically detailed that I sometimes wish that memory would effect the distortion with which it is commonly credited. For a lot of the time I was in New York I used a perfume called *Fleurs de Rocaille,* and then *L'Air du Temps,* and now the slightest trace of either can short-circuit my connections for the rest of the day. Nor can I smell Henri Bendel jasmine soap without falling back into the past, or the particular mixture of spices used for boiling crabs. There were barrels of crab boil in a Czech place in the Eighties where I once shopped. Smells, of course, are notorious memory stimuli, but there are other things which affect me the same way. Blue-and-white striped sheets. Vermouth cassis. Some faded nightgowns which were new in 1959 or 1960, and some chiffon scarves I bought about the same time.

I suppose that a lot of us who have been young in New York have the same scenes on our home screens. I remember sitting in a lot of apartments with a slight headache about five o'clock in the morning. I had a friend who could not sleep, and he knew a few other people who had the same trouble, and we would watch the sky lighten and have a last drink with no ice and then go home in the early morning light, when the streets were clean and wet (had it rained in the night? we never knew) and the few cruising taxis still had their headlights on and the only color was the red and green of traffic signals. The White Rose bars opened very early in the morning; I recall waiting in one of them to watch an astronaut go into space, waiting so long that at the moment it actually happened I had my eyes not on the television screen but on a cockroach on the tile floor. I liked the bleak branches above Washington Square at dawn, and the monochromatic flatness of Second Avenue, the fire escapes and the grilled storefronts peculiar and empty in their perspective.

It is relatively hard to fight at six-thirty or seven in the morning, without any sleep, which was perhaps one reason we stayed up all night, and it seemed to me a pleasant time of day. The windows were shuttered in that apartment in the Nineties and I could sleep a few hours and then go to work. I could work then on two or three hours' sleep and a container of coffee from Chock Full O'Nuts. I liked going to work, liked the soothing and satisfactory rhythm of getting out a magazine, liked the orderly progression of four-color closings and two-color closings and black-and-white closings and then The Product, no abstraction but something which looked effortlessly glossy and could be picked up on a newsstand and weighed in the hand. I liked all the minutiae of proofs and layouts, liked working late on the nights the magazine went to press, sitting and reading *Variety* and waiting for the copy desk to call. From my office I could look across town to the weather signal on the Mutual of New York Building and the lights that alternately spelled out TIME and LIFE above Rockefeller Plaza; that pleased me obscurely, and so did walking uptown in the mauve eight o'clocks of early summer evenings and looking at things, Lowestoft tureens in Fifty-seventh Street windows, people in evening clothes trying to get taxis, the trees just coming into full leaf, the lambent air, all the sweet promises of money and summer.

Some years passed, but I still did not lose that sense of wonder about New York. I began to cherish the loneliness of it, the sense that at any given time no one need know where I was or what I was doing. I liked walking, from the East River over to the Hudson and back on brisk days, down around the Village on warm days. A friend would leave me the key to her apartment in the West Village when she was out of town, and sometimes I would just move down there, because by that time the telephone was beginning to bother me (the canker, you see, was already in the rose) and not many people had that number. I remember one day when someone who did have the West Village number came to pick me up for lunch there, and we both had hangovers, and I cut my finger opening him a beer and burst into tears, and we walked to a Spanish restaurant and drank Bloody Marys and *gazpacho* until we felt better. I was not then guilt-ridden about spending afternoons that way, because I still had all the afternoons in the world.

And even that late in the game I still liked going to parties, all parties, bad parties, Saturday-afternoon parties given by recently married couples who lived in Stuyvesant Town, West Side parties given by unpublished or failed writers who served cheap red wine and talked about going to Guadalajara, Village parties where all the guests worked for advertising agencies and voted for Reform Democrats, press parties at Sardi's, the worst kinds of parties. You will have perceived by now that I was not one to profit by the experience of others, that it was a very long time indeed before I stopped believing in new faces and began to understand the lesson in that story, which was that it is distinctly possible to stay too long at the Fair.

I could not tell you when I began to understand that. All I know is that it was very bad when I was twenty-eight. Everything that was said to me I seemed to have heard before, and I could no longer listen. I could no longer sit in little bars near Grand Central and listen to someone complaining of his wife's inability to cope with the help while he missed another train to Connecticut. I no longer had any interest in hearing about the advances other people had received from their publishers, about plays which were having second-act trouble in Philadelphia, or about people I would like very much if only I would come out and meet them. I had already met them, always. There were certain parts of the city which I had to avoid. I could not bear upper Madison Avenue on weekday mornings (this was a particularly inconvenient aversion, since I then lived just fifty or sixty feet east of Madison), because I would see women walking Yorkshire terriers and shopping at Gristede's, and some Veblenesque gorge would rise in my throat. I could not go to Times Square in the afternoon, or to the New York Public Library for any reason whatsoever. One day I could not go into a Schrafft's; the next day it would be Bonwit Teller.

I hurt the people I cared about, and insulted those I did not. I cut myself off from the one person who was closer to me than any other. I cried until I was not even aware when I was crying and when I was not, cried in elevators and in taxis and in Chinese laundries, and when I went to the doctor he said only that I seemed to be depressed, and should see a "specialist." He wrote down a psychiatrist's name and address for me, but I did not go.

Instead I got married, which as it turned out was a very good thing to do but badly timed, since I still could not walk on upper Madison Avenue in the mornings and still could not talk to people and still cried in Chinese laundries. I had never before understood what "despair" meant, and I am not sure that I understand now, but I understood that year. Of course I could not work. I could not even get dinner with any degree of certainty, and I would sit in the apartment on Seventy-fifth Street paralyzed until my husband would call from his office and say gently that I did not have to get dinner, that I could meet him at Michael's Pub or at Toots Shor's or at Sardi's East. And then one morning in April (we had been married in January) he called and told me that he wanted to get out of New York for a while, that he would take a six-month leave of absence, that we would go somewhere.

It was three years ago that he told me that, and we have lived in Los Angeles since. Many of the people we knew in New York think this a curious aberration, and in fact tell us so. There is no possible, no adequate answer to that, and so we give certain stock answers, the answers everyone gives. I talk about how difficult it would be for us to "afford" to live in New York right now, about how much "space" we need. All I mean is that I was very young in New York, and that at some point the golden rhythm was broken, and I am not that young any more. The last time I was in New York was in a cold January, and everyone was ill and tired. Many of the people I used to know there had moved to Dallas or had gone on Antabuse or had bought a farm in New Hampshire. We stayed ten days, and then we took an afternoon flight back to Los Angeles, and on the way home from the airport that night I could see the moon on the Pacific and smell jasmine all around and we both knew that there was no longer any point in keeping the apartment we still kept in New York. There were years when I called Los Angeles "the Coast," but they seem a long time ago.　　[1967]

On Going Home

I AM HOME FOR MY DAUGHTER'S FIRST birthday. By "home" I do not mean the house in Los Angeles where my husband and I and the baby live, but the place where my family is, in the Central Valley of California. It is a vital although troublesome distinction. My husband likes my family but is uneasy in their house, because once there I fall into their ways, which are difficult, oblique, deliberately inarticulate, not my husband's ways. We live in dusty houses ("D-U-S-T," he once wrote with his finger on surfaces all over the house, but no one noticed it) filled with mementos quite without value to him (what could the Canton dessert plates mean to him? how could he have known about the assay scales, why should he care if he did know?), and we appear to talk exclusively about people we know who have been committed to mental hospitals, about people we know who have been booked on drunk-driving charges, and about property, particularly about property, land, price per acre and C-2 zoning and assessments and freeway access. My brother does not understand my husband's inablility to perceive the advantage in the rather common real-estate transaction known as "sale-leaseback," and my husband in turn does not understand why so many of the people he hears about in my father's house have recently been committed to mental hospitals or booked on drunk-driving charges. Nor does he understand that when we talk about sale-leasebacks and right-of-way condemnations we are talking in code about the things we like best, the yellow fields and the cottonwoods and the rivers rising and falling and the mountain roads closing when the heavy snow comes in. We miss each other's points, have another drink and regard the fire. My brother refers to my husband, in his presence, as "Joan's husband." Marriage is the classic betrayal.

Or perhaps it is not any more. Sometimes I think that those of us who are now in our thirties were born into the last generation to carry the burden of "home," to find in family life the source of all tension and drama. I had by all objective accounts a "normal" and a "happy" family situation, and yet I was almost thirty years old before I could talk to my family on the telephone without crying after I had hung up. We did not fight. Nothing was wrong. And yet some nameless anxiety colored the emotional charges between me and the place that I came from. The question of whether or not you could go home again was a very real part of the sentimental and largely literary baggage with which we left home in

the fifties; I suspect that it is irrelevant to the children born of the frag-
mentation after World War II. A few weeks ago in a San Francisco bar
I saw a pretty young girl on crystal take off her clothes and dance for the
cash prize in an "amateur-topless" contest. There was no particular sense
of moment about this, none of the effect of romantic degradation, of
"dark journey," for which my generation strived so assiduously. What sense
could that girl possibly make of, say, Long Day's Journey into Night? Who
is beside the point?

That I am trapped in this particular irrelevancy is never more apparent
to me than when I am home. Paralyzed by the neurotic lassitude engen-
dered by meeting one's past at every turn, around every corner, inside every
cupboard, I go aimlessly from room to room. I decide to meet it head-on
and clean out a drawer, and I spread the contents on the bed. A bathing suit
I wore the summer I was seventeen. A letter of rejection from The Nation,
an aerial photograph of the site for a shopping center my father did not
build in 1954. Three teacups hand-painted with cabbage roses and signed
"E.M.," my grandmother's initials. There is no final solution for letters of
rejection from The Nation and teacups hand-painted in 1900. Nor is there
any answer to snapshots of one's grandfather as a young man on skis,
surveying around Donner Pass in the year 1910. I smooth out the snapshot
and look into his face, and do and do not see my own. I close the drawer,
and have another cup of coffee with my mother. We get along very well,
veterans of a guerrilla war we never understood.

Days pass. I see no one. I come to dread my husband's evening call, not
only because he is full of news of what by now seems to me our remote life
in Los Angeles, people he has seen, letters which require attention, but
because he asks what I have been doing, suggests uneasily that I get out,
drive to San Francisco or Berkeley. Instead I drive across the river to a family graveyard. It has been vandalized since my last visit and the monuments
are broken, overturned in the dry grass. Because I once saw a rattlesnake in
the grass I stay in the car and listen to a country-and-Western station. Later
I drive with my father to a ranch he has in the foothills. The man who runs
his cattle on it asks us to the roundup, a week from Sunday, and although
I know that I will be in Los Angeles I say, in the oblique way my family
talks, that I will come. Once home I mention the broken monuments in
the graveyard. My mother shrugs.

I go to visit my great-aunts. A few of them think now that I am my
cousin, or their daughter who died young. We recall an anecdote about a
relative last seen in 1948, and they ask if I still like living in New York City.
I have lived in Los Angeles for three years, but I say that I do. The baby

is offered a horehound drop, and I am slipped a dollar bill "to buy a treat." Questions trail off, answers are abandoned, the baby plays with the dust motes in a shaft of afternoon sun.

It is time for the baby's birthday party: a white cake, strawberry-marshmallow ice cream, a bottle of champagne saved from another party. In the evening, after she has gone to sleep, I kneel beside the crib and touch her face, where it is pressed against the slats, with mine. She is an open and trusting child, unprepared for and unaccustomed to the ambushes of family life, and perhaps it is just as well that I can offer her little of that life. I would like to give her more. I would like to promise her that she will grow up with a sense of her cousins and of rivers and of her great-grandmother's teacups, would like to pledge her a picnic on a river with fried chicken and her hair uncombed, would like to give her *home* for her birthday, but we live differently now and I can promise her nothing like that. I give her a xylophone and a sundress from Madeira, and promise to tell her a funny story. [1967]

On Morality

As it happens I am in Death Valley, in a room at the Enterprise Motel and Trailer Park, and it is July, and it is hot. In fact it is 119°. I cannot seem to make the air conditioner work, but there is a small refrigerator, and I can wrap ice cubes in a towel and hold them against the small of my back. With the help of the ice cubes I have been trying to think, because *The American Scholar* asked me to, in some abstract way about "morality," a word I distrust more every day, but my mind veers inflexibly toward the particular.

Here are some particulars. At midnight last night, on the road in from Las Vegas to Death Valley Junction, a car hit a shoulder and turned over.

The driver, very young and apparently drunk, was killed instantly. His girl was found alive but bleeding internally, deep in shock. I talked this afternoon to the nurse who had driven the girl to the nearest doctor, 185 miles across the floor of the Valley and three ranges of lethal mountain road. The nurse explained that her husband, a talc miner, had stayed on the highway with the boy's body until the coroner could get over the mountains from Bishop, at dawn today. "You can't just leave a body on the highway," she said. "It's immoral."

It was one instance in which I did not distrust the word, because she meant something quite specific. She meant that if a body is left alone for even a few minutes on the desert, the coyotes close in and eat the flesh. Whether or not a corpse is torn apart by coyotes may seem only a sentimental consideration, but of course it is more: one of the promises we make to one another is that we will try to retrieve our casualties, try not to abandon our dead to the coyotes. If we have been taught to keep our promises—if, in the simplest terms, our upbringing is good enough—we stay with the body, or have bad dreams.

I am talking, of course, about the kind of social code that is sometimes called, usually pejoratively, "wagon-train morality." In fact that is precisely what it is. For better or worse, we are what we learned as children: my own childhood was illuminated by graphic litanies of the grief awaiting those who failed in their loyalties to each other. The Donner-Reed Party, starving in the Sierra snows, all the ephemera of civilization gone save that one vestigial taboo, the provision that no one should eat his own blood kin. The Jayhawkers, who quarreled and separated not far from where I am tonight. Some of them died in the Funerals and some of them died down near Badwater and most of the rest of them died in the Panamints. A woman who got through gave the Valley its name. Some might say that the Jayhawkers were killed by the desert summer, and the Donner Party by the mountain winter, by circumstances beyond control; we were taught instead that they had somewhere abdicated their responsibilities, somehow breached their primary loyalties, or they would not have found themselves helpless in the mountain winter or the desert summer, would not have given way to acrimony, would not have deserted one another, would not have *failed*. In brief, we heard such stories as cautionary tales, and they still suggest the only kind of "morality" that seems to me to have any but the most potentially mendacious meaning.

You are quite possibly impatient with me by now; I am talking, you want to say, about a "morality" so primitive that it scarcely deserves the name, a code that has as its point only survival, not the attainment of the ideal good. Exactly. Particularly out here tonight, in this country so ominous and terrible that to live in it is to live with antimatter, it is difficult to believe that "the good" is a knowable quantity. Let me tell you what it is like out here tonight. Stories travel at night on the desert. Someone gets in his pickup and drives a couple of hundred miles for a beer, and he carries news of what is happening, back wherever he came from. Then he drives another hundred miles for another beer, and passes along stories from the last place as well as from the one before; it is a network kept alive by people whose instincts tell them that if they do not keep moving at night in the desert they will lose all reason. Here is a story that is going around the desert tonight: over across the Nevada line, sheriff's deputies are diving in some underground pools, trying to retrieve a couple of bodies known to be in the hole. The widow of one of the drowned boys is over there; she is eighteen, and pregnant, and is said not to leave the hole. The divers go down and come up, and she just stands there and stares into the water. They have been diving for ten days but have found no bottom to the caves, no bodies and no trace of them, only the black 90° water going down and down and down, and a single translucent fish, not classified. The story tonight is that one of the divers has been hauled up incoherent, out of his head, shouting—until they got him out of there so that the widow could not here—about water that got hotter instead of cooler as he went down, about light flickering through the water, about magma, about underground nuclear testing.

That is the tone stories take out here, and there are quite a few of them. And it is more than the stories alone. Across the road at the Faith Community Church a couple of dozen old people, come here to live in trailers and die in the sun, are holding a prayer sing. I cannot hear them and do not want to. What I can hear are occasional coyotes and a constant chorus of "Baby the Rain Must Fall" from the jukebox in the Snake Room next door, and if I were also to hear those dying voices, those Midwestern voices drawn to this lunar country for some unimaginable atavistic rites, *rock of ages cleft for me*, I think I would lose my own reason. Every now and then I imagine I hear a rattlesnake, but my husband says that it is a faucet, a paper rustling, the wind. Then he stands by a window, and plays a flashlight over the dry wash outside.

What does it mean? It means nothing manageable. There is some sinister hysteria in the air out here tonight, some hint of the monstrous perversion to which any human idea can come. "I followed my own conscience." "I did what I thought was right." How many madmen have said it and meant it? How many murderers? Klaus Fuchs said it, and the men who committed the Mountain Meadows Massacre said it, and Alfred Rosenberg said it. And, as we are rotely and rather presumptuously reminded by those who would say it now, Jesus said it. Maybe we have all said it, and maybe we have been wrong. Except on that most primitive level—our loyalties to those we love—what could be more arrogant than to claim the primacy of personal conscience? ("Tell me," a rabbi asked Daniel Bell when he said, as a child, that he did not believe in God, "Do you think God cares?") At least some of the time, the world appears to me as a painting by Hieronymous Bosch; were I to follow my conscience then, it would lead me out onto the desert with Marion Faye, out to where he stood in *The Deer Park* looking east to Los Alamos and praying, as if for rain, that it would happen: ". . . *let it come and clear the rot and the stench and the stink, let it come for all of everywhere, just so it comes and the world stands clear in the white dead dawn.*"

Of course you will say that I do not have the right, even if I had the power, to inflict that unreasonable conscience upon you; nor do I want you to inflict your conscience, however reasonable, however enlightened, upon me. ("We must be aware of the dangers which lie in our most generous wishes," Lionel Trilling once wrote. "Some paradox of our nature leads us, when once we have made our fellow men the objects of our enlightened interest, to go on to make them the objects of our pity, then of our wisdom, ultimately of our coercion.") That the ethic of conscience is intrinsically insidious seems scarcely a revelatory point, but it is one raised with increasing infrequency; even those who do raise it tend to *segue* with troubling readiness into the quite contradictory position that the ethic of conscience is dangerous when it is "wrong," and admirable when it is "right."

You see I want to be quite obstinate about insisting that we have no way of knowing—beyond that fundamental loyalty to the social code—what is "right" and what is "wrong," what is "good" and what "evil." I dwell so upon this because the most disturbing aspect of "morality" seems to me to be the frequency with which the word now appears; in the press, on television, in the most perfunctory kinds of conversation. Questions of straightforward power (or survival) politics, questions of quite indifferent public policy, questions of almost anything: they are all assigned these factitious moral burdens. There is something facile going on, some self-indulgence at work. Of course we would all like to "believe" in something, like to assuage our private guilts in public causes, like to lose our tiresome selves; like, perhaps, to transform the white flag of defeat at home into the brave white banner of battle away from home. And of course it is all right to do that; that is how, immemorially, things have gotten done. But I think it is all right only so long as we do not delude ourselves about what we are doing, and why. It is all right only so long as we remember that all the *ad hoc* committees, all the picket lines, all the brave signatures in *The New York Times,* all the tools of agitprop straight across the spectrum, do not confer upon anyone any *ipso facto* virtue. It is all right only so long as we recognize that the end may or may not be expedient, may or may not be a good idea, but in any case has nothing to do with "morality." Because when we start deceiving ourselves into thinking not that we want something or need something, not that it is a pragmatic necessity for us to have it, but that it is a *moral imperative* that we have it, then is when we join the fashionable madmen, and then is when the thin whine of hysteria is heard in the land, and then is when we are in bad trouble. And I suspect we are already there. [1965]

Why I Write

Oᴲ course I stole the title for this talk from George Orwell. One reason I stole it was that I like the sound of the words: *Why I Write.* There you have three short unambiguous words that share a sound, and the sound they share is this:

I

I

I

In many ways writing is the act of saying *I,* of imposing oneself upon other people, of saying *listen to me, see it my way, change your mind.* It's an aggressive, even a hostile act. You can disguise its aggressiveness all you want with veils of subordinate clauses and qualifiers and tentative subjunctives, with ellipses and evasions—with the whole manner of intimating rather than claiming, of alluding rather than stating—but there's no getting around the fact that setting words on paper is the tactic of a secret bully, an invasion, an imposition of the writer's sensibility on the reader's most private space.

I stole the title not only because the words sounded right but because they seemed to sum up, in a no-nonsense way, all I have to tell you. Like many writers I have only this one "subject," this one "area": the act of writing. I can bring you no reports from any other front. I may have other interests: I am "interested," for example, in marine biology, but I don't flatter myself that you would come out to hear me talk about it. I am not a scholar. I am not in the least an intellectual, which is not to say that when I hear the word "intellectual" I reach for my gun, but only to say that I do not think in abstracts. During the years when I was an undergraduate at Berkeley I tried, with a kind of hopeless late-adolescent energy, to buy some temporary visa into the world of ideas, to forge for myself a mind that could deal with the abstract.

In short I tried to think. I failed. My attention veered inexorably back to the specific, to the tangible, to what was generally considered, by everyone I knew then and for that matter have known since, the peripheral. I would try to contemplate the Hegelian dialectic and would find myself concentrating instead on a flowering pear tree outside my window and the particular way the petals fell on my floor. I would try to read linguistic theory and would find myself wondering instead if the lights were on in the bevatron up the hill. When I say that I was wondering if the lights were on in the bevatron you might immediately suspect, if you deal in ideas at all, that I was registering the bevatron as a political symbol, thinking in short-hand about the military-industrial complex and its role in the university community, but you would be wrong. I was only wondering if the lights were on in the bevatron, and how they looked. A physical fact.

I had trouble graduating from Berkeley, not because of this inability to deal with ideas—I was majoring in English, and I could locate the house-and-garden imagery in *The Portrait of a Lady* as well as the next person, "imagery" being by definition the kind of specific that got my attention—but simply because I had neglected to take a course in Milton. For reasons which now sound baroque I needed a degree by the end of that summer, and the English department finally agreed, if I would come down from Sacramento every Friday and talk about the cosmology of *Paradise Lost*, to certify me proficient in Milton. I did this. Some Fridays I took the Greyhound bus, other Fridays I caught the Southern Pacific's City of San

Francisco on the last leg of its transcontinental trip. I can no longer tell you whether Milton put the sun or the earth at the center of his universe in *Paradise Lost,* the central question of at least one century and a topic about which I wrote 10,000 words that summer, but I can still recall the exact rancidity of the butter in the City of San Francisco's dining car, and the way the tinted windows on the Greyhound bus cast the oil refineries around Carquinez Straits into a grayed and obscurely sinister light. In short my attention was always on the periphery, on what I would see and taste and touch, on the butter, and the Greyhound bus. During those years I was traveling on what I knew to be a very shaky passport, forged papers: I knew that I was no legitimate resident in any world of ideas. I knew I couldn't think. All I knew then was what I couldn't do. All I knew then was what I wasn't, and it took me some years to discover what I was.

Which was a writer.

By which I mean not a "good" writer or a "bad" writer but simply a writer, a person whose most absorbed and passionate hours are spent arranging words on pieces of paper. Had my credentials been in order I would never have become a writer. Had I been blessed with even limited access to my own mind there would have been no reason to write. I write entirely to find out what I'm thinking, what I'm looking at, what I see and what it means. What I want and what I fear. Why did the oil refineries around Carquinez Straits seem sinister to me in the summer of 1956? Why have the night lights in the bevatron burned in my mind for twenty years? *What is going on in these pictures in my mind?*

When I talk about pictures in my mind I am talking, quite specifically, about images that shimmer around the edges. There used to be an illustration in every elementary psychology book showing a cat drawn by a patient in varying stages of schizophrenia. This cat had a shimmer around it. You could see the molecular structure breaking down at the very edges of the cat: the cat became the background and the background the cat, everything interacting, exchanging ions. People on hallucinogens describe the same perception of objects. I'm not a schizophrenic, nor do I take hallucinogens, but certain images do shimmer for me. Look hard enough, and you can't miss the shimmer. It's there. You can't think too much about these pictures that shimmer. You just lie low and let them develop. You stay quiet. You don't talk to many people and you keep your nervous system from shorting out and you try to locate the cat in the shimmer, the grammar in the picture.

Just as I meant "shimmer" literally I mean "grammar" literally. Grammar is a piano I play by ear, since I seem to have been out of school the year the rules were mentioned. All I know about grammar is its infinite power. To shift the structure of a sentence alters the meaning of that sentence, as definitely and infexibly as the position of a camera alters the meaning of the object photographed. Many people know about camera angles now, but not so many know about sentences. The arrangement of the words matters, and the arrangement you want can be found in the picture in your mind. The picture dictates the arrangement. The picture dictates whether this will be a sentence with or without clauses, a sentence that ends hard or a dying-fall sentence, long or short, active or passive. The picture tells you how to arrange the words and the arrangement of the words tells you, or tells me, what's going on in the picture. *Nota bene:*

It tells you.

You don't tell it.

Let me show you what I mean by pictures in the mind. I began *Play It as It Lays* just as I have begun each of my novels, with no notion of "character" or "plot" or even "incident." I had only two pictures in my mind, more about which later, and a technical intention, which was to write a novel so elliptical and fast that it would be over before you noticed it, a novel so fast that it would scarcely exist on the page at all. About the pictures: the first was of white space. Empty space. This was clearly the picture that dictated the narrative intention of the book—a book in which anything that happened would happen off the page, a "white" book to which the reader would have to bring his or her own bad dreams—and yet this picture told me no "story," suggested no situation. The second picture did. This second picture was of something actually witnessed. A young woman with long hair and a short white halter dress walks through the casino at the Riviera in Las Vegas at one in the morning. She crosses the casino alone and picks up a house telephone. I watch her because I have heard her paged, and recognize her name: she is a minor actress I see around Los Angeles from time to time, in places like Jax and once in a gynecologist's office in the Beverly Hills Clinic, but have never met. I know nothing about her. Who is paging her? Why is she here to be paged? How exactly did she come to this? It was precisely this moment in Las Vegas that made *Play It as It Lays* begin to tell itself to me, but the moment appears in the novel only obliquely, in a chapter which begins:

> Maria made a list of things she would never do. She would never: walk through the Sands or Caesar's alone after midnight. She would never: ball at a party, do S-M unless she wanted to, borrow furs from Abe Lipsey, deal. She would never: carry a Yorkshire in Beverly Hills.

That is the beginning of the chapter and that is also the end of the chapter, which may suggest what I meant by "white space."

I recall having a number of pictures in my mind when I began the novel I just finished, *A Book of Common Prayer*. As a matter of fact one of these pictures was of that bevatron I mentioned, although I would be hard put to tell you a story in which nuclear energy figured. Another was a newspaper photograph of a hijacked 707 burning on the desert in the Middle East. Another was the night view from a room in which I once spent a week with paratyphoid, a hotel room on the Colombian coast. My husband and I seemed to be on the Colombian coast representing the United States of America at a film festival (I recall invoking the name "Jack Valenti" a lot, as if its reiteration could make me well), and it was a bad place to have fever, not only because my indisposition offended our hosts but because every night in this hotel the generator failed. The lights went out. The elevator stopped. My husband would go to the event of the evening and make excuses for me and I would stay alone in this hotel room, in the dark. I remember standing at the window trying to call Bogotá (the telephone seemed to work on the same principle as the generator) and watching the night wind come up and wondering what I was doing eleven degrees off the equator with a fever of 103. The view from that window definitely figures in *A Book of Common Prayer*, as does the burning 707, and yet none of these pictures told me the story I needed.

The picture that did, the picture that shimmered and made these other images coalesce, was the Panama airport at 6 A.M. I was in this airport only once, on a plane to Bogotá that stopped for an hour to refuel, but the way it looked that morning remained superimposed on everything I saw until the day I finished *A Book of Common Prayer*. I lived in that airport for several years. I can still feel the hot air when I step off the plane, can see the heat already rising off the tarmac at 6 A.M. I can feel my skirt damp and wrinkled on my legs. I can feel the asphalt stick to my sandals. I remember the big tail of a Pan American plane floating motionless down at the end of the tarmac. I remember the sound of a slot machine in the waiting room. I could tell you that I remember a particular woman in the airport, an American woman, a *norteamericana*, a thin *norteamericana* about 40 who wore a big square emerald in lieu of a wedding ring, but there was no such woman there.

I put this woman in the airport later. I made this woman up, just as I later made up a country to put the airport in, and a family to run the country. This woman in the airport is neither catching a plane nor meeting one. She is ordering tea in the airport coffee shop. In fact she is not simply "ordering" tea but insisting that the water be boiled, in front of her, for twenty minutes. Why is this woman in this airport? Why is she going nowhere, where has she been? Where did she get that big emerald? What derangement, or disassociation, makes her believe that her will to see the water boiled can possibly prevail?

> She had been going to one airport or another for four months, one could see it, looking at the visas on her passport. All those airports where Charlotte Douglas's passport had been stamped would have looked alike. Sometimes the sign on the tower would say "Bienvenidos" and sometimes the sign on the tower would say "Bienvenue," some places were wet and hot and others dry and hot, but at each of these airports the pastel concrete walls would rust and stain and the swamp off the runway would be littered with the fuselages of cannibalized Fairchild F-227's and the water would need boiling.
> "I knew why Charlotte went to the airport even if Victor did not.
> "I knew about airports."

These lines appear about halfway through *A Book of Common Prayer,* but I wrote them during the second week I worked on the book, long before I had any idea where Charlotte Douglas had been or why she went to airports. Until I wrote these lines I had no character called "Victor" in mind: the necessity for mentioning a name, and the name "Victor," occurred to me as I wrote the sentence. *I knew why Charlotte went to the airport* sounded incomplete. *I knew why Charlotte went to the airport even if Victor did not* carried a little more narrative drive. Most important of all, until I wrote these lines I did not know who "I" was, who was telling the story. I had intended until that moment that the "I" be no more than the voice of the author, a 19th-century omniscient narrator. But there it was:

> "I knew why Charlotte went to the airport even if Victor did not.
> "I knew about airports."

This "I" was the voice of no author in my house. This "I" was someone who not only knew why Charlotte went to the airport but also knew someone called "Victor." Who was Victor? Who was this narrator? Why was this narrator telling me this story? Let me tell you one thing about why writers write: had I known the answer to any of these questions I would never have needed to write a novel.   [1976]

John Wayne: A Love Song

In the summer of 1943 I was eight, and my father and mother and small brother and I were at Peterson Field in Colorado Springs. A hot wind blew through that summer, blew until it seemed that before August broke, all the dust in Kansas would be in Colorado, would have drifted over the tar-paper barracks and the temporary strip and stopped only when it hit Pikes Peak. There was not much to do, a summer like that: there was the day they brought in the first B-29, an event to remember but scarcely a vacation program. There was an Officers' Club, but no swimming pool; all the Officers' Club had of interest was artificial blue rain behind the bar. The rain interested me a good deal, but I could not spend the summer watching it, and so we went, my brother and I, to the movies.

We went three and four afternoons a week, sat on folding chairs in the darkened Quonset hut which served as a theater, and it was there, that summer of 1943 while the hot wind blew outside, that I first saw John Wayne. Saw the walk, heard the voice. Heard him tell the girl in a picture called *War of the Wildcats* that he would build her a house, "at the bend in the river where the cottonwoods grow." As it happened I did not grow up to be the kind of woman who is the heroine in a Western, and although the men I have known have had many virtues and have taken me to live in many places I have come to love, they have never been John Wayne, and they have never taken me to that bend in the river where the cottonwoods grow. Deep in that part of my heart where the artificial rain forever falls, that is still the line I wait to hear.

I tell you this neither in a spirit of self-revelation nor as an exercise in total recall, but simply to demonstrate that when John Wayne rode through my childhood, and perhaps through yours, he determined forever the shape of certain of our dreams. It did not seem possible that such a man could fall ill, could carry within him that most inexplicable and ungovernable of diseases. The rumor struck some obscure anxiety, threw our very childhoods into question. In John Wayne's world, John Wayne was supposed to give the orders. "Let's ride," he said, and "Saddle up." "Forward *ho*," and "A man's gotta do what he's got to do." "Hello, there," he said when he first saw the girl, in a construction camp or on a train or just standing around on the front porch waiting for somebody to ride up through the tall grass. When John Wayne spoke, there was no mistaking his intentions; he had a sexual authority so strong that even a child could perceive it. And in a world we understood early to be characterized by venality and doubt and paralyzing ambiguities, he suggested another world, one which may or may not have existed ever but in any case existed no more: a place where a man could move free, could make his own code and live by it; a world in which, if a man did what he had to do, he could one day take the girl and go riding through the draw and find himself home free, not in a hospital with something going wrong inside, not in a high bed with the flowers and the drugs and the forced smiles, but there at the bend in the bright river, the cottonwoods shimmering in the early morning sun.

"Hello, there." Where did he come from, before the tall grass? Even his history seemed right, for it was no history at all, nothing to intrude upon the dream. Born Marion Morrison in Winterset, Iowa, the son of a druggist. Moved as a child to Lancaster, California, part of the migration to that promised land sometimes called "the west coast of Iowa." Not that Lancaster was the promise fulfilled; Lancaster was a town on the Mojave where the dust blew through. But Lancaster was still California, and it was only a year from there to Glendale, where desolation had a different flavor: antimacassars among the orange groves, a middle-class prelude to Forest Lawn. Imagine Marion Morrison in Glendale. A Boy Scout, then a student at Glendale High. A tackle for U.S.C., a Sigma Chi. Summer vacations, a job moving props on the old Fox lot. There, a meeting with John Ford, one of the several directors who were to sense that into this perfect mold might be poured the inarticulate longings of a nation wondering at just what pass the trail had been lost. "Dammit," said Raoul Walsh later, "the son of a bitch looked like a man." And so after a while the boy from Glendale became a star. He did not become an actor, as he has always been careful to point out to interviewers ("How many times do I gotta tell you, I don't act at all, I re-act"), but a star, and the star called John Wayne would spend most of the rest of his life with one or another of those directors, out on some forsaken location, in search of the dream.

> Out where the skies are a trifle bluer
> Out where friendship's a little truer
> That's where the West begins.

Nothing very bad could happen in the dream, nothing a man could not face down. But something did. There it was, the rumor, and after a while the headlines. "I licked the Big C," John Wayne announced, as John Wayne would, reducing those outlaw cells to the level of any other outlaws, but even so we all sensed that this would be the one unpredictable confrontation, the one shoot-out Wayne could lose. I have as much trouble as the next person with illusion and reality, and I did not much want to see John Wayne when he must be (or so I thought) having some trouble with it himself, but I did, and it was down in Mexico when he was making the picture his illness had so long delayed, down in the very country of the dream.

It was John Wayne's 165th picture. It was Henry Hathaway's 84th. It was number 34 for Dean Martin, who was working off an old contract to Hal Wallis, for whom it was independent production number 65. It was called *The Sons of Katie Elder,* and it was a Western, and after the three-month delay they had finally shot the exteriors up in Durango, and now they were in the waning days of interior shooting at Estudio Churubusco outside Mexico City, and the sun was hot and the air was clear and it was lunchtime. Out under the pepper trees the boys from the Mexican crew sat around sucking caramels, and down the road some of the technical men sat around a place which served a stuffed lobster and a glass of tequila for one dollar American, but it was inside the cavernous empty commissary where the talent sat around, the reasons for the exercise, all sitting around the big table picking at *huevos con queso* and Carta Blanca beer. Dean Martin, unshaven. Mack Gray, who goes where Martin goes. Bob Goodfried, who was in charge of Paramount publicity and who had flown down to arrange for a trailer and who had a delicate stomach. "Tea and toast," he warned repeatedly. "That's the ticket. You can't trust the lettuce." And Henry Hathaway, the director, who did not seem to be listening to Goodfried. And John Wayne, who did not seem to be listening to anyone.

"This week's gone slow," Dean Martin said, for the third time.

"How can you say that?" Mack Gray demanded.

"This . . . week's . . . gone . . . slow, that's how I can say it."

"You don't mean you want it to end."

"I'll say it right out, Mack, I want it to *end.* Tomorrow night I shave this beard, I head for the airport, I say *adios amigos!* Bye-bye *muchachos!"*

Henry Hathaway lit a cigar and patted Martin's arm fondly. "Not to-morrow, Dino."

"Henry, what are you planning to add? A World War?"

Hathaway patted Martin's arm again and gazed into the middle distance. At the end of the table someone mentioned a man who, some years before, had tried unsuccessfully to blow up an airplane.

"He's still in jail," Hathaway said suddenly.

"In jail?" Martin was momentarily distracted from the question whether to send his golf clubs back with Bob Goodfried or consign them to Mack Gray. "What's he in jail for if nobody got killed?"

"Attempted murder, Dino," Hathaway said gently. "A felony."

"You mean some guy just *tried* to kill me he'd end up in jail?"

Hathaway removed the cigar from his mouth and looked across the table. "Some guy just tried to kill *me* he wouldn't end up in jail. How about you, Duke?"

Very slowly, the object of Hathaway's query wiped his mouth, pushed back his chair, and stood up. It was the real thing, the authentic article, the move which had climaxed a thousand scenes on 165 flickering frontiers and phantasmagoric battlefields before, and it was about to climax this one, in the commissary at Estudio Churubusco outside Mexico City. "Right," John Wayne drawled. "I'd kill him."

Almost all the cast of *Katie Elder* had gone home, that last week; only the principals were left, Wayne, and Martin, and Earl Holliman, and Michael Anderson, Jr., and Martha Hyer. Martha Hyer was not around much, but every now and then someone referred to her, usually as "the girl." They had all been together nine weeks, six of them in Durango. Mexico City was not quite Durango; wives like to come along to places like Mexico City, like to shop for handbags, go to parties at Merle Oberon Pagliai's, like to look at her paintings. But Durango. The very name hallucinates. Man's country. Out where the West begins. There had been ahuehuete trees in Durango; a waterfall, rattlesnakes. There had been weather, nights so cold that they had postponed one or two exteriors until they could shoot inside at Churubusco. "It was the girl," they explained. "You couldn't keep the girl out in cold like that." Henry Hathaway had cooked in Durango, *gazpacho* and ribs and the steaks that Dean Martin had ordered flown down from the Sands; he had wanted to cook in Mexico City, but the management of the Hotel Bamer refused to let him set up a brick barbecue in his room. "You really missed something, *Durango*," they would say, sometimes joking and sometimes not, until it became a refrain, Eden lost.

But if Mexico City was not Durango, neither was it Beverly Hills. No one else was using Churubusco that week, and there inside the big sound stage that said LOS HIJOS DE KATIE ELDER on the door, there with the pepper trees and the bright sun outside, they could still, for just so long as the picture lasted, maintain a world peculiar to men who liked to make Westerns, a world of loyalties and fond raillery, of sentiment and shared cigars, of interminable desultory recollections; campfire talk, its only point to keep a human voice raised against the night, the wind, the rustlings in the brush.

"Stuntman got hit accidentally on a picture of mine once," Hathaway would say between takes of an elaborately choreographed fight scene. "What was his name, married Estelle Taylor, met her down in Arizona." The circle would close around him, the cigars would be fingered. The delicate art of the staged fight was to be contemplated.

"I only hit one guy in my life," Wayne would say. "Accidentally, I mean. That was Mike Mazurki."

"Some guy. Hey, Duke says he only hit one guy in his life, Mike Mazurki."

"Some choice." Murmurings, assent.

"It wasn't a choice, it was an accident."

"I can believe it."

"You bet."

"Oh boy. Mike Mazurki."

And so it would go. There was Web Overlander, Wayne's makeup man for twenty years, hunched in a blue Windbreaker, passing out sticks of Juicy Fruit. "*Insect* spray," he would say. "Don't tell us about insect spray. We saw insect spray in Africa, all right. Remember Africa?" Or, "*Steamer* clams. Don't tell us about steamer clams. We got our fill of steamer clams all right, on the *Hatari!* appearance tour. Remember Bookbinder's?" There was Ralph Volkie, Wayne's trainer for eleven years, wearing a red baseball cap and carrying around a clipping from Hedda Hopper, a tribute to Wayne. "This Hopper's some lady," he would say again and again. "Not like some of these guys, all they write is sick, sick, sick, how can you call that guy *sick*, when he's got pains, coughs, works all day, *never complains.* That guy's got the best hook since Dempsey, not *sick.*"

And there was Wayne himself, fighting through number 165. There was Wayne, in his thirty-three-year-old spurs, his dusty neckerchief, his blue shirt. "You don't have too many worries about what to wear in these things," he said. "You can wear a blue shirt, or, if you're down in Monument Valley, you can wear a yellow shirt." There was Wayne, in a relatively new hat, a hat which made him look curiously like William S. Hart. "I had this old cavalry hat I loved, but I lent it to Sammy Davis. I got it back, it was unwearable. I think they all pushed it down on his head and said *O.K., John Wayne*—you know, a joke."

There was Wayne, working too soon, finishing the picture with a bad cold and a racking cough, so tired by late afternoon that he kept an oxygen inhalator on the set. And still nothing mattered but the Code. "That guy," he muttered of a reporter who had incurred his displeasure. "I admit I'm balding. I admit I got a tire around my middle. What man fifty-seven doesn't? Big news. Anyway, that guy."

He paused, about to expose the heart of the matter, the root of the distaste, the fracture of the rules that bothered him more than the alleged misquotations, more than the intimation that he was no longer the Ringo Kid. "He comes down, uninvited, but I ask him over anyway. So we're sitting around drinking mescal out of a water jug."

He paused again and looked meaningfully at Hathaway, readying him for the unthinkable denouement. "He had to be *assisted* to his room."

They argued about the virtues of various prizefighters, they argued about the price of J & B in pesos. They argued about dialogue.

"As rough a guy as he is, Henry, I still don't think he'd raffle off his mother's *Bible*."

"I like a shocker, Duke."

They exchanged endless training-table jokes. "You know why they call this memory sauce?" Martin asked, holding up a bowl of chili.

"Why?"

"Because you *remember it in the morning*."

"Hear that Duke? Hear why they call this memory sauce?"

They delighted one another by blocking out minute variations in the free-for-all fight which is a set piece in Wayne pictures; motivated or totally gratuitous, the fight sequence has to be in the picture, because they so enjoy making it. "Listen—this'll really be funny. Duke picks up the kid, see, and then it takes both Dino and Earl to throw him out the door—*how's that?*"

They communicated by sharing old jokes; they sealed their camaraderie by making gentle, old-fashioned fun of wives, those civilizers, those tamers. "So Señora Wayne takes it into her head to stay up and have one brandy. So for the rest of the night it's 'Yes, Pilar, you're right, dear. I'm a bully, Pilar, you're right, I'm impossible.'"

"You hear that? Duke says Pilar threw a table at him."

"Hey, Duke, here's something funny. That finger you hurt today, get the Doc to bandage it up, go home tonight, show it to Pilar, tell her she did it when she threw the table. You know, make her think she was really cutting up."

They treated the oldest among them respectfully; they treated the youngest fondly. "You see that kid?" they said of Michael Anderson, Jr. "What a kid."

"He don't act, it's right from the heart," said Hathaway, patting his heart.

"Hey kid," Martin said. "You're gonna be in my next picture. We'll have the whole thing, no beards. The striped shirts, the girls, the hi-fi, the eye lights."

They ordered Michael Anderson his own chair, with "BIG MIKE" tooled on the back. When it arrived on the set, Hathaway hugged him. "You see that?" Anderson asked Wayne, suddenly too shy to look him in the eye. Wayne gave him the smile, the nod, the final accolade. "I saw it, kid."

On the morning of the day they were to finish *Katie Elder*, Web Overlander showed up not in his Windbreaker but in a blue blazer. "Home, Mama," he said, passing out the last of his Juicy Fruit. "I got on my getaway clothes." But he was subdued. At noon, Henry Hathaway's wife dropped by the commissary to tell him that she might fly over to Acapulco. "Go ahead," he told her. "I get through here, all I'm gonna do is take Seconal to a point just this side of suicide." They were all subdued. After Mrs. Hathaway left, there were desultory attempts at reminiscing, but man's country was receding fast; they were already halfway home, and all they could call up was the 1961 Bel Air fire, during which Henry Hathaway had ordered the Los Angeles Fire Department off his property and saved the place himself by, among other measures, throwing everything flammable into the swimming pool. "Those fire guys might've just given it up," Wayne said. "Just let it burn." In fact this was a good story, and one incorporating several of their favorite themes, but a Bel Air story was still not a Durango story.

In the early afternoon they began the last scene, and although they spent as much time as possible setting it up, the moment finally came when there was nothing to do but shoot it. "Second team out, first team in, *doors closed*," the assistant director shouted one last time. The stand-ins walked off the set, John Wayne and Martha Hyer walked on. "All right, boys, *silencio*, this is a picture." They took it twice. Twice the girl offered John Wayne the tattered Bible. Twice John Wayne told her that "there's a lot of places I go where that wouldn't fit in." Everyone was very still. And at 2:30 that Friday afternoon Henry Hathaway turned away from the camera, and in the hush that followed he ground out his cigar in a sand bucket. "O.K.," he said. "That's it."

Since that summer of 1943 I had thought of John Wayne in a number of ways. I had thought of him driving cattle up from Texas, and bringing airplanes in on a single engine, thought of him telling the girl at the Alamo that "Republic is a beautiful word." I had never thought of him having dinner with his family and with me and my husband in an expensive restaurant in Chapultepec Park, but time brings odd mutations, and there we were, one night that last week in Mexico. For a while it was only a nice evening, an evening anywhere. We had a lot of drinks and I lost the sense that the face across the table was in certain ways more familiar than my husband's.

And then something happened. Suddenly the room seemed suffused with the dream, and I could not think why. Three men appeared out of nowhere, playing guitars. Pilar Wayne leaned slightly forward, and John Wayne lifted his glass almost imperceptibly toward her. "We'll need some Pouilly-Fuissé for the rest of the table," he said "and some red Bordeaux for the Duke." We all smiled, and drank the Pouilly-Fuissé for the rest of the table and the red Bordeaux for the Duke, and all the while the men with the guitars kept playing, until finally I realized what they were playing, what they had been playing all along: "The Red River Valley" and the theme from *The High and the Mighty*. They did not quite get the beat right, but even now I can hear them, in another country and a long time later, even as I tell you this.   [1965]

JAMES McCONKEY

Kathy Morris

J AMES MCCONKEY BEGINS *COURT OF MEM-
ory,* his 1982 collection of essays, with a statement of his credo as a writer, and
how he arrived at it:

> One night more than twenty years ago, as I sat in the basement study of
> my former home in Ithaca, New York, I underwent a change so radical
> that it transformed my apprehension both of the world and of valid modes
> for writing about it. . . . The story I had [just finished writing] was unsatis-
> factory because it was 'made up,' a fiction, one devoid of the sacredness
> I saw everywhere about me. The only way open to me to communicate
> the strength of my feelings was through myself—through my intimate ex-
> periences, through memory, and personal observation. . . . At that mo-
> ment in my own life, I began an autobiographical account of the meaning
> implicit in one of the humblest objects imaginable. A botched-up night-
> stand I had built as a child for my mother.

The essay he wrote that night in 1960, "A Night Stand," begins: "I no
longer have the desire, on this immense and silent winter's night, to dissemble,
to fabricate tales." In the passionate, but coldly rational articulation of that
sentence lies the essential quality of McConkey's essays. He writes about the
"ordinary and commonplace" not with the poetic piety of many writers who
wish to celebrate the sacredness of life, but with unsentimental clarity, objective
analysis, and unflinching honesty. He writes about his own life, he says, as if it
were fiction and himself his main character.

Born in Lakewood, Ohio, in 1921, James McConkey grew up throughout the
midwest—in Ohio, Arkansas, Kentucky, Illinois, and Michigan—as his family
disintegrated, became impoverished, and finally came back together again.
The story of these years is a frequent subject of his essays. To help his mother
financially, during high school and college McConkey wrote stories he hoped
to sell, worked nights as a copyboy for a Cleveland newspaper, and edited
a small-town paper. He worked his way through Cleveland College doing
janitorial duties, graduated in 1943, was drafted and trained to be a rifleman.
McConkey married his wife on a furlough and soon after was sent to Europe in
an infantry company. Shortly before the war ended, McConkey was injured in
Germany when his jeep hit a landmine; he was operated on in a field hospital
and evacuated to England where he recovered.

After the war, McConkey and his wife enrolled in graduate school at the University of Iowa, where they lived for a while in a trailer in a cornfield, not so unusual in those days for young veterans studying on the G.I. Bill. From 1950 to 1956 he taught English at Morehead State University in eastern Kentucky. In 1956 he moved to Cornell University as an assistant professor of English and there he has remained, retiring in 1992 as the Goldwin Smith Professor of English Literature, emeritus. For most of those years he and his wife and their three sons have lived in a farmhouse north of Ithaca, New York, and it is there that most of McConkey's essays begin, with an event that recalls an analogous event from a time earlier in his life.

"Of all the writers who have influenced my life," McConkey says, "Forster and Chekhov remain the most important." There are no excesses or superfluities in Forster and Chekhov. They both write lean prose, nothing "literary" about them, with the greatest respect for their readers' perceptions. "The writer who moves me most deeply," McConkey says, "is Chekhov." In the late seventies McConkey organized a literary festival at Cornell on Chekhov, the papers from which he edited under the title *Chekhov and Our Age*. In 1984 he wrote a book-length, speculative essay on a trip Chekhov had made in 1890 from Moscow to Sakhalin Island, a Russian penal colony lying off the east coast of Siberia. This book, *To a Distant Island*, is one of the most unusual biographical studies ever written, an imaginary narrative of Chekhov's journey, both physical and psychological.

McConkey has published several novels—*A Journey to Sahalin* (1971), *The Tree House Confessions* (1979), and *Kayo: The Authentic and Annotated Autobiographical Novel from Outer Space* (1987)—and a nonfiction study of Rowan County, Kentucky, titled *Rowan's Progress* (1992). His greatest achievement, however, lies in his personal, autobiographical essays, all of which can be found in two collections, *Court of Memory* (1982) and *Stories from My Life with the Other Animals* (1993).

McConkey's essays do not form a chronological autobiography nor are they a series of mere reminiscences. Rather, they are intense, separate explorations of the most meaningful events in a life he himself says has not been particularly remarkable. He explores his past in order to discover the deepest meanings implicit in his experiences. He says in one place that "to have invented *any* event or person would have been a violation of my most crucial rule for this

kind of writing" and in another that "Artlessness has always appealed to me."
The two statements would seem to imply that he places more value on honesty
than artfulness. But in fact James McConkey—like Anton Chekhov and E. M.
Forster—is one of the most *artful* writers of our time, and his autobiographical
essays are simultaneously both "true" and as highly crafted as fiction. ■

A Night Stand

I NO LONGER HAVE THE DESIRE, ON this immense and silent winter's night, to dissemble, to fabricate tales. When I turn out the little lamp on my desk and stare out my study window, at first I see only the faint whiteness of the snow in the yard: but what is it that illuminates the snow, what makes it faintly shimmer? There is not a light visible anywhere. My neighbor on the left, an elderly bachelor, a retired college dean, may still be at work in *his* study, for he keeps his interest in his profession, engineering, despite his retirement; but his windows always are darkened by heavy blinds—he is thorough in every respect, and would not possess a blind that permitted the tiniest rip of light to escape outward. My neighbors on the right are certainly asleep; the wife, who not long ago underwent her third operation for cancer, reads a great deal, mainly fiction and verse, but is allowed only the daylight hours.

As I watch from my darkened study, I see the patches of snow on the dark pines, then the little white mound that rises absurdly from the deserted robin's nest in the maple; and then, above the maple, above the pines, suddenly rides Orion. Other stars appear. Mars, wondrously alive this season, follows the Seven Sisters. . . . Scattered on my desk are sheets of paper, palely shimmering like the snow. A completed manuscript, a story: words follow words across each sheet in thin little rows. Can I read those words in the light from Betelgeuse and Regel, in the glow from Orion's great nebula—that hazy spot, there, in the hunter's sword? But on the couch to my right, the dog whimpers: Black Judy, my children's German shepherd, wondering why I sit in the dark.

And so I switch on the lamp again, and reach over to stroke the dog. Immediately she stretches out her hind legs, closes her eyes and sleeps. Her coat is lustrous in its blackness, it is a pleasure to stroke her soft fur and to touch her cold nose, to listen as she slowly breathes in and out, in and out.

Mine is a most comfortable study, finished in its present state by the former owner of the house, a professor of philosophy. It is hidden away at the rear of the basement; but since the house is built on a slope in this town of hills, the study is actually higher than ground level. Two flights above me, wife and children sleep. My wife and I repainted this room, to cover the marks left by the former occupant's book shelves. A reprint—a Miró—which he had firmly taped to the plasterboard of one wall is the only reminder that the room has belonged to another. Once the shelves in this room had countless volumes stamped in gold print with the single word: MIND. Now the shelves—the new ones, which I built of soft pine, that lumber of the novice—sag with novels good and indifferent, volumes of poetry, a broken camera, a pipe rack, a box of telescope lenses, and some odd-shaped rocks my older boy found in the creek bed.

And again I think of my neighbors.

Every afternoon for the past few months, at precisely the same moment—four o'clock—I have looked out my study window to see my neighbor the dean, cane in hand, walk the asphalt road behind our house. Our back yard adjoins a little park which is, in reality, only the landscaped grounds of the water filtration plant; the asphalt road circles the filtration plant. Seven times around, says my neighbor, is exactly one mile: and seven times around he briskly marches each winter day, scarf flying in the breeze, cane tapping the ice and snow. He smiles at the children, he dodges deftly between the hurtling sleds that slice down the slopes and across the road: his cheeks are red, his disposition jovial, and he knows that an emeritus professor must have his daily exercise. If, half an hour later on any day, I had climbed the steps for a cup of coffee and had thought to peer through the living room window while waiting for the pot to warm, I would probably have seen my other neighbor, the woman who recently has undergone surgery. For on the hill across the street is a pleasant old Irish Catholic cemetery, and here my other neighbor slowly but surely regains her health, each day climbing the path one headstone further. This week she has passed the Hersons (Patrick, 1818–1900; Catherine Morgan *His Wife,* 1834–1910, *Children,* 1854–John–1884, 1861–Patrick–1895, 1869–Mathew–1901, 1856–James–1906) and is well into the Shannons.

In these past few months I have been more deeply involved in making stories than I have for several years. And so—until tonight—I have been aware only that my neighbors have been dwelling in another world than mine; their oddity has been their significance; I have watched them curiously, thinking, *I ought to get them both in a story some day,* and then I have turned quickly back into *my* realm, that world where the people and the paragraphs containing them are fixed and forever on typing paper—as forever, at any rate, as the low rag content will permit them to be.

Where have I been these past few months? It is difficult to say; yet in recent nights—as writing slowly has become more chore than pleasure, as the glandular juices that excite one into creativity have begun to subside—I have waked to recall the identical dream, an image of a clumsy little table, a night stand I built as a child. My writing has not been dealing with my childhood, it has not been consciously autobiographical; nevertheless my mind must have been dipping back to an earlier period, collecting what it would. The night stand—of what use is a night stand in a story?—had been rejected, but there it rose into my dreams, haunting me for my neglect of it. And now that my writing has begun to ebb, it has taken precedence. Like the neighbors, the books, the dog, it has become important. Wretched little night stand! Acting as if *its* turn has come, as if it won't be satisfied until given its due!

All right.

I had made it in the ninth grade. In the previous summer, despair had settled upon my family; sudden poverty—for the Depression had reached us at last—was the cause. I shall say only that my parents were so distracted that they moved here and there and finally to Arkansas, and that my father—a Northern businessman—seriously considered pig raising as an occupation and ordered the proper leaflet from the government. An impossibility, of course, but so was everything else; in their chaos, my parents separated. My father asked for a divorce, and soon married a widow in Texas. My brother, my mother, and I sold all the furniture for gasoline and traveled halfway across the nation in an old Packard—symbol of former opulence—to knock, without warning or invitation, one midnight upon the door of the nearest relatives too tender to deny us admission. They took us in, that most kind uncle and aunt—took not only us, the three of us prickled and small with shame, but my dog as well, a thin and ravenous German shepherd not unlike the one sleeping on the couch as I recall the past on another midnight.

For months thereafter, I was continually drowsy, my mind occupied with lassitudinous dreams. Full of humiliation and self-pity, I was pleased whenever someone spoke to me harshly for having neglected an assigned task. But let me pass over this year with my uncle and aunt simply by saying that my two semesters of ninth-grade manual training produced only that one wobbly night stand, its legs spindlier than any previous night stand had been known to be. For I had planed them down, down, down, day after day, with eyes shut: once I opened them to see the instructor and the rest of the class standing in a half-circle before my bench, laughing silently. The blueprint called for a drawer which I had neither the time nor the aptitude to build. Nor, after the legs had been screwed to the top, did I even have time for paint or stain. I gave the night stand to my mother on her birthday: my gift, a year's toil; she—do you believe it?—cried.

Keep your eyes, whoever you are who may be following this reminiscence, keep your eyes on that night stand; some sudden travels take place, but the night stand is the theme of these chronicles of my youth; never lose sight of it. My mother, certainly, didn't. After this year with my relatives, my brother took a job in Michigan; we accompanied him. The dog, the night stand, and my mother occupied the back of the car during the journey. Misfortune ensues once more, and once more as the result of insufficient cash. The finance company—the old opulence, after all, had been based on credit—took the Packard; a relative in Ohio, the dog. *I* cried when he was carted off in his Railway Express cage.

My mother, always strongly religious, now went with unfailing regularity to church for spiritual counsel; as one less benighted, I refused to accompany her. I would make us rich writing fiction; on Saturdays and Sundays, all weekend long, even after school during the week, I would furiously write—sometimes one story a week, sometimes two, sometimes three or even more. I would make us rich, yes—but even more than that I was playing God, creating little dream worlds in which I could impose the pattern, in which I could bring love to hate, peace to violence, unity to chaos. The paper, the pencils, and the typewriter ribbons took money from food, and the stories—ten-page thrillers, tales of suicide, rape, and murder, but all with happy endings—never sold; even I knew they were poor. Such a succession of failures only made me increasingly belligerent when my mother continued to ask me to attend Sunday services with her.

And so we would quarrel; I was incensed by her mild, even meek, determination to salvage my soul. Hiding behind the curtains of our second-story apartment—a small apartment in a frame dwelling on the fringes of the downtown area—I would watch as she stepped off the curb—*Careful of that car, little momma!*—and walked quickly, without a backward look, toward the Presbyterian church six or eight blocks away. But not until early morning—in those gray and heavy hours before sunrise when a child, awakening, can sense death waiting for others if not for himself—would I feel truly contrite, alone and frightened. I would tiptoe into her room, then wake her gently: "Mother, I'm sorry. Next Sunday I'll go." She would smile, clasp my hand and fall back into sleep. The clock by her bed stood on the miserable night stand I had made.

This little idyl of my youth came to an end when we were no longer able to pay the modest rent for our apartment. My brother found other lodgings in town; eventually, after staying half a year in Chicago with my father and his second wife, I returned to live with my uncle and aunt; my mother—how it anguished me at the time!—took employment as a maid with still another relative, one insufferably rich and inexcusably distant in the blood line. I need not comment on my intense loneliness, my bitterness; indeed, they soon began to vanish, for my uncle and aunt gave me the love and care of parents. And then, finally, the Depression began to retreat, to disperse, the way a shrouding cloud does before the moist winds of spring; pockets slowly filled with cash again, madness departed the world, and my parents, as in my happy endings, were reunited. My father's second wife gladly resumed her widowhood, and at the second wedding of my parents I was the best man. Yet I still recall a letter from my mother, one written soon after she took her job as maid: *My room is cheerful, in a separate wing above the garage, and with private bath. It is home for me though I look forward to the time our whole family can be together again. The photographs of you, your father and your brother are on my bureau; the night stand you made is of course by the bed. . . .*

That wretched, miserable night stand: wobbly, unpainted, without a drawer! I read the letter as many times as it was capable of imparting pain; I carried it in my pocket to my high-school classes, it lay under my pillow at night. In my dreams I saw my mother's face in sleep at the moment before I had wakened her in my remorse; I had visions of tortured tables with twisted tops, with legs warped and wobbly as bent pins. And I tried to imagine her long bus trip from Michigan: where had she put the night stand? Would the driver have argued that she couldn't take it, that it could travel with propriety neither in the luggage compartment nor in the racks? Later, I discovered that he *had* argued; and that she, in her mild perseverance, her gentle and maddening obstinacy, had won. It had occupied the seat next to her for the entire trip.

There it is.

The true adventure of a night stand.

It is odd that I should remember it so fully this night, that all of the associations which once surrounded that night stand should return with its image; that the night stand should impinge so sharply on my mind that the recently completed manuscript on my desk fades in importance before it. Yet I had been wholly involved in that story while writing it. So involved that I locked my study door against my children, refused to bandage cut knees, made no response to bells, ignored my family at dinner and saw my neighbors only as characters in a proposed dream. There is a pleasure in locking out the actual world and in populating another world with bits of one's own self. It is, I have heard, a noble thing to do: to attempt an order and a pattern that will emulate God's own dream, if in smaller scope.

But one needs to escape from dreams, even though the real world may seem but a bubble in which nobility is hard to find. The dog, Black Judy, whimpers again: now she wants to go out into the night, to sniff the trees and shrubs in the park and graveyard, to relieve her bladder and intestine.

Upstairs, my older boy—he is ten—may have wet the bed: though he has a wonderful pose of self-sufficiency, he is nervous and unsure at times and hence there are many sheets to hang on the line. He is deaf in one ear, the consequence of a severe case of mumps when he was five. It is, to be sure, a minor disability, one not affecting either his love for music—he practices the violin and the piano with great enthusiasm—or for such sports as ice skating and baseball. And perhaps the bad ear will keep him from military service. The younger boy, the seven-year-old, is attracted less by baseball than he is by butterflies; for that matter, he watches intently the doings of all small forms of animal and vegetable life—the flowering plants, the birds, the insects. Still, he is concerned, as is typical of children his age, with death. When spring comes, he will pick every flower he can; yet he intentionally has killed no breathing thing; last summer, on our walks in the deep gorge behind the park, he would shout loudly to scare the fish away whenever we saw in the creek the earnestly patient men with hip boots and poles. But his concern with death is not wholly unselfish. "If I am good, I will live again after I die," he says; it is a belief he has picked up at school, either from other children or from a young grade-school teacher desperate for some new means of discipline. "And if I'm good when I live again, I'll live once *again*. Three lives," and he holds up three fingers.

Black Judy jumps down from the couch and lifts her paw into my lap. I put on my coat, snap on her leash and snap out the light; I walk her first in the graveyard and then in the park. "Heel," I say, marching this way and then that, for she is wild as a puppy and must learn discipline and control if she is to survive both the busy thoroughfare before our house and the wrath of the gardener down the block. "Heel, sit, stay, come." She tugs at the leash, nearly pulling me over into the snow. *"Heel,"* I say sternly, now walking the asphalt road that circles the filtration plant.

Obedient to my cry, she trots now by my side, her front paws even with my feet; her ears up, alertly she awaits the next command. I look at the stars: Andromeda has long since vanished over the northwestern horizon, and Orion touches the land to the west. Except for the Big Dipper, the stars above me form no familiar constellation; and yet they are everywhere. The night is frigid but still, and the air hangs heavy with the cold: it magnifies the stars and makes them shimmer as through water. And as I watch, the dog pacing at my side, they form into dozens of constellations, each one a perfect table, each a flawless little night stand. It is, I suppose, my imagination. But I marvel, and am pleased. And, as I circle the filtration plant for the second time, I think I see my neighbor the dean plodding ahead of me, his cane tapping into the ice; upon the hill across the road, ghostly in the starlight, my other neighbor glides softly among the tombstones.

[1960]

■

The Bullfrog Pond

IT WAS THE SECOND AND FINAL EVE-ning of a visit by Sigurd, the Icelander, and Jennifer, his California-born wife, who now taught with him in a secondary school in Reykjavik. As young men, Sigurd and I were colleagues at Cornell, but it was twenty years since he and Jennifer had sold their isolated Finger Lakes house near a stone quarry and gone off with their two children to Sigurd's native land, and ten years since Jean and I and our three boys had most recently visited them in Iceland.

The last decade had aged the four of us while bringing our children to maturity. Jennifer and Sigurd now had three grandchildren—two in Reykjavik, where their son lived, and the third in Scotland, where their daughter and her husband were teachers. Jean and I were not yet grandparents. Though two of our sons still lived with us, Jimmy, our youngest, would be entering college in the fall, and this summer was away, wilderness-camping with high-school friends in the Adirondacks. Cris, who worked the second shift at the Morse Chain plant, in Ithaca, never got home until after midnight. He was twenty-five. Of our children, Cris was the one most interested in using the farmland surrounding the old country house that all three had grown up in. He kept a herd of goats that he milked in the early-morning hours, and he hoped someday to earn his living through the sale of dairy products; he spent his weekends experimenting with various methods of making cheese.

Waiting for our wives to return from Ithaca, where they had gone after dinner to see one of Jennifer's acquaintances, Sigurd and I sat talking in the living room. He was tired and vaguely depressed, as one is apt to be near the end of a long vacation. On a walk Jennifer and he and I had taken that morning along the rim of Taughannock Gorge, he shouted angrily at her for standing on a rock jutting from the gorge wall. They quarreled. He apologized, but he remained upset by his bossiness, his tendency to transfer to his wife the feelings of protection he'd once had for his children: it was, he said, the habit he would most like to break. I said that I, too, found it difficult to outgrow fatherhood. I supposed my inability to counsel any of my children, now that they were grown, accounted for the degree to which I remembered the days in which all of them had depended upon my some-times faulty guardianship. For example, I often found myself reliving the events of the year I had spent with my family in France and Italy. One boy or another—their ages then had ranged from just three to thirteen—was always teetering in the window of a tower, balancing himself on a parapet, peering into a deep and unprotected well.

If I were to choose one day that seemed a perfect metaphor of father-hood, I said, it would be our last full day in Europe. Jean and I and our two older children, helped by the desk clerk and porter and chambermaid, spent much of the morning extricating our three-year-old from the Naples hotel bedroom into which he had locked himself. We visited Pompeii in the noonday heat, and in the late afternoon climbed Vesuvius to walk the lip of the cone with a group of other tourists. It wasn't simply the height that I found frightening; it was a sense of desolation, emptiness, and waste. I felt I particularly had to keep Jimmy—he was so young—from that mam-moth but constricting cone on one side of us, from the empty sky on the other; I shamed all my children with my panic and anger. Ultimately, Larry, the oldest boy, put Jimmy on his shoulders and—either to prove me too cautionary or just to get away—went right down that mountain of ash, sometimes standing, sometimes using his bottom for a sled and sending up great spumes of dust. "Look at that boy sliding down the mountain with a baby on his shoulders!" another tourist exclaimed, as if it were the chief spectacle Vesuvius provided. Covered with soot but behaving as if nothing extraordinary had happened, they were sitting next to the locked car and drinking from a shared bottle of Coca-Cola when Jean and Cris and I finally made it down the zigzagging trail to the parking lot.

Sigurd remarked that all fathers had some variation of that story to tell. "I'm not through," I said. "I drove back to Naples in the dark, the children in back and Jean beside me, with none of us saying a word. Then I got lost trying to find the garage at the hotel. 'A simple matter,' you might say. 'Here's the front of the hotel—just drive to the garage in back.' But get off those main streets, and Naples is nothing but a maze of branching alleys so narrow that the fenders of a VW nearly scrape the walls. I had to make three attempts—"

"And fathers, we know, aren't supposed to get lost."

"So our children think. On the first try we came around a bend to discover a family of six or so celebrating a feast day or some other occasion with a dinner on a candlelit table set out in the middle of the alley. They had to remove the dishes and the wine bottles and the candles and a vase of flowers—a lace tablecloth, too!—and cart the table and chairs partway up a staircase in the nearest building to let us by. They were singing and smiling; they bowed to us as we passed, they bore us no grudge. A fine Italian family. We felt almost as if we were part of the celebration. On the second try—"

"I can guess what happened."

"Of course. I entered another alley but came around a bend to see the same candlelit table before us. They weren't so happy this time to remove the dishes and flowers and candles and so on and to retreat up the stairs with the table and chairs. And then, when I took yet another alley and *still* found myself going around a familiar bend to see the candles—well, I turned off the car lights and tried to back up, but managed only to bash a fender in my nervousness. There was no turning back, Sigurd! Our children were all on the floor behind the front seat, piled on top of each other, and hissing at me; even Jean was slumped as far down as you can get in the front of a VW. As the rest of that Italian family moved everything away again, the husband put his head in the car window and asked, in English, 'Why? Why? Why?'"

"One 'why' for each attempt," Sigurd observed. He softly repeated the word three times himself, and then sighed.

I wanted to make him laugh, to return both of us to the light-hearted spirit of the parties he and Jennifer had given in their house by the quarry so many years before. But, as had been true of so many of our conversations during this brief visit, each of us, while feeling our old affection for the other, ended up solemn and discontented. Even to me my tale had seemed lugubrious. "You and I—at least we always tried to be responsible fathers," I said.

The windows were open; the breeze occasionally carried the tinkling of goat bells or the twanging of frogs in our pond. We listened to those sounds. "Tell me," Sigurd said. "Isn't it time our wives came back?"

But it was only ten. We had been sipping Scotch; I refilled our glasses. Idly talking, we wandered from room to room, upstairs and down, using one staircase or another—we have three in this sprawling house. I was more or less looking for an album of photographs taken during our three visits to Iceland, but it was nowhere to be found. Nearly every room in the house has at least one bookcase, and old school texts (Jean's and mine as well as those of our children), juvenile fiction, encyclopedias, scrapbooks, scholarly treatises, novels, and volumes of poetry are all jumbled together in them. At one time I carried a memory of the color and shape of each book and where it most likely had been shelved, but the constant addition of new titles, combined with the increased use of my books by the children as they grew, finally resulted in the same kind of disorder that had developed earlier in the closets. At the end of a second-floor hallway, Sigurd and I bent down to go through a small door to enter a large room with a platform; in the nineteenth century it had served as a circuit-court chamber for the judges who traveled about on horseback.

"When the boys were small and had disobeyed Jean or me, I would say to them, 'Let's go to the judge's chamber so I can try the case,'" I said as Sigurd and I sat down on the edge of the platform. "Now look at the room," and I pointed to the various unmade beds. "It's become a bunk-house!" I told him that Cris often brought out young people in need of guidance or just food; they helped him milk the goats and clean the barn. Sometimes they stayed a night, sometimes a week or longer. One boy named Sam, who frequently returned, was adept at fixing farm machinery, but equally adept at breaking things with it. "Even worse than that, Sigurd, Sam loses all my tools. Not just my hammer. The socket set, the wrenches, the screwdrivers—they're all rusting out there somewhere," and I gestured in the direction of the dark fields.

"A house the size of yours needs people," Sigurd said reasonably. "What would you ever do with a place like this without Cris? You're lucky to have a son still at home, one interested in putting a farm to its proper use."

When Cris was a young child, I said, he helped Larry and Jean and me build the horse barn to replace a much larger barn that had burned down. He remarked at the time that he thought we should construct the barn like a house, so that Jean and I could live in it when we got as old as his grand-parents; Larry or Jimmy or he could then live in the farmhouse with a wife and children, and look after us. That a boy hammering next to his father would be dreaming such generous thoughts had given me the kind of hap-piness that makes one's eyes too blurred to drive a nail properly; but Jean and I, in our late fifties, certainly found no pleasure in contemplating some future retirement to a horse barn while goats wandered about eating our shrubs and the house became a deteriorating and untidy commune.

"Since I became a grandfather, I think in platitudes," Sigurd said, with another sigh. "Still, it's true enough that we can't impose our sense of what's fit on the younger ones."

I felt threatened by the reverse of that, I said. Not long ago, an editor had wanted to know if I would do a book. What she had in mind wasn't quite *Zen and the Art of Goat Raising,* she said, but such a title might suggest certain possibilities. . . . "I'm a professor of English," I said to Sigurd, "with courses to teach, with programs to direct. I don't look to goats for spiritual sustenance! When I was younger I was in control of my life. If a roof needed replacing, I replaced it. I built barns, I could pull a screw out of a horse's hoof when my boys weren't strong enough to do it, I painted one side of the house every summer. Now things are getting out of hand, and I *don't like it at all.*"

Jean and Jennifer had come back and were chatting in the living room with Sigurd and me when Cris arrived with Sam, whom he'd found at a downtown corner. Cris had driven directly home from his job—without even washing the grease from his hands—just in case we might still be up. Smiling, he was full of memories of our visits to Iceland—of the sheep and horses that wandered on the mountain slopes and seemed so free; of the lava flow from Hekla that had ponderously moved forward, bathing us in its shimmering heat as we watched; of cold lakes set in volcanic basins. If discontent had led me from one long story to the next, simple happiness had loosened Cris's tongue; he usually came home, as he told Sigurd, to a dark house. He spoke of the sagas he had read as a child, after our first stay in Iceland, and of parallels between them and Greek myths; the latter brought him, by way of Pan, to the subject of goats. As he talked, his excitement and pleasure made him pace the room and pull at his reddish beard—a beard not yet so luxuriant as Sigurd's, which he had always admired. Suddenly aware that he had forgotten the conventional amenities, he introduced Sam to Sigurd and Jennifer and asked us all what we had been doing, how we had been passing the hours.

I said that Jean and Jennifer had been away and that Sigurd and I hadn't done much other than to listen to the sound of the bullfrogs.

"What bullfrogs?" Cris asked.

"The ones in the pond," I said. "Listen," and we all sat quietly until we heard a twang, as if a rubber band had snapped, and then another.

Sam had remained standing uncertainly in the doorway even after his introduction, but now he laughed, contemptuous of the sound. "Them ain't *bull*frogs," he said, with a knowing look at Cris.

Sam often contradicted me, and everybody else. He was a pudgy boy who had spent his childhood in a series of foster homes. That spring, after quarreling with a teacher and other students, he had dropped out of his senior year of high school. I could understand his need to be stubborn and assertive; still, his dismissal of that twang irritated me, and I said that for twenty years I had told people bullfrogs twanged like that, and nobody had argued.

Cris said that Sam was right: he and Sam had found a pond with genuine bullfrogs and would be happy to lead us there, if we would like to hear them. I asked him where the pond was; he pointed out the window at the lights blinking from the radio tower on Connecticut Hill, six miles away. "You go almost there, turn right on the Cayutaville Road, make a left, and—well, none of the roads have names."

It was 1:00 A.M. Sigurd and Jennifer would be leaving for Iceland soon after breakfast. I began, in my old fatherly manner, "I really don't think, Cris—" but Jennifer said she wanted to go. Though she was fond of Iceland, I knew she still had strong attachments not only to her relatives and friends in the United States but to the natural world she once had known—the trees and plants and animal life. (That morning, on our walk along the rim of the gorge, she had stopped to touch and to name ferns and wild flowers that she remembered from the ravine behind their old house by the stone quarry.) Sigurd said he would also like to hear frogs that did more than just twang; he had been cheerful ever since Cris's arrival, and now, eager to be off in search of frogs, he reached for the cane he needed because of back trouble.

"Don't you need to milk your goats?" I asked Cris.

"Never mind!" He was laughing and already heading out the door with Sam, beckoning for us to come.

Cris took Sam in his pickup truck; I followed with the others. Our route consisted chiefly of a succession of roads barely more than fire trails or cart paths, the trees and underbrush so close that branches occasionally scraped the car. Most of these roads, I had been told, were once surrounded by pastures and cornfields, but the land, never very productive, had gradually been abandoned, the owners leaving during the Depression or in the later years of urban prosperity brought about by the Second World War. The New York Department of Conservation managed thousands of acres here, permitting the habitat gradually to revert to its original state. Three or four old sugar maples in a row, their thick boles illuminated in our headlights, meant that a house had stood behind them: how odd that houses and barns, and all the life they had contained, could be gone—and so soon! Though all of our children were fascinated by the region, Jean and I never much liked it; the young trees blocked the views and made us feel uneasy and confined. Even the vaguest memory of the Connecticut Hill area, as I mowed a field or replaced a section of rotten house siding, would give me the awareness of both the urgency of my task and its ultimate uselessness.

Now Cris drove through it, flashing his lights to indicate for us passages of some danger or difficulty—a fallen tree partly obstructing the road, a washed-out section, a boulder. Two or three miles into that wilderness, he stopped the truck and came to our car to say apologetically that he had made a wrong turn; he guided me back to a gap in the underbrush, where both vehicles could reverse their direction. After leading us along another road, he stopped again, at what might have been the identical place. "Lost forever!" I said to my passengers as Cris approached once more. He said, "We're here. Turn off your lights."

Then, in the darkness, we stood with Cris and Sam by the side of the road. "Be careful of the drop-off," Cris whispered.

"What drop-off?" The question was a chorus.

"Well, don't move until you can see."

Slowly the blackness took on various unfamiliar shapes. Below us, a few feet away, tiny lights began to shimmer and to spread, as if over a large field.

"What's that, shining everywhere?" Jean asked.

"Glowworms, I think," I said.

"Stars, on the pond," Cris said; and even as he was saying those words I felt as if all of us had moved an immense distance away, and were staring down at our universe. On a summer's night at our farmhouse, one can see friendly lights on distant hills and hear many sounds—a truck backfiring, a dog barking in the hamlet of Mecklenburg, the twanging of *our* frogs, and, of course, the comforting tinkling of goat bells. Here the absolute stillness and tiny points of light were frightening.

"Your frogs, Sam—" I began; but Cris hushed me, a hand on my arm. Then a horn blared: though we were miles from the nearest railroad track, I thought for an instant that a diesel locomotive was bearing down upon us.

"Lord!" Sigurd cried.

"Bullfrogs!" Sam said triumphantly. "I told you, didn't I?"

The horn below us blared again; another replied from the opposite bank. "Cassiopeia answering the Dog Star," Cris said.

The fancy so pleased me that I smiled at the mirrored stars.

"You were scared, weren't you?" Cris asked, his hand still restraining me.

"Oh, not really. Not much. It was Sigurd who cried, 'Lord.'"

We stood on the bank, teasing each other like that and listening. Jennifer said she would remember this pond and its sounds during the long nights of the coming Icelandic winter. As for me, I was, for the moment, happy as a child.   [1979]

■

Passages Early and Late

IN JUNE OF ONE OF MY FIRST YEARS AS a teacher, my wife and I and the drama teacher at my college and his wife made a daylong excursion from our eastern Kentucky town of Morehead to a state park. The children of both families had been left with friends. The spring term had just ended, and even Linda, the drama teacher's wife, was more relaxed than usual—she was normally the most intense and active of the four of us and was on medication for her high blood pressure. The day was cool and misty in the early morning, but bright and hot by noon: the kind of day in Kentucky in which meadowlarks sing in the hedgerows in the morning, wild roses bloom on the crumbling stone fences, and everything perceived between mid-morning and dusk is so sharply outlined that the viewer feels gifted with a strange power to look into the very essence of things—a bud, a thorn, a vulture on a rock, the rock itself.

We had brought food and cooking equipment for breakfast, but even hunger was pleasurable, something we didn't wish to satiate too quickly. And so we rented horses at the park stable as soon as it opened. We rode through the trails in the dark woods, trotting whenever we came to the sunny glades; and, in the green fields above the lake, we galloped abreast.

The smell and warmth of sweating horses, the sound that hooves and leather make, the feeling that from the waist down the rider has become one with the animal while the chest and head remain free and wholly human—these sensations, so sensuous and agreeable, are particularly exhilarating for one who is young and a reasonably good horseman.

At a picnic site we finally dismounted, leading the horses back and forth until they were cooled enough to be tethered to saplings at the edge of the clearing. Linda and my wife walked to the car for the breakfast supplies while I gathered brush and branches into a pile for P.C., the drama teacher, who had offered to build the fire. P.C. was tall and thin and had the pale complexion of people who haunt dark theaters and basement studios. On his knees, patiently tending his small fire, he looked to me more an ascetic than an outdoorsman; but in his gentle voice he began reminiscing about his childhood in North Carolina, and about various experiences with bears and other wildlife in the Great Smokies. He spoke of moments of recklessness and danger. Once, as a boy, he had rescued a man whose car had plummeted from a cliff. . . .

It was characteristic of P.C. in his intervals of happiness—after, say, an opening performance of *The Tempest* in which his student actors from Neon and Salt Lick had conjured up more magic than he had believed possible—to talk about himself, to mention certain of his childhood adventures and to speak of famous actors with whom he'd had a beer or two during a season of summer stock; but he always did so in such a soft and apologetic voice that anybody not familiar with him would think he was telling one little lie after another. It is the fact of P.C.'s happiness, his shy garrulousness, that I remember from this day. I cannot remember what he said about bears, or about how he had managed to rescue a motorist whose car might or might not have been cradled in the branches of a tree; if he described for me some action of his adolescence in which his sense of abandon had nearly cost him his life, I have only a faint recollection that probably this is so.

For, while I can remember from this day everything that gave me a personal pleasure—including such a tableau as P.C. kneeling before a fire while four horses watched him—I can recall almost nothing of what any of my companions said, and nothing whatsoever of what particularly pleased them. What did my wife say, and what gave her the most delight? Did she smile at me? Was she wearing the boots and breeches from her high school days? My memory, usually so reliable in regard to what has made her happy, tells me much too little about my wife and the couple who for six years were among our closest friends.

I most regret my inability to recollect Linda's responses. She had wanted to be an actress. In a way, she was an unpaid drama teacher at the college, for she helped P.C. coach the student performers, designed costumes, and once or twice a year—whenever a play had a role for a woman that required a maturity and emotional response beyond the experience and ability of the available students—acted in the productions. Restless, she needed always to be planning parties or arranging social events for charitable purposes. A month before we went to the park, I had returned to my graduate school in Iowa to take the final oral examination for my doctoral degree. On the night immediately preceding my departure, Linda, aware of my anxiety, gathered all the members of my department and their wives before our front door to sing "Your Ph.D., your Ph.D., you're going to get . . . your Ph.D.," to the tune of "Aloha." Some years after my wife and I had left eastern Kentucky for upstate New York, Linda suffered a stroke that deprived her of speech. P.C. gave up the theater for less demanding work so that he would have the time to teach her word after word of her lost language. Following another stroke, Linda died, "knowing at least, thank God, how to speak," as P.C. told my wife and me in a late-night long-distance call following her burial.

On that day at the park, the four of us—after breakfast and further riding—walked the nature trails, dived into the cold water of a blue lake surrounded by green hills, raced our companions to the dam and back in foot-driven paddleboats, lay in the sand in our wet swimming suits and later in the grass of the meadow above the lake, and explored in the heat of late afternoon a cool cave whose roof was furred with sleeping bats. All day I kept saying to myself, "How happy I am! How good I feel!" My body felt lean and capable of the most strenuous physical task; at rest it was loose-limbed, drowsy, sensual.

Toward evening, we started home. I was driving; my wife rested her head on my shoulder. Nobody spoke, for we were all tired; but when I saw an intriguing road—the narrow kind, with gravel or sand only in the single pair of tracks, that curves as it climbs a forested hill—I swerved off the blacktop to take it. Roads of this kind often appear in my most mysterious dreams; and if I actually come upon such a road and do not take it, thinking that I can't spare the time or that my desire to follow it is merely superstitious, I suffer the nostalgia we feel for something of large value that we have willfully lost. I took such a road on that day at least partly because I didn't want my personal happiness to end. Not only was the term over, but I had just been granted my doctoral degree. Regardless of the lateness of the hour, of the fact that the families who were caring for our children were expecting us to retrieve them before supper, none of the others protested when I left the highway; perhaps they slept, perhaps they were as unwilling as I to admit that our excursion was almost completed.

I drove past several abandoned cabins. Beyond them, the road dipped to ford a rocky creek and climbed again into further woods. The uphill tracks had been eroded by the rivulets of the preceding rainy season; dry and snake-like channels now, they held large stones against which the frame of the car occasionally scraped. My companions had become alert. "Hadn't we better turn back?" my wife asked. I said maybe we could, at the top of the hill. At the crest, though, facing a huge sun just beginning to descend behind a ridge that paralleled ours, we looked down into a green and level valley. A wide stream divided the fields; and beneath us, at the edge of the stream, stood a small, white-painted church. Here the road stopped; there was no bridge. It was such an improbable destination for this rarely traveled and wretchedly maintained road that it reminded me at once of the end of such roads in my dreams; I wanted to see whether the church truly existed, and, if so, whether it really was as immaculate as it appeared to be from our height.

I remember no further ruts, no further rocky obstructions. By the side of the church, the road looped back upon itself like the terminus of a streetcar line. On the other bank of the stream, a somewhat wider and neatly-graveled road led to a parking lot. A barge—a simple ferry boat for passengers—was tied to the opposite shore; a cable fastened to trees on both banks and connected by a pulley and smaller cable to the boat obviously was intended to keep the worshipers from floating downstream during the flood season. How was the boat propelled? Did the worshipers sling a rope across the water to a solitary person who took our road for the purpose of pulling the others to his side? Were long poles hidden in the barge? While we marveled and built our theories, twilight came. There were no power lines in the valley—that was part of its charm—but such a lack meant no electricity in the church. Freshly painted, it shimmered and grew larger in the vanishing light.

The door unlatched easily; it had been kept shut by a hasp with a whittled stick through the staple. The interior was not yet dark; the walls and ceiling were white and the many-paned windows large. The unvarnished floor had the bleached and sanded look that comes from countless scrubbings. Six rows of pews faced the pulpit. Next to the lectern stood a bulky black piano and a stool. No religious objects or pictures decorated the little room; no sign existed outside or within the building to denote a sect. But the hymnals in the racks and on the piano were those of my childhood—and apparently of the childhoods of my companions too. Sitting on the stool, P.C. looked at the page to which the hymnal was opened and immediately began to play "I Walk in the Garden Alone," and then "The Old Rugged Cross" and "Come to the Church in the Wild Wood." Grouped around him, the rest of us, needing to see the words no more than he needed to see the musical notations, sang as if we had been invited into the church to do so; as if the purely physical and no doubt self-centered happiness we individually had experienced earlier that day had been an intentional and necessary preparation for this activity which otherwise was as isolated from everything in the past and from everything in the future as the church itself was isolated from our habitual world. The room slowly became one with the darkness gathering outside and each of the singers became only a face and a voice—a face almost indistinguishable from the other faces floating in the night, a voice merging with the melodic stream arising from a nearly invisible instrument.

In my sixth and last year of teaching in Kentucky, I gave a talk before a group of about thirty people, all of them considerably older than I, in the banquet hall of a hotel in Huntington, West Virginia. The occasion was West Virginia Poetry Day; I had been chosen to be the banquet speaker, and my wife had been invited to attend. I felt honored; not only was I a young and unknown teacher who never before had made a public address, but I had been plucked out of a neighboring state, as if nobody in West Virginia were quite up to the task.

The trip to Huntington took place in October rather than June, and my wife and I left our home in early afternoon rather than early morning—but this day, like the day we had spent at the state park, was one of unusual clarity. The trees were changing color; maples and oaks stood out sharply in the sunlight against the dark green of the pines. Our road led past the brick kilns and American Legion Post of Olive Hill and past the entrance to the park; a few miles beyond the entrance, it descended from the hills into a wide valley. Here the land was more fertile, the barns larger and in better repair. Steep-roofed farmhouses replaced the cabins with their rusty washing machines and refrigerators on the slanting porches. The streets of Huntington were broad and lined with trees; stately houses were set back in landscaped grounds. Our town of three thousand seemed a peasant hamlet to which Huntington was the provincial capital. The five-or-six-story hotel with its uniformed porter waiting beneath the marquee was large enough to be the palace of an archduke.

Although we arrived on time, most of the guests were already seated at the U-shaped table beneath the chandelier, and were speaking to each other in subdued voices. A photographer wandered about, taking pictures. The president of the poetry society, a tall woman wearing a long dress and a corsage that matched the flowers on the table, introduced us to several people. One was the society editor of the Huntington newspaper, another the chairman of the English department at the local university. As my wife and I were escorted to our central places at the bottom of the U, I felt my new suit to be shoddy and ill-fitting.

The event began with a reading by the president of a poem written for the occasion by the governor of West Virginia; he was honorary chairman of the poetry society and had been responsible for the proclamation giving West Virginia its annual Poetry Day. Following his poem, which praised the state's beauty and its poets, the president began a roll call. As each name was pronounced, a man or woman would rise to recite a poem he or she had composed since the last banquet. Some of the members had memorized their work; others pulled folded sheets from pockets or purses, adjusted their glasses, and carefully read their verses. Halfway through the readings I realized that their own words were more important to the members than any speech of mine; I knew also that my prepared talk was much too long and full of quotations, and that to read it aloud would be a disaster.

Indigestion kept me from eating the fried chicken. I put my manuscript next to my plate; with a pen I deleted large segments, drawing connecting arrows between the remaining paragraphs, and put asterisks next to phrases I was so fond of that I wanted to make sure I would give them exactly as written. Once I began to speak, though, I abandoned the typed text almost completely. The subject of my address was "The Creative Process." I talked of divine and human love. My references were to Dante and Virgil and Beatrice and the stars that end each part of *The Divine Comedy;* to the speculations of the mathematician Henri Poincaré about the "aesthetic sieve" possessed by all creators, a sieve permitting only those combinations that are beautiful (and hence usually true) to escape from their dreaming to their conscious states; and to Hindu metaphysics. I was able to speak so readily, I think, because my subject, being both large and noble, assured me of the amplitude and generosity of my own mind. The occasional flash-bulbs persuaded me of my status as a celebrity, and my voice became nearly as deep and resonant as that of Dylan Thomas. The ovation I received so gratified me that I immediately gave away my manuscript, though I had made no carbon of it, to the poetry society member who told me she regretted only the brevity of my remarks. For some years I kept a copy of the full page the Huntington newspaper had devoted to the banquet. In a note accompanying the copy she had mailed to me, the president of the society wrote that she thought the headline—"Mankind Equipped for Love, Poetry Speaker Says"—somewhat unfortunate, but that she felt I might like to see the pictures. They included one of me, hand raised as I made a point. The brief text said that I had been inspirational.

After we left the hotel, my wife and I walked the streets of downtown Huntington, looking at the window displays of the now-closed department and furniture stores. Huntington, while still seeming exotic—the chairs and clothing in the windows were beyond our income—had managed to become friendlier; it was quite possible that someday we would be residents of such a city. Perhaps the chairman of the English department at the university had been so impressed by my talk that at this moment he was sitting before his desk in the study of one of those stately houses, writing me to find out if I would be interested in a position. Would it be in my best interest to accept such an offer immediately, or should I hold off while inquiring about possibilities elsewhere?

As we drove homeward, the wide valley was blue and shimmering in the light of a full moon. Mists rose from swamps and ponds, little exhalations of a drowsing and comfortable world tumbling through space with its moon. We closed our windows against the rapidly cooling night air and turned on the car heater. The large farmhouses with their brightly lit windows disappeared as we began the rise into the hills; instead we saw now and then a kerosene lamp glowing dimly in a cabin close to the road. Coming around a bend between Olive Hill and Morehead—we were that close to home—we saw what appeared to be a bonfire in the field to our left. I slowed the car and then stopped. Three figures stood before the fire. Beyond it, and illuminated more by the moon than the flames, a mule attached to a pole plodded in a circle. How marvelous to see, from this lonely road, a moonlit field with three men, a fire, and a mule!

"What do you suppose they're doing?" my wife asked.

"Why don't we find out?" I said. Normally I would never have suggested anything like that; I was usually too self-conscious, too uncertain of the propriety of intruding upon people I didn't know. I had never become acquainted with any of the hill farmers—nothing more than a word or two with them in the hardware or shoe store, a few phrases exchanged once with a family my wife and I had picked up after their Model A truck had broken down on the highway. The region was theirs, not mine, a fact I could tell simply by looking at the gaunt faces and bony bodies of the farmers who came to town: these men resembled the very fields they tilled. My clothes, my manner of speaking, my literary interests, my occupation as a teacher, all constituted a barrier I had never known how to surmount. I had been told by the older professors at the college that the hill people of our county were as proud as they were poor, and that their shyness or reticence was far in excess of any that I might feel; I had also been told that if they felt themselves victimized or insulted, particularly on a Saturday night in town, they were apt to respond with quick violence—among them were descendants of the survivors of the Tolliver and Martin feud, the most devastating in Kentucky history. Indeed, my college had been founded to bring understanding to these passionate families; the first president had almost been hit by a bullet as he stepped from the railroad car.

My wife and I walked slowly toward the fire. The men were apparently a farmer and his two almost-grown sons. The father, the shortest of the three, was bearded. They knew, of course, that we were approaching; but they never looked our way or gave us a greeting. We stopped a short distance from the fire and whispered to each other our conjectures about the equipment. The mule, as it plodded, was operating some kind of mill or press. One of the sons dropped an armful of cane into the hopper. A long and shallow cast-iron vat stood over the flames; two of its legs were shorter than the other pair, giving it a slight tilt. Much like the partitions in a labyrinth or maze, metal strips of various lengths welded to the floor of the open vat served to impede the flow of the dark liquid oozing from the upper side to the lower. Steam rose from the bubbling syrup.

"They're making molasses," my wife said. "It must be sorghum molasses. Look, they must have just cut the cane," and she pointed to the rows of stubble.

Slowly reaching into his baggy overalls, the father pulled a large knife from an inner pocket and unclasped the blade. He bent over and picked up a section of cane and cut two equal lengths of it; before handing them to the younger son, he scraped and whittled them a bit and considered them carefully in his open palm. These grave and deliberate actions were without seeming reference to us; but with an equal solemnity the son approached us and placed one piece of cane in my hand and the other in my wife's. At last the father looked at us, at our bodies and our faces; and we, in turn, looked expectantly at him, wondering what we were to do with our gifts. He said quietly, "It's better at the other end," motioning us to the lower part of the vat. The simplicity of the words gave the invitation the clarity and symbolic nature of a dream, and so we will probably remember it all our lives.

We dipped the cane into the heavy syrup collecting and cooling at the lower end, and sucked the sweetness from the surface of the cane and its pith. "Oh yes, this is *very* good," I said, dipping my cane again into the vat, and yet again. Our lips and fingers became sticky, but we found it pleasurable to lick our fingers, to run a tongue over our lips. When we had finished, we stood with the farmer and his sons, looking with them at the fire and the mule still patiently turning in his circle; listening with them to the crackling of the logs, the creaking of the press, the baying of a distant moonstruck hound. The taste of molasses lingered on my teeth and tongue. The fire warmed my stomach and thighs.

"You folks from up North?" the younger son asked.

"No," I said. "We've been on a little trip. We live in Morehead."

"Then you're almost home."

"Almost," I said.

Beyond our backs, a car droned past on the highway without slowing. After the sound had disappeared, I thought that the driver must have seen five figures and a mule. A few minutes later, we thanked our hosts and drove home in silence.

Our son Cris's thirty goats share a pasture with the two fat and elderly horses my wife and I bought when we moved from Ithaca to the Finger Lakes countryside in 1962. Eventually Cris would like to earn his livelihood through the sale of milk and cheese; for the present he works a late shift—3:30 P.M. until midnight—in an Ithaca factory. He does his chores, including the milking, in the early-morning hours, gets whatever sleep he can, repeats the chores, bathes, and dashes out the door to his pickup truck, buttoning his shirt as he goes.

For several weeks this past winter, during a period of the heaviest snowfalls, he was both nearly sleepless and always late for work. In August, the billy had managed to jump the fence and reach the nannies; eleven kids arrived in late January and early February, the worst possible season for their survival. Two of the births were difficult ones; Cris had to alter the position of the kids in the womb before pulling them from their mothers. Because the nights were too bitter for the kids to remain in the barn, he brought them into the house as they were born, one or two or three at a time.

All eleven were in the kitchen for a week. My wife and I fed them with nursing bottles or pans of warmed milk two or three times a day, and grew so fond of them that after the feedings we let them romp about the kitchen, all eleven at once, even though it meant a considerable amount of cleaning up with paper towels and pails of hot soapy water smelling of disinfectant. The one I liked best was a small white doe. If she were removed from her box, she would vigorously flap her ears and then jump as high as she could; because her muscles were still weak and the linoleum floor was slick, her legs would splay out and she would have to be helped onto her tiny brown hooves.

I have been on sabbatical leave from my university this academic year, and have been working at home, in my study. Several times (after my wife had left for her job in Ithaca and while Cris was still sleeping) I brought that favorite kid into the study, closed the door, placed her on the rug, and let her jump as much as she wanted to; I would lie on the rug and let her nibble at my hair and ears as well as my shirt. I was fond of that kid not only because she was alert and spunky, but because I had helped to save her life. Cris had brought her into the house early one afternoon. Still wet from the fluid in the sac, her body was nearly frozen. We filled the kitchen sink with warm water. While Cris prepared a mixture of glucose and water in a syringe, I immersed the kid: one of my hands supported her belly and chest, the other her limp head. The umbilical cord was still connected to her belly and floated, red and stringy, beside her. Some fecal matter that had been caught in her soft fur floated about, too. It seemed as if my hand were cupped against her heart, so intense was the throbbing.

And yet for a moment that heart faltered and stopped. I massaged the kid's chest while swishing her body back and forth in the water, and the beat came back into my palm as if it were the pulsing of my own blood. Cris pried open the jaws, inserted the tube of the syringe over the tongue and as far back as it would go and squeezed the warm syrup into the throat. In a few moments the legs jerked and the kid's eyes opened. My face must have been the first object she saw. The possibility that imprinting might work two ways has not been generally acknowledged.

That night my wife and I drove between high banks of snow the ten miles to Ithaca to hear a concert at Barnes Hall on the Cornell campus. The small auditorium, a former chapel on the second floor, has several stained-glass windows in the apse and organ pipes against one wall; the sloping sides of its high ceiling are connected by an intricate arrangement of wooden beams. It has become as familiar an environment to me as a room in my own house. On this evening, the selections were for violin and viola. The violist was a young woman I did not know, but the violinist was an old friend whose playing I always look forward to.

Despite the weather, the auditorium was filled. My wife and I sat in the tier of seats to the left of the stage. The occasional chattering of steam pipes, the single chime every fifteen minutes of the library tower clock, were subsumed into the rhythms of the more central instruments. I was attracted by the fluidity of the dresses worn by both performers. At some point I became aware that I was concentrating upon the slight indentation of the violist's navel; it came and went in the taut and silky fabric of her dress as her arm moved. Such a fixation bothered me; surely no other member of the audience could be so preoccupied. Two wholly serious and bearded youths nearby were following the score as best they could in the dim light; an elderly woman, resting her head within the furry nest of her coat collar, had closed her eyes either to sleep or the better to listen; a trio of girls in jeans in the front row leaned forward—chins cupped in their hands, elbows on their knees—in homage to such superb female talent.

During Mozart's Duo in G Major, the final selection of the evening, I forgot for a time both the audience and the physical presence of the performers and remembered—as I so often have done on this sabbatical leave, perhaps because it is my next to last before retirement—the Kentucky church, the ferryboat, and the faces of the singers (one now dead) in the dark; the circling of a mule under the full October moon and the figures before the fire. My body once had been young enough, my mind naïve enough, to permit me the illusion of self-containment, as if the external world existed for the gratification of my senses; and yet the very vigor of my responses had enabled me (so it seemed, listening to Mozart on a cold night in a warm hall in my fifty-seventh year) to vault beyond myself like an athlete of pure being. It was as if all that could be glorious for me had already occurred, as if my past signified far more than my future; and so I was returned to the violist and violinist in their sinuous dresses. Was it my sadness, my resignation, that made me aware then that my concentration on the violist all along had been caused by my feelings toward the limp and new-born kid I had immersed in the kitchen sink earlier that day?

The moment I saw, superimposed on the body of the violist, that of the kid—for I saw her drifting in somnolence there, the red cord streaming out, an image with the truth that dreams possess—I experienced an acceptance of pure physicality, a sensation quite unlike any of those of my desirous younger days; it permitted me an immediate tenderness for bodies, human and animal, in all their biological manifestations and changes. This acceptance altered the way I looked at the two performers, the older and the younger, and the way I looked at all the members of the audience, the children, the students, the middle-aged, the elderly; it was in harmony not only with the remembrance of warm molasses on the tongue and images of figures in a field, singers in a church, but with the fluid memories that must have been deep in Mozart's dreaming self as he put certain symbols on paper, symbols that these two performers now were faithfully recreating as spiritual sounds.   [1978]

■

A Family Record

ONE DAY THIS PAST SUMMER, I RE-
ceived a phone call from a staff member of the Division of Unclaimed Funds of the Ohio Department of Commerce in Columbus, who had managed to trace me to my Finger Lakes farmhouse, ten miles from Ithaca, New York; he wanted to know if I was the only survivor of my childhood family. I said yes—that my father, Clayton; my mother, Grace; and my older brother and only sibling, Jack, had all died. He said that eighteen hundred dollars remained in an Olmsted Falls, Ohio, bank account in the name of Grace McConkey and her son Jack, and that he required some verification that Jack as well as Grace was dead, and proof that I was indeed the younger son. I surprised myself by being able to recall for him the dates of the deaths of my parents and brother, as well as their ages. I told him that my father had died in 1972 in Olmsted Falls on his seventy-seventh birthday, November 24th—which also, though I didn't tell him this, was the date of my parents' first marriage, in 1915, and of their remarriage, in 1938, a ceremony at which I was the only witness; that my brother had died, at fifty-six, on July 15, 1974, in a car accident at the entrance to O'Hare Airport, near Chicago; and that my mother, who in her final decade had lived with my wife and me and two of our sons, had died on December 13, 1982, a few weeks after her grandchildren and great-grandchildren—the latter all on my brother's side—had joined my family at our farmhouse for a celebration of her hundredth birthday. On the day that my mother left Olmsted Falls to live with us, she withdrew the funds

from her major account there to transfer them to another in an Ithaca bank; apparently, I said, she had forgotten about the other account, which I assumed had been set up for the monthly sums my brother and I had sent to our parents as a supplement to their Social Security checks. The caller asked me to forward to his office whatever evidence I had that I was indeed Grace's only surviving child—including, if I could find any of her correspondence, a letter containing her Olmsted Falls address. I told him I would try. But for some weeks I put it off, not wanting, especially for something so grubby as cash, to burrow into the boxes in the closet of my mother's former bedroom, which was where my wife, Jean, knowing I wasn't up to sorting through them in the Christmas season following my mother's death, had put all of Grace's possessions.

Long before I heard from the man at the Division of Unclaimed Funds, I believed I had found whatever order and meaning I could in the lives of my father, brother, and mother, since their deaths separately had recalled, with a vividness that seemed greater than actual experience, everything that bound me to each. And the death of my mother had brought all three together into a relationship with me, the survivor, that was as satisfactory as possible, existing as it did as a feeling, generalized but not abstract, that transcribed the past into a kind of complex harmony. When at last I decided to look for the documents, I found them—luckily, almost at once—among the first papers in the top box on the closet shelf. I also found, just beneath those papers, a battered little book called "By Our Fireside: A Family Record," which contains, on its opening page, a signed certificate of my parents' first marriage. The following pages are intended for the names of the wedding guests and a description of the events of the wedding trip. Later sections are for drawings of the "family crest or coat of arms" of husband and wife and for their genealogical records, details about the births and adventures of the children, and so on. Many pages are simply titled "Noteworthy Events;" others, for "Wedding Anniversaries," have a subtitle that is partially blank: "Years married _____." The entries are mainly the work of my mother, written in a script whose appearance varies with the decades; in the early years my father sometimes amplifies her remarks.

Even while I was standing on the ladder in the closet, the book in my hand, I recognized that from her middle years on my mother had put down in it, often without comment, only matters of great importance to her. Except for two entries, all of those pages that were supposed to be devoted to "Noteworthy Events" are empty. Those entries are for the deaths of my father and brother. The latter—"Jack killed," followed by the date—was in a shaky script, for my mother was ninety-two, and living with us, when the accident happened: those blunt words were probably written later during that terrible morning on which I had lain next to her on her bed to tell her over and over the news I had been awakened some hours earlier to hear on the telephone. All her faculties were acute: not fearing in the slightest her own end, she simply found it difficult to believe that one of her children had preceded her.

I sat in my mother's upholstered rocker and read the record that I had not known she kept. Sitting in this chair on rainy summer mornings or days of winter storms, my mother looked for hours at the photographs on the opposite wall, perhaps hearing in them the melody or rhythms of her own past, for they consisted of pictures of her parents; of her sister and brother, who died before she came to live with us; of her young husband; and of Jack and me as babies, young boys, and adolescents.

Those pictures are now buried in one of the boxes, but I can see all of them, and two with particular clarity. In one, taken by my mother when I was thirteen, my father is combing my hair as I sit on the stone railing of the only house—a grand half-timbered English Tudor model, in a new subdivision of Little Rock—my parents ever owned. They owned it briefly—it was lost to the bank after my father deserted his family. In the picture my ankle is bandaged, and my brother is standing behind us, holding the .22 rifle he had secretly used his school lunch money to buy, his face swollen and his mouth tightly closed so that the space where he was missing teeth would not show. I have never liked this photograph; it reminds me not only of my father's imminent departure but of my own carelessness: sitting on the handlebars while Jack gave me a downhill ride on his bicycle, I let my foot become entangled in the spokes of the front wheel. The bicycle skidded to such a quick stop that my brother was hurled over me and landed on his jaw on the pavement, splintering his upper front teeth, a harbinger of that fatal accident four decades later in which he was hurled from the back seat into the dashboard of the limousine taking him and his crew—he was captain of a commercial airliner—from the Palmer House to O'Hare Airport.

The other is a photograph of my mother and me that my brother took the following summer, after the three of us, having no money and no other place to go, went a thousand miles north to knock, without advance notice, on the front door of the Ohio house of my mother's sister and her family. To help pay for our room and board there, Jack, who had just finished high school and hoped to enter college, found a job at a dime-store hamburger stand in downtown Cleveland. My mother joined my aunt in doing the washing and ironing she took in during those Depression years to augment her husband's meager salary, and I had a newspaper route to pay for my clothes and other personal expenses. The setting of this photograph is the Lake Erie island my uncle and aunt and their children visited for a week or so at the beginning of each summer season; a relative of my uncle's gave him the use of his house on the island in return for cleaning it and starting up the old car that was kept there. In this photograph, my mother and I are sitting on the stony beach, smiling at my brother; I am, at fourteen, already much larger than my mother, who was about five feet tall.

Surprisingly, she looks not much different in the photograph from the way she looked in her nineties, maybe because her hair, still brown in Little Rock, had turned to a pure white within the year. If in her last decades she seemed to me to appear much younger than her age, as a child I knew her to look much older than the mothers of my friends. For one thing, she was thirty-eight when I was born, and, for another, her wish not to spend money unnecessarily kept her from having a missing front tooth replaced (though, of course, she insisted at once on a bridge for Jack). My father, who was thirteen years younger than she, had fallen in love with her when he was nineteen, and they were married when he was twenty; when he left her, after another nineteen years, for a younger woman, a widow who had inherited some money, my mother thought at first he had deserted her because of her missing tooth, and considered his departure her fault, for not having had it replaced. What I like about the photograph of the two of us on the beach is that my arm is around her shoulders and we both look happy.

Neither of my parents had much interest in their family trees, for my mother (except for the years of the divorce) lived for the present and my father always for the future, and so the pages in "By Our Fireside" for family crests and genealogical records are blank. In making her initial entries—those under "Wedding Guests" and "Our Wedding Trip"—my mother apparently felt the need to be faithful to certain of the book's demands; to explain the lack of names of wedding guests, for example, she wrote that she and Clayton, at least in the sense assumed by the book, "had no wedding—just went to church and were married." She went on, "My sister and Clayton's father [James, for whom I was named] only ones there. After wedding, sister went to station to meet [and here is inscribed the name of the man my aunt was later to marry], and Father came home and had dinner with us." There is no mention in that entry of what I once heard from my father: that at the dinner my grandfather said sternly to him, "Young man, you are at the table!" as he in his new happiness began to sing, or that my grandfather, then an insurance agent, had given the couple as a wedding present an insurance policy for which he had paid only the first month's premium—an unusually canny gift from a man who later, having come into some money, set up a loan agency, handed out to all clients whatever they wanted, until he had nothing left, and thenceforth lived with one or another of his children.

On the first of the pages for "Our Wedding Journey," my mother writes, much as she did for the wedding itself, "Had no wedding journey, but did have a pleasant little trip [from Cleveland] to Akron the day we were married"—a trip obviously made before the ceremony, probably so that my father could apply for a job, since they moved at once to Akron, where he became a laborer in the Goodyear plant. He held that job until he became a car salesman. Then—when he was about twenty-three—he was hired as the manager of the Cleveland Marmon agency, above whose showroom he had erected what a local newspaper referred to as "the largest advertising sign in the Western Hemisphere." (The yellowed clipping is buried in one of the boxes.) To my mother's comment about the lack of a wedding trip, my father adds a note the following summer, after a brief holiday from the Goodyear plant: "Saturday, July 1st, 1916, we took our 'wedding trip,' to Ruggles Grove, Huron, Ohio, where we ate, slept, and enjoyed ourselves for *two* days"—a vacation that, given the wages of a beginning laborer in that period, he had reason to boast of.

A section of the book called "Where We Have Lived" has space for pictures of only three houses, their addresses, and dates of occupancy, so it is just as well that my mother made no attempt to fill in this part; my parents moved a number of times before my birth, and, during my childhood, at least once a year, to cities in the North, Midwest, and South. I began the first grade in P S 99 on Long Island, for my father then managed the Brooklyn Studebaker agency, which might have had a smaller sign than did the Cleveland Marmon agency but sold more automobiles than any other Studebaker outlet in the country. Dissatisfied despite his success, he quit to help establish Michelin-tire distributorships throughout the eastern United States when that French company made its first attempt to compete with American firms in this country. He must have been an extraordinarily good salesman, for, even after Michelin shrank back to France in the early Depression years, he managed, in much the same sort of position for various American tire firms, to increase both outlets and sales. Once, as an explanation to me when I wondered at his success, he gave me a book to read, *The Man Nobody Knows*, by Bruce Barton, a New York advertising executive and United States congressman, which finds Christ to be the greatest salesman of all time, able to win disciples through his belief in his message. It was clear enough from his enthusiasm that my father believed, if but briefly, in each product he sold, but he thought that there was always a better product somewhere—one that would enable him to find his "bracket."

Despite the injury he inflicted upon his family, particularly upon his wife, I now think of him as both an innocent and the quintessential American of his period, believing as he did that one should look forward, never back, and that spiritual goals can be achieved through material ends. His ever-unfulfilled spiritual desires found a solace in organ music, which both he and my mother liked above all other forms of art, and which even as a child I thought to be crucial to the bond between them. In his annual search for a new house, he always looked for one with a fireplace, before which he could sit, an arm around my mother, while they listened to organ-music records or, on the radio, those two popular organists of the day, Al Carney and Irma Glynn.

The lovely place he finally bought for us in Normandy, the fashionable Little Rock subdivision, was the closest approximation of his bracket that he ever found in a house, for it had, in addition to a fireplace, three bathrooms and a maid's room, this last large enough for Jack and me to play pool in, on the table my father bought us. But that house also represented one last, grandiose effort on my father's part, since by then the Depression had reached its lowest depth and even a superb salesman with the finest merchandise could find nobody to buy his wares.

On the Sundays that he was at home, he always took us to a Presbyterian church that he said had the finest pipe organ in the state of Arkansas. Early one Monday morning, he kissed us all goodbye, got into his Packard, and drove away from that English Tudor house in Normandy, never to return to it. Two weeks later, he telephoned my mother from San Antonio, to say that he had fallen in love with another woman and wanted a divorce; she didn't tell Jack or me anything about that call, though we knew, from the tears she couldn't hide, that she was concealing something dreadful. Within another week, she received a letter from the woman. Disturbed by the depth of her grief, I searched for it until I found it buried beneath stockings and undergarments in her bureau drawer. The last sentence read, "Obviously, if you love your husband as much as you say you do, you will agree to a divorce out of the knowledge that he finds a greater happiness with me."

Grace hated the word "obviously" for a number of years after that, because the logic of it in that sentence entrapped her—she *did* love Clayton, and so acquiesced in the divorce. His betrayal would have been less of a shock to her had he given at any time the slightest hint that he didn't love all of us as deeply as a husband and father ever loved his wife and their children.

In the "Wedding Anniversaries" section, my mother made four entries. Here are the first three:

YEARS MARRIED 10
Grand Ave., Wauwatosa, Wis. I met Clayton at office. We had dinner at the Sky Room in the Plankinton Hotel, then we went to the Palace. On the way to the hotel, in the auto, Clayton gave me a beautiful patent leather bag. He also sent me a lovely bunch of chrysanthemums. The prettiest bouquet I ever had.

YEARS MARRIED 15
We are living at 424 South Cedar St., Little Rock, Ark. Clayton gave me another bag. A pretty brown leather one. I still liked the one he gave me 5 years ago but it looked shabby beside the new one. Had a happy anniversary.

YEARS MARRIED 19
[By November 24th of this year, 1934, the divorce papers would have been filed. We had returned to Little Rock after stays in Fort Smith and Paducah, Kentucky.] 1801 North Arthur St., Little Rock, Ark. Clayton in Louisiana. Sent him the following telegram—
"Have had nineteen gloriously happy years *with* you. May the next nineteen be as happy *for* you. With all my love,
Your wife,
Grace"

At the bottom of this page, she adds, for herself alone, these words: "The *end*."

How strange it is, to be a man of sixty-three, married for forty years and the father of three grown sons, a man who carries in his memory what he considers to be the completed melody of the family he was born into—to be such a man, reading the words of a mother who, when she wrote them, was younger than he is now, and married not quite half as long! But for a moment that last entry brought me back to a time before the melody existed, to the years during which my father was not forgiven by me, and my brother was serving as a kind of surrogate for him, and I, as the younger son, was drawn, by our loss, into an ever-closer bond with my mother. In

Let Us Now Praise Famous Men, James Agee finds it but a "small wonder" that in her "dry agony of despair a mother may fasten her talons and her vampire mouth upon the soul of her struggling son and drain him empty, light as a locust shell." This did not happen to me, perhaps because my mother kept her steadfast love for and loyalty to the absent Clayton, and lived always for the possibility of his return. Again and again, she spoke to me of the happiness and fulfillment that would come to me (as it did, as it does) in marriage—without such love, she said, life would be empty, sterile.

My brother was awarded a scholarship to General Motors Institute—an engineering college that augmented classroom studies with industrial experience—in Flint, Michigan, and my mother and I accompanied him there, hoping, vainly, that my father would send the small monthly sums of money that, in addition to the pay Jack received as a part-time worker in a spark-plug factory, would support us. Ultimately, my mother left for Cleveland to be a live-in maid for a well-to-do relative, while I, out of necessity, went to Chicago to stay with my father and stepmother, who were living beyond their means in a skyscraper apartment building on the Lake Shore. Apparently, they had already exhausted my stepmother's inheritance, for I saw at once a tension between them over the money she had brought to the marriage, and in the second month I was with them they were evicted from their luxurious suite for nonpayment of rent.

They moved into cheap quarters in a brick building on a streetcar line; it had but a single bedroom, which my stepmother insisted should be mine, even though she complained about the daybed in the living room. Whatever her motives, her generosity toward me made me feel guilty; even to smile at her was to me a betrayal of my mother. That Clayton had made his second wife unhappy seemed partly my responsibility, too, since I was his son. Sometimes at night I was awakened by the illusion that my mother was standing on the sidewalk beneath my open window, calling my name. My growing personal distress caused me to write the uncle and aunt who had taken in my mother and brother and me, to see if I could return; my aunt telephoned, telling me they loved me, and to come immediately.

Soon after I left, my stepmother divorced my father, and he continued his search for what even he at this period of his life must have recognized as unobtainable. Perhaps one who will not, or cannot, be sustained by the past, who has no present hope in his dreams, and yet whose lifelong habit is to be in motion, inevitably will move in the direction of self-destruction, toward a kind of willed defeat. My father drove his Packard south, to places where he was remembered in hotels as a valued customer. At one hotel near the Mexican border, he wrote a check for cash, using it to buy pesos, for he had heard that either the dollar or the peso was to rise in value in respect to the other, and he hoped to make a profit if he converted his currency the right way. But he converted it the wrong way. He had an insufficient sum in his bank account to cover that check, and so he drove blindly on, from city to city, staying at the best hotels and paying for his rooms with checks written on various nonexistent accounts. After six months of such frantic travel, he was, quite possibly to his relief, caught and sentenced to a three-year term at the Mansfield, Ohio, state reformatory. Upon the intercession of an industrialist grateful for his past services, he was paroled in less than a year, with the understanding that he would remarry Grace (she write, I know, a letter in his support), and with the requirement that he repay the hotels in accordance with an agreed-upon schedule. And so I was witness to my parents' second marriage—by the same clergyman who later, during my last furlough before being shipped overseas with my infantry division in the Second World War, was to marry Jean and me. My mother's final entry under "Wedding Anniversaries":

YEARS MARRIED _____
November 24, 1938. Married in Olmsted Falls, O. So very happy.

In reading the last two entries, I was surprised to discover that my parents were divorced for only four years—it means that they lived as husband and wife, usually in much harmony, for more than half a century. To me, those four years still seem a near-eternity, in which my adult nature was formed.

Despite my mother's happiness, my parents' new life together continued for several years to be troubled, for to the problems occasioned by the Depression were added those brought by the record of my father's recent past. He could not obtain, at first, any job other than as a manager of a used-car lot, his pay coming only from commissions. After much trying, he found a not much better position—one that again sent him from city to city with a salesman's valise. Since he was behind in those payments so necessary to his parole, my mother moved to a house belonging to a pair of unmarried sisters—friends of my parents from the time of their first marriage; in exchange for caring for the younger sister, who had cancer, she received free room and board for herself and for my father on weekends.

By this time, I was supporting myself while attending college by working nights as a copyboy for an afternoon Cleveland newspaper. I shared a large apartment with a reporter, a Lucky Strike salesman, and a middle-aged stenographer, and owned a secondhand car—I had paid my father a small sum for it while he was still at the used-car lot and thought I had given him the full price, but I discovered much later that he had paid out of his own pocket much more than I had given him. It was an example of a kindness that always existed within him (when, as a child, I developed a fondness for turtles, he picked them up from the highways, keeping them alive with food and water in his hotel rooms so that I could add them to my collection) but that his desertion had obscured from me.

My mother, of course, always saw that generous aspect of his character, her knowledge of it nourishing her love. She saw it even after, having found yet another woman of means, he telephoned my mother from a hotel in a central-Illinois town to ask for a second divorce. When she called me with that news, I cried, "That God-damned stupid son of a bitch," and for the only time I can remember she became angry with me, both for the sacrilege and for the attack on my father. I replied that he was at least stupid, since he needed her even more than she needed him, and that if he weren't stopped he'd end up in a greater mess than ever.

"What should we do, Jim?" my mother asked me. "He wants me to phone him tomorrow night."

"Pack your bag," I said. "I'll be at your place at six in the morning."

"What about Yvonne?"

"To hell with Yvonne. . . . No, I don't mean that. Tell her sister to take care of her or to find somebody else."

It rained throughout our journey. Neither of us spoke much, though occasionally my mother reached for my hand, and smiled at me. She was so small that I felt during that strange trip more like her father than her son. I was chiefly worried about what I would do if there was a woman with my father in the hotel room; I thought I would ask her to leave. But what if she wouldn't? At the hotel, I took my mother's bag, found out my father's room number, and escorted her to it. The door opened to my knock; my father was alone. "Here's your wife," I said, dropping the bag and pushing her so quickly into his arms that his embrace of her was part of his moment of astonishment; and then I ran downstairs to my car. It was still raining. I turned on the radio; Joe Louis was fighting somebody, I'm not sure who— though I do know that I was wrong, years later, in telling my parents that while they resolved their problems successfully enough to have decades of happiness, I was listening as Louis defeated Max Schmeling in fifteen rounds. All I really remember is that sometime after the fight ended my father was standing on the sidewalk in the rain, tapping at my closed and steamy window. "Grace is spending the night, and I've reserved a room for you," he said, pretending it was the rain that made him rub his eyes as he turned away. "I don't know why I've been a fool so long. Thanks for bringing her."

My life remained entwined with that of my parents, for, when the other occupants left my Cleveland apartment, my mother and father moved in. Upon my induction into the Army, they made it wholly their own, and they lived there for fifteen years—their longest stay at one address. During the war, my father operated a turret lathe in a defense plant. He joined the union and became a shop steward. One afternoon he lost part of a thumb to his machine but was back at work the following morning. When the war ended, he returned to salesmanship, and my mother became a bookkeeper for a painting contractor. She liked the job—particularly the task of making out checks for the painting crew. (Perhaps she enjoyed that task too much. Once, while the owner was out of town, she mailed a small Christmas bonus to all the painters, because, in her opinion, they deserved it, and the books she kept led her to know the company could readily afford such a present. Upon his return, the owner indignantly demanded that she recall all the checks. He waited until the following year to institute Christmas bonuses as a company policy.) At holiday times, the apartment would become crowded, for both Jack and I brought our families. I think of the decade and a half that my parents lived in the Cleveland apartment as a particularly fulfilling period for them, one in which my father at last was able to separate his domestic life from his dreams. That is to say, he was happy at home and faithful in his affections. He was still restless enough outside it to change jobs as rapidly as ever, but my strongest recollection of those years is of rooms filled with laughter and talk and the smells of cinnamon and yeasty cloverleaf rolls.

In his later years, my father's eagerness to have at last a business of his own led him to a final error in judgment. He bought a Kaiser-Frazer dealership in Ashtabula, Ohio, at the time that car manufacturer was failing. I was teaching in Kentucky then—it was my first full-time position— and Jean had given birth to our second son. Her mother had recently died, and she had inherited a couple of thousand dollars. Since we needed a new car, we thought we'd drive up to Ashtabula, to help my father's new business along by buying one from him. My parents were living, temporarily, in the single house along a particular, and most pleasant, section of Lake Erie shoreline that had not been boarded up. (The whole area was soon to be razed for industrial development.) As we pulled into the driveway, I saw my mother smiling at us from a little swing my father had just hung from an apple bough for our older child; it was mid-May. Some apple blossoms—reddened by a sun disappearing into the lake—had fallen on her shoulders and hair, and the sense of the transience of all things saddened me.

Instead of selling us a car, my father sold us two thousand dollars' worth of stock in his new company, for he needed the money to meet his payroll. I believe he thought he was doing us a favor; he was optimistic, and had any number of ingenious plans for making the business profitable. When the Internal Revenue Service locked the company's doors, Jean and I worried that, as stockholders, we might be held liable for some of the debts. But my father, proud of the good credit rating that he had struggled over the years to gain and that had enabled him to buy the dealership, refused to enter bankruptcy, convincing both the bank and the IRS much as he once had the parole board—of his ability to repay his debts; he was almost seventy before he paid the last of them.

Several months before my father showed the initial symptoms of cancer, my family and I visited my parents in Olmsted Falls; they had returned to the town of their second wedding to share a house with my mother's now widowed sister. During that visit, my mother took me aside to say that Clayton was worried that I had never forgiven him for his treatment of his family so many years ago; and she added, almost wistfully, "I hope, Jimmy, that he's wrong." I said, with indignation, that the courage and determination he had displayed over the years made me proud to be his son. But it was less his anxiety than her uncertainty about my ability to forgive that rankled me, and made my response close to an angry one. Though she never knew it, the seemingly infinite nature of her own mercy was a formidable quality, against which the other members of her family were forced to measure themselves; and if, at this moment, I felt defensive before that quality in her, what effect had it had upon my father in his transgressions? Since in our conversations neither he nor I ever brought up the subject of those painful years, I had thought his apparent obliviousness of them a continuing indication of a faulty or selective memory. Until she spoke to me that day of his feelings, I had not realized that he could be so vulnerable to the past to sense in me, through those subtle and unspoken ways in which family members can communicate with each other, a coldness or wariness I had refused to acknowledge in myself.

His dreams, though, remained invulnerable. While recovering from his first cancer operation, he made plans for a new business, and was still dreaming of the future at the time of his second operation. My mother, who was then about ninety, nursed him after both surgeries. The injustices and sufferings visited upon him by his illness became one in my mind with those he had visited upon his family so long ago, and I found I had truly forgiven him. Intimacy, like disdain, needs no words, and I believe he understood that I had been released from a burden I had been stubbornly carrying for decades.

Jean and I were with my parents, to celebrate my father's birthday and their twin wedding anniversaries, on the day he died. His last words were a defiant denial of reality: "I don't have cancer!" he cried, shortly after the blood began to gush from his mouth. Despite that nadir following his second wife's departure, he was no Willy Loman, and the indomitable nature of his dreams gave him a victory of spirit over death itself.

Tucked between the pages of "By Our Fireside" is a note—undated, without either salutation or signature—that my mother wrote to my father. From her handwriting, and from the references to the sunset and to my brother and me, I can attribute that note to the days after my parents left Ashtabula for an Akron apartment and my father was managing a dismal bureau of women who sold subscriptions to *Life* and *Time* through telephone solicitations; the words are my mother's way of letting him know that the loss of his business is of no consequence to her:

> The view from our home was most wonderful at all times but when the sun was setting and the sky a riot of gorgeous colors, what more could one ask for when beauty so satisfied the soul? Of course to hear Al Carney or Irma Glynn play the organ happiness is complete especially when you have a true lover husband and two fine young boys who bid fair to become well known in their chosen life work. To me boys and girls are wondrous with their youth, beauty, and enthusiasm. Roses round the door, babies on the floor, may sound soothing and sweet but I prefer them grown as our boys are. I have always preferred them as they were, tiny or big. This is my heart throb. See ya in the morning.

That note would have been written in the mid-fifties, many years after Al Carney and Irma Glynn had ceased their radio broadcasts; so my mother's preference for a given moment of her family present over any moment in the past was strengthened—even made possible—by her ability to carry into the present those values kept within her memory: sunsets of the immediate past and organ music of a more distant time. We tend to think of youth as flexible, and of age as rigid, but this is more a matter of bones than of psyches: as any longtime teacher knows, youth, always looking forward, can break before those unexpected tragedies to which age, looking back, only bends.

In her last decade with us, Grace possessed an extraordinary inner suppleness. On the dreadful morning that I had to tell her of my brother's death, she said, "Jackie," remembering him as the laughing child who on more than one occasion had slipped away from her after a bath or soaking himself with a garden hose to go running, naked and wet, down the street—an event I found faithfully recorded under "The Children" section of her book. If memories of this sort at first intensify one's sense of loss, they serve as an ultimate solace, much as do pictures on a wall.

Fortunate in the possession of sharp eyesight as well as hearing, my mother enjoyed wandering over the large back lawn on pleasant summer days, finding so many four-leaf clovers (neither Jean nor I ever found any) that they became miniature bouquets in cream pitchers or shot glasses on the dining-room table. Certain of our linguistic tendencies, including a gift for word-play, can develop with age; a sip of wine at dinner enabled her to make puns the dexterity of which I could not match until I had drunk three full glasses. She liked the summer visits that Bill, Jean's father, paid us nearly every year until his death. Although he had a pacemaker and suffered from emphysema, he smoked cigarette after cigarette. "Don't smoke," she would tell him as he reached for his pack at the breakfast table. He would grumble, "That's my gracious Gracie, always cracking the whip," and she would respond, "Somebody has to, bilious Bill," and they would both laugh, and he would put away his cigarettes for a while.

Her age allowed her—it was the only advantage she made of it—to say whatever was on her mind. When Larry, our oldest son, brought home from Philadelphia the young black woman he planned to marry, I worried that Grace, though I had never known her to display prejudice of any kind, might say something inappropriate. My mother was asleep by the time the two of them arrived, so the meeting occurred the next morning. Larry was frying bacon as his wife-to-be entered the kitchen, where Grace was sipping her coffee.

"Hello, I'm Jackie," the young woman said.

"That was the name of my older son," my mother said.

Jackie said sympathetically, "I know."

"And you're Larry's girl?"

"Yes."

"Do you love him?"

"Yes. Very much."

Perhaps feeling that such questioning might be making her nervous, Larry told Jackie to take an egg from the refrigerator. As she was bringing it to the stove, Grace said to her, "That egg looks beautiful in your hand."

Since my mother refused to take seriously any questions about her health, Jean and I found it difficult to tell if she ever was ill. One November night a few weeks before her hundredth birthday, she mysteriously slipped into a coma; we called for an ambulance to take her to the hospital. The next day, I found her in much the same condition—unconscious, or too deeply asleep to respond to my presence or words except by a barely perceptible flick of the eyelids; she was receiving oxygen and glucose through plastic tubes. While I was sitting by her bedside, her doctor arrived. He said that twice during the night she had come out of her sleep to pull the tubes loose, as if she wanted to get through her dying as quickly as possible. I said that such a wish ought to be respected, but he replied that there was a slim chance that the results of some lab tests he had ordered might provide him with a clue that could lead to her recovery.

I sat there for maybe four hours, thinking of how remote and childlike she seemed, and of how, in pulling out the life-support systems, she was behaving as I had guessed she would while I was writing a novel several years earlier. It may seem absurd that a man in his late fifties, as I was at the time I began that novel, would be worried about the grief he expected to suffer over the death of a mother thirty-eight years older than himself—a woman whose life had long since seemed as nearly complete as it could get—but one of my reasons for writing that manuscript was to imagine, as best I could, how a woman like her would die, and the effect that her death would have on a son somewhat like me, so that I would be prepared for the actual moment. Since she didn't die on this occasion, it, like the novel, was an aid to me when death did come, about six weeks later—death that, in the manner of its occurrence, brought me more happiness than I would have believed possible had I not already attributed some such feeling to the middle-aged son of my fiction.

Early on the second morning of my mother's hospital stay, her doctor phoned to say that she had made what seemed to him a remarkable recovery—for it had been without treatment of any kind—and that she was her alert former self and probably could go home in a day or so. (On the previous night, as I later was to be told, a nurse came out of my mother's room to say in astonishment to a colleague, "That dying old woman just spoke to me. I was checking to see how well she was breathing, and I whispered, 'See you later,' thinking she was comatose and wouldn't hear me even if she weren't, and she whispered back at me, 'Alligator.'")

And so she lived to greet her grandchildren and great-grandchildren on her hundredth birthday, to drink a small glass of champagne, and to munch on a piece of birthday cake. She could eat only soft foods, for an orderly at the hospital in obeying the regulation to remove the false teeth of all bed patients, had accidentally broken off the single natural tooth that kept her upper dental plate in place—the plate that, when she finally consented to having it made, filled in all the gaps in her front teeth. On the snowy day in the second week of December that she once again suddenly became comatose, I entered her bedroom to check on her condition; I was hoping, really, that she would die in her own bed before the ambulance arrived. Somehow, she knew I was there; she opened her eyes, groped for my hand, and gave me the most radiant (and the gummiest) smile that a son ever received from a dying parent. As I have said, my father's last words were "I don't have cancer!"; my mother's, which followed that smile, were "I love you."

My parents' appreciation of organ music traced back to their pleasure in the melodies played on the organs of the silent- and early talking-picture houses as well as on those of their childhood churches, and so their taste in music written or arranged for that instrument was not circumscribed. They delighted in tunes by Irving Berlin, including "Alexander's Ragtime Band" and "Always"; songs of the American West and South; lighthearted Depression ditties such as "Keep Your Sunny Side Up"; Viennese and American waltzes; Schubert's "Ave Maria"; and traditional hymns like "O God, Our Help in Ages Past." They enjoyed the humming in the organ pipes of virtuoso performances of "Flight of the Bumble Bee" and another kind of resonance to be found in Bach and Handel and Mozart.

What a mélange of tunes, unified only by the instrument upon which each piece was played! I suppose that memory, like the organ, is an instrument capable of infusing the most secular music with spiritual sounds. Despite the sadness in some of its chords, the melody of the family I was born into reverberates in my memory as if Al Carney and Irma Glynn are rendering on dual organs a song of such steadfast hope (his console) and such steadfast love (hers) that it ends up as a hallelujah.   [1985]

CYNTHIA OZICK

Julius Ozick

$$\blacksquare$$

Born in New York City in 1928, both parents Russian Jews, Cynthia Ozick grew up in the Pelham Bay section of the Bronx, a largely Irish Catholic neighborhood at the time. Isolated from her classmates at school, Ozick immersed herself in books and listened to the stories her grandmother told of the village she had left in Russia. Though her father was a pharmacist, their life during the Depression was a constant economic struggle.

By the time Ozick entered New York University in the winter of 1946, she was already caught by the allure of the intellectual world. Staring at a copy of *Partisan Review*—"the table of the gods," whose authors included all the New York intellectuals of the time—Ozick felt "their small conflagration flaming in the gray street: the succulent hotness of their promise," and was determined to "penetrate every one of them." "Listening to the 'Lesson of the Master' at the wrong time," she says, she confused the merits of Life and Art, opting in her own life for Art, abandoning human involvement, passion, and distraction for the sake of literature. Years later she described herself as "an Extreme and Hideous Example of Premature Exposure to Henry James."

After earning a B.A. in English Literature in 1949 (cum laude, Phi Beta Kappa), Cynthia Ozick went to Ohio State University, where she earned an M.A. in Literature in 1951, writing her master's thesis on the later novels of Henry James. She spent a year as a copywriter in a department store in Boston, then married and settled with her husband in New Rochelle, New York. Over the next fourteen years Cynthia Ozick wrote two long novels in the Jamesian manner, the second of which was published in 1966 with the title *Trust*. Several reviewers praised Ozick for her linguistic virtuosity, but shared critic Martin Tucker's opinion that "sometimes the cleverness of her style is obtrusive." Still, *Trust* received more attention than many first novels and Ozick became a writer worth watching.

Throughout the 1970s Ozick wrote short stories and essays. The stories were published in three collections: *The Pagan Rabbi and Other Stories* (1971), *Bloodshed and Three Novellas* (1976), and *Levitation: Five Fictions* (1982), and received a great deal of critical acclaim. Although the stories are often challenging because of their use of Jewish themes, and frequently contain fantastical elements, they nevertheless reveal Ozick as one of the best writers of serious fiction in our time. As a consequence she has received many honors, among them the O. Henry First Prize Award in fiction three times. Although she has taught occasionally as a visiting writer, most of her life Cynthia Ozick has been able, with the support of grants, to write full-time.

Her essays have been published in two collections, *Art and Ardor: Essays* (1983) and *Memory and Metaphor* (1988). The rich mandarin style that is sometimes seen as "extravagant rhetoric" in her fiction proves to be the perfect vehicle for the exotic world she recreates in her autobiographical essays. Indeed, the mandarin style often serves autobiography well, as in Vladimir Nabokov's *Speak, Memory,* Alfred Kazin's *A Walker in the City,* and James Agee's "Knoxville: Summer 1915." In the essay "Washington Square, 1946" Ozick can write "The air is smoky with New York winter grit, and on clogged Broadway a mob of trucks shifts squawking gears" and it is fine; but in fiction, where the narrator's voice should never be precisely the author's, elevated language tends to be obtrusive and distracting.

In the 1980s Ozick published two more novels, *The Cannibal Galaxy* (1983) and *The Messiah of Stockholm* (1987), both of which are compressed, rigorously conceived novels of ideas, and a very welcome return to a form she had not worked in for many years. "It is one of my life's regrets that I haven't written enough fiction; certainly not enough novels," Cynthia Ozick said in response to praise of *The Messiah of Stockholm,* and one can hope not only for more fiction, but more autobiographical essays. ∎

Washington Square, 1946

... this portion of New York appears to many persons the most delectable. It has a kind of established repose which is not of frequent occurrence in other quarters of the long, shrill city; it has a riper, richer, more honorable look than any of the upper ramifications of the great longitudinal thoroughfare—the look of having had something of a social history.
                                    – HENRY JAMES, *Washington Square*

I FIRST CAME DOWN TO WASHINGTON Square on a colorless February morning in 1946. I was seventeen and a half years old and was carrying my lunch in a brown paper bag, just as I had carried it to high school only a month before. It was—I thought it was—the opening day of spring term at Washington Square College, my initiation into my freshman year at New York University. All I knew of N.Y.U. then was that my science-minded brother had gone there; he had written from the Army that I ought to go there too. With master-of-ceremonies zest he described the Browsing Room on the second floor of the Main Building as a paradisal chamber whose bookish loungers leafed languidly through magazines and exchanged high-principled witticisms between classes. It had the sound of a carpeted Olympian club in Oliver Wendell Holmes's Boston, Hub of the Universe, strewn with leather chairs and delectable old copies of *The Yellow Book.*

On that day I had never heard of Oliver Wendell Holmes or *The Yellow Book,* and Washington Square was a faraway bower where wounded birds fell out of trees. My brother had once brought home from Washington Square Park a baby sparrow with a broken leg, to be nurtured back to flight. It died instead, emitting in its last hours melancholy faint cheeps, and leaving behind a dense recognition of the minute explicitness of mortality. All the same, in the February grayness Washington Square had the allure of the celestial unknown. A sparrow might die, but my own life was luminously new: I felt my youth like a nimbus.

Which dissolves into the dun gauze of a low and sullen city sky. And here I am flying out of the Lexington Avenue subway at Astor Place, just a few yards from Wanamaker's, here I am turning the corner past a secondhand bookstore and a union hall; already late, I begin walking very fast toward the park. The air is smoky with New York winter grit, and on clogged Broadway a mob of trucks shifts squawking gears. But there, just ahead, crisscrossed by paths under high branches, is Washington Square; and on a single sidewalk, three clear omens; or call them riddles, intricate and redolent. These I will disclose in a moment, but before that you must push open the heavy brass-and-glass doors of the Main Building, and come with me, at a hard and panting pace, into the lobby of Washington Square College on the earliest morning of the freshman year.

On the left, a bank of elevators. Straight ahead, a long burnished corridor, spooky as a lit tunnel. And empty, all empty. I can hear my solitary footsteps reverberate, as in a radio mystery drama: they lead me up a short staircase into a big dark ghost-town cafeteria. My brother's letter, along with an account of the physics and chemistry laboratories (I will never see them), has already explained that this place is called Commons—and here my heart will learn to shake with the merciless newness of life. But not today; today there is nothing. Tables and chairs squat in dead silhouette. I race back through a silent maze of halls and stairways to the brass-and-glass doors—there stands a lonely guard. From the pocket of my coat I retrieve a scrap with a classroom number on it and ask the way. The guard announces in a sly croak that the first day of school is not yet; come back tomorrow, he says.

A dumb bad joke: I'm humiliated. I've journeyed the whole way down from the end of the line—Pelham Bay, in the northeast Bronx—to find myself in desolation, all because of a muddle: Tuesday isn't Wednesday. The nimbus of expectation fades off. The lunch bag in my fist takes on a greasy sadness. I'm not ready to dive back into the subway—I'll have a look around.

Across the street from the Main Building, the three omens. First, a pretzel man with a cart. He's wearing a sweater, a cap that keeps him faceless—he's nothing but the shadows of his creases—and wool gloves with the fingertips cut off. He never moves; he might as well be made of papier-mâché, set up and left out in the open since spring. There are now almost no pretzels for sale, and this gives me a chance to inspect the construction of his bare pretzel poles. The pretzels are hooked over a column of gray cardboard cylinders, themselves looped around a stick, the way horseshoes drop around a post. The cardboard cylinders are the insides of toilet paper rolls.

The pretzel man is rooted between a Chock Full o'Nuts (that's the second omen) and a newsstand (that's the third).

The Chock Full: the doors are like fans, whirling remnants of conversation. *She will marry him. She will not marry him.* Fragrance of coffee and hot chocolate. *We can prove that the senses are partial and unreliable vehicles of information, but who is to say that reason is not equally the product of human limitation?* Powdered doughnut sugar on their lips.

Attached to a candy store, the newsstand. Copies of *Partisan Review:* the table of the gods. Jean Stafford, Mary McCarthy, Elizabeth Hardwick, Irving Howe, Delmore Schwartz, Alfred Kazin, Clement Greenberg, Stephen Spender, William Phillips, John Berryman, Saul Bellow, Philip Rahv, Richard Chase, Randall Jarrell, Simone de Beauvoir, Karl Shapiro, George Orwell! I don't know a single one of these names, but I feel their small conflagration flaming in the gray street: the succulent hotness of their promise. I mean to penetrate every one of them. Since all the money I have is my subway fare—two nickels—I don't buy a copy (the price of *Partisan* in 1946 is fifty cents); I pass on.

I pass on to the row of houses on the north side of the Square. Henry James was born in one of these, but I don't know that either. Still, they are plainly old, though no longer aristocratic: haughty last-century shabbies with shut eyelids, built of rosy-ripe respectable brick, down on their luck. Across the park bulks Judson Church, with its squat squarish bell tower; by the end of the week I will be languishing at the margins of a basketball game in its basement, forlorn in my blue left-over-from-high-school gym suit and mooning over Emily Dickinson:

> There's a certain Slant of light,
> Winter Afternoons—
> That oppresses, like the Heft
> Of Cathedral Tunes—

There is more I don't know. I don't know that W. H. Auden lives just down *there,* and might at any moment be seen striding toward home under his tall rumpled hunch; I don't know that Marianne Moore is only up the block, her doffed tricorn resting on her bedroom dresser. It's Greenwich Village—I know *that*—no more than twenty years after Edna St. Vincent Millay has sent the music of her name (her best, perhaps her only, poem) into these bohemian streets: bohemia, the honey pot of poets.

On that first day in the tea-leafed cup of the town I am ignorant, ignorant! But the three riddle-omens are soon to erupt, and all of them together will illumine Washington Square.

Begin with the benches in the Park. Here, side by side with students and their loose-leafs, lean or lie the shadows of the pretzel man, his creased ghosts or doubles: all those pitiables, half-women and half-men, neither awake nor asleep, the discountable, the repudiated, the unseen. No more notice is taken of any of them than of a scudding fragment of newspaper in the path. Even then, even so long ago, the benches of Washington Square are pimpled with this hell-tossed crew, these Mad Margarets and Cokey Joes, these volcanic coughers, shakers, groaners, tremblers, droolers, blasphemers, these public urinators with vomitous breath and rusted teeth-stumps, dead-eyed and self-abandoned, dragging their makeshift junkyard shoes, their buttonless layers of raggedy ratfur. The pretzel man with his toilet paper rolls conjures and spews them all—he is a loftier brother to these citizens of the lower pox, he is guardian of the garden of the jettisoned. They rattle along all the seams of Washington Square. They are the pickled City, the true and universal City-below-Cities, the wolfish vinegar-Babylon that dogs the spittled skirts of bohemia. The toilet paper rolls are the temple-columns of this sacred grove.

Next, the whirling doors of Chock Full o'Nuts. Here is the marketplace of Washington Square, its bazaar, its roiling gossip parlor, its matchmaker's office and arena—the outermost wing, so to speak, evolved from the Commons. On a day like today, when the Commons is closed, the Chock Full is thronged with extra power, a cello making up for a missing viola. Until now, the fire of my vitals has been for the imperious tragedians of the *Aeneid;* I have lived in the narrow throat of poetry. Another year or so of this oblivion, until at last I am hammer-struck with the shock of Europe's skull, the bled planet of death camp and war. Eleanor Roosevelt has not yet written her famous column announcing the discovery of Anne Frank's diary. The term "cold war" is new. The Commons, like the college itself, is overcrowded, veterans in their pragmatic thirties mingling with the reluctant dreamy young. And the Commons is convulsed with politics: a march to the docks is organized, no one knows by whom, to protest the arrival of Walter Gieseking, the German musician who flourished among Nazis. The Communists—two or three readily recognizable cantankerous zealots—stomp through with their daily leaflets and sneers. There is even a Monarchist, a small poker-faced rectangle of a man with secretive tireless eyes who, when approached for his views, always demands, in perfect Bronx tones, the restoration of his king. The engaged girls—how many of them there seem to be!—flash their rings and tangle their ankles in their long New Look skirts. There is no feminism and no feminists; I am, I think, the only one. The Commons is a tide: it washes up the cold war, it washes up the engaged girls' rings, it washes up the several philosophers and the numerous poets. The philosophers are all Existentialists; the poets are all influenced by "The Waste Land." When the Commons overflows, the engaged girls cross the street to show their rings at the Chock Full.

Call it density, call it intensity, call it continuity: call it, finally, society. The Commons belongs to the satirists. Here, one afternoon, is Alfred Chester, holding up a hair, a single strand, before a crowd. (He will one day write stories and novels. He will die young.) "What is that hair?" I innocently ask, having come late on the scene. "A pubic hair," he replies, and I feel as Virginia Woolf did when she declared human nature to have "changed in or about December 1910"—soon after her sister Vanessa explained away a spot on her dress as "semen."

In or about February 1946 human nature does not change; it keeps on. On my bedroom wall I tack—cut out from *Life* magazine—the wildest Picasso I can find: a face that is also a belly. Mr. George E. Mutch, a lyrical young English teacher twenty-seven years old, writes on the blackboard: "When lilacs last in the dooryard bloom'd," and "Bare, ruined choirs, where late the sweet birds sang," and "A green thought in a green shade"; he tells us to burn, like Pater, with a hard, gemlike flame. Another English teacher—his name is Emerson—compares Walt Whitman to a plumber; next year he will shoot himself in a wood. The initial letters of Washington Square College are a device to recall three of the Seven Deadly Sins: Wantonness, Sloth, Covetousness. In Commons they argue the efficacy of the orgone box. Eda Lou Walton, sprightly as a bird, knows all the Village bards, and is a Village bard herself. Sidney Hook is an intellectual rumble in the logical middle distance. Homer Watt, chairman of the English Department, is the very soul who, in a far-off time of bewitchment, hired Thomas Wolfe.

And so, in February 1946, I make my first purchase of a "real" book—which is to say, not for the classroom. It is displayed in the window of the secondhand bookstore between the Astor Place subway station and the union hall, and for weeks I have been coveting it: *Of Time and the River.* I am transfigured; I am pierced through with rapture; skipping gym, I sit among morning mists on a windy bench a foot from the stench of Mad Margaret, sinking into that cascading syrup: "Man's youth is a wonderful thing: It is so full of anguish and of magic and he never comes to know it as it is, until it is gone from him forever . . . . And what is the essence of that strange and bitter miracle of life which we feel so poignantly, so unutterably, with such a bitter pain and joy, when we are young?" Thomas Wolfe, lost, and by the wind grieved, ghost, come back again! In Washington Square I am appareled in the "numb exultant secrecies of fog, fog-numb air filled with solemn joy of nameless and impending prophecy, an ancient yellow light, the old smoke-ochre of the morning. . . ."

The smoke-ochre of the morning. Ah, you who have flung Thomas Wolfe, along with your strange and magical youth, onto the ash heap of juvenilia and excess, myself among you, isn't this a lovely phrase still? It rises out of the old pavements of Washington Square as delicately colored as an eggshell.

The veterans in their pragmatic thirties are nailed to Need; they have families and futures to attend to. When Mr. George E. Mutch exhorts them to burn with a hard, gemlike flame, and writes across the blackboard the line that reveals his own name,

> The world is too much with us; late and soon,
> Getting and spending, we lay waste our powers,

one of the veterans heckles, "What about getting a Buick, what about spending a buck?" Chester, at sixteen, is a whole year younger than I; he has transparent eyes and a rosebud mouth, and is in love with a poet named Diana. He has already found his way to the Village bars, and keeps in his wallet Truman Capote's secret telephone number. We tie our scarves tight against the cold and walk up and down Fourth Avenue, winding in and out of the rows of secondhand bookshops crammed one against the other. The proprietors sit reading their wares and never look up. The books in all their thousands smell sleepily of cellar. Our envy of them is speckled with longing; our longing is sick with envy. We are the sorrowful literary young.

Every day, month after month, I hang around the newsstand near the candy store, drilling through the enigmatic pages of *Partisan Review.* I still haven't bought a copy; I still can't understand a word. I don't know what "cold war" means. Who is Trotsky? I haven't read *Ulysses;* my adolescent phantoms are rowing in the ablative absolute with *pius* Aeneas. I'm in my mind's cradle, veiled by the exultant secrecies of fog.

Washington Square will wake me. In a lecture room in the Main Building, Dylan Thomas will cry his webwork syllables. Afterward he'll warm himself at the White Horse Tavern. Across the corridor I will see Sidney Hook plain. I will read the Bhagavad Gita and Catullus and Lessing, and, in Hebrew, a novel eerily called *Whither?* It will be years and years before I am smart enough, worldly enough, to read Alfred Kazin and Mary McCarthy.

In the spring, all of worldly Washington Square will wake up to the luster of little green leaves. [1985]

The Seam of the Snail

In my depression childhood, whenever I had a new dress, my cousin Sarah would get suspicious. The nicer the dress was, and especially the more expensive it looked, the more suspicious she would get. Finally she would lift the hem and check the seams. This was to see if the dress had been bought or if my mother had sewed it. Sarah could always tell. My mother's sewing had elegant outsides, but there was something catch-as-catch-can about the insides. Sarah's sewing, by contrast, was as impeccably finished inside as out; not one stray thread dangled.

My uncle Jake built meticulous grandfather clocks out of rosewood; he was a perfectionist, and sent to England for the clockworks. My mother built serviceable radiator covers and a serviceable cabinet, with hinged doors, for the pantry. She built a pair of bookcases for the living room. Once, after I was grown and in a house of my own, she fixed the sewer pipe. She painted ceilings, and also landscapes; she reupholstered chairs. One summer she planted a whole yard of tall corn. She thought herself capable of doing anything, and did everything she imagined. But nothing was perfect. There was always some clear flaw, never visible head-on. You had to look underneath, where the seams were. The corn thrived, though not in rows. The stalks elbowed one another like gossips in a dense little village.

"Miss Brrrroooobaker," my mother used to mock, rolling her Russian *r*'s, whenever I crossed a *t* she had left uncrossed, or corrected a word she had misspelled, or became impatient with a *v* that had tangled itself up with a *w* in her speech. ("*Vvv*entriloquist," I would say. "*Vvv*entriloquist," she would obediently repeat. And the next time it would come out "wiolinist.") Miss Brubaker was my high school English teacher, and my mother invoked her name as an emblem of raging finical obsession. "Miss Brrrroooobaker," my mother's voice hoots at me down the years, as I go on casting and recasting sentences in a tiny handwriting on monomaniacally uniform paper. The loops of my mother's handwriting—it was the Palmer Method—were as big as soup bowls, spilling generous splashy ebullience. She could pull off, at five minutes' notice, a satisfying dinner for ten concocted out of nothing more than originality and panache. But the napkin would be folded a little off center, and the spoon might be on the wrong side of the knife. She was an optimist who ignored trifles; for her, God was not in the details but in the intent. And all these culinary and agricultural efflorescences were extracurricular, accomplished in the crevices and niches of a fourteen-hour business day. When she scribbled out her family memoirs, in heaps of dog-eared notebooks, or on the backs of old bills, or on the margins of last year's calendar, I would resist typing them; in the speed of the chase she often omitted words like "the," "and," "will." The same flashing and bountiful hand fashioned and fired ceramic pots, and painted brilliant autumn views and vases of imaginary flowers and ferns, and decorated ordinary Woolworth platters with lavish enameled gardens. But bits of the painted petals would chip away.

Lavish: my mother was as lavish as nature. She woke early and saturated the hours with work and inventiveness, and read late into the night. She was all profusion, abundance, fabrication. Angry at her children, she would run after us whirling the cord of the electric iron, like a lasso or a whip; but she never caught us. When, in seventh grade, I was afraid of failing the Music Appreciation final exam because I could not tell the difference between "To a Wild Rose" and "Barcarole," she got the idea of sending me to school with a gauze sling rigged up on my writing arm, and an explanatory note that was purest fiction. But the sling kept slipping off. My mother gave advice like mad—she boiled over with so much passion for the predicaments of strangers that they turned into permanent cronies. She told intimate stories about people I had never heard of.

Despite the gargantuan Palmer loops (or possibly because of them), I have always known that my mother's was a life of—intricately abashing word!—excellence: insofar as excellence means ripe generosity. She burgeoned, she proliferated; she was endlessly leafy and flowering. She wore red hats, and called herself a gypsy. In her girlhood she marched with the suffragettes and for Margaret Sanger and called herself a Red. She made me laugh, she was so varied: like a tree on which lemons, pomegranates, and prickly pears absurdly all hang together. She had the comedy of prodigality.

My own way is a thousand times more confined. I am a pinched perfectionist, the ultimate fruition of Miss Brubaker; I attend to crabbed minutiae and am self-trammeled through taking pains. I am a kind of human snail, locked in and condemned by my own nature. The ancients believed that the moist track left by the snail as it crept was the snail's own essence, depleting its body little by little; the farther the snail toiled, the smaller it became, until it finally rubbed itself out. That is how perfectionists are. Say to us Excellence, and we will show you how we use up our substance and wear ourselves away, while making scarcely any progress at all. The fact that I am an exacting perfectionist in a narrow strait only, and nowhere else, is hardly to the point, since nothing matters to me so much as a comely and muscular sentence. It is my narrow strait, this snail's road; the track of the sentence I am writing now; and when I have eked out the wet substance, ink or blood that is its mark, I will begin the next sentence. Only in treading out sentences am I perfectionist; but then there is nothing else I know how to do, or take much interest in. I miter every pair of abutting sentences as scrupulously as Uncle Jake fitted one strip of rosewood against another. My mother's worldly and bountiful hand has escaped me. The sentence I am writing is my cabin and my shell, compact, self-sufficient. It is the burnished horizon—a merciless planet where flawlessness is the single standard, where even the inmost seams, however hidden from a laxer eye, must meet perfection. Here "excellence" is not strewn casually from a tipped cornucopia, here disorder does not account for charm, here trifles rule like tyrants.

I measure my life in sentences pressed out, line by line, like the lustrous ooze on the underside of the snail, the snail's secret open seam, its wound, leaking attar. My mother was too mettlesome to feel the force of a comma. She scorned minutiae. She measured her life according to what poured from the horn of plenty, which was her own seamless, ample, cascading, elastic, susceptible, inexact heart. My narrower heart rides between the tiny twin horns of the snail, dwindling as it goes.

And out of this thinnest thread, this ink-wet line of words, must rise a visionary fog, a mist, a smoke, forging cities, histories, sorrows, quagmires, entanglements, lives of sinners, even the life of my furnace-hearted mother: so much wilderness, waywardness, plenitude on the head of the precise and impeccable snail, between the horns. (Ah, if this could be!)   [1985]

A Drugstore in Winter

This is about reading; a drugstore in winter; the gold leaf on the dome of the Boston State House; also loss, panic, and dread.

First, the gold leaf. (This part is a little like a turn-of-the-century pulp tale, though only a little. The ending is a surprise, but there is no plot.) Thirty years ago I burrowed in the Boston Public Library one whole afternoon, to find out—not out of curiosity—how the State House got its gold roof. The answer, like the answer to most Bostonian questions, was Paul Revere. So I put Paul Revere's gold dome into an "article," and took it (though I was just as scared by recklessness then as I am now) to the *Boston Globe,* on Washington Street. The Features Editor had a bare severe head, a closed parenthesis mouth, and silver Dickensian spectacles. He made me wait, standing, at the side of his desk while he read; there was no bone in me that did not rattle. Then he opened a drawer and handed me fifteen dollars. Ah, joy of Homer, joy of Milton! Grub Street bliss!

The very next Sunday, Paul Revere's gold dome saw print. Appetite for more led me to a top-floor chamber in Filene's department store: Window Dressing. But no one was in the least bit dressed—it was a dumbstruck nudist colony up there, a mob of naked frozen enigmatic manikins, tall enameled skinny ladies with bald breasts and skulls, and legs and wrists and necks that horribly unscrewed. Paul Revere's dome paled beside this gold mine! A sight—mute numb Walpurgisnacht—easily worth another fifteen dollars. I had a Master's degree (thesis topic: "Parable in the Later Novels of Henry James") and a job as an advertising copywriter (9 A.M. to 6 P.M. six days a week, forty dollars per week; if you were male and had no degree at all, sixty dollars.) Filene's Sale Days—Crib Bolsters! Lulla-Buys! Jonnie-Mops! Maternity Skirts with Expanding Invisible Trick Waist! And a company show; gold watches to mark the retirement of elderly Irish salesladies; for me the chance to write song lyrics (to the tune of "On Top of Old Smoky") honoring our Store. But "Mute Numb Walpurgisnacht in Secret Downtown Chamber" never reached the *Globe.* Melancholy and meaning business, the Advertising Director forbade it. Grub Street was bad form, and I had to promise never again to sink to another article. Thus ended my life in journalism.

Next: reading, and certain drugstore winter dusks. These come together. It is an aeon before Filene's, years and years before the Later Novels of

Henry James. I am scrunched on my knees at a round glass table near a plate glass door on which is inscribed, in gold leaf Paul Revere never put there, letters that must be read backward: PARK VIEW PHARMACY There is an evening smell of late coffee from the fountain, and all the librarians are lined up in a row on the tall stools, sipping and chattering. They have just stepped in from the cold of the Traveling Library, and so have I. The Traveling Library is a big green truck that stops, once every two weeks, on the corner of Continental Avenue, just a little way in from Westchester Avenue, not far from a house that keeps a pig. Other houses fly pigeons from their roofs, other yards have chickens, and down on Mayflower there is even a goat. This is Pelham Bay, the Bronx, in the middle of the Depression, all cattails and weeds, such a lovely place and tender hour! Even though my mother takes me on the subway far, far downtown to buy my winter coat in the frenzy of Klein's on Fourteenth Street, and even though I can recognize the heavy power of a quarter, I don't know it's the Depression. On the trolley on the way to Westchester Square I see the children who live in the boxcar strangely set down in an empty lot some distance from Spy Oak (where a Revolutionary traitor was hanged—served him right for siding with redcoats); the lucky boxcar children dangle their stick-legs from their trainhouse maw and wave; how I envy them! I envy the orphans of the Gould Foundation, who have their own private swings and seesaws. Sometimes I imagine I am an orphan, and my father is an impostor pretending to be my father.

My father writes in his prescription book: *#59330 Dr. O'Flaherty Pow .60/ #59331 Dr. Mulligan Gtt. .65/ #59332 Dr. Thron Tab .90.* Ninety cents! A terrifically expensive medicine; someone is really sick. When I deliver a prescription around the corner or down the block, I am offered a nickel tip. I always refuse, out of conscience; I am, after all, the Park View Pharmacy's own daughter, and it wouldn't be seemly. My father grinds and mixes powders, weighs them out in tiny snowy heaps on an apothecary scale, folds them into delicate translucent papers or meticulously drops them into gelatin capsules.

In the big front window of the Park View Pharmacy there is a startling display—goldfish bowls, balanced one on the other in amazing pyramids. A German lady enters, one of my father's cronies—his cronies are both women and men. My quiet father's eyes are water-color blue, he wears his small skeptical quiet smile and receives the neighborhood's life-secrets. My father is discreet and inscrutable. The German lady pokes a punchboard with a pin, pushes up a bit of rolled paper, and cries out—she has just won a goldfish bowl, with two swimming goldfish in it! Mr. Jaffe, the salesman from McKesson & Robbins, arrives, trailing two mists: winter steaminess and the animal fog of his cigar, which melts into the coffee smell, the tarpaper smell, the eerie honeyed tangled drugstore smell. Mr. Jaffe and my mother and father are intimates by now, but because it is the 1930s, so long ago, and the old manners still survive, they address one another gravely as Mr. Jaffe, Mrs. Ozick, Mr. Ozick. My mother calls my father Mr. O, even at home, as in a Victorian novel. In the street my father tips his hat to ladies. In the winter his hat is a regular fedora; in the summer it is a straw boater with a black ribbon and a jot of blue feather.

What am I doing at this round glass table, both listening and not listening to my mother and father tell Mr. Jaffe about their struggle with "Tessie," the lion-eyed landlady who has just raised, threefold, in the middle of that Depression I have never heard of, the Park View Pharmacy's devouring rent? My mother, not yet forty, wears bandages on her ankles, covering oozing varicose veins, back and forth she strides, dashes, runs, climbing cellar stairs or ladders; she unpacks cartons, she toils behind drug counters and fountain counters. Like my father, she is on her feet until one in the morning, the Park View's closing hour. My mother and father are in trouble, and I don't know it. I am too happy. I feel the secret center of eternity, nothing will ever alter, no one will ever die. Through the window, past the lit goldfish, the gray oval sky deepens over our neighborhood wood, where all the dirt paths lead down to seagull-specked water. I am familiar with every frog-haunted monument: Pelham Bay Park is thronged with WPA art—statuary, fountains, immense rococo staircases cascading down a hillside, Bacchus-faced stelae—stone Roman glories afterward mysteriously razed by an avenging Robert Moses. One year—how distant it seems now, as if even the climate is past returning—the bay froze so hard that whole families, mine among them, crossed back and forth to City Island, strangers saluting and calling out in the ecstasy of the bright trudge over such a sudden wilderness of ice.

In the Park View Pharmacy, in the winter dusk, the heart in my body is revolving like the goldfish fleet-finned in their clear bowls. The librarians are still warming up over their coffee. They do not recognize me, though only half an hour ago I was scrabbling in the mud around the two heavy boxes from the Traveling Library—oafish crates tossed with a thump to the ground. One box contains magazines—*Boy's Life, The American Girl, Popular Mechanix*. But the other, the other! The other transforms me. It is tumbled with storybooks, with clandestine intimations and transfigurations. In school I am a luckless goosegirl, friendless and forlorn. In P.S. 71 I carry, weighty as a cloak, the ineradicable knowledge of my scandal—I am cross-eyed, dumb, an imbecile at arithmetic; in P.S. 71 I am publicly shamed in Assembly because I am caught not singing Christmas carols; in P.S. 71 I am repeatedly accused of deicide. But in the Park View Pharmacy, in the winter dusk, branches blackening in the park across the road, I am driving in rapture through the Violet Fairy Book and the Yellow Fairy Book, insubstantial chariots snatched from the box in the mud. I have never been *inside* the Traveling Library; only grownups are allowed. The boxes are for the children. No more than two books may be borrowed, so I have picked the fattest ones, to last. All the same, the Violet and the Yellow are melting away. Their pages dwindle. I sit at the round glass table, dreaming, dreaming. Mr. Jaffe is murmuring advice. He tells a joke about Wrong-Way Corrigan. The librarians are buttoning up their coats. A princess, captive of an ogre, receives a letter from her swain and hides it in her bosom. I can visualize her bosom exactly—she clutches it against her chest. It is a tall and shapely vase, with a hand-painted flower on it, like the vase on the secondhand piano at home.

I am incognito. No one knows who I truly am. The teachers in P.S. 71 don't know. Rabbi Meskin, my *cheder* teacher, doesn't know. Tessie the lion-eyed landlady doesn't know. Even Hymie the fountain clerk can't know—though he understands other things better than anyone: how to tighten roller skates with a skatekey, for instance, and how to ride a horse. On Friday afternoons, when the new issue is out, Hymie and my brother fight hard over who gets to see *Life* magazine first. My brother is older than I am, and doesn't like me; he builds radios in his bedroom, he is already W2LOM, and operates his transmitter (*da-di-da-dit, da-da-di-da*) so penetratingly on Sunday mornings that Mrs. Eva Brady, across the way, complains. Mrs. Eva Brady has a subscription to *The Writer;* I fill a closet with her old copies. How to Find a Plot. Narrative and Character, the Writer's Tools. Because my brother has his ham license, I say, "I have a license too." "What kind of license?" my brother asks, falling into the trap. "Poetic license," I reply; my brother hates me, but anyhow his birthday presents are transporting: one year *Alice in Wonderland, Pinocchio* the next, then *Tom Sawyer.* I go after Mark Twain, and find *Joan of Arc* and my first satire, *Christian Science.* My mother surprises me with *Pollyanna,* the admiration of her Lower East Side childhood, along with *The Lady of the Lake.* Mrs. Eva Brady's daughter Jeannie has outgrown her Nancy Drews and Judy Boltons, so on rainy afternoons I cross the street and borrow them, trying not to march away with too many—the child of immigrants, I worry that the Bradys, true and virtuous Americans, will judge me greedy or careless. I wrap the Nancy Drews in paper covers to protect them. Old Mrs. Brady,

Jeannie's grandmother, invites me back for more. I am so timid I can hardly speak a word, but I love her dark parlor; I love its black bookcases. Old Mrs. Brady sees me off, embracing books under an umbrella; perhaps she divines who I truly am. My brother doesn't care. My father doesn't notice. I think my mother knows. My mother reads the *Saturday Evening Post* and the *Woman's Home Companion;* sometimes the *Ladies' Home Journal,* but never *Good Housekeeping.* I read all my mother's magazines. My father reads *Drug Topics* and *Der Tog,* the Yiddish daily. In Louie Davidowitz's house (waiting our turn for the rabbi's lesson, he teaches me chess in *cheder*) there is a piece of furniture I am in awe of: a shining circular table that is also a revolving bookshelf holding a complete set of Charles Dickens. I borrow *Oliver Twist.* My cousins turn up with *Gulliver's Travels, Just So Stories, Don Quixote,* Oscar Wilde's *Fairy Tales,* uncannily different from the usual kind. Blindfolded, I reach into a Thanksgiving grabbag and pull out *Mrs. Leicester's School,* Mary Lamb's desolate stories of rejected children. Books spill out of rumor, exchange, miracle. In the Park View Pharmacy's lending library I discover, among the nurse romances, a browning, brittle miracle: *Jane Eyre.* Uncle Morris comes to visit (*his* drugstore is on the other side of the Bronx) and leaves behind, just like that, a three-volume Shakespeare. Peggy and Betty Provan, Scottish sisters around the corner, lend me their *Swiss Family Robinson.* Norma Foti, a whole year older, transmits a rumor about Louisa May Alcott; afterward I read *Little Women* a thousand times. Ten thousand! I am no longer incognito, not even to myself. I am Jo in her "vortex"; not Jo exactly, but some Jo-of-the-future. I am under an enchantment: who I truly am must be deferred, waited for and waited for. My father, silently filling capsules, is grieving over his mother in Moscow. I write letters in Yiddish to my Moscow grandmother, whom I will never know. I will know my Russian aunts, uncles, cousins. In Moscow there is suffering, deprivation, poverty. My mother, threadbare, goes without a new winter coat so that packages can be sent to Moscow. Her fiery justice-eyes are semaphores I cannot decipher.

Someday, when I am free of P.S. 71, I will write stories; meanwhile, in winter dusk, in the Park View, in the secret bliss of the Violet Fairy Book, I both see and do not see how these grains of life will stay forever, papa and mama will live forever, Hymie will always turn my skatekey.

Hymie, after Italy, after the Battle of the Bulge, comes back from the war with a present: *From Here to Eternity.* Then he dies, young. Mama reads *Pride and Prejudice* and every single word of Willa Cather. Papa reads, in Yiddish, all of Sholem Aleichem and Peretz. He reads Malamud's *The Assistant* when I ask him to.

Papa and mama, in Staten Island, are under the ground. Some other family sits transfixed in the sun parlor where I read *Jane Eyre* and *Little Women* and, long afterward, *Middlemarch*. The Park View Pharmacy is dismantled, turned into a Hallmark card shop. It doesn't matter! I close my eyes, or else only stare, and everything is in its place again, and everyone.

A writer is dreamed and transfigured into being by spells, wishes, goldfish, silhouettes of trees, boxes of fairy tales dropped in the mud, uncles' and cousins' books, tablets and capsules and powders, papa's Moscow ache, his drugstore jacket with his special fountain pen in the pocket, his beautiful Hebrew paragraphs, his Talmudist's rationalism, his Russian-Gymnasium Latin and German, mama's furnace-heart, her masses of memoirs, her paintings of autumn walks down to the sunny water, her braveries, her reveries, her old, old school hurts.

A writer is buffeted into being by school hurts—Orwell, Forster, Mann!—but after a while other ambushes begin: sorrows, deaths, disappointments, subtle diseases, delays, guilts, the spite of the private haters of the poetry side of life, the snubs of the glamorous, the bitterness of those for whom resentment is a daily gruel, and so on and so on; and then one day you find yourself leaning here, writing at that selfsame round glass table salvaged from the Park View Pharmacy—writing this, an impossibility, a summary of how you came to be where you are now, and where, God knows, is that? Your hair is whitening, you are a well of tears, what you meant to do (beauty and justice) you have not done, papa and mama are under the earth, you live in panic and dread, the future shrinks and darkens, stories are only vapor, your inmost craving is for nothing but an old scarred pen, and what, God knows, is that?   [1982]

On Permission to Write

> I hate everything that does not relate to literature, conversations bore me
> (even when they relate to literature), to visit people bores me, the joys and
> sorrows of my relatives bore me to my soul. Conversation takes the im-
> portance, the seriousness, the truth, out of everything I think.
>
> — FRANZ KAFKA, from his diary, 1918

IN A SMALL AND DEPRESSING CITY IN A
nearby state there lives a young man (I will call him David) whom I have
never met and with whom I sometimes correspond. David's letters are volu-
minous, vehemently bookish, and—in obedience to literary modernism—
without capitals. When David says "I," he writes "i." This does not mean
that he is insecure in his identity or that he suffers from a weakness of
confidence—David cannot be characterized by thumbnail psychologizing.
He is like no one else (except maybe Jane Austen). He describes himself
mostly as poor and provincial, as in Balzac, and occasionally as poor and
black. He lives alone with his forbearing and bewildered mother in a flat
"with imaginary paintings on the walls in barren rooms," writes stories and
novels, has not yet published, and appears to spend his days hauling heaps
of books back and forth from the public library.

He has read, it seems, everything. His pages are masses of flashy literary
allusions—nevertheless entirely lucid, witty, learned, and sane. David is not
exactly a crank who writes to writers, although he is probably a bit of that
too. I don't know how he gets his living, or whether his letters romanti-
cize either his poverty (he reports only a hunger for books) or his passion
(ditto); still, David is a free intellect, a free imagination. It is possible that
he hides his manuscripts under a blotter, Jane-Austenly, when his mother
creeps mutely in to collect his discarded socks. (A week's worth, perhaps,
curled on the floor next to Faulkner and Updike and Cummings and
Tristram Shandy. Of the latter he remarks: "a worthy book. dare any man
get offspring on less?")

On the other hand, David wants to be noticed. He wants to be paid
attention to. Otherwise, why would he address charming letters to writers
(I am not the only one) he has never met? Like Joyce in "dirty provincial
Dublin," he says, he means to announce his "inevitable arrival on the
mainland." A stranger's eye, even for a letter, is a kind of publication.

David, far from insisting on privacy, is a would-be public man. It may be that he pants after fame. And yet in his immediate position—his secret literary life, whether or not he intends it to remain secret—there is something delectable. He thirsts to read, so he reads; he thirsts to write, so he writes. He is in the private cave of his freedom, an eremite, a solitary; he orders his mind as he pleases. In this condition he is prolific. He writes and writes. Ah, he is poor and provincial, in a dim lost corner of the world. But his lonely place (a bare cubicle joyfully tumbling with library books) and his lonely situation (the liberty to be zealous) have given him the permission to write. To be, in fact, prolific.

I am not like David. I am not poor, or provincial (except in the New York way), or unpublished, or black. (David, the sovereign of his life, invents an aloofness from social disabilities, at least in his letters, and I have not heard him mythologize "negritude"; he admires poets for their words and cadences.) But all this is not the essential reason I am not like David. I am not like him because I do not own his permission to write freely, and zealously, and at will, and however I damn please; and abundantly; and always.

There is this difference between the prolific and the non-prolific: the prolific have arrogated to themselves the permission to write.

By permission I suppose I ought to mean *inner* permission. Now "inner permission" is a phrase requiring high caution: it was handed to me by a Freudian dogmatist, a writer whose energy and confidence depend on regular visits to his psychoanalyst. In a useful essay called "Art and Neurosis," Lionel Trilling warns against the misapplication of Freud's dictum that "we are all ill, i.e., neurotic," and insists that a writer's productivity derives from "the one part of him that is healthy, by any conceivable definition of health . . . that which gives him the power to conceive, to plan, to work, and to bring his work to a conclusion." The capacity to write, in short, comes from an uncharted space over which even all-prevailing neurosis can have no jurisdiction or dominion. "The use to which [the artist] puts his power . . . may be discussed with reference to his particular neurosis," Trilling concedes; yet Trilling's verdict is finally steel: "But its essence is irreducible. It is, as we say, a gift."

If permission to write (and for a writer this is exactly equal to the power to write) is a gift, then what of the lack of permission? Does the missing "Go ahead" mean neurosis? I am at heart one of those hapless pre-moderns who believe that the light bulb is the head of a demon called forth by the light switch, and that Freud is a German word for pleasure; so I am not equipped to speak about principles of electricity or psychoanalysis. All the same, it seems to me that the electrifying idea of inward obstacle—neurosis—is not nearly so often responsible for low productivity as we are told. Writer's permission is not something that is switched off by helpless forces inside the writer, but by social currents—human beings and their ordinary predilections and prejudices—outside. If David writes freely and others don't, the reason might be that, at least for a while, David has kidnapped himself beyond the pinch of society. He is Jane Austen with her hidden manuscript momentarily slipped out from under the blotter; he is Thoreau in his cabin. He is a free man alone in a room with imaginary pictures on the walls, reading and writing in a private rapture.

There are some writers who think of themselves as shamans, dervishes of inspiration, divinely possessed ecstatics—writers who believe with Emerson that the artist "has cast off the common motives of humanity and has ventured to trust himself for a taskmaster": himself above everyone. Emerson it is who advises writers to aspire, through isolation, to "a simple purpose . . . as strong as iron necessity is to others," and who—in reply to every contingency—exhorts, "O father, O mother, O wife, O brother, O friend, I have lived with you after appearances hitherto. Henceforward I am the truth's." These shaman-writers, with their cult of individual genius and romantic egoism, may be self-glamorizing holy madmen, but they are not maniacs; they know what is good for them, and what is good for them is fences. You cannot get near them, whatever your need or demand. O father, O mother, O wife, O brother, O friend, they will tell you—*beat it*. They call themselves caviar, and for the general their caviar is a caveat.

Most writers are more modest than this, and more reasonable, and don't style themselves as unbridled creatures celestially privileged and driven. They know that they are citizens like other citizens, and have simply chosen a profession, as others have. These are the writers who go docilely to gatherings where they are required to marvel at every baby; who yield slavishly to the ukase that sends them out for days at a time to scout a samovar for the birthday of an elderly great-uncle; who pretend to overnight guests that they are capable of sitting at the breakfast table without being consumed by print; who craftily let on to in-laws that they are diligent cooks and sheltering wives, though they would sacrifice a husband to a hurricane to fetch them a typewriter ribbon; and so on. In short, they work at appearances, trust others for taskmasters, and do not insist too rigorously on whose truth they will live after. And they are honorable enough. In company, they do their best to dress like everyone else: if they are women they will tolerate panty hose and high-heeled shoes, if they are men they will show up in a three-piece suit; but in either case they will be concealing the fact that during any ordinary row of days they sleep in their clothes. In the same company they lend themselves, decade after decade, to the expectation that they will not lay claim to unusual passions, that they will believe the average belief, that they will take pleasure in the average pleasure. Dickens, foreseeing the pain of relinquishing his pen at a time not of his choosing, reportedly would not accept an invitation. "Thank God for books," Auden said, "as an alternative to conversation." Good-citizen writers, by contrast, year after year decline no summons, refuse no banquet, turn away from no tedium, willingly enter into every anecdote and brook the assault of any amplified band. They will put down their pens for a noodle pudding.

And with all this sterling obedience, this strenuous courtliness and congeniality, this anxious flattery of unspoken coercion down to the third generation, something goes wrong. One dinner in twenty years is missed. Or no dinner at all is missed, but an "attitude" is somehow detected. No one is fooled; the cordiality is pronounced insincere, the smile a fake, the goodwill a dud, the talk a fib, the cosseting a cozening. These sweating citizen-writers are in the end always found out and accused. They are accused of elitism. They are accused of snobbery. They are accused of loving books and bookishness more feelingly than flesh and blood.

Edith Wharton, in her cool and bitter way, remarked of the literary life that "in my own family it created a kind of restraint that grew with the years. None of my relations ever spoke to me of my books, either to praise or to blame—they simply ignored them; . . . the subject was avoided as if it were a kind of family disgrace, which might be condoned but could not be forgotten."

Good-citizen writers are not read by their accusers; perhaps they cannot be. "If I succeed," said Conrad, "you shall find there according to your deserts: encouragement, consolation, fear, charm—all you demand—and, perhaps, also that glimpse of truth for which you have forgotten to ask." But some never demand, or demand less. "If you simplified your style," a strict but kindly aunt will advise, "you might come up to par," and her standard does not exempt Conrad.

The muse-inspired shaman-writers are never called snobs, for the plain reason that no strict but kindly aunt will ever get within a foot of any of them. But the good-citizen writers—by virtue of their very try at citizenship—are suspect and resented. Their work will not be taken for work. They will always be condemned for not being interchangeable with nurses or salesmen or schoolteachers or accountants or brokers. They will always be found out. They will always be seen to turn longingly after a torn peacock's tail left over from a fugitive sighting of paradise. They will always have hanging from a back pocket a telltale shred of idealism, or a cache of a few grains of noble importuning, or, if nothing so grandly quizzical, then a single beautiful word, in Latin or Hebrew; or else they will tip their hand at the wedding feast by complaining meekly of the raging horn that obliterates the human voice; or else they will forget not to fall into Montaigne over the morning toast; or else they will embarrass everyone by oafishly banging on the kettle of history; or else, while the room fills up with small talk, they will glaze over and inwardly chant "This Lime-Tree Bower My Prison"; or else—but never mind. What is not understood is not allowed. These citizen-pretenders will never be respectable. They will never come up to par. They will always be blamed for their airs. They will always be charged with superiority, disloyalty, coldness, want of family feeling. They will always be charged with estranging their wives, husbands, children. They will always be called snob.

They will never be granted the permission to write as serious writers are obliged to write: fanatically, obsessively, consumingly, torrentially, above all comically—and for life.

And therefore: enviable blissful provincial prolific lonesome David!

[1984]

ALICE WALKER

Jean Weisinger

ALICE WALKER WAS BORN IN EATONTON, Georgia, on February 9, 1944, the eighth child of Willie Lee and Minnie Lou Walker, black sharecroppers. In many of her essays Walker documents the harshness of their life in those days, the "hard work in the fields, the shabby houses, the evil greedy men who worked my father to death and almost broke the courage" of her mother, and of how "on hot Saturday afternoons of my childhood I gazed longingly through the window of the corner drugstore where white youngsters sat on stools in air-conditioned comfort and drank Cokes and nibbled ice-cream cones." And yet, looking back on her childhood, she also recalls "neighborly kindness and sustaining love" and "the Georgia countryside where I fished and swam and walked through fields of black-eyed Susans."

Early in her teens Alice Walker began seeing the world beyond Eatonton, spending her summers in Boston with older brothers and sisters who had already moved north. In 1961 she was awarded a scholarship to attend Spelman College in Atlanta, and the following summer was selected to attend a World Youth Peace Festival in Helsinki, Finland. It was also during her freshman year at Spelman that she heard Dr. Martin Luther King, Jr., for the first time: "I have often thought that if it had not been for . . . Dr. King, I would have come of age believing in nothing and no one. As it was, my life, like that of millions of black young Southerners, seemed to find its beginning and its purpose at the precise moment I first heard him speak." In the summer of 1963 she rode a bus from Boston to Washington to sit "perched on the limb of a tree far from the Lincoln Center" while Dr. King delivered his eloquent "I Have a Dream" speech to hundreds of thousands of Freedom Marchers.

In 1964, disillusioned with the conservative, middle-class values she found at Spelman, Walker transferred to Sarah Lawrence College, and it was there, during an intense week of writing in the winter of her senior year, that she wrote her first book of poems. "Each morning, the poems finished during the night were stuffed under Muriel Rukeyser's door—her classroom was an old gardener's cottage in the middle of the campus. Then I would hurry back to my room to write some more. I didn't care what she did with the poems. I only knew I wanted someone to read them as if they were new leaves sprouting from an old tree." What Muriel Rukeyser, a distinguished poet, did with the poems was to send them to her agent, who gave them to an editor at a major publishing house, who immediately accepted them for publication. Alice Walker had just turned twenty-one.

Following her graduation from Sarah Lawrence in 1965, Walker went back to Georgia for the summer to register black voters, then returned north to attend the Bread Loaf Writers' Conference on a scholarship. She took a job with the New York City Welfare Department, but left in 1967 when she won a writing fellowship from the Ingram Merrill Foundation. By now her stories and essays were beginning to appear in magazines and anthologies (such as *Voices of the Revolution* and *The Best Short Stories by Negro Writers from 1899 to the Present,* both published in 1967), and she was awarded a residency at The MacDowell Colony, an artists' retreat.

That same year, 1967, she married Mel Leventhal, a young lawyer, and they moved to Jackson, Mississippi, where Leventhal prosecuted the Jackson school-desegregation cases. As "the only interracial, married, home-owning couple in Mississippi," their life in Jackson was one of constant taunts and threats: "All the while," Walker has written, "there was the fear that my young husband would not return from one of his trips to visit his clients in the Mississippi backwoods." Though Walker was also involved with the civil rights movement—working in the Head Start program, teaching black studies at Jackson State College—she does not consider herself to have been a "true activist." Rather, she says that she "sat in a book-lined study and wrote" and "when I was working well and the poems and stories grew, I had no time to think of" social and political issues. During the late sixties and early seventies she wrote her first novel, *The Third Life of George Copeland* (1970); her second poetry collection, *Revolutionary Petunias and Other Poems* (1973); her first collection of short stories, *In Love and Trouble: Stories of Black Women* (1973); and a biography of Langston Hughes for young readers.

In 1971, needing "a change from Mississippi," Alice Walker moved to Boston with her infant daughter and spent the next year-and-a-half supported by a fellowship from the Radcliffe Institute and teaching part-time at Wellesley College and the Boston campus of the University of Massachusetts. Returning to Mississippi in 1973—ten years after the March on Washington—Walker found that since most of the civil rights battles had been won, the new black middle class—"the very class that owes its new affluence to the Movement"—had "abandoned itself to the pursuit of cars, expensive furniture, large houses, and the finest Scotch," and "now refuses to support the organizations that made its success possible, and has retreated from its concern for black people who are poor." Disillusioned, Walker and Leventhal left Mississippi and moved to Brooklyn, where he now sued racist landlords and she wrote an elegiac novel about the Movement (*Meridian*, 1976).

In 1974 Alice Walker began a long association with *Ms.* magazine when it published her essay "In Search of Our Mothers' Gardens." Focusing on the neglect and mistreatment of black women throughout history, Walker became a leading spokesperson for black feminism, and coined a word to describe the characteristics of such a person: *womanist.* (See *In Search of Our Mothers' Gardens*, 1983.) In 1976 Walker and Leventhal were divorced.

By 1979 her next novel began forming itself in her mind: she speaks of her characters "trying to contact me, to speak *through* me." But being "country people," they "refused even to visit" her in New York. So Walker disposed of the house she had only three months earlier bought and moved west to California, settling finally in the countryside north of San Francisco, in a place that "looked a lot like the town in Georgia most of them were from." And there they came freely, and the novel flowed. *The Color Purple* was published in 1982 and won both the Pulitzer Prize and American Book Award for fiction in 1983. The quality that most distinguishes *The Color Purple* is the voice of its narrator, Celie, and the other characters who speak through her; and even though the things that happen to them are tragic, the voices are joyous. And that is the same quality one finds in Alice Walker's own voice, and which raises it above polemics, despite the gravity of her subject matter.

Over the past few years Alice Walker has continued to publish prolifically: in 1987 a new collection of essays, *Living by the Word;* in 1989, a novel, *The Temple of My Familiar;* in 1991, her complete poems from 1965 to 1990, *Her Blue Body Everything We Know: Earthling Poems;* and in 1992, *Possessing the Secret of Joy,* a novel about a tribal African woman who suffers the trauma of genital mutilation. ∎

Brothers and Sisters

WE LIVED ON A FARM IN THE SOUTH in the fifties, and my brothers, the four of them I knew (the fifth had left home when I was three years old), were allowed to watch animals being mated. This was not unusual; nor was it considered unusual that my older sister and I were frowned upon if we even asked, innocently, what was going on. One of my brothers explained the mating one day, using words my father had given him: "The bull is getting a little something on his stick," he said. And he laughed. "What stick?" I wanted to know. "Where did he get it? How did he pick it up? Where did he put it?" All my brothers laughed.

I believe my mother's theory about raising a large family of five boys and three girls was that the father should teach the boys and the mother teach the girls the facts, as one says, of life. So my father went around talking about bulls getting something on their sticks and she went around saying girls did not need to know about such things. They were "womanish" (a very bad way to be in those days) if they asked.

The thing was, watching the matings filled my brothers with an aimless sort of lust, as dangerous as it was unintentional. They knew enough to know that cows, months after mating, produced calves, but they were not bright enough to make the same connection between women and their offspring.

Sometimes, when I think of my childhood, it seems to me a particularly hard one. But in reality, everything awful that happened to me didn't seem to happen to *me* at all, but to my older sister. Through some incredible power to negate my presence around people I did not like, which produced invisibility (as well as an ability to appear mentally vacant when I was nothing of the kind), I was spared the humiliation she was subjected to, though at the same time, I felt every bit of it. It was as if she suffered for my benefit, and I vowed early in my life that none of the things that made existence so miserable for her would happen to me.

The fact that she was not allowed at official matings did not mean she never saw any. While my brothers followed my father to the mating pens on the other side of the road near the barn, she stationed herself near the pigpen, or followed our many dogs until they were in a mating mood, or, failing to witness something there, she watched the chickens. On a farm it is impossible *not* to be conscious of sex, to wonder about it, to dream . . . but to whom was she to speak of her feelings? Not to my father, who thought all young women perverse. Not to my mother, who pretended all her children grew out of stumps she magically found in the forest. Not to me, who never found anything wrong with this lie.

When my sister menstruated she wore a thick packet of clean rags between her legs. It stuck out in front like a penis. The boys laughed at her as she served them at the table. Not knowing any better, and because our parents did not dream of actually *discussing* what was going on, she would giggle nervously at herself. I hated her for giggling, and it was at those times I would think of her as dim-witted. She never complained, but she began to have strange fainting fits whenever she had her period. Her head felt as if it were splitting, she said, and everything she ate came up again. And her cramps were so severe she could not stand. She was forced to spend several days of each month in bed.

My father expected all of his sons to have sex with women. "Like bulls," he said, "a man *needs* to get a little something on his stick." And so, on Saturday nights, into town they went, chasing the girls. My sister was rarely allowed into town alone, and if the dress she wore fit too snugly at the waist, or if her cleavage dipped too far below her collarbone, she was made to stay home.

"But why can't I go too," she would cry, her face screwed up with the effort not to wail.

"They're boys, your brothers, *that's* why they can go."

Naturally, when she got the chance, she responded eagerly to boys. But when this was discovered she was whipped and locked up in her room.

I would go in to visit her.

"Straight Pine," she would say, "you don't know what it *feels* like to want to be loved by a man."

"And if this is what you get for feeling like it I never will," I said, with—I hoped—the right combination of sympathy and disgust.

"Men smell so good," she would whisper ecstatically. "And when they look into your eyes, you just melt."

Since they were so hard to catch, naturally she thought almost any of them terrific.

"Oh, that Alfred!" she would moon over some mediocre, square-headed boy, "he's so *sweet!*" And she would take his ugly picture out of her bosom and kiss it.

My father was always warning her not to come home if she ever found herself pregnant. My mother constantly reminded her that abortion was a sin. Later, although she never became pregnant, her period would not come for months at a time. The painful symptoms, however, never varied or ceased. She fell for the first man who loved her enough to beat her for looking at someone else, and when I was still in high school, she married him.

My fifth brother, the one I never knew, was said to be different from the rest. He had not liked matings. He would not watch them. He thought the cows should be given a choice. My father had disliked him because he was soft. My mother took up for him. "Jason is just tender-hearted," she would say in a way that made me know he was her favorite; "he takes after me." It was true that my mother cried about almost anything.

Who was this oldest brother? I wondered.

"Well," said my mother, "he was someone who always loved you. Of course he was a great big boy when you were born and out working on his own. He worked on a road gang building roads. Every morning before he left he would come in the room where you were and pick you up and give you the biggest kisses. He used to look at you and just smile. It's a pity you don't remember him."

I agreed.

At my father's funeral I finally "met" my oldest brother. He is tall and black with thick gray hair above a young-looking face. I watched my sister cry over my father until she blacked out from grief. I saw my brothers sobbing, reminding each other of what a great father he had been. My oldest brother and I did not shed a tear between us. When I left my father's grave he came up and introduced himself. "You don't ever have to walk alone," he said, and put his arms around me.

One out of five ain't *too* bad, I thought, snuggling up.

But I didn't discover until recently his true uniqueness: He is the only one of my brothers who assumes responsibility for all his children. The other four all fathered children during those Saturday-night chases of twenty years ago. Children—my nieces and nephews whom I will probably never know—they neither acknowledge as their own, provide for, or even see.

It was not until I became a student of women's liberation ideology that I could understand and forgive my father. I needed an ideology that would define his behavior in context. The black movement had given me an ideology that helped explain his colorism (he *did* fall in love with my mother partly because she was so light; he never denied it). Feminism helped explain his sexism. I was relieved to know his sexist behavior was not something uniquely his own, but, rather, an imitation of the behavior of the society around us.

All partisan movements add to the fullness of our understanding of society as a whole. They never detract; or, in any case, one must not allow them to do so. Experience adds to experience. "The more things the better," as O'Connor and Welty both have said, speaking, one of marriage, the other of Catholicism.

I desperately needed my father and brothers to give me male models I could respect, because white men (for example; being particularly handy in this sort of comparison)—whether in films or in person—offered man as dominator, as killer, and always as hypocrite.

My father failed because he copied the hypocrisy. And my brothers—except for one—never understood they must represent half the world to me, as I must represent the other half to them.   [1975]

Beauty: When the Other Dancer Is the Self

IT IS A BRIGHT SUMMER DAY IN 1947. My father, a fat, funny man with beautiful eyes and a subversive wit, is trying to decide which of his eight children he will take with him to the county fair. My mother, of course, will not go. She is knocked out from getting most of us ready: I hold my neck stiff against the pressure of her knuckles as she hastily completes the braiding and then beribboning of my hair.

My father is the driver for the rich old white lady up the road. Her name is Miss Mey. She owns all the land for miles around, as well as the house in which we live. All I remember about her is that she once offered to pay my mother thirty-five cents for cleaning her house, raking up piles of her magnolia leaves, and washing her family's clothes, and that my mother—she of no money, eight children, and a chronic earache—refused it. But I do not think of this in 1947. I am two and a half years old. I want to go everywhere my daddy goes. I am excited at the prospect of riding in a car. Someone has told me fairs are fun. That there is room in the car for only three of us doesn't faze me at all. Whirling happily in my starchy frock, showing off my biscuit-polished patent-leather shoes and lavender socks, tossing my head in a way that makes my ribbons bounce, I stand, hands on hips, before my father. "Take me, Daddy," I say with assurance: "I'm the prettiest!"

Later, it does not surprise me to find myself in Miss Mey's shiny black car, sharing the back seat with the other lucky ones. Does not surprise me that I thoroughly enjoy the fair. At home that night I tell the unlucky ones all I can remember about the merry-go-round, the man who eats live chickens, and the teddy bears, until they say: that's enough, baby Alice. Shut up now, and go to sleep.

It is Easter Sunday, 1950. I am dressed in a green, flocked, scalloped-hem dress (handmade by my adoring sister, Ruth) that has its own smooth satin petticoat and tiny hot-pink roses tucked into each scallop. My shoes, new T-strap patent leather, again highly biscuit-polished. I am six years old and have learned one of the longest Easter speeches to be heard that day, totally unlike the speech I said when I was two: "Easter lilies/pure and white/blossom in/the morning light." When I rise to give my speech I do so on a great wave of love and pride and expectation. People in the church stop rustling their new crinolines. They seem to hold their breath. I can tell they admire my dress, but it is my spirit, bordering on sassiness (woman-ishness), they secretly applaud.

"That girl's a little *mess*," they whisper to each other, pleased.

Naturally I say my speech without stammer or pause, unlike those who stutter, stammer, or, worst of all, forget. This is before the word "beautiful" exists in people's vocabulary, but "Oh, isn't she the *cutest* thing!" frequently floats my way. "And got so much sense!" they gratefully add . . . for which thoughtful addition I thank them to this day.

It was great fun being cute. But then, one day, it ended.

I am eight years old and a tomboy. I have a cowboy hat, cowboy boots, checkered shirt and pants, all red. My playmates are my brothers, two and four years older than I. Their colors are black and green, the only difference in the way we are dressed. On Saturday nights we all go to the picture show, even my mother; Westerns are her favorite kind of movie. Back home, "on the ranch," we pretend we are Tom Mix, Hopalong Cassidy, Lash LaRue (we've even named one of our dogs Lash LaRue); we chase each other for hours rustling cattle, being outlaws, delivering damsels from distress. Then my parents decide to buy my brothers guns. These are not "real" guns. They shoot "BBs," copper pellets my brothers say will kill birds. Because I am a girl, I do not get a gun. Instantly I am relegated to the position of Indian. Now there appears a great distance between us. They shoot and shoot at everything with their new guns. I try to keep up with my bow and arrows.

One day while I am standing on top of our makeshift "garage"—pieces of tin nailed across some poles—holding my bow and arrow and looking out toward the fields, I feel an incredible blow in my right eye. I look down just in time to see my brother lower his gun.

Both brothers rush to my side. My eye stings, and I cover it with my hand. "If you tell," they say, "we will get a whipping. You don't want that to happen, do you?" I do not. "Here is a piece of wire," says the older brother, picking it up from the roof; "say you stepped on one end of it and the other flew up and hit you." The pain is beginning to start. "Yes," I say. "Yes, I will say that is what happened." If I do not say this is what happened, I know my brothers will find ways to make me wish I had. But now I will say anything that gets me to my mother.

Confronted by our parents we stick to the lie agreed upon. They place me on a bench on the porch and I close my left eye while they examine the right. There is a tree growing from underneath the porch that climbs past the railing to the roof. It is the last thing my right eye sees. I watch as its trunk, its branches, and then its leaves are blotted out by the rising blood.

I am in shock. First there is intense fever, which my father tries to break using lily leaves bound around my head. Then there are chills: my mother tries to get me to eat soup. Eventually, I do not know how, my parents learn what has happened. A week after the "accident" they take me to see a doctor. "Why did you wait so long to come?" he asks, looking into my eye and shaking his head. "Eyes are sympathetic," he says. "If one is blind, the other will likely become blind too."

This comment of the doctor's terrifies me. But it is really how I look that bothers me most. Where the BB pellet struck there is a glob of whitish scar tissue, a hideous cataract, on my eye. Now when I stare at people—a favorite pastime, up to now—they will stare back. Not at the "cute" little girl, but at her scar. For six years I do not stare at anyone, because I do not raise my head.

Years later, in the throes of a mid-life crisis, I ask my mother and sister whether I changed after the "accident." "No," they say, puzzled. "What do you mean?"

What do I mean?

I am eight, and, for the first time, doing poorly in school, where I have been something of a whiz since I was four. We have just moved to the place where the "accident" occurred. We do not know any of the people around us because this is a different county. The only time I see the friends I knew is when we go back to our old church. The new school is the former state penitentiary. It is a large stone building, cold and drafty, crammed to overflowing with boisterous, ill-disciplined children. On the third floor there is a huge circular imprint of some partition that has been torn out.

"What used to be here?" I ask a sullen girl next to me on our way past it to lunch.

"The electric chair," says she.

At night I have nightmares about the electric chair, and about all the people reputedly "fried" in it. I am afraid of the school, where all the students seem to be budding criminals.

"What's the matter with your eye?" they ask, critically.

When I don't answer (I cannot decide whether it was an "accident" or not), they shove me, insist on a fight.

My brother, the one who created the story about the wire, comes to my rescue. But then brags so much about "protecting" me, I become sick.

After months of torture at the school, my parents decide to send me back to our old community, to my old school. I live with my grandparents and the teacher they board. But there is no room for Phoebe, my cat. By the time my grandparents decide there *is* room, and I ask for my cat, she cannot be found. Miss Yarborough, the boarding teacher, takes me under her wing, and begins to teach me to play the piano. But soon she marries an African—a "prince," she says—and is whisked away to his continent.

At my old school there is at least one teacher who loves me. She is the teacher who "knew me before I was born" and bought my first baby clothes. It is she who makes life bearable. It is her presence that finally helps me turn on the one child at the school who continually calls me "one-eyed bitch." One day I simply grab him by his coat and beat him until I am satisfied. It is my teacher who tells me my mother is ill.

My mother is lying in bed in the middle of the day, something I have never seen. She is in too much pain to speak. She has an abscess in her ear. I stand looking down on her, knowing that if she dies, I cannot live. She is being treated with warm oils and hot bricks held against her cheek. Finally a doctor comes. But I must go back to my grandparents' house. The weeks pass but I am hardly aware of it. All I know is that my mother might die, my father is not so jolly, my brothers still have their guns, and I am the one sent away from home.

"You did not change," they say.

Did I imagine the anguish of never looking up?

I am twelve. When relatives come to visit I hide in my room. My cousin Brenda, just my age, whose father works in the post office and whose mother is a nurse, comes to find me. "Hello," she says. And then she asks, looking at my recent school picture, which I did not want taken, and on which the "glob," as I think of it, is clearly visible, "You still can't see out of that eye?"

"No," I say, and flop back on the bed over my book.

That night, as I do almost every night, I abuse my eye. I rant and rave at it, in front of the mirror. I plead with it to clear up before morning. I tell it I hate and despise it. I do not pray for sight. I pray for beauty.

"You did not change," they say.

I am fourteen and baby-sitting for my brother Bill, who lives in Boston. He is my favorite brother and there is a strong bond between us. Understanding my feelings of shame and ugliness he and his wife take me to a local hospital, where the "glob" is removed by a doctor named O. Henry. There is still a small bluish crater where the scar tissue was, but the ugly white stuff is gone. Almost immediately I become a different person from the girl who does not raise her head. Or so I think. Now that I've raised my head I win the boyfriend of my dreams. Now that I've raised my head I have plenty of friends. Now that I've raised my head classwork comes from my lips as faultlessly as Easter speeches did, and I leave high school as valedictorian, most popular student, and *queen,* hardly believing my luck. Ironically, the girl who was voted most beautiful in our class (and was) was later shot twice through the chest by a male companion, using a "real" gun, while she was pregnant. But that's another story in itself. Or is it?

"You did not change," they say.

It is now thirty years since the "accident." A beautiful journalist comes to visit and to interview me. She is going to write a cover story for her magazine that focuses on my latest book. "Decide how you want to look on the cover," she says. "Glamorous, or whatever."

Never mind "glamorous," it is the "whatever" that I hear. Suddenly all I can think of is whether I will get enough sleep the night before the photography session: if I don't, my eye will be tired and wander, as blind eyes will.

At night in bed with my lover I think up reasons why I should not appear on the cover of a magazine. "My meanest critics will say I've sold out," I say. "My family will now realize I write scandalous books."

"But what's the real reason you don't want to do this?" he asks.

"Because in all probability," I say in a rush, "my eye won't be straight."

"It will be straight enough," he says. Then, "Besides, I thought you'd made your peace with that."

And I suddenly remember that I have.

I remember:

I am talking to my brother Jimmy, asking if he remembers anything unusual about the day I was shot. He does not know I consider that day the last time my father, with his sweet home remedy of cool lily leaves, chose me, and that I suffered and raged inside because of this. "Well," he says, "all I remember is standing by the side of the highway with Daddy, trying to flag down a car. A white man stopped, but when Daddy said he needed somebody to take his little girl to the doctor, he drove off."

I remember:

I am in the desert for the first time. I fall totally in love with it. I am so overwhelmed by its beauty, I confront for the first time, consciously, the meaning of the doctor's words years ago: "Eyes are sympathetic. If one is blind, the other will likely become blind too." I realize I have dashed about the world madly, looking at this, looking at that, storing up images against the fading of the light. *But I might have missed seeing the desert!* The shock of that possibility—and gratitude for over twenty-five years of sight—sends me literally to my knees. Poem after poem comes—which is perhaps how poets pray.

ON SIGHT

I am so thankful I have seen
The Desert
And the creatures in the desert
And the desert Itself.

The desert has its own moon
Which I have seen
With my own eye.
There is no flag on it.

Trees of the desert have arms
All of which are always up

That is because the moon is up
The sun is up
Also the sky
The stars
Clouds
None with flags.

If there *were* flags, I doubt
the trees would point.
Would you?

But mostly, I remember this:
I am twenty-seven, and my baby daughter is almost three. Since her birth I have worried about her discovery that her mother's eyes are different from other people's. Will she be embarrassed? I think. What will she say? Every day she watches a television program called "Big Blue Marble." It begins with a picture of the earth as it appears from the moon. It is bluish, a little battered-looking, but full of light, with whitish clouds swirling around it. Every time I see it I weep with love, as if it is a picture of Grandma's house. One day when I am putting Rebecca down for her nap, she suddenly focuses on my eye. Something inside me cringes, gets ready to try to protect myself. All children are cruel about physical differences, I know from experience, and that they don't always mean to be is another matter. I assume Rebecca will be the same.

But no-o-o-o. She studies my face intently as we stand, her inside and me outside her crib. She even holds my face maternally between her dimpled little hands. Then, looking every bit as serious and lawyerlike as her father, she says, as if it may just possibly have slipped my attention: "Mommy, there's a *world* in your eye." (As in, "Don't be alarmed, or do anything crazy.") And then, gently, but with great interest: "Mommy, where did you *get* that world in your eye?"

For the most part, the pain left then. (So what, if my brothers grew up to buy even more powerful pellet guns for their sons and to carry real guns themselves. So what, if a young "Morehouse man" once nearly fell off the steps of Trevor Arnett Library because he thought my eyes were blue.) Crying and laughing I ran to the bathroom, while Rebecca mumbled and sang herself off to sleep. Yes indeed, I realized, looking into the mirror. There *was* a world in my eye. And I saw that it was possible to love it: that in fact, for all it had taught me of shame and anger and inner vision, I *did* love it. Even to see it drifting out of orbit in boredom, or rolling up out of fatigue, not to mention floating back at attention in excitement (bearing witness, a friend has called it), deeply suitable to my personality, and even characteristic of me.

That night I dream I am dancing to Stevie Wonder's song "Always" (the name of the song is really "As," but I hear it as "Always"). As I dance, whirling and joyous, happier than I've ever been in my life, another bright-faced dancer joins me. We dance and kiss each other and hold each other through the night. The other dancer has obviously come through all right, as I have done. She is beautiful, whole and free. And she is also me.   [1983]

In Search of Our Mothers' Gardens

I described her own nature and temperament. Told how they needed a larger life for their expression. . . . I pointed out that in lieu of proper channels, her emotions had overflowed into paths that dissipated them. I talked, beautifully I thought, about an art that would be born, an art that would open the way for women the likes of her. I asked her to hope, and build up an inner life against the coming of that day. . . . I sang, with a strange quiver in my voice, a promise song.

— JEAN TOOMER, "Avey," *Cane*

THE POET SPEAKING TO A PROSTITUTE who falls asleep while he's talking—

When the poet Jean Toomer walked through the South in the early twenties, he discovered a curious thing: black women whose spirituality was so intense, so deep, so *unconscious,* that they were themselves unaware of the richness they held. They stumbled blindly through their lives: creatures so abused and mutilated in body, so dimmed and confused by pain, that they considered themselves unworthy even of hope. In the selfless abstractions their bodies became to the men who used them, they became more than "sexual objects," more even than mere women: they became "Saints." Instead of being perceived as whole persons, their bodies became shrines: what was thought to be their minds became temples suitable for worship. These crazy Saints stared out at the world, wildly, like lunatics— or quietly, like suicides; and the "God" that was in their gaze was as mute as a great stone.

Who were these Saints? These crazy, loony, pitiful women?

Some of them, without a doubt, were our mothers and grandmothers.

In the still heat of the post-Reconstruction South, this is how they seemed to Jean Toomer: exquisite butterflies trapped in an evil honey, toiling away their lives in an era, a century, that did not acknowledge them, except as "the *mule* of the world." They dreamed dreams that no one knew—not even themselves, in any coherent fashion—and saw visions no one could understand. They wandered or sat about the countryside crooning lullabies to ghosts, and drawing the mother of Christ in charcoal on courthouse walls.

They forced their minds to desert their bodies and their striving spirits sought to rise, like frail whirlwinds from the hard red clay. And when those frail whirlwinds fell, in scattered particles, upon the ground, no one mourned. Instead, men lit candles to celebrate the emptiness that remained, as people do who enter a beautiful but vacant space to resurrect a God.

Our mothers and grandmothers, some of them: moving to music not yet written. And they waited.

They waited for a day when the unknown thing that was in them would be made known; but guessed, somehow in their darkness, that on the day of their revelation they would be long dead. Therefore to Toomer they walked, and even ran, in slow motion. For they were going nowhere immediate, and the future was not yet within their grasp. And men took our mothers and grandmothers, "but got no pleasure from it." So complex was their passion and their calm.

To Toomer, they lay vacant and fallow as autumn fields, with harvest time never in sight: and he saw them enter loveless marriages, without joy; and become prostitutes, without resistance; and become mothers of children, without fulfillment.

For these grandmothers and mothers of ours were not Saints, but Artists; driven to a numb and bleeding madness by the springs of creativity in them for which there was no release. They were Creators, who lived lives of spiritual waste, because they were so rich in spirituality—which is the basis of Art—that the strain of enduring their unused and unwanted talent drove them insane. Throwing away this spirituality was their pathetic attempt to lighten the soul to a weight their work-worn, sexually abused bodies could bear.

What did it mean for a black woman to be an artist in our grandmothers' time? In our great-grandmothers' day? It is a question with an answer cruel enough to stop the blood.

Did you have a genius of a great-great-grandmother who died under some ignorant and depraved white overseer's lash? Or was she required to bake biscuits for a lazy backwater tramp, when she cried out in her soul to paint watercolors of sunsets, or the rain falling on the green and peaceful pasturelands? Or was her body broken and forced to bear children (who were more often than not sold away from her)—eight, ten, fifteen, twenty children—when her one joy was the thought of modeling heroic figures of rebellion, in stone or clay?

How was the creativity of the black woman kept alive, year after year and century after century, when for most of the years black people have been in America, it was a punishable crime for a black person to read or write? And the freedom to paint, to sculpt, to expand the mind with action did not exist. Consider, if you can bear to imagine it, what might have been the result if singing, too, had been forbidden by law. Listen to the voices of Bessie Smith, Billie Holiday, Nina Simone, Roberta Flack, and Aretha Franklin, among others, and imagine those voices muzzled for life. Then you may begin to comprehend the lives of our "crazy," "Sainted" mothers and grandmothers. The agony of the lives of women who might have been Poets, Novelists, Essayists, and Short-Story Writers (over a period of centuries), who died with their real gifts stifled within them.

And, if this were the end of the story, we would have cause to cry out in my paraphrase of Okot p'Bitek's great poem:

> O, my clanswomen
> Let us all cry together!
> Come,
> Let us mourn the death of our mother,
> The death of a Queen
> The ash that was produced
> By a great fire!
> O, this homestead is utterly dead
> Close the gates

With *lacari* thorns,
For our mother
The creator of the Stool is lost!
And all the young women
Have perished in the wilderness!

But this is not the end of the story, for all the young women—our mothers and grandmothers, *ourselves*—have not perished in the wilderness. And if we ask ourselves why, and search for and find the answer, we will know beyond all efforts to erase it from our minds, just exactly who, and of what, we black American women are.

One example, perhaps the most pathetic, most misunderstood one, can provide a backdrop for our mothers' work: Phillis Wheatley, a slave in the 1700s.

Virginia Woolf, in her book *A Room of One's Own,* wrote that in order for a woman to write fiction she must have two things, certainly: a room of her own (with key and lock) and enough money to support herself.

What then are we to make of Phillis Wheatley, a slave, who owned not even herself? This sickly, frail black girl who required a servant of her own at times—her health was so precarious—and who, had she been white, would have been easily considered the intellectual superior of all the women and most of the men in the society of her day.

Virginia Woolf wrote further, speaking of course not of our Phillis, that "any woman born with a great gift in the sixteenth century [insert "eighteenth century," insert "black woman," insert "born or made a slave"] would certainly have gone crazed, shot herself, or ended her days in some lonely cottage outside the village, half witch, half wizard [insert "Saint"], feared and mocked at. For it needs little skill and psychology to be sure that a highly gifted girl who had tried to use her gift for poetry would have been so thwarted and hindered by contrary instincts [add "chains, guns, the lash, the ownership of one's body by someone else, submission to an alien religion"], that she must have lost her health and sanity to a certainty."

The key words, as they relate to Phillis, are "contrary instincts." For when we read the poetry of Phillis Wheatley—as when we read the novels of Nella Larsen or the oddly false-sounding autobiography of that freest of all black women writers, Zora Hurston—evidence of "contrary instincts" is everywhere. Her loyalties were completely divided, as was, without question, her mind.

But how could this be otherwise? Captured at seven, a slave of wealthy, doting whites who instilled in her the "savagery" of the Africa they "rescued" her from . . . one wonders if she was even able to remember her homeland as she had known it, or as it really was.

Yet, because she did try to use her gift for poetry in a world that made her a slave, she was "so thwarted and hindered by . . . contrary instincts, that she . . . lost her health. . . ." In the last years of her brief life, burdened not only with the need to express her gift but also with a penniless, friendless "freedom" and several small children for whom she was forced to do strenuous work to feed, she lost her health, certainly. Suffering from malnutrition and neglect and who knows what mental agonies, Phillis Wheatley died.

So torn by "contrary instincts" was black, kidnapped, enslaved Phillis that her description of "the Goddess"—as she poetically called the Liberty she did not have—is ironically, cruelly humorous. And, in fact, has held Phillis up to ridicule for more than a century. It is usually read prior to hanging Phillis's memory as that of a fool. She wrote:

> The Goddess comes, she moves divinely fair,
> Olive and laurel binds her *golden* hair.
> Wherever shines this native of the skies,
> Unnumber'd charms and recent graces rise. [My italics]

It is obvious that Phillis, the slave, combed the "Goddess's" hair every morning; prior, perhaps, to bringing in the milk, or fixing her mistress's lunch. She took her imagery from the one thing she saw elevated above all others.

With the benefit of hindsight we ask, "How could she?"

But at last, Phillis, we understand. No more snickering when your stiff, struggling, ambivalent lines are forced on us. We know now that you were not an idiot or a traitor; only a sickly little black girl, snatched from your home and country and made a slave; a woman who still struggled to sing the song that was your gift, although in a land of barbarians who praised you for your bewildered tongue. It is not so much what you sang, as that you kept alive, in so many of our ancestors, *the notion of song.*

Black women are called, in the folklore that so aptly identifies one's status in society, "the *mule* of the world," because we have been handed the burdens that everyone else—*everyone* else—refused to carry. We have also been called "Matriarchs," "Superwomen," and "Mean and Evil Bitches." Not to mention "Castraters" and "Sapphire's Mama." When we have pleaded for understanding, our character has been distorted; when we have asked for simple caring, we have been handed empty inspirational appellations, then stuck in the farthest corner. When we have asked for love, we have been given children. In short, even our plainer gifts, our labors of fidelity and love, have been knocked down our throats. To be an artist and a black woman, even today, lowers our status in many respects, rather than raises it: and yet, artists we will be.

Therefore we must fearlessly pull out of ourselves and look at and identify with our lives the living creativity some of our great-grandmothers were not allowed to know. I stress *some* of them because it is well known that the majority of our great-grandmothers knew, even without "knowing" it, the reality of their spirituality, even if they didn't recognize it beyond what happened in the singing at church—and they never had any intention of giving it up.

How they did it—those millions of black women who were not Phillis Wheatley, or Lucy Terry or Frances Harper or Zora Hurston or Nella Larsen or Bessie Smith; or Elizabeth Catlett, or Katherine Dunham, either—brings me to the title of this essay, "In Search of Our Mothers' Gardens," which is a personal account that is yet shared, in its theme and its meaning, by all of us. I found, while thinking about the far-reaching world of the creative black woman, that often the truest answer to a question that really matters can be found very close.

In the late 1920s my mother ran away from home to marry my father. Marriage, if not running away, was expected of seventeen-year-old girls. By the time she was twenty, she had two children and was pregnant with a third. Five children later, I was born. And this is how I came to know my mother: she seemed a large, soft, loving-eyed woman who was rarely impatient in our home. Her quick, violent temper was on view only a few times a year, when she battled with the white landlord who had the misfortune to suggest to her that her children did not need to go to school.

She made all the clothes we wore, even my brothers' overalls. She made all the towels and sheets we used. She spent the summers canning vegetables and fruits. She spent the winter evenings making quilts enough to cover all our beds.

During the "working" day, she labored beside—not behind—my father in the fields. Her day began before sunup, and did not end until late at night. There was never a moment for her to sit down, undisturbed, to unravel her own private thoughts; never a time free from interruption—by work or the noisy inquiries of her many children. And yet, it is to my mother—and all our mothers who were not famous—that I went in search of the secret of what has fed that muzzled and often mutilated, but vibrant, creative spirit that the black woman has inherited, and that pops out in wild and unlikely places to this day.

But when, you will ask, did my overworked mother have time to know or care about feeding the creative spirit?

The answer is so simple that many of us have spent years discovering it. We have constantly looked high, when we should have looked high—and low.

For example: in the Smithsonian Institution in Washington, D.C., there hangs a quilt unlike any other in the world. In fanciful, inspired, and yet simple and identifiable figures, it portrays the story of the Crucifixion. It is considered rare, beyond price. Though it follows no known pattern of quilt-making, and though it is made of bits and pieces of worthless rags, it is obviously the work of a person of powerful imagination and deep spiritual feeling. Below this quilt I saw a note that says it was made by "an anonymous Black woman in Alabama, a hundred years ago."

If we could locate this "anonymous" black woman from Alabama, she would turn out to be one of our grandmothers—an artist who left her mark in the only materials she could afford, and in the only medium her position in society allowed her to use.

As Virginia Woolf wrote further, in *A Room of One's Own:*

> Yet genius of a sort must have existed among women as it must have existed among the working class. [Change this to "slaves" and "the wives and daughters of sharecroppers."] Now and again an Emily Brontë or a Robert Burns [change this to "a Zora Hurston or a Richard Wright"] blazes out and proves its presence. But certainly it never got itself on to paper. When, however, one reads of a witch being ducked, of a woman possessed by devils [or "Sainthood"], of a wise woman selling herbs [our root workers], or even a very remarkable man who had a mother, then I think we are on the track of a lost novelist, a suppressed poet, of some mute and inglorious Jane Austen. . . . Indeed, I would venture to guess that Anon, who wrote so many poems without signing them, was often a woman. . . .

And so our mothers and grandmothers have, more often than not anonymously, handed on the creative spark, the seed of the flower they themselves never hoped to see: or like a sealed letter they could not plainly read.

And so it is, certainly, with my own mother. Unlike "Ma" Rainey's songs, which retained their creator's name even while blasting forth from Bessie Smith's mouth, no song or poem will bear my mother's name. Yet so many of the stories that I write, that we all write, are my mother's stories. Only recently did I fully realize this: that through years of listening to my mother's stories of her life, I have absorbed not only the stories themselves, but something of the manner in which she spoke, something of the urgency that involves the knowledge that her stories—like her life—must be recorded. It is probably for this reason that so much of what I have written is about characters whose counterparts in real life are so much older than I am.

But the telling of these stories, which came from my mother's lips as naturally as breathing, was not the only way my mother showed herself as an artist. For stories, too, were subject to being distracted, to dying without conclusion. Dinners must be started, and cotton must be gathered before the big rains. The artist that was and is my mother showed itself to me only after many years. This is what I finally noticed:

Like Mem, a character in *The Third Life of Grange Copeland,* my mother adorned with flowers whatever shabby house we were forced to live in. And not just your typical straggly country stand of zinnias, either. She planted ambitious gardens—and still does—with over fifty different varieties of plants that bloom profusely from early March until late November. Before she left home for the fields, she watered her flowers, chopped up the grass, and laid out new beds. When she returned from the fields she might divide clumps of bulbs, dig a cold pit, uproot and replant roses, or prune branches from her taller bushes or trees—until night came and it was too dark to see.

Whatever she planted grew as if by magic, and her fame as a grower of flowers spread over three counties. Because of her creativity with her flowers, even my memories of poverty are seen through a screen of blooms—sunflowers, petunias, roses, dahlias, forsythia, spirea, delphiniums, verbena . . . and on and on.

And I remember people coming to my mother's yard to be given cuttings from her flowers; I hear again the praise showered on her because whatever rocky soil she landed on, she turned into a garden. A garden so brilliant with colors, so original in its design, so magnificent with life and creativity, that to this day people drive by our house in Georgia—perfect strangers and imperfect strangers—and ask to stand or walk among my mother's art.

I notice that it is only when my mother is working in her flowers that she is radiant, almost to the point of being invisible—except as Creator: hand and eye. She is involved in work her soul must have. Ordering the universe in the image of her personal conception of Beauty.

Her face, as she prepares the Art that is her gift, is a legacy of respect she leaves to me, for all that illuminates and cherishes life. She has handed down respect for the possibilities—and the will to grasp them.

For her, so hindered and intruded upon in so many ways, being an artist has still been a daily part of her life. This ability to hold on, even in very simple ways, is work black women have done for a very long time.

This poem is not enough, but it is something, for the woman who literally covered the holes in our walls with sunflowers:

> They were women then
> My mama's generation
> Husky of voice—Stout of
> Step
> With fists as well as
> Hands
> How they battered down
> Doors
> And ironed
> Starched white
> Shirts
> How they led
> Armies
> Headragged Generals
> Across mined
> Fields
> Booby-trapped
> Kitchens
> To discover books
> Desks
> A place for us
> How they knew what we
> *Must* know
> Without knowing a page
> Of it
> Themselves.

Guided by my heritage of a love of beauty and a respect for strength—in search of my mother's garden, I found my own.

And perhaps in Africa over two hundred years ago, there was just such a mother; perhaps she painted vivid and daring decorations in oranges and yellows and greens on the walls of her hut; perhaps she sang—in a voice like

Roberta Flack's —*sweetly* over the compounds of her village; perhaps she wove the most stunning mats or told the most ingenious stories of all the village storytellers. Perhaps she was herself a poet—though only her daughter's name is signed to the poems that we know.

Perhaps Phillis Wheatley's mother was also an artist.

Perhaps in more than Phillis Wheatley's biological life is her mother's signature made clear.   [1974]

Journey to Nine Miles

By five o'clock we were awake, listening to the soothing slapping of the surf, and watching the sky redden over the ocean. By six we were dressed and knocking on my daughter's door. She and her friend Kevin were going with us (Robert and me) to visit Nine Miles, the birthplace of someone we all loved, Bob Marley. It was Christmas Day, bright, sunny, and very warm and the traditional day of thanksgiving for the birth of someone sacred.

I missed Bob Marley when his body was alive, and I have often wondered how that could possibly be. It happened, though, because when he was singing all over the world, I was living in Mississippi, being political, digging into my own his/herstory, writing books, having a baby—and listening to local music, B. B. King, and the Beatles. I liked dreadlocks, but only because I am an Aquarian; I was unwilling to look beyond the sexism of Rastafarianism. The music stayed outside my consciousness. It didn't help either that the most political and spiritual of reggae music was suppressed in the United States, so that "Stir It Up," and not "Natty Dread" or "Lively Up Yourself" or "Exodus," was what one heard. And then, of course, there *was* disco, a music so blatantly soulless as to be frightening, and impossible to do anything to but exercise.

I first really *heard* Bob Marley when I was in the throes of writing a draft of the screenplay for *The Color Purple*. Each Monday I drove up to my studio in the country, a taxing three-hour drive, worked steadily until Friday, drove back to the city, and tried to be two parents to my daughter on weekends. We kept in touch by phone during the week, and I had the impression that she was late for school every day and living on chocolates. (No *way*! She always smiled innocently.)

My friends Jan and Chris, a white couple nearby, seeing my stress, offered their help, which I accepted in the form of dinner at their house every night after a day's work on the script. One night after yet another sumptuous meal, we pushed back the table and, in our frustration at the pain that rides on the seat next to joy in life (cancer, pollution, invasions, the bomb), began dancing to reggae records: UB-40, Black Uhuru . . . Bob Marley. I was transfixed. It was hard to believe the beauty of the soul I heard in "No Woman No Cry," "Coming In from the Cold," "Could You Be Loved?," "Three Little Birds," and "Redemption Song." Here was a man who loved his roots, even after he'd been nearly assassinated in his own country, and knew they extended to the ends of the earth. Here was a soul who loved Jamaica and loved Jamaicans and loved *being* a Jamaican (nobody got more pleasure out of the history, myths, traditions, and language of Jamaica than Bob Marley) but who knew it was not meant to limit itself, or even could, to an island of any sort. Here was the radical peasant-class, working-class consciousness that fearlessly denounced the Wasichus (the greedy and destructive) and did it with such grace you could dance to it. Here was a man of extraordinary sensitivity, political acumen, spiritual power, and sexual wildness; a free spirit if ever there was one. Here, I felt, was my brother. It was as if there had been a great and gorgeous light on all over the world, and somehow I'd missed it. Every night for the next two months I listened to Bob Marley. I danced with his spirit—so much more alive still than many people walking around. I felt my own dreadlocks begin to grow.

Over time, the draft of the script I was writing was finished. My evenings with my friends came to an end. My love of Marley spread easily over my family, and it was as neophyte rastas, having decided that "rasta" for us meant a commitment to a religion of attentiveness and joy, that we appeared when we visited Jamaica in 1984.

What we saw is a ravaged land, a place where people, often rastas, eat out of garbage cans and where, one afternoon in a beach café during a rainstorm, I overheard a thirteen-year-old boy offer, along with some Jamaican pot, his eleven-year-old sister (whose grownup's earrings looked larger, almost, than her face) to a large, hirsute American white man (who blushingly declined).

The car we rented, from a harried, hostile dealer who didn't even seem to want to tell us where to buy gas, had already had two flats. On the way to Nine Miles it had three more. Eventually, however, after an agonizing seven hours from Negril, where we were staying, blessing the car at every bump in the road, to encourage it to live through the trip, we arrived.

Nine Miles, because it is nine miles from the nearest village of any size, is one of the stillest and most isolated spots on the face of the earth. It is only several houses, spread out around the top of a hill. There are small, poor farms, with bananas appearing to be the predominant crop.

Several men and many children come down the hill to meet our car. They know we've come to visit Bob. They walk with us up the hill where Bob Marley's body is entombed in a small mausoleum with stained-glass windows; the nicest building in Nine Miles. Next to it is a small one-room house where Bob and his wife, Rita, lived briefly during their marriage. I think of how much energy Bob Marley had to generate to project himself into the world beyond this materially impoverished place; and of how exhausted, in so many of his later photographs, he looked. On the other hand, it is easy to understand—listening to the deep stillness that makes a jet soaring overhead sound like the buzzing of a fly—why he wanted to be brought back to his home village, back to Nine Miles, to rest. We see the tomb from a distance of about fifty feet, because we cannot pass through, or climb over, an immense chain-link fence that has recently been erected to keep the too eager (and apparently destructive and kleptomaniacal) tourists at bay. One thing that I like very much: built into the hill facing Bob's tomb is a permanent stage. On his birthday, February 6, someone tells us, people from all over the world come to Nine Miles to sing to him.

The villagers around us are obviously sorry about the fence. Perhaps we were not the ones intended to be kept out? Their faces seem to say as much. They are all men and boys. No women or girls among them. On a front porch below the hill I see some women and girls, studiously avoiding us.

One young man, the caretaker, tells us that, though we can't go in, there *is* a way we can get closer to Bob. I almost tell him I could hardly *be* any closer to Bob and still be alive, but I don't want to try to explain. He points out a path that climbs the side of the hill, and we—assisted by half a dozen of the more agile villagers—take it. It passes through bananas and weeds, flowers, past goats tethered out of the sun, past chickens. Past the home, one says, of Bob Marley's cousin, a broken but gallant-looking man in his fifties, nearly toothless, and with a gentle and generous smile. He sits in his tiny, bare house and watches us. His face is radiant with the pride of relationship.

From within the compound now we hear singing. Bob's songs come from the lips of the caretaker, who says he and Bob were friends. That he loved Bob. Loved his music. He sings terribly. But perhaps this is only because he is, though about the age Bob would have been now, early forties, lacking his front teeth. He is very dark, and quite handsome, teeth or no. And it is his humble, terrible singing—as he moves proprietarily about the yard where his friend is enshrined—that makes him so. It is as if he sings Bob's songs *for* Bob, in an attempt to animate the tomb. The little children are all about us, nearly underfoot. Beautiful children. One little boy is right beside me. He is about six, of browner skin than the rest—who are nearer to black—with curlier hair. He looks like Bob.

I ask his name. He tells me. I have since forgotten it. As we linger by the fence, our fingers touch. For a while we hold hands. I notice that over the door to the tomb someone has plastered a bumper sticker with the name of Rita Marley's latest album. It reads: "Good Girls Culture." I am offended by it; there are so many possible meanings. For a moment I try to imagine the sticker plastered across Bob's forehead. It drops off immediately, washed away by his sweat (as he sings and dances in the shamanistic trance I so love) and his spirit's inability to be possessed by anyone other than itself, and Jah. The caretaker says Rita erected the fence. I understand the necessity.

Soon it is time to go. We clamber back down the hill to the car. On the way down the little boy who looks like Bob asks for money. Thinking of our hands together and how he is so like Bob must have been at his age, I don't want to give him money. But what else can I give him, I wonder.

I consult "the elders," the little band of adults who've gathered about us.

"The children are asking for money," I say. "What should we do?"

"You should give it" is the prompt reply. So swift and unstudied is the answer, in fact, that suddenly the question seems absurd.

"They ask because they have none. There is nothing here."

"Would Bob approve?" I ask. Then I think, Probably. The man has had himself planted here to fund the village.

"Yes" is the reply. "Because he would understand."

Starting with the children, but by no means stopping there, because the grownups look as expectant as they, we part with some of our "tourist" dollars, realizing that tourism is a dead thing, a thing of the past; that no one can be a tourist anymore, and that, like Bob, all of us can find our deepest rest at home.

It is a long, hot, anxious drive that we have ahead of us. We make our usual supplications to our little tin car and its four shiny tires. But even when we have another flat, bringing us to our fourth for the trip, it hardly touches us. Jamaica is a poor country reduced to selling its living and its dead while much of the world thinks of it as "real estate" and a great place to lie in the sun; but Jamaicans as a people have been seen in all their imperfections and beauty by one of their own and fiercely affirmed, even from the grave, and loved. There is no poverty, only richness in this. We sing "Redemption Song" as we change the tire; feeling very Jamaica, very Bob, very rasta, very *no woman no cry*. [1986]

A SAMPLER OF ESSAYS
FROM PREVIOUS EDITIONS

MAX BEERBOHM
A Relic

E. M. FORSTER
My Wood

D. H. LAWRENCE
Adolf

JAMES THURBER
The Dog That Bit People

EDMUND WILSON
The Old Stone House

NORMAN MAILER
Miami Beach

LEWIS THOMAS
On Natural Death

PAUL FUSSELL
The Boy Scout Handbook

CAROL BLY
Getting Tired

EDWARD HOAGLAND
The Courage of Turtles

MAX BEERBOHM

A Relic

Y ESTERDAY I FOUND IN A CUPBOARD
an old, small, battered portmanteau which, by the initials on it, I recognized as my own property. The lock appeared to have been forced. I
dimly remembered having forced it myself, with a poker, in my hot youth,
after some journey in which I had lost the key; and this act of violence was
probably the reason why the trunk had so long ago ceased to travel. I un-
strapped it, not without dust; it exhaled the faint scent of its long closure;
it contained a tweed suit of Late Victorian pattern, some bills, some letters,
a collar-stud, and—something which, after I had wondered for a moment
or two what on earth it was, caused me suddenly to murmur, "Down
below, the sea rustled to and fro over the shingle."

Strange that these words had, year after long year, been existing in some
obscure cell at the back of my brain!—forgotten but all the while existing,
like the trunk in that cupboard. What released them, what threw open the
cell door, was nothing but the fragment of a fan; just the butt-end of an
inexpensive fan. The sticks are of white bone, clipped together with a semi-
circular ring that is not silver. They are neatly oval at the base, but variously
jagged at the other end. The longest of them measures perhaps two inches.
Ring and all, they have no market value; for a farthing is the least coin in
our currency. And yet, though I had so long forgotten them, for me they
are not worthless. They touch a chord . . . Lest this confession raise false
hopes in the reader, I add that I did not know their owner.

I did once see her, and in Normandy, and by moonlight, and her name
was Angélique. She was graceful, she was even beautiful. I was but nineteen
years old. Yet even so I cannot say that she impressed me favorably. I was
seated at a table of a café on the terrace of a casino. I sat facing the sea, with
my back to the casino. I sat listening to the quiet sea, which I had crossed
that morning. The hour was late, there were few people about. I heard the
swing-door behind me flap open, and was aware of a sharp snapping and
crackling sound as a lady in white passed quickly by me. I stared at her erect
thin back and her agitated elbows. A short fat man passed in pursuit of
her—an elderly man in a black alpaca jacket that billowed. I saw that she
had left a trail of little white things on the asphalt. I watched the efforts of
the agonized short fat man to overtake her as she swept wraithlike away to
the distant end of the terrace. What was the matter? What had made her

so spectacularly angry with him? The three or four waiters of the café were exchanging cynical smiles and shrugs, as waiters will. I tried to feel cynical, but was thrilled with excitement, with wonder and curiosity. The woman out yonder had doubled on her tracks. She had not slackened her furious speed, but the man waddlingly contrived to keep pace with her now. With every moment they became more distinct, and the prospect that they would presently pass by me, back into the casino, gave me that physical tension which one feels on a wayside platform at the imminent passing of an express. In the rushingly enlarged vision I had of them, the wrath on the woman's face was even more saliently the main thing than I had supposed it would be. That very hard Parisian face must have been as white as the powder that coated it. "Écoute, Angélique," gasped the perspiring bourgeois, "écoute, je te supplie—" The swing-door received them and was left swinging to and fro. I wanted to follow, but had not paid for my bock. I beckoned my waiter. On his way to me he stooped down and picked up something which, with a smile and a shrug, he laid on my table: "Il semble que Mademoiselle ne s'en servira plus." This is the thing I now write of, and at sight of it I understood why there had been that snapping and crackling, and what the white fragments on the ground were.

I hurried through the rooms, hoping to see a continuation of that drama—a scene of appeasement, perhaps, or of fury still implacable. But the two oddly assorted players were not performing there. My waiter had told me he had not seen either of them before. I suppose they had arrived that day. But I was not destined to see either of them again. They went away, I suppose, next morning; jointly or singly; singly, I imagine.

They made, however, a prolonged stay in my young memory, and would have done so even had I not had that tangible memento of them. Who were they, those two of whom that one strange glimpse had befallen me? What, I wondered, was the previous history of each? What, in particular, had all that tragic pother been about? Mlle. Angélique I guessed to be thirty years old, her friend perhaps fifty-five. Each of their faces was as clear to me as in the moment of actual vision—the man's fat shiny bewildered face; the taut white face of the woman, the hard red line of her mouth, the eyes that were not flashing, but positively dull, with rage. I presumed that the fan had been a present from him, and a recent present—bought perhaps that very day, after their arrival in the town. But what, *what* had he done that she should break it between her hands, scattering the splinters as who should sow dragon's teeth? I could not believe he had done anything much amiss. I imagined her grievance a trivial one. But this did not make the case less engrossing. Again and again I would take the fan-stump from my pocket, examining it on the palm of my hand, or between finger and thumb, hoping to read the mystery it had been mixed up in, so that I might reveal that mystery to the world. To the world, yes; nothing less than that. I was determined to make a story of what I had seen—a *conte* in the manner of great Guy de Maupassant. Now and again, in the course of the past year or so, it had occurred to me that I might be a writer. But I had not felt the impulse to sit down and write something. I did feel that impulse now. It would indeed have been an irresistible impulse if I had known just what to write.

I felt I might know at any moment, and had but to give my mind to it. Maupassant was an impeccable artist, but I think the secret of the hold he had on the young men of my day was not so much that we discerned his cunning as that we delighted in the simplicity which his cunning achieved. I had read a great number of his short stories, but none that had made me feel as though I, if I were a writer, mightn't have written it myself. Maupassant had an European reputation. It was pleasing, it was soothing and gratifying, to feel that one could at any time win an equal fame if one chose to set pen to paper. And now, suddenly, the spring had been touched in me, the time was come. I was grateful for the fluke by which I had witnessed on the terrace that evocative scene. I looked forward to reading the MS. of "The Fan"—tomorrow, at latest. I was not wildly ambitious. I was not inordinately vain. I knew I couldn't ever, with the best will in the world, write like Mr. George Meredith. Those wondrous works of his, seething with wit, with poetry and philosophy and what not, never had beguiled me with the sense that I might do something similar. I had full consciousness of not being a philosopher, of not being a poet, and of not being a wit. Well, Maupassant was none of these things. He was just an observer like me. Of course he was a good deal older than I, and had observed a good deal more. But it seemed to me that he was not my superior in knowledge of life. I knew all about life through *him*.

Dimly, the initial paragraph of my tale floated in my mind. I—not exactly I myself, but rather that impersonal *je* familiar to me through Maupassant—was to be sitting at that table, with a book before me, just as I *had* sat. Four or five short sentences would give the whole scene. One of these I had quite definitely composed. You have already heard it. "Down below, the sea rustled to and fro over the shingle."

These words, which pleased me much, were to do double duty. They were to recur. They were to be, by a fine stroke, the very last words of my tale, their tranquillity striking a sharp ironic contrast with the stress of what had just been narrated. I had, you see, advanced further in the form of my tale than in the substance. But even the form was as yet vague. What, exactly, was to happen after Mlle. Angélique and M. Joumand (as I provisionally called him) had rushed back past me into the casino? It was clear that I must hear the whole inner history from the lips of one or the other of them. Which? Should M. Joumand stagger out on to the terrace, sit down heavily at the table next to mine, bury his head in his hands, and presently, in broken words, blurt out to me all that might be of interest? . . .

"'And I tell you I gave up everything for her—everything.' He stared at me with his old hopeless eyes. 'She is more than the fiend I have described to you. Yet I swear to you, monsieur, that if I had anything left to give, it should be hers.'

"Down below, the sea rustled to and fro over the shingle."

Or should the lady herself be my informant? For a while, I rather leaned to this alternative. It was more exciting, it seemed to make the writer more signally a man of the world. On the other hand, it was less simple to manage. Wronged persons might be ever so communicative, but I surmised that persons in the wrong were reticent. Mlle. Angélique, therefore, would have to be modified by me in appearance and behavior, toned down, touched up; and poor M. Joumand must look like a man of whom one could believe anything. . . .

"She ceased speaking. She gazed down at the fragments of her fan, and then, as though finding in them an image of her own life, whispered, 'To think what I once was, monsieur!—what, but for him, I might be, even now!' She buried her face in her hands, then stared out into the night. Suddenly she uttered a short, harsh laugh.

"Down below, the sea rustled to and fro over the shingle."

I decided that I must choose the first of these two ways. It was the less chivalrous as well as the less lurid way, but clearly it was the more artistic as well as the easier. The "chose vue," the "tranche de la vie"—this was the thing to aim at. Honesty was the best policy. I must be nothing if not merciless. Maupassant was nothing if not merciless. He would not have spared Mlle. Angélique. Besides, why should I libel M. Joumand? Poor—no, not *poor* M. Joumand! I warned myself against pitying him. One touch of "sentimentality," and I should be lost. M. Joumand was ridiculous. I must keep him so. But—what was his position in life? Was he a lawyer perhaps?—or the proprietor of a shop in the Rue de Rivoli? I toyed with the possibility that he kept a fan shop—that the business had once been a prosperous one, but had gone down, down, because of his infatuation for this woman to whom he was always giving fans—which she *always* smashed. . . . "'Ah monsieur, cruel and ungrateful to me though she is, I swear to you that if I had anything left to give, it should be hers; but,' he stared at me with his old hopeless eyes, 'the fan she broke tonight was the last—the last, monsieur—of my stock.' Down below,"—but I pulled myself together, and asked pardon of my Muse.

It may be that I had offended her by my fooling. Or it may be that she had a sisterly desire to shield Mlle. Angélique from my mordant art. Or it may be that she was bent on saving M. de Maupassant from a dangerous rivalry. Anyway, she withheld from me the inspiration I had so confidently solicited. I *could not* think what had led up to that scene on the terrace. I tried hard and soberly. I turned the "chose vue" over and over in my mind, day by day, and the fan-stump over and over in my hand. But the "chose à figurer"—what, oh what, was that? Nightly I revisited the café, and sat there with an open mind—a mind wide open to catch the idea that should drop into it like a ripe golden plum. The plum did not ripen. The mind remained wide open for a week or more, but nothing except that phrase about the sea rustled to and fro in it.

A full quarter of a century has gone by. M. Joumand's death, so far too fat was he all those years ago, may be presumed. A temper so violent as Mlle. Angélique's must surely have brought its owner to the grave, long since. But here, all unchanged, the stump of her fan is; and once more I turn it over and over in my hand, not learning its secret—no, nor even trying to, now. The chord this relic strikes in me is not one of curiosity as to that old quarrel, but (if you will forgive me) one of tenderness for my first effort to write, and for my first hopes of excellence.   [1918]

E. M. FORSTER

My Wood

A FEW YEARS AGO I WROTE A BOOK which dealt in part with the difficulties of the English in India. Feeling that they would have had no difficulties in India themselves, the Americans read the book freely. The more they read it the better it made them feel, and a check to the author was the result. I bought a wood with the check. It is not a large wood—it contains scarcely any trees, and it is intersected, blast it, by a public footpath. Still, it is the first property that I have owned, so it is right that other people should participate in my shame, and should ask themselves, in accents that will vary in horror, this very important question: What is the effect of property upon the character? Don't let's touch economics; the effect of private ownership upon the community as a whole is another question—a more important question, perhaps, but another one. Let's keep to psychology. If you own things, what's their effect on you? What's the effect on me of my wood?

In the first place, it makes me feel heavy. Property does have this effect. Property produces men of weight, and it was a man of weight who failed to get into the Kingdom of Heaven. He was not wicked, that unfortunate millionaire in the parable, he was only stout; he stuck out in front, not to mention behind, and as he wedged himself this way and that in the crystalline entrance and bruised his well-fed flanks, he saw beneath him a comparatively slim camel passing through the eye of a needle and being woven into the robe of God. The Gospels all through couple stoutness and slowness. They point out what is perfectly obvious, yet seldom realized: that if you have a lot of things you cannot move about a lot, that furniture requires dusting, dusters require servants, servants require insurance stamps, and the whole tangle of them makes you think twice before you accept an invitation to dinner or go for a bathe in the Jordan. Sometimes the Gospels proceed further and say with Tolstoy that property is sinful; they approach the difficult ground of asceticism here, where I cannot follow them. But as to the immediate effects of property on people, they just show straightforward logic. It produces men of weight. Men of weight cannot, by definition, move like the lightning from the East unto the West, and the ascent of a fourteen-stone bishop into a pulpit is thus the exact antithesis of the coming of the Son of Man. My wood makes me feel heavy.

In the second place, it makes me feel it ought to be larger.

The other day I heard a twig snap in it. I was annoyed at first, for I thought that someone was blackberrying, and depreciating the value of the undergrowth. On coming nearer, I saw it was not a man who had trodden on the twig and snapped it, but a bird, and I felt pleased. My bird. The bird was not equally pleased. Ignoring the relation between us, it took fright as soon as it saw the shape of my face, and flew straight over the boundary hedge into a field, the property of Mrs. Henessy, where it sat down with a loud squawk. It had become Mrs. Henessy's bird. Something seemed grossly amiss here, something that would not have occurred had the wood been larger. I could not afford to buy Mrs. Henessy out, I dared not murder her, and limitations of this sort beset me on every side. Ahab did not want that vineyard—he only needed it to round off his property, preparatory to plotting a new curve—and all the land around my wood has become necessary to me in order to round off the wood. A boundary protects. But—poor little thing—the boundary ought in its turn to be protected. Noises on the edge of it. Children throw stones. A little more, and then a little more, until we reach the sea. Happy Canute! Happier Alexander! And after all, why should even the world be the limit of possession? A rocket containing a Union Jack, will, it is hoped, be shortly fired at the moon. Mars. Sirius. Beyond which . . . But these immensities ended by saddening me. I could not suppose that my wood was the destined nucleus of universal dominion—it is so small and contains no mineral wealth beyond the blackberries. Nor was I comforted when Mrs. Henessy's bird took alarm for the second time and flew clean away from us all, under the belief that it belonged to itself.

In the third place, property makes its owner feel that he ought to do something to it. Yet he isn't sure what. A restlessness comes over him, a vague sense that he has a personality to express—the same sense which, without any vagueness, leads the artist to an act of creation. Sometimes I think I will cut down such trees as remain in the wood, at other times I want to fill up the gaps between them with new trees. Both impulses are pretentious and empty. They are not honest movements towards money-making or beauty. They spring from a foolish desire to express myself and from an inability to enjoy what I have got. Creation, property, enjoyment form a sinister trinity in the human mind. Creation and enjoyment are both very very good, yet they are often unattainable without a material basis, and at such moments property pushes itself in as a substitute, saying, "Accept me instead—I'm good enough for all three." It is not enough. It is, as Shakespeare said of lust, "The expense of spirit in a waste of shame": it is "Before, a joy proposed; behind, a dream." Yet we don't know how to shun it. It is forced on us by our economic system as the alternative to starvation. It is also forced on us by an internal defect in the soul, by the feeling that in property may lie the germs of self-development and of exquisite or heroic deeds. Our life on earth is, and ought to be, material and carnal. But we have not yet learned to manage our materialism and carnality properly; they are still entangled with the desire for ownership, where (in the words of Dante) "Possession is one with loss."

And this brings us to our fourth and final point: the blackberries.

Blackberries are not plentiful in this meagre grove, but they are easily seen from the public footpath which traverses it, and all too easily gathered. Foxgloves, too—people will pull up the foxgloves, and ladies of an educational tendency even grub for toadstools to show them on the Monday in class. Other ladies, less educated, roll down the bracken in the arms of their gentlemen friends. There is paper, there are tins. Pray, does my wood belong to me or doesn't it? And, if it does, should I not own it best by allowing no one else to walk there? There is a wood near Lyme Regis, also cursed by a public footpath, where the owner has not hesitated on this point. He has built high stone walls each side of the path, and has spanned it by bridges, so that the public circulate like termites while he gorges on the blackberries unseen. He really does own his wood, this able chap. Dives in Hell did pretty well, but the gulf dividing him from Lazarus could be traversed by vision, and nothing traverses it here. And perhaps I shall come to this in time. I shall wall in and fence out until I really taste the sweets of property. Enormously stout, endlessly avaricious, pseudo-creative, intensely selfish, I shall weave upon my forehead the quadruple crown of possession until those nasty Bolshies come and take it off again and thrust me aside into the outer darkness. [1926]

D. H. LAWRENCE

Adolf

When we were children our fa-
ther often worked on the nightshift. Once it was spring-time, and he used
to arrive home, black and tired, just as we were downstairs in our night-
dresses. Then night met morning face to face, and the contact was not
always happy. Perhaps it was painful to my father to see us gaily entering
upon the day into which he dragged himself soiled and weary. He didn't
like going to bed in the spring morning sunshine.

But sometimes he was happy, because of his long walk through the dewy
fields in the first daybreak. He loved the open morning, the crystal and the
space, after a night down pit. He watched every bird, every stir in the
trembling grass, answered the whinnying of the pewits and tweeted to the
wrens. If he could, he also would have whinnied and tweeted and whistled
in a native language that was not human. He liked non-human things best.

One sunny morning we were all sitting at table when we heard his heavy
slurring walk up the entry. We became uneasy. His was always a disturbing
presence, trammelling. He passed the window darkly, and we heard him go
into the scullery and put down his tin bottle. But directly he came into the
kitchen. We felt at once that he had something to communicate. No one
spoke. We watched his black face for a second.

"Give me a drink," he said.

My mother hastily poured out his tea. He went to pour it out into his
saucer. But instead of drinking he suddenly put something on the table
among the teacups. A tiny brown rabbit! A small rabbit, a mere morsel,
sitting against the bread as still as if it were a made thing.

"A rabbit! A young one! Who gave it you, father?"

But he laughed enigmatically, with a sliding motion of his yellow-grey
eyes, and went to take off his coat. We pounced on the rabbit.

"Is it alive? Can you feel its heart beat?"

My father came back and sat down heavily in his armchair. He dragged
his saucer to him, and blew his tea, pushing out his red lips under his black
moustache.

"Where did you get it, father?"

"I picked it up," he said, wiping his naked forearm over his mouth and
beard.

"Where?"

"It is a wild one!" came my mother's quick voice.

"Yes, it is."

"Then why did you bring it?" cried my mother.

"Oh, we wanted it," came our cry.

"Yes, I've no doubt you did—" retorted my mother. But she was drowned in our clamour of questions.

On the field path my father had found a dead mother rabbit and three dead little ones—this one alive, but unmoving.

"But what had killed them, daddy?"

"I couldn't say, my child. I s'd think she'd aten something."

"Why did you bring it!" again my mother's voice of condemnation. "You know what it will be."

My father made no answer, but we were loud in protest.

"He must bring it. It's not big enough to live by itself. It would die," we shouted.

"Yes, and it will die now. And then there'll be *another* outcry."

My mother set her face against the tragedy of dead pets. Our hearts sank.

"It won't die, father, will it? Why will it? It won't."

"I s'd think not," said my father.

"You know well enough it will. Haven't we had it all before!" said my mother.

"They dunna always pine," replied my father testily.

But my mother reminded him of other little wild animals he had brought, which had sulked and refused to live, and brought storms of tears and trouble in our house of lunatics.

Trouble fell on us. The little rabbit sat on our lap, unmoving, its eye wide and dark. We brought it milk, warm milk, and held it to its nose. It sat as still as if it was far away, retreated down some deep burrow, hidden, oblivious. We wetted its mouth and whiskers with drops of milk. It gave no sign, did not even shake off the wet white drops. Somebody began to shed a few secret tears.

"What did I say?" cried my mother. "Take it and put it down in the field."

Her command was in vain. We were driven to get dressed for school. There sat the rabbit. It was like a tiny obscure cloud. Watching it, the emotions died out of our breast. Useless to love it, to yearn over it. Its little feelings were all ambushed. They must be circumvented. Love and affection were a trespass upon it. A little wild thing, it became more mute and asphyxiated still in its own arrest, when we approached with love. We must not love it. We must circumvent it, for its own existence.

So I passed the order to my sister and my mother. The rabbit was not to be spoken to, nor even looked at. Wrapping it in a piece of flannel I put it in an obscure corner of the cold parlour, and put a saucer of milk before its nose. My mother was forbidden to enter the parlour whilst we were at school.

"As if I should take any notice of your nonsense," she cried affronted. Yet I doubt if she ventured into the parlour.

At midday, after school, creeping into the front room, there we saw the rabbit still and unmoving in the piece of flannel. Strange grey-brown neutralization of life, still living! It was a sore problem to us.

"Why won't it drink its milk, mother?" we whispered. Our father was asleep.

"It prefers to sulk its life away, silly little thing." A profound problem. Prefers to sulk its life away! We put young dandelion leaves to its nose. The sphinx was not more oblivious. Yet its eye was bright.

At tea-time, however, it had hopped a few inches, out of its flannel, and there it sat again, uncovered, a little solid cloud of muteness, brown, with unmoving whiskers. Only its side palpitated slightly with life.

Darkness came; my father set off to work. The rabbit was still unmoving. Dumb despair was coming over the sisters, a threat of tears before bedtime. Clouds of my mother's anger gathered as she muttered against my father's wantonness.

Once more the rabbit was wrapped in the old pit-singlet. But now it was carried into the scullery and put under the copper fireplace, that it might imagine itself inside a burrow. The saucers were placed about, four or five, here and there on the floor, so that if the little creature *should* chance to hop abroad, it could not fail to come upon some food. After this my mother was allowed to take from the scullery what she wanted and then she was forbidden to open the door.

When morning came and it was light, I went downstairs. Opening the scullery door, I heard a slight scuffle. Then I saw dabbles of milk all over the floor and tiny rabbit-droppings in the saucers. And there the miscreant, the tips of his ears showing behind a pair of boots. I peeped at him. He sat bright-eyed and askance, twitching his nose and looking at me while not looking at me.

He was alive—very much alive. But still we were afraid to trespass much on his confidence.

"Father!" My father was arrested at the door. "Father, the rabbit's alive."

"Back your life it is," said my father.

"Mind how you go in."

By evening, however, the little creature was tame, quite tame. He was christened Adolf. We were enchanted by him. We couldn't really love him, because he was wild and loveless to the end. But he was an unmixed delight.

We decided he was too small to live in a hutch—he must live at large in the house. My mother protested, but in vain. He was so tiny. So we had him upstairs, and he dropped his tiny pills on the bed and we were enchanted.

Adolf made himself instantly at home. He had the run of the house, and was perfectly happy, with his tunnels and his holes behind the furniture.

We loved him to take meals with us. He would sit on the table humping his back, sipping his milk, shaking his whiskers and his tender ears, hopping off and hobbling back to his saucer, with an air of supreme unconcern. Suddenly he was alert. He hobbled a few tiny paces, and reared himself up inquisitively at the sugar basin. He fluttered his tiny fore-paws, and then reached and laid them on the edge of the basin, whilst he craned his thin neck and peeped in. He trembled his whiskers at the sugar, then did his best to lift down a lump.

"*Do* you think I will have it! Animals in the sugar pot!" cried my mother, with a rap of her hand on the table.

Which so delighted the electric Adolf that he flung his hind-quarters and knocked over a cup.

"It's your own fault, mother. If you left him alone—"

He continued to take tea with us. He rather liked warm tea. And he loved sugar. Having nibbled a lump, he would turn to the butter. There he was shooed off by our parent. He soon learned to treat her shooing with indifference. Still, she hated him to put his nose in the food. And he loved to do it. And one day between them they overturned the cream-jug. Adolf deluged his little chest, bounced back in terror, was seized by his little ears by my mother and bounced down on the hearth-rug. There he shivered in momentary discomfort, and suddenly set off in a wild flight to the parlour.

This last was his happy hunting ground. He had cultivated the bad habit of pensively nibbling certain bits of cloth in the hearth-rug. When chased from this pasture he would retreat under the sofa. There he would twinkle in Buddhist meditation until suddenly, no one knew why, he would go off like an alarm clock. With a sudden bumping scuffle he would whirl out of the room, going through the doorway with his little ears flying. Then we would hear his thunderbolt hurtling in the parlour, but before we could follow, the wild streak of Adolf would flash past us, on an electric wind that swept him round the scullery and carried him back, a little mad thing, flying possessed like a ball round the parlour. After which ebullition he would sit in a corner composed and distant, twitching his whiskers in abstract meditation. And it was in vain we questioned him about his outbursts. He just went off like a gun, and was as calm after it as a gun that smokes placidly.

Alas, he grew up rapidly. It was almost impossible to keep him from the outer door.

One day, as we were playing by the stile, I saw his brown shadow loiter across the road and pass into the field that faced the houses. Instantly a cry of "Adolf!"—a cry he knew full well. And instantly a wind swept him away down the sloping meadow, his tail twinkling and zigzagging through the grass. After him we pelted. It was a strange sight to see him, ears back, his little loins so powerful, flinging the world behind him. We ran ourselves out of breath, but could not catch him. Then somebody headed him off, and he sat with sudden unconcern, twitching his nose under a bunch of nettles.

His wanderings cost him a shock. One Sunday morning my father had just been quarrelling with a pedlar, and we were hearing the aftermath indoors, when there came a sudden unearthly scream from the yard. We flew out. There sat Adolf cowering under a bench, whilst a great black and white cat glowered intently at him, a few yards away. Sight not to be forgotten. Adolf rolling back his eyes and parting his strange muzzle in another scream, the cat stretching forward in a slow elongation.

Ha, how we hated that cat! How we pursued him over the chapel wall and across the neighbours' gardens.

Adolf was still only half grown.

"Cats!" said my mother. "Hideous detestable animals, why do people harbour them?"

But Adolf was becoming too much for her. He dropped too many pills. And suddenly to hear him clumping downstairs when she was alone in the house was startling. And to keep him from the door was impossible. Cats prowled outside. It was worse than having a child to look after.

Yet we would not have him shut up. He became more lusty, more callous than ever. He was a strong kicker, and many a scratch on face and arms did we owe to him. But he brought his own doom on himself. The lace curtains in the parlour—my mother was rather proud of them—fell on the floor very full. One of Adolf's joys was to scuffle wildly through them as though through some foamy undergrowth. He had already torn rents in them.

One day he entangled himself altogether. He kicked, he whirled round in a mad nebulous inferno. He screamed—and brought down the curtain-rod with a smash, right on the best beloved pelargonium, just as my mother rushed in. She extricated him, but she never forgave him. And he never forgave either. A heartless wildness had come over him.

Even we understood that he must go. It was decided, after a long deliberation, that my father should carry him back to the wildwoods. Once again he was stowed into the great pocket of the pit-jacket.

"Best pop him i' th' pot," said my father, who enjoyed raising the wind of indignation.

And so, next day, our father said that Adolf, set down on the edge of the coppice, had hopped away with utmost indifference, neither elated nor moved. We heard it and believed. But many, many were the heartsearchings. How would the other rabbits receive him? Would they smell his tameness, his humanized degradation, and rend him? My mother poohpoohed the extravagant idea.

However, he was gone, and we were rather relieved. My father kept an eye open for him. He declared that several times passing the coppice in the early morning, he had seen Adolf peeping through the nettle-stalks. He had called him, in an odd, high-voiced, cajoling fashion. But Adolf had not responded. Wildness gains so soon upon its creatures. And they become so contemptuous then of our tame presence. So it seemed to me. I myself would go to the edge of the coppice, and call softly. I myself would imagine bright eyes between the nettle-stalks, flash of a white, scornful tail past the bracken. That insolent white tail, as Adolf turned his flank on us! It reminded me always of a certain rude gesture, and a certain unprintable phrase, which may not even be suggested.

But when naturalists discuss the meaning of the rabbit's white tail, that rude gesture and still ruder phrase always come to my mind. Naturalists say that the rabbit shows his white tail in order to guide his young safely after him, as a nursemaid's flying strings are the signal to her toddling charges to follow on. How nice and naïve! I only know that my Adolf wasn't naïve. He used to whisk his flank at me, push his white feather in my eye, and say *"Merde!"* It's a rude word—but one which Adolf was always semaphoring at me, flag-wagging it with all the derision of his narrow haunches.

That's a rabbit all over—insolence, and the white flag of spiteful derision. Yes, and he keeps his flag flying to the bitter end, sporting, insolent little devil that he is. See him running for his life. Oh, how his soul is fanned to an ecstasy of fright, a fugitive whirlwind of panic. Gone mad, he throws the world behind him, with astonishing hind legs. He puts back his head and lays his ears on his sides and rolls the white of his eyes in sheer ecstatic agony of speed. He knows the awful approach behind him; bullet or stoat. He knows! He knows, his eyes are turned back almost into his head. It is agony. But it is also ecstasy. Ecstasy! See the insolent white flag bobbing. He whirls on the magic wind of terror. All his pent-up soul rushes into agonized electric emotion of fear. He flings himself on, like a falling star swooping into extinction. White heat of the agony of fear. And at the same time, bob! bob! bob! goes the white tail, *merde! merde! merde!* it says to the pursuer. The rabbit can't help it. In his utmost extremity he still flings the insult at the pursuer. He is the inconquerable fugitive, the in-domitable meek. No wonder the stoat becomes vindictive.

And if he escapes, this precious rabbit! Don't you see him sitting there, in his earthly nook, a little ball of silence and rabbit triumph? Don't you see the glint on his black eye? Don't you see, in his very immobility, how the whole world is *merde* to him? No conceit like the conceit of the meek. And if the avenging angel in the shape of the ghostly ferret steals down on him, there comes a shriek of terror out of that little hump of self-satisfaction sitting motionless in a corner. Falls the fugitive. But even fallen, his white feather floats. Even in death it seems to say: "I am the meek, I am the righteous, I am the rabbit. All you rest, you are evil doers, and you shall be *bien emmerdés!*"   [1920]

The Dog That Bit People

PROBABLY NO ONE MAN SHOULD HAVE as many dogs in his life as I have had, but there was more pleasure than distress in them for me except in the case of an Airedale named Muggs. He gave me more trouble than all the other fifty-four or -five put together, although my moment of keenest embarrassment was the time a Scotch terrier named Jeannie, who had just had six puppies in the clothes closet of a fourth floor apartment in New York, had the unexpected seventh and last at the corner of Eleventh Street and Fifth Avenue during a walk she had insisted on taking. Then, too, there was the prize winning French poodle, a great big black poodle—none of your little, untroublesome white miniatures—who got sick riding in the rumble seat of a car with me on her way to the Greenwich Dog Show. She had a red rubber bib tucked around her throat and, since a rain storm came up when we were halfway through the Bronx, I had to hold over her a small green umbrella, really more of a parasol. The rain beat down fearfully and suddenly the driver of the car drove into a big garage, filled with mechanics. It happened so quickly that I forgot to put the umbrella down and I will always remember, with sickening distress, the look of incredulity mixed with hatred that came over the face of the particular hardened garage man that came over to see what we wanted, when he took a look at me and the poodle. All garage men, and people of that intolerant stripe, hate poodles with their curious haircut, especially the pom-poms that you've got to leave on their hips if you expect the dogs to win a prize.

But the Airedale, as I have said, was the worst of all my dogs. He really wasn't my dog, as a matter of fact: I came home from a vacation one summer to find that my brother Roy had bought him while I was away. A big, burly, choleric dog, he always acted as if he thought I wasn't one of the family. There was a slight advantage in being one of the family, for he didn't bite the family as often as he bit strangers. Still, in the years that we had him he bit everybody but mother, and he made a pass at her once but missed. That was during the month when we suddenly had mice, and Muggs refused to do anything about them. Nobody ever had mice exactly like the mice we had that month. They acted like pet mice, almost like mice somebody had trained. They were so friendly that one night when mother entertained at dinner the Friraliras, a club she and my father had

belonged to for twenty years, she put down a lot of little dishes with food
in them on the pantry floor so that the mice would be satisfied with that
and wouldn't come into the dining room. Muggs stayed out in the pantry
with the mice, lying on the floor, growling to himself—not at the mice, but
about all the people in the next room that he would have liked to get at.
Mother slipped out into the pantry once to see how everything was going.
Everything was going fine. It made her so mad to see Muggs lying there,
oblivious of the mice—they came running up to her—that she slapped him
and he slashed at her, but didn't make it. He was sorry immediately, mother
said. He was always sorry, she said, after he bit someone, but we could not
understand how she figured this out. He didn't act sorry.

Mother used to send a box of candy every Christmas to the people the
Airedale bit. The list finally contained forty or more names. Nobody could
understand why we didn't get rid of the dog. I didn't understand it very
well myself, but we didn't get rid of him. I think that one or two people
tried to poison Muggs—he acted poisoned once in a while—and old Major
Moberly fired at him once with his service revolver near the Seneca Hotel
in East Broad Street—but Muggs lived to be almost eleven years old and
even when he could hardly get around he bit a Congressman who had
called to see my father on business. My mother had never liked the
Congressman—she said the signs of his horoscope showed he couldn't be
trusted (he was Saturn with the moon in Virgo)—but she sent him a box
of candy that Christmas. He sent it right back, probably because he suspected it was trick candy. Mother persuaded herself it was all for the best
that the dog had bitten him, even though father lost an important business
association because of it. "I wouldn't be associated with such a man,"
mother said. "Muggs could read him like a book."

We used to take turns feeding Muggs to be on his good side, but that
didn't always work. He was never in a very good humor, even after a meal.
Nobody knew exactly what was the matter with him, but whatever it was
it made him irascible, especially in the mornings. Roy never felt very well
in the morning, either, especially before breakfast, and once when he came
downstairs and found that Muggs had moodily chewed up the morning
paper he hit him in the face with a grapefruit and then jumped upon the
dining room table, scattering dishes and silverware and spilling the coffee.
Muggs' first free leap carried him all the way across the table and into a
brass fire screen in front of the gas grate but he was back on his feet in a
moment and in the end he got Roy and gave him a pretty vicious bite in
the leg. Then he was all over it; he never bit anyone more than once at a
time. Mother always mentioned that as an argument in his favor; she said

he had a quick temper but that he didn't hold a grudge. She was forever defending him. I think she liked him because he wasn't well. "He's not strong," she would say, pityingly, but that was inaccurate; he may not have been well but he was terribly strong.

One time my mother went to the Chittenden Hotel to call on a woman mental healer who was lecturing in Columbus on the subject of "Harmonious Vibrations." She wanted to find out if it was possible to get harmonious vibrations into a dog. "He's a large tan-colored Airedale," mother explained. The woman said that she had never treated a dog but she advised my mother to hold the thought that he did not bite and would not bite. Mother was holding the thought the very next morning when Muggs got the iceman but she blamed that slip-up on the iceman. "If you didn't think he would bite you, he wouldn't," mother told him. He stomped out of the house in a terrible jangle of vibrations.

One morning when Muggs bit me slightly, more or less in passing, I reached down and grabbed his short stumpy tail and hoisted him into the air. It was a foolhardy thing to do and the last time I saw my mother, about six months ago, she said she didn't know what possessed me. I don't either, except that I was pretty mad. As long as I held the dog off the floor by his tail he couldn't get at me, but he twisted and jerked so, snarling all the time, that I realized I couldn't hold him that way very long. I carried him to the kitchen and flung him onto the floor and shut the door on him just as he crashed against it. But I forgot about the backstairs. Muggs went up the backstairs and down the frontstairs and had me cornered in the living room. I managed to get up onto the mantelpiece above the fireplace, but it gave way and came down with a tremendous crash throwing a large marble clock, several vases, and myself heavily to the floor. Muggs was so alarmed by the racket that when I picked myself up he had disappeared. We couldn't find him anywhere, although we whistled and shouted, until old Mrs. Detweiler called after dinner that night. Muggs had bitten her once, in the leg, and she came into the living room only after we assured her that Muggs had run away. She had just seated herself when, with a great growling and scratching of claws, Muggs emerged from under a davenport where he had been quietly hiding all the time, and bit her again. Mother examined the bite and put arnica on it and told Mrs. Detweiler that it was only a bruise. "He just bumped you," she said. But Mrs. Detweiler left the house in a nasty state of mind.

Lots of people reported our Airedale to the police but my father held a municipal office at the time and was on friendly terms with the police. Even so, the cops had been out a couple times—once when Muggs bit Mrs.

Rufus Sturtevant and again when he bit Lieutenant-Governor Malloy—but mother told them that it hadn't been Muggs' fault but the fault of the people who were bitten. "When he starts for them, they scream," she explained, "and that excites him." The cops suggested that it might be a good idea to tie the dog up, but mother said that it mortified him to be tied up and that he wouldn't eat when he was tied up.

Muggs at his meals was an unusual sight. Because of the fact that if you reached toward the floor he would bite you, we usually put his food plate on top of an old kitchen table with a bench alongside the table. Muggs would stand on the bench and eat. I remember that my mother's Uncle Horatio, who boasted that he was the third man up Missionary Ridge, was splutteringly indignant when he found out that we fed the dog on a table because we were afraid to put his plate on the floor. He said he wasn't afraid of any dog that ever lived and that he would put the dog's plate on the floor if we would give it to him. Roy said that if Uncle Horatio had fed Muggs on the ground just before the battle he would have been the first man up Missionary Ridge. Uncle Horatio was furious. "Bring him in! Bring him in now!" he shouted. "I'll feed the --- on the floor!" Roy was all for giving him a chance, but my father wouldn't hear of it. He said that Muggs had already been fed. "I'll feed him again!" bawled Uncle Horatio. We had quite a time quieting him.

In his last year Muggs used to spend practically all of his time outdoors. He didn't like to stay in the house for some reason or other—perhaps it held too many unpleasant memories for him. Anyway, it was hard to get him to come in and as a result the garbage man, the iceman, and the laundryman wouldn't come near the house. We had to haul the garbage down to the corner, take the laundry out and bring it back, and meet the iceman a block from home. After this had gone on for some time we hit on an ingenious arrangement for getting the dog in the house so that we could lock him up while the gas meter was read, and so on. Muggs was afraid of only one thing, an electrical storm. Thunder and lightning frightened him out of his senses (I think he thought a storm had broken the day the mantelpiece fell). He would rush into the house and hide under a bed or in a clothes closet. So we fixed up a thunder machine out of a long narrow piece of sheet iron with a wooden handle on one end. Mother would shake this vigorously when she wanted to get Muggs into the house. It made an excellent imitation of thunder, but I suppose it was the most round-about system for running a household that was ever devised. It took a lot out of mother.

A few months before Muggs died, he got to "seeing things." He would rise slowly from the floor, growling low, and stalk stiff-legged and menacing toward nothing at all. Sometimes the Thing would be just a little to the right or left of a visitor. Once a Fuller Brush salesman got hysterics. Muggs came wandering into the room like Hamlet following his father's ghost. His eyes were fixed on a spot just to the left of the Fuller Brush man, who stood it until Muggs was about three slow, creeping paces from him. Then he shouted. Muggs wavered on past him into the hallway grumbling to himself but the Fuller man went on shouting. I think mother had to throw a pan of cold water on him before he stopped. That was the way she used to stop us boys when we got into fights.

Muggs died quite suddenly one night. Mother wanted to bury him in the family lot under a marble stone with some such inscription as "Flights of angels sing thee to thy rest" but we persuaded her it was against the law. In the end we just put up a smooth board above his grave along a lonely road. On the board I wrote with an indelible pencil "Cave Canem." Mother was quite pleased with the simple classic dignity of the old Latin epitaph.   [1933]

EDMUND WILSON

The Old Stone House

As I go north for the first time in years, in the slow, the constantly stopping, milk train—which carries passengers only in the back part of the hind car and has an old stove to heat it in winter—I look out through the dirt-yellowed double pane and remember how once, as a child, I used to feel thwarted in summer till I had got the windows open and there was nothing between me and the widening pastures, the great boulders, the black and white cattle, the rivers, stony and thin, the lone elms like feather-dusters, the high air which sharpens all outlines, makes all colors so breathtakingly vivid, in the clear light of late afternoon.

The little stations again: Barneveld, Stittville, Steuben—a tribute to the Prussian general who helped drill our troops for the Revolution. The woman behind me in the train talks to the conductor with a German accent. They came over here for land and freedom.

Boonville: that pale boxlike building, smooth gray, with three floors of slots that look in on darkness and a roof like a flat overlapping lid—cold dark clear air, fresh water. Like nothing else but upstate New York. Rivers that run quick among stones, or, deeper, stained dark with dead leaves. I used to love to follow them—should still. A fresh breath of water off the Black River, where the blue closed gentians grow. Those forests, those boulder-strewn pastures, those fabulous distant falls!

There was never any train to Talcottville. Our house was the center of the town. It is strange to get back to this now: it seems not quite like anything else that I have ever known. But is this merely the apparent uniqueness of places associated with childhood?

The settlers of this part of New York were a first westward migration from New England. At the end of the eighteenth century, they drove ox-teams from Connecticut and Massachusetts over into the wild northern country below Lake Ontario and the St. Lawrence River, and they established here an extension of New England.

Yet an extension that was already something new. I happened last week to be in Ipswich, Mass., the town from which one branch of my family came; and, for all the New England pride of white houses and green blinds, I was oppressed by the ancient crampedness. Even the House of the Seven

Gables, which stimulated the imagination of Hawthorne, though it is grim perhaps, is not romantic. It, too, has the tightness and the self-sufficiency of that little provincial merchant society, which at its best produced an intense little culture, quite English in its concreteness and practicality—as the block letters of the signs along the docks made Boston look like Liverpool. But life must have hit its head on those close and low-ceilinged coops. That narrowness, that meagerness, that stinginess, still grips New England today: the drab summer cottages along the shore seem almost as slit-windowed and pinched as the gray twin-houses of a mill town like Lawrence or Fall River. I can feel the relief myself of coming away from Boston to these first uplands of the Adirondacks, where, discarding the New England religion but still speaking the language of New England, the settlers found limitless space. They were a part of the new America, now forever for a century on the move; and they were to move on themselves before they would be able to build here anything comparable to the New England civilization. The country, magnificent and vast, has never really been humanized as New England has: the landscape still overwhelms the people. But this house, one of the few of its kind among later wooden houses and towns, was an attempt to found a civilization. It blends in a peculiar fashion the amenities of the eastern seaboard with the rudeness and toughness of the new frontier.

It was built at the end of the eighteenth century: the first event recorded in connection with it is a memorial service for General Washington. It took four or five years in the building. The stone had to be quarried and brought out of the river. The walls are a foot and a half thick, and the plaster was applied to the stone without any intervening lattice. The beams were secured by enormous nails, made by hand and some of them eighteen inches long. Solid and simple as a fortress, the place has also the charm of something which has been made to order. There is a front porch with white wooden columns which support a white wooden balcony that runs along the second floor. The roof comes down close over the balcony, and the balcony and the porch are draped with vines. Large ferns grow along the porch, and there are stone hitching-posts and curious stone ornaments, cut out of the quarry like the house: on one side, a round bottomed bowl in which red geraniums bloom, and on the other, an unnamable object, crudely sculptured and vaguely pagoda-like. The front door is especially handsome: the door itself is dark green and equipped with a brass knocker, and the woodwork which frames it is white; it is crowned with a wide fanlight and flanked by two narrow panes of glass, in which a white filigree of ironwork makes a webbing like ice over winter ponds. On one of the broad sides of the building, where the mortar has come off the stone, there is a dappling of dark gray under pale gray like the dappling of light in shallow water, and the feathers of the elms make dapplings of sun among their shadows of large lace on the grass.

The lawn is ungraded and uneven like the pastures, and it merges eventually with the fields. Behind, there are great clotted masses of myrtle-beds, lilac-bushes, clumps of pink phlox and other things I cannot identify; pink and white hollyhocks, some of them leaning, fine blue and purple dye of larkspur; a considerable vegetable garden, with long rows of ripe gooseberries and currants, a patch of yellow pumpkin flowers, and bushes of raspberries, both white and red—among which are sprinkled like confetti the little flimsy California poppies, pink, orange, white and red. In an old dark red barn behind, where the hayloft is almost collapsing, I find spinning-wheels, a carder, candle-molds, a patent bootjack, obsolete implements of carpentry, little clusters of baskets for berry-picking and a gigantic pair of scales such as is nowadays only seen in the hands of allegorical figures.

The house was built by the Talcotts, after whom the town was named. They owned the large farm in front of the house, which stretches down to the river and beyond. They also had a profitable grist mill, but—I learn from the county history—were thought to have "adopted a policy adverse to the building up of the village at the point where natural advantages greatly favored," since they "refused to sell village lots to mechanics, and retained the water power on Sugar River, although parties offered to invest liberally in manufactures." In time, there were only two Talcotts left, an old maid and her widowed sister. My great-grandfather, Thomas Baker, who lived across the street and had been left by the death of his wife with a son and eight daughters, paid court to Miss Talcott and married her. She was kind to the children, and they remembered her with affection. My great-grandfather acquired in this way the house, the farm and the quarry.

All but two of my great-grandfather's daughters, of whom my grandmother was one—"six of them beauties," I understand—got married and went away. Only one of them was left in the house at the time when I first remember Talcottville: my great-aunt Rosalind, a more or less professional invalid and a figure of romantic melancholy, whose fiancé had been lost at sea. When I knew her, she was very old. It was impressive and rather frightening to call on her—you did it only by special arrangement, since she had to prepare herself to be seen. She would be beautifully dressed in a lace cap, a lavender dress and a white crocheted shawl, but she had become so bloodless and shrunken as dreadfully to resemble a mummy and reminded one uncomfortably of Miss Haversham in Dickens' *Great Expectations*. She had a certain high and formal coquetry and was the only person I ever knew who really talked like the characters in old novels. When she had been able to get about, she had habitually treated the townspeople with a condescension almost baronial. According to the family legend, the great-grandmother of great-grandmother Baker had been a daughter of one of the Earls of Essex, who had eloped with a gardener to America.

Another of my Baker great-aunts, who was one of my favorite relatives, had married and lived in the town and had suffered tragic disappointments. Only her strong intellectual interests and a mind capable of philosophic pessimism had maintained her through the wreck of her domestic life. She used to tell me how, a young married woman, she had taught herself French by the dictionary and grammar, sitting up at night alone by the stove through one of their cold and dark winters. She had read a great deal of French, subscribed to French magazines, without ever having learned to pronounce it. She had rejected revealed religion and did not believe in immortality; and when she felt that she had been relieved of the last of her family obligations—though her hair was now turning gray—she came on to New York City and lived there alone for years, occupying herself with the theater, reading, visits to her nephews and nieces—with whom she was extremely popular—and all the spectacle and news of the larger world which she had always loved so much but from which she had spent most of her life removed.

When she died, only the youngest of the family was left, the sole brother, my great-uncle Tom. His mother must have been worn out with childbearing—she died after the birth of this ninth child—and he had not turned out so well as the others. He had been born with no roof to his mouth and was obliged to wear a false gold palate, and it was difficult to understand him. He was not really simple-minded—he had held a small political job under Cleveland, and he usually beat me at checkers—but he was childlike and ill-equipped to deal with life in any very effective way. He sold the farm to a German and the quarry to the town. Then he died, and the house was empty, except when my mother and father would come here to open it up for two or three months in the summer.

I have not been back here in years, and I have never before examined the place carefully. It has become for me something like a remembered dream—unearthly with the powerful impressions of childhood. Even now that I am here again, I find I have to shake off the dream. I keep walking from room to room, inside and outside, upstairs and down, with uneasy sensations of complacency that are always falling through to depression.

These rooms are very well proportioned; the white mantelpieces are elegant and chaste, and the carving on each one is different. The larger of the two living rooms now seems a little bare because the various members of the family have claimed and taken away so many things; and there are some disagreeable curtains and carpets, for which the wife of my great-uncle Tom is to blame. But here are all the things, I take note, that are nowadays sold in antique stores: red Bohemian-glass decanters; a rusty silver snuff-box; a mirror with the American eagle painted at the top of the glass. Little mahogany tables with slim legs; a set of curly-maple furniture, deep seasoned yellow like satin; a yellow comb-backed rocker, with a design of green conch-shells that look like snails. A small bust of Dante with the nose chipped, left behind as defective by one of my cousins when its companion piece, Beethoven, was taken away; a little mahogany melodeon on which my Aunt "Lin" once played. Large engravings of the family of Washington and of the "Reformers Presenting Their Famous Protest before the Diet of Spires"; a later engraving of Dickens. Old tongs and poker, impossibly heavy. A brown mahogany desk inlaid with yellow birdwood, which contains a pair of steel-rimmed spectacles and a thing for shaking sand on wet ink. Daguerrotypes in fancy cases: they seem to last much better than photographs—my grandmother looks fresh and cunning—I remember that I used to hear that the first time my grandfather saw her, she was riding on a load of hay—he came back up here to marry her as soon as he had got out of medical school. An old wooden flute—originally brought over from New England, I remember my great-uncle's telling me, at the time when they traveled by ox-team—he used to get a lonely piping out of it—I try it but cannot make a sound. Two big oval paintings, in tarnished gilt frames, of landscapes romantic and mountainous: they came from the Utica house of my great-grandfather Baker's brother—he married a rich wife and invented excelsior—made out of the northern lumber—and was presented with a solid-silver table service by the grateful city of Utica.

Wallpaper molded by the damp from the stone; uninviting old black haircloth furniture. A bowl of those enormous up-country sweet peas, incredibly fragrant and bright—they used to awe and trouble me—why?

In the dining room, a mahogany china closet, which originally—in the days when letters were few and great-grandfather Baker was postmaster—was the whole of the village post office. My grandmother's pewter tea-service, with its design of oak-leaves and acorns, which I remember from her house in New Jersey. Black iron cranes, pipkins and kettles for cooking in the fireplace; a kind of flat iron pitchfork for lifting the bread in and out, when they baked at the back of the hearth. On the sideboard, a glass decanter with a gilt blackletter label: "J. Rum." If there were only some rum in the decanter!—if the life of the house were not now all past!—the kitchens that trail out behind are almost too old-smelling, too long deserted, to make them agreeable to visit—in spite of the delightful brown crocks with long-tailed blue birds painted on them, a different kind of bird on each crock.

In the ample hall with its staircase, two large colored pictures of trout, one rising to bait, one leaping. Upstairs, a wooden pestle and mortar; a perforated tin box for hot coals to keep the feet warm in church or on sleigh-rides; a stuffed heron; a horrible bust of my cousin Dorothy Read in her girlhood, which her mother had done of her in Germany. The hair-ribbon and the ruffles are faithfully reproduced in marble, and the eyes have engraved pupils. It stands on a high pedestal, and it used to be possible, by pressing a button, to make it turn around. My Cousin Grace, Dorothy's mother, used to show it off and invite comparison with the original, especially calling attention to the nose; but what her mother had never known was that Dorothy had injured her nose in some rather disgraceful row with her sister. One day when the family were making an excursion, Dorothy pleaded indisposition and bribed a man with a truck to take the bust away and drop it into a pond. But Uncle Tom got this out of the man, dredged the statue up and replaced it on its pedestal. An ugly chair with a round rag back; an ugly bed with the head of Columbus sticking out above the pillows like a figurehead. Charming old bedquilts, with patterns of rhomboids in softened browns, greens and pinks, or of blue polka-dotted hearts that ray out on stiff phallic stalks. A footstool covered in white, which, however, when you step on a tab at the side, opens up into a cuspidor—some relic, no doubt, of the times when the house was used for local meetings. (There used to be a musical chair, also brought back from Germany, but it seems to have disappeared.) A jar of hardly odorous dried rose-leaves, and a jar of little pebbles and shells that keep their bright colors in alcohol.

The original old panes up here have wavy lines in the glass. There are cobweb-filthy books, which I try to examine: many religious works, the annals of the state legislature, a book called *The Young Wife, or Duties of Women in the Marriage Relation,* published in Boston in 1838 and containing a warning against tea and coffee, which "loosen the tongue, fire the eye, produce mirth and wit, excite the animal passions, and lead to remarks about ourselves and others, that we should not have made in other circumstances, and which it were better for us and the world, never to have made." But there is also, I noticed downstairs, Grant Allan's *The Woman Who Did* from 1893.

I come upon the *History of Lewis County* and read it with a certain pride. I am glad to say to myself that it is a creditable piece of work—admirably full in its information on geology, flora and fauna, on history and local politics; diversified with anecdotes and biographies never overflattering and often pungent; and written in a sound English style. Could anyone in the country today, I wonder, command such a sound English style? I note with gratification that the bone of a prehistoric cuttlefish, discovered in one of the limestone caves, is the largest of its kind on record, and that a flock of wild swans was seen here in 1821. In the eighties, there were still wolves and panthers. There are still bears and deer today.

I also look into the proceedings of the New York State Assembly. My great-grandfather Thomas Baker was primarily a politician and at that time a member of the Assembly. I have heard that he was a Jacksonian Democrat, and that he made a furious scene when my grandmother came back from New Jersey and announced that she had become a Republican: it "spoiled her whole visit." There is a photograph of great-grandfather Baker in an oval gilt frame, with his hair sticking out in three spikes and a wide and declamatory mouth. I look through the Assembly record to see what sort of role he played. It is the forties; the Democrats are still angry over the Bank of United States. But when I look up Thomas Baker in the index, it turns out that he figures solely as either not being present or as requesting leave of absence. They tell me he used to go West to buy cattle.

That sealed-up space on the second floor which my father had knocked out—who did they tell me was hidden in it? I have just learned from one of the new road-signs which explain historical associations that there are caves somewhere here in which slaves were hidden. Could this have been a part of the underground route for smuggling Negroes over the border into Canada? Is the attic, the "kitchen chamber," which is always so suffocating in summer, still full of those carpetbags and crinolines and bonnets and beaver-hats that we used to get out of the old cowhide trunks and use to dress up for charades?

It was the custom for the married Baker daughters to bring their children back in the summer; and their children in time brought their children. In those days, how I loved coming up here! It was a reunion with cousins from Boston and New York, Ohio and Wisconsin, as well as with the Talcottville and Utica ones: we fished and swam in the rivers, had all sorts of excursions and games. Later on, I got to dislike it: the older generation died, the younger did not much come. I wanted to be elsewhere, too. The very fullness with life of the past, the memory of those many families of cousins and uncles and aunts, made the emptiness of the present more oppressive. Isn't it still?—didn't my gloom come from that, the night of my first arrival? Wasn't it the dread of that that kept me away? I am aware, as I walk through the rooms, of the amplitude and completeness of the place—the home of a big old-fashioned family that had to be a city in itself. And not merely did it house a clan: the whole life of the community passed through it. And now for five sixths of the year it is nothing but an unheated shell, a storehouse of unused antiques, with no intimate relation to the county.

The community itself today is somewhat smaller than the community of those days, and its condition has very much changed. It must seem to the summer traveler merely one of the clusters of houses that he shoots through along the state highway; and there may presently be little left save our house confronting, across the road, the hot-dog stand and the gasoline station.*

For years I have had a recurrent dream. I take a road that runs toward the west. It is summer; I pass by a strange summer forest, in which there are mysterious beings, though I know that, on the whole, they are shy and benign. If I am fortunate and find the way, I arrive at a wonderful river, which runs among boulders, with rapids, between alders and high weedy trees, through a countryside fresh, green and wide. We go in swimming; it is miles away from anywhere. We plunge in the smooth flowing pools. We make our way to the middle of the stream and climb up on the pale round gray stones and sit naked in the sun and the air, while the river glides away below us. And I know that it is the place for which I have always longed, the place of wildness and freedom, to find which is the height of what one may hope for—the place of unalloyed delight.

As I walk about Talcottville now, I discover that the being-haunted forest is a big grove which even in daytime used to be lonely and dark and where great white Canadian violets used to grow out of the deep black leaf-mold. Today it is no longer dark, because half the trees have been cut down. The river of my dream, I see, is simply an idealized version of the farther and less frequented and more adventurous bank of Sugar River,

---

*This description may seem inconsistent with my account of our Talcottville location in another book, *A Piece of My Mind,* but the main highway was later shifted, put through along another road, and my mother had succeeded, in the meantime, in getting rid of the hot-dog stand by buying back the lot across the street.

which had to be reached by wading. Both river and forest are west of the road that runs through the village, which accounts for my always taking that direction in my dream. I remember how Sugar River—out of the stone of which our house is built—used, in my boyhood, so to fascinate me that I had an enlargement made of one of the photographs I had taken of it—a view of "the Big Falls"—and kept it in my room all winter. Today the nearer bank has been largely blasted away to get stone for the new state highway, and what we used to call "the Little Falls" is gone.

I visit the house of my favorite great-aunt, and my gloom returns and overwhelms me. The huge root of an elm has split the thick slabs of the pavement so that you have to walk over a hump; and one of the big square stone fence-posts is toppling. Her flowers, with no one to tend them, go on raggedly blooming in their seasons. There has been nobody in her house since she died. It is all too appropriate to her pessimism—that dead end she always foresaw. As I walk around the house, I remember how, once on the back porch there, she sang me old English ballads, including that gruesome one, "Oh, where have you been, Randall, my son?"—about the man who had gone to Pretty Peggy's house and been given snakes to eat:

> "What had you for supper, Randall, my son?"
> "Fresh fish fried in butter. Oh, make my bed soon!
> For I'm sick at my heart and I fain would lie down!"

She was old then—round-shouldered and dumpy—after the years when she had looked so handsome, straight-backed and with the fashionable aigrette in her hair. And the song she sang seemed to have been drawn out of such barbarous reaches of the past, out of something so surprisingly different from the college-women's hotels in New York in which I had always known her as living: that England to which, far though she had some from it, she was yet so much nearer than I—that queer troubling world of legend which I knew from Percy's *Reliques* but with which she had maintained a real contact through centuries of women's voices—for she sang it without a smile, completely possessed by its spirit—that it made my flesh creep, disconcerted me.

My great-aunt is dead, and all her generation are dead—and the new generations of the family have long ago left Talcottville behind and have turned into something quite different. They were already headed for the cities by the middle of the last century, as can be seen by the rapid dispersal of great grandfather Baker's daughters. Yet there were still, in my childhood, a few who stayed on in this country as farmers. They were very impressive people, the survivors of a sovereign race who had owned their own pastures and fields and governed their own community. Today the descendants of these are performing mainly minor functions in a machine which they do not control. They have most of them become thoroughly urbanized, and they are farther from great-grandfather Baker than my grandmother, his daughter, was when she came back from New Jersey a Republican. One of her children, a retired importer in New York, was complaining to me the other day that the outrageous demands of the farmers were making business recovery impossible, and protesting that if the advocates of the income tax had their way, the best people would no longer be able to live up to their social positions. A cousin, who bears the name of one of his Ipswich ancestors, a mining engineer on the Coast and a classmate and admirer of Hoover, invested and has lost heavily in Mexican real estate and the industrial speculations of the boom. Another, with another of the old local names, is now at the head of an organization whose frankly avowed purpose is to rescue the New York manufacturers from taxation and social legislation. He has seen his native city of Utica decline as a textile center through the removal of its mills to the South, where taxes are lighter and labor is cheaper; and he is honestly convinced that his efforts are directed toward civic betterment.

Thus the family has come imperceptibly to identify its interests with those of what my great-grandfather Baker would have called the "money power." They work for it and acquiesce in it—they are no longer the sovereign race of the first settlers of Lewis County, and in the cities they have achieved no sovereignty. They are much too scrupulous and decent, and their tastes are too comparatively simple for them ever to have rolled up great fortunes during the years of expansion and plunder. They have still the frank accent and the friendly eye of the older American world, and they seem rather taken aback by the turn that things have been taking.

And what about me? As I come back in the train, I find that—other causes contributing—my depression of Talcottville deepens. I did not find the river and the forest of my dream—I did not find the magic of the past. I have been too close to the past: there in that house, in that remote little town which has never known industrial progress since the Talcotts first obstructed the development of the water power of Sugar River, you can see exactly how rural Americans were living a century and a half ago. And who would go back to it? Not I. Let people who have never known country life complain that the farmer has been spoiled by his radio and his Ford. Along with the memory of exaltation at the immensity and freedom of that countryside, I have memories of horror at its loneliness: houses burning down at night, sometimes with people in them, where there was no fire department to save them, and husbands or wives left alone by death—the dark nights and the prisoning winters. I do not grudge the sacrifice of the Sugar River falls for the building of the new state highway, and I do not resent the hot-dog stand. I am at first a little shocked at the sight of a transformer on the road between Talcottville and Boonville, but when I get to the Talcottville house, I am obliged to be thankful for it—no more oil-lamps in the evenings! And I would not go back to that old life if I could: that civilization of northern New York—why should I idealize it?—was too lonely, too poor, too provincial.

I look out across the Hudson and see Newburgh: with the neat-windowed cubes of its dwellings and docks, distinct as if cut by a burin, built so densely up the slope of the bank and pierced by an occasional steeple, undwarfed by tall modern buildings and with only the little old-fashioned ferry to connect it with the opposite bank, it might still be an eighteenth-century city. My father's mother came from there. She was the granddaughter of a carpet-importer from Rotterdam. From him came the thick Spanish coins which the children of my father's family were supposed to cut their teeth on. The business, which had been a con-siderable one, declined as the sea trade of the Hudson became concentrated in New York. My father and mother went once—a good many years ago—to visit the old store by the docks, and were amazed to find a solitary old clerk still scratching up orders and sales on a slate that hung behind the counter.

And the slate and the Spanish coins, though they symbolize a kind of life somewhat different from that evoked by Talcottville, associate them-selves in my mind with such things as the old post office turned china closet. And as I happen to be reading Herndon's *Life of Lincoln,* that, too, goes to flood out the vision with its extension still further west, still further from the civilized seaboard, of the life of the early frontier. Through Hern-don's extraordinary memoir, one of the few really great American books of its kind, which America has never accepted, preferring to it the sentimen-talities of Sandburg and the ladies who write Christmas stories—the past confronts me even more plainly than through the bootjacks and daguerre-otypes of Talcottville, and makes me even more uneasy. Here you are back again amid the crudeness and the poverty of the American frontier, and here is a man of genius coming out of it and perfecting himself. The story is not merely moving, it becomes almost agonizing. The ungainly boorish boy from the settler's clearing, with nobody and nothing behind him, hoping that his grandfather had been a planter as my great-aunt Rosalind hoped that she was a descendant of the Earls of Essex, the morbid young man looking passionately toward the refinement and the training of the East but unable to bring himself to marry the women who represented it for him—rejoining across days in country stores, nights in godforsaken hotels, rejoining by heroic self-discipline the creative intelligence of the race, to find himself the conscious focus of its terrible unconscious parturition—his miseries burden his grandeur. At least they do for me at this moment.

> Old Abe Lincoln came out of the wilderness,
> Out of the wilderness, out of the wilderness—

The echo of the song in my mind inspires me with a kind of awe—I can hardly bear the thought of Lincoln.

Great-grandfather Baker's politics and the Talcottville general store, in which people sat around and talked before the new chain store took its place—Lincoln's school was not so very much different. And I would not go back to that.

Yet as I walk up the steps of my house in New York, I am forced to recognize, with a sinking, that I have never been able to leave it. This old wooden booth I have taken between First and Second Avenues—what is it but the same old provincial America? And as I open the door with its loose knob and breathe in the musty smell of the stair-carpet, it seems to me that I have not merely stuck in the world where my fathers lived but have actually, in some ways, lost ground in it. This gray paintless clapboarded front, these lumpy and rubbed yellow walls—they were probably once respectable, but they must always have been commonplace. They have never had even the dignity of the house in Lewis County. But I have rented them because, in my youth, I had been used to living in houses and have grown to loathe city apartments.

So here, it seems, is where I must live: in an old cramped and sour frame-house—having failed even worse than my relatives at getting out of the American big-business era the luxuries and the prestige that I unquestionably should very much have enjoyed. Here is where I end by living—among the worst instead of the best of this city that took the trade away from Newburgh—the sordid and unhealthy children of my sordid and unhealthy neighbors, who howl outside my windows night and day. It is this, in the last analysis—there is no doubt about it now!—which has been rankling and causing my gloom: to have left that early world behind yet never to have really succeeded in what was till yesterday the new. [1933]

NORMAN MAILER

Miami Beach

THEY SNIPPED THE RIBBON IN 1915, they popped the cork, Miami Beach was born. A modest burg they called a city, nine-tenths jungle. An island. It ran along a coastal barrier the other side of Biscayne Bay from young Miami—in 1868 when Henry Lum, a California 'forty-niner, first glimpsed the island from a schooner, you may be certain it was jungle, coconut palms on the sand, mangrove swamp and palmetto thicket ten feet off the beach. But by 1915, they were working the vein. John S. Collins, a New Jersey nurseryman (after whom Collins Avenue is kindly named) brought in bean fields and avocado groves; a gent named Fisher, Carl G., a Hoosier—he invented Prestolite, a millionaire—bought up acres from Collins, brought in a work-load of machinery, men, even two elephants, and jungle was cleared, swamps were filled, small residential islands were made out of baybottom mud, dredged, then relocated, somewhat larger natural islands adjacent to the barrier island found themselves improved, streets were paved, sidewalks put in with other amenities—by 1968, one hundred years after Lum first glommed the beach, large areas of the original coastal strip were covered over altogether with macadam, white condominium, white luxury hotel and white stucco flea-bag. Over hundreds, then thousands of acres, white sidewalks, streets and white buildings covered the earth where the jungle had been. Is it so dissimilar from covering your poor pubic hair with adhesive tape for fifty years? The vegetal memories of that excised jungle haunted Miami Beach in a steam-pot of miasmas. Ghosts of expunged flora, the never-born groaning in vegetative chancery beneath the asphalt came up with a tropical curse, an equatorial leaden wet sweat of air which rose from the earth itself, rose right up through the baked asphalt and into the heated air which entered the lungs like a hand slipping into a rubber glove.

The temperature was not that insane. It hung around 87° day after day, at night it went down to 82°, back to the same 87° in the A.M.—the claims of the News Bureau for Miami Beach promised that in 1967 temperature exceeded 90° only four times. (Which the Island of Manhattan could never begin to say.) But of course Miami Beach did not have to go that high, for its humidity was up to 87° as well—it was, on any and every day of the Republican Convention of 1968, one of the hottest cities in the world. The reporter was no expert on tropical heats—he had had, he would admit, the island of Luzon for a summer in World War II; and basic training in the pine woods of Fort Bragg, North Carolina, in August; he had put in a week at Las Vegas during July—temperatures to 110°; he had crossed the Mojave Desert once by day; he was familiar with the New York subway in the rush hour on the hottest day of the year. These were awesome immersions—one did not have to hit the Congo to know what it was like in a hothouse in hell—but that 87° in Miami Beach day after day held up in competition against other sulphuric encounters. Traveling for five miles up the broken-down, forever in-a-state-of-alteration and repair of Collins Avenue, crawling through 5 P.M. Miami Beach traffic in the pure miserable fortune of catching an old taxi without air conditioning, dressed in shirt and tie and jacket—formal and implicitly demanded uniform of political journalists—the sensation of breathing, then living, was not unlike being obliged to make love to a 300-pound woman who has decided to get on top. Got it? You could not dominate a thing. That uprooted jungle had to be screaming beneath.

Of course it could have been the air conditioning: natural climate transmogrified by technological climate. They say that in Miami Beach the air conditioning is pushed to that icy point where women may wear fur coats over their diamonds in the tropics. For ten miles, from the Diplomat to the Di Lido, above Hallandale Beach Boulevard down to Lincoln Mall, all the white refrigerators stood, piles of white refrigerators six and eight and twelve stories high, twenty stories high, shaped like sugar cubes and ice-cube trays on edge, like mosques and palaces, shaped like matched white luggage and portable radios, stereos, plastic compacts and plastic rings, Moorish castles shaped like waffle irons, shaped like the baffle plates on white plastic electric heaters, and cylinders like Waring blenders, building looking like giant op art and pop art paintings, and sweet wedding cakes, cottons of kitsch and piles of dirty cotton stucco, yes, for ten miles the hotels for the delegates stood on the beach side of Collins Avenue: the Eden Roc and the Fontainebleau (Press Headquarters), the Di Lido and the De Lano, the Ivanhoe, Deauville, Sherry Frontenac and the Monte Carlo, the Cadillac, Caribbean and the Balmoral, the Lucerne, Hilton Plaza, Doral Beach, the Sorrento, Marco Polo, Casablanca, and Atlantis, the Hilyard Manor, Sans Souci, Algiers, Carillon, Seville, the Gaylord, the Shore Club, the Nautilus, Montmartre, and the Promenade, the Bal Harbour on North Bay Causeway, and the Twelve Caesars, the Regency and the Americana, the Diplomat, Versailles, Coronado, Sovereign, the Waldman (dig!), the Beau Rivage, the Crown Hotel, even Holiday Inn, all oases for technological man. Deep air conditioning down to 68°, ice-palaces to chill the fevered brain—when the air conditioning worked. And their furnishings were monumentally materialistic. Not all of them: the cheaper downtown hotels like the Di Lido and the Nautilus were bare and mean with vinyl coverings on the sofas and the glare of plastic off the rugs and tables and tiles, inexpensive hotel colors of pale brown and buff and dingy cream, sodden gray, but the diadems like the Fontainebleau and the Eden Roc, the Doral Beach, the Hilton Plaza (Headquarters for Nixon), the Deauville (Hq for Reagan) or the Americana—Rockefeller and the New York State delegation's own ground—were lavish with interlockings, curves, vaults and runs of furnishings as intertwined as serpents in the roots of a mangrove tree. All the rivers of the very worst taste twisted down to the delta of each lobby in each grand Miami Beach hotel—rare was the central room which did not look like the lobby of a movie palace, imitation of late-Renaissance imitations of Greek and Roman statues, imitations of baroque and rococo and brothel Victorian and Art Nouveau and Bauhaus with gold grapes and cornucopias welded to the modern bronze tubing of the chair, golden moldings which ran like ivy from room to room, chandeliers complex as the armature of dynamos, and curvilinear steps in the shape of amoebas and palettes, cocktail lounge bars in deep rose or maroon with spun-sugar white tubes of plaster decor to twist around the ceiling. There was every color of iridescence, rainbows of vulgarity, aureoles of gorgeous taste, opium den of a middle-class dollar, materialistic as meat, sweat, and the cigar. It is said that people born under Taurus and Capricorn are the most materialistic of us all. Take a sample of the residents in the census of Miami B.—does Taurus predominate more than one-twelfth of its share? It must, or astrology is done, for the Republicans, Grand Old Party with a philosophy rather than a program, had chosen what must certainly be the materialistic capital of the world for their convention. Las Vegas might offer competition, but Las Vegas was materialism in the service of electricity—fortunes could be lost in the spark of the dice. Miami was materialism baking in the sun, then stepping back to air-conditioned caverns where ice could nestle in the fur. It was the first of a hundred curiosities—that in a year when the Republic hovered on the edge of revolution, nihilism, and lines of police on file to the horizon, visions of future Vietnams in our own cities upon us, the party of conservatism and principle, of corporate wealth and personal frugality, the party of cleanliness, hygiene, and balanced budget, should have set itself down on a sultan's strip.

That was the first of a hundred curiosities, but there were mysteries as well. The reporter had moved through the convention quietly, as anonymously as possible, wan, depressed, troubled. Something profoundly un-classifiable was going on among the Republicans and he did not know if it was conceivably good or a concealment of something bad—which was the first time a major social phenomenon like a convention had confused him so. He had covered others. The Democratic Convention in 1960 in Los Angeles which nominated John F. Kennedy, and the Republican in San Francisco in 1964 which installed Barry Goldwater, had encouraged some of his very best writing. He had felt a gift for comprehending those conventions. But the Republican assembly in Miami Beach in 1968 was a different affair—one could not tell if nothing much was going on, or to the contrary, nothing much was going on near the surface but everything was shifting down below. So dialogue with other journalists merely depressed him—the complaints were unanimous that this was the dullest convention anyone could remember. Complaints took his mind away from the slow brooding infusion he desired in the enigmas of conservatism and/or Republicanism, and any hope of perspective on the problem beyond. The country was in a throe, a species of eschatological heave. The novelist John Updike was not necessarily one of his favorite authors, but after the assassination of Robert F. Kennedy, it was Updike who had made the remark that God might have withdrawn His blessing from America. It was a thought which could not be forgotten for it gave insight to the perspectives of the Devil and his political pincers: Left-wing demons, white and Black, working to inflame the conservative heart of America, while Right-wing devils exacerbated Blacks and drove the mind of the New Left and liberal middle class into prides of hopeless position. And the country roaring like a bull in its wounds, coughing like a sick lung in the smog, turning over in sleep at the sound of motorcycles, shivering at its need for new phalanxes of order. Where were the new phalanxes one could trust? The reporter had seen the faces of too many police to balm his dreams with the sleep they promised. Even the drinks tasted bad in Miami in the fever and the chill.

[1968]

LEWIS THOMAS

On Natural Death

THERE ARE SO MANY NEW BOOKS about dying that there are now special shelves set aside for them in book-shops, along with the health-diet and home-repair paperbacks and the sex manuals. Some of them are so packed with detailed information and step-by-step instructions for performing the function that you'd think this was a new sort of skill which all of us are now required to learn. The strongest impression the casual reader gets, leafing through, is that proper dying has become an extraordinary, even an exotic experience, something only the specially trained get to do.

Also, you could be led to believe that we are the only creatures capable of the awareness of death, that when all the rest of nature is being cycled through dying, one generation after another, it is a different kind of pro-cess, done automatically and trivially, more "natural," as we say.

An elm in our backyard caught the blight this summer and dropped stone dead, leafless, almost overnight. One weekend it was a normal-looking elm, maybe a little bare in spots but nothing alarming, and the next weekend it was gone, passed over, departed, taken. Taken is right, for the tree surgeon came by yesterday with his crew of young helpers and their cherry picker, and took it down branch by branch and carted it off in the back of a red truck, everyone singing.

The dying of a field mouse, at the jaws of an amiable household cat, is a spectacle I have beheld many times. It used to make me wince. Early in life I gave up throwing sticks at the cat to make him drop the mouse, because the dropped mouse regularly went ahead and died anyway, but I always shouted unaffections at the cat to let him know the sort of animal he had become. Nature, I thought, was an abomination.

Recently I've done some thinking about that mouse, and I wonder if his dying is necessarily all that different from the passing of our elm. The main difference, if there is one, would be in the matter of pain. I do not believe that an elm tree has pain receptors, and even so, the blight seems to me a relatively painless way to go even if there were nerve endings in a tree, which there are not. But the mouse dangling tail-down from the teeth of a gray cat is something else again, with pain beyond bearing, you'd think, all over his small body.

There are now some plausible reasons for thinking it is not like that at all, and you can make up an entirely different story about the mouse and his dying if you like. At the instant of being trapped and penetrated by teeth, peptide hormones are released by cells in the hypothalamus and the pituitary gland; instantly these substances, called endorphins, are attached to the surface of other cells responsible for pain perception; the hormones have the pharmacologic properties of opium; there is no pain. Thus it is that the mouse seems always to dangle so languidly from the jaws, lies there so quietly when dropped, dies of his injuries without a struggle. If a mouse could shrug, he's shrug.

I do not know if this is true or not, nor do I know how to prove it if it is true. Maybe if you could get in there quickly enough and administer naloxone, a specific morphine antagonist, you could turn off the endorphins and observe the restoration of pain, but this is not something I would care to do or see. I think I will leave it there, as a good guess about the dying of a cat-chewed mouse, perhaps about dying in general.

Montaigne had a hunch about dying, based on his own close call in a riding accident. He was so badly injured as to be believed dead by his companions, and was carried home with lamentations, "all bloody, stained all over with the blood I had thrown up." He remembers the entire episode, despite having been "dead, for two full hours," with wonderment:

> It seemed to me that my life was hanging only by the tip of my lips. I closed my eyes in order, it seemed to me, to help push it out, and took pleasure in growing languid and letting myself go. It was an idea that was only floating on the surface of my soul, as delicate and feeble as all the rest, but in truth not only free from distress but mingled with that sweet feeling that people have who have let themselves slide into sleep. I believe that this is the same state in which people find themselves whom we see fainting in the agony of death, and I maintain that we pity them without cause. . . . In order to get used to the idea of death, I find there is nothing like coming close to it.

Later, in another essay, Montaigne returns to it:

> If you know not how to die, never trouble yourself; Nature will in a moment fully and sufficiently instruct you; she will exactly do that business for you; take you no care for it.

The worst accident I've ever seen was in Okinawa, in the early days of the invasion, when a jeep ran into a troop carrier and was crushed nearly flat. Inside were two young MPs, trapped in bent steel, both mortally hurt, with only their heads and shoulders visible. We had a conversation while people with the right tools were prying them free. Sorry about the accident, they said. No, they said, they felt fine. Is everyone else okay, one of them said. Well, the other one said, no hurry now. And then they died.

Pain is useful for avoidance, for getting away when there's time to get away, but when it is end game, and no way back, pain is likely to be turned off, and the mechanisms for this are wonderfully precise and quick. If I had to design an ecosystem in which creatures had to live off each other and in which dying was an indispensable part of living, I could not think of a better way to manage.   [1979]

PAUL FUSSELL

The Boy Scout Handbook

IT'S AMAZING HOW MANY INTEREST-
ing books humanistic criticism manages not to notice. Staring fixedly at
its handful of teachable masterpieces, it seems content not to recognize
that a vigorous literary-moral life constantly takes place just below (sometimes above) its vision. What a pity Lionel Trilling or Kenneth Burke never
paused to examine the intersection of rhetoric and social motive among,
say, the Knights of Columbus or the Elks. That these are their fellow citizens is less important than that the desires and rituals of these groups are
desires and rituals, and thus of permanent social and psychological consequence. The culture of the Boy Scouts deserves this sort of look-in,
especially since the right sort of people don't know much about it.

The right sort consists, of course, of liberal intellectuals. They have
often gazed uneasily at the Boy Scout movement. After all, a general, the
scourge of the Boers, invented it; Kipling admired it; the Hitler-jugend
(and the Soviet Pioneers) aped it. If its insistence that there is a God has
not sufficed to alienate the enlightened, its khaki uniforms, lanyards,
salutes, badges, and flag-worship have seemed to argue incipient militarism,
if not outright fascism. The movement has often seemed its own worst
enemy. Its appropriation of Norman Rockwell as its official Apelles has not
endeared it to those of exquisite taste. Nor has its cause been promoted by
events like the TV appearance a couple of years ago of the Chief Pardoner,
Gerald Ford, rigged out in scout neckerchief, assuring us from the tele-
prompter that a Scout is Reverent. Then there are the leers and giggles
triggered by the very word "scoutmaster," which in knowing circles is alone
sufficient to promise comic pederastic narrative. "*All* scoutmasters are
homosexuals," asserted George Orwell, who also insisted that "*All* tobac-
conists are Fascists."

But anyone who imagines that the scouting movement is either sinister
or stupid or funny should spend a few hours with the latest edition of *The
Official Boy Scout Handbook* (1979). Social, cultural, and literary historians
could attend to it profitably as well, for after *The Red Cross First Aid
Manual, The World Almanac,* and the Gideon Bible, it is probably the best-
known book in this country. Since the first edition in 1910, twenty-nine
million copies have been read in bed by flashlight. The first printing of this
ninth edition is 600,000. We needn't take too seriously the ascription of

authorship to William ("Green Bar Bill") Hillcourt, depicted on the title page as an elderly gentleman bare-kneed in scout uniform and identified as Author, Naturalist, and World Scouter. He is clearly the Ann Page or Reddy Kilowatt of the movement, and although he's doubtless contributed to this handbook (by the same author is *Baden-Powell: The Two Lives of a Hero* [1965]), it bears all the marks of composition by committee, or "task force," as it's called here. But for all that, it's admirably written. And although a complex sentence is as rare as a reference to girls, the rhetoric of this new edition has made no compromise with what we are told is the new illiteracy of the young. The book assumes an audience prepared by a very good high-school education, undaunted by terms like *biosphere, ideology,* and *ecosystem.*

The pliability and adaptability of the scout movement explains its remarkable longevity, its capacity to flourish in a world dramatically different from its founder's. Like the Roman Catholic Church, the scout movement knows the difference between cosmetic and real change, and it happily embraces the one to avoid any truck with the other. Witness the new American flag patch, now worn at the top of the right sleeve. It betokens no access of jingoism or threat to a civilized internationalism. It simply conduces to dignity by imitating a similar affectation of police and fire departments in anarchic towns like New York City. The message of the flag patch is not "I am a fascist, straining to become old enough to purchase and wield guns." It is, rather, "I can be put to quasi-official use, and like a fireman or policeman I am trained in first aid and ready to help."

There are other innovations, none of them essential. The breeches of thirty years ago have yielded to trousers, although shorts are still in. The wide-brimmed army field hat of the First World War is a fixture still occasionally seen, but it is now augmented by headwear deriving from succeeding mass patriotic exercises: overseas caps and berets from World War II, and visor caps of the sort worn by General Westmoreland and sunbelt retirees. The scout handclasp has been changed, perhaps because it was discovered in the context of the new internationalism that the former one, in which the little finger was separated from the other three on the right hand, transmitted inappropriate suggestions in the Third World. The handclasp is now the normal civilian one, but given with the left hand. There's now much less emphasis on knots than formerly; as if to signal this change, the neckerchief is no longer religiously knotted at the tips. What used to be known as artificial respiration ("Out goes the bad air, in comes the good") has given way to "rescue breathing." The young are now being familiarized with the metric system. Some bright empiric has discovered that a paste made of meat tenderizer is the best remedy for painful insect stings. Constipation is not the bugbear it was a generation ago. And throughout there is a striking new lyricism. "Feel the wind blowing through your hair," the scout is adjured, just as he is exhorted to perceive that Being Prepared for life means learning "to live happy" and—equally important—"to die happy." There's more emphasis now on fun and less on duty; or rather, duty is validated because, properly viewed, it is a pleasure. (If that sounds like advice useful to grown-ups as well as to sprouts, you're beginning to get the point.)

There are only two possible causes of complaint. The term "free world" surfaces too often, although the phrase is mercifully uncapitalized. And the Deism is a bit insistent. The United States is defined as a country "whose people believe in a supreme being." The words "In God We Trust" on the coinage and currency are taken almost as a constitutional injunction. The camper is told to carry along the "Bible, Testament, or prayer book of your faith," even though, for light backpacking, he is advised to leave behind air mattress, knife and fork, and pancake turner. When the scout finds himself lost in the woods, he is to "stay put and have faith that someone will find you." In aid of this end, "Prayer will help." But the religiosity is so broad that it's harmless. The words "your church" are followed always by the phrase "or synagogue." The writers have done as well as they can considering that they're saddled with the immutable twelve points of Baden-Powell's Scout Law, stating unambiguously that "A Scout is Reverent" and "faithful to his religious duties." But if "You have the right to worship God in your own way," you must see to it that "others retain their right to worship God in their way." Likewise, if "you have the right to speak your mind without fear of prison or punishment," you must "ensure that right for others, even when you do not agree with them." If the book adheres to any politics, they can hardly be described as conservative; they are better described as slightly archaic liberal. It is broadly hinted that industrial corporations are prime threats to clean air and conservation. In every illustration depicting more than three boys, one is black. The section introducing the reader to some Great Americans pays respects not only to Franklin and Edison and John D. Rockefeller and Einstein; it also makes much of Walter Reuther and Samuel Gompers, as well as Harriet Tubman, Martin Luther King, and Whitney Young. There is a post-Watergate awareness that public officials must be watched closely. One's civic duties include the obligation to "keep up on what is going on around you" in order to "get involved" and "help change things that are not good."

Few books these days could be called compendia of good sense. This is one such, and its good sense is not merely about swimming safely and putting campfires "cold out." The good sense is psychological and ethical as well. Indeed, this handbook is among the very few remaining popular repositories of something like classical ethics, deriving from Aristotle and Cicero. Except for the handbook's adhesions to the motif of scenic beauty, it reads as if the Romantic movement had never taken place. The constant moral theme is the inestimable benefits of looking objectively outward and losing consciousness of self in the work to be done. To its young audience vulnerable to invitations to "trips" and trances and anxious self-absorption, the book calmly says: "Forget yourself." What a shame the psychobabblers of Marin County will never read it.

There is other invaluable advice, applicable to adults as well as to scouts. Some is practical, like "Never use flammable fluids to start a charcoal fire. They burn off fast, lighting only a little of the charcoal." Some is civic-moral: "Take a 2-hour walk where you live. Make a list of things that please you, another of things that should be improved." And then the kicker: "Set out to improve them." Some advice is even intellectual, and pleasantly uncompromising: "Reading trash all the time makes it impossible for anyone to be anything but a second-rate person." But the best advice is ethical: "Learn to think." "Gather knowledge." "Have initiative." "Respect the rights of others." Actually, there's hardly a better gauge for measuring the gross official misbehavior of the seventies than the ethics enshrined in this handbook. From its explicit ethics you can infer such propositions as "A scout does not tap his acquaintances' telephones," or "A scout does not bomb and invade a neutral country, and then lie about it," or "A scout does not prosecute war unless, as the Constitution provides, it has been declared by the Congress." Not to mention that because a scout is clean in thought, word, and deed, he does not, like Richard Nixon, designate his fellow citizens "shits" and then both record his filth and lie about the recordings ("A scout tells the truth").

Responding to Orwell's satiric analysis of "Boys' Weeklies" forty years ago, the boys' author Frank Richards, stigmatized by Orwell as a manufacturer of excessively optimistic and falsely wholesome stories, observed that "The writer for young people should . . . endeavor to give his young readers a sense of stability and solid security, because it is good for them, and makes for happiness and peace of mind." Even if it is true, as Orwell objects, that the happiness of youth is a cruel delusion, then, says Richards, "Let youth be happy, or as happy as possible. Happiness is the best preparation for misery, if misery must come. At least the poor kid will have had something." In the current world of Making It and Getting Away with It, there are not many books devoted to associating happiness with virtue. The shelves of the CIA and the State Department must be bare of them. "Horror swells around us like an oil spill," Terrence Des Pres said recently. "Not a day passes without more savagery and harm." He was commenting on Philip Hallie's *Lest Innocent Blood Be Shed,* an account of a whole French village's trustworthiness, loyalty, helpfulness, friendliness, courtesy, kindness, cheerfulness, and bravery in hiding scores of Jews during the Occupation. Des Pres concludes: "*Goodness.* When was the last time anyone used that word in earnest, without irony, as anything more than a doubtful cliché?" *The Official Boy Scout Handbook,* for all its focus on Axmanship, Backpacking, Cooking, First Aid, Flowers, Hiking, Map and Compass, Semaphore, Trees, and Weather, is another book about goodness. No home, and certainly no government office, should be without a copy. The generously low price of $3.50 is enticing, and so is the place on the back cover where you're invited to inscribe your name.   [1982]

CAROL BLY

Getting Tired

THE MEN HAVE LEFT A GIGANTIC 6600 combine a few yards from our grove, at the edge of the stubble. For days it was working around the farm; we heard it on the east, later on the west, and finally we could see it grinding back and forth over the windrows on the south. But now it has been simply squatting at the field's edge, huge, tremendously still, very professional, slightly dangerous.

We all have the correct feelings about this new combine: this isn't the good old farming where man and soil are dusted together all day; this isn't farming a poor man can afford, either, and therefore it further threatens his hold on the American "family farm" operation. We have been sneering at this machine for days, as its transistor radio, amplified well over the engine roar, has been grinding up our silence, spreading a kind of shrill ghetto evening all over the farm.

But now it is parked, and after a while I walk over to it and climb up its neat little John Deere-green ladder on the left. Entering the big cab up there is like coming up into a large ship's bridge on visitors' day—heady stuff to see the inside workings of a huge operation like the Queen Elizabeth II. On the other hand I feel left out, being only a dumbfounded passenger. The combine cab has huge windows flaring wider at the top; they lean forward over the ground, and the driver sits so high behind the glass in its rubber moldings it is like a movie-set spaceship. He has obviously come to dominate the field, whether he farms it or not.

The value of the 66 is that it can do anything, and to change it from a combine into a cornpicker takes one man about half an hour, whereas most machine conversions on farms take several men a half day. It frees its owner from a lot of monkeying.

Monkeying, in city life, is what little boys do to clocks so they never run again. In farming it has two quite different meanings. The first is small side projects. You monkey with poultry, unless you're a major egg handler. Or you monkey with ducks or geese. If you have a very small milk herd, and finally decide that prices plus state regulations don't make your few Holsteins worthwhile, you "quit monkeying with them." There is a hidden dignity in this word: it precludes mention of money. It lets the wife of a very marginal farmer have a conversation with a woman who may be helping her husband run fifteen hundred acres. "How you coming with those geese?" "Oh, we've been real disgusted. We're thinking of quitting monkeying with them." It saves her having to say, "We lost our shirts on those darn geese."

The other meaning of monkeying is wrestling with and maintaining machinery, such as changing heads from combining to cornpicking. Farmers who cornpick the old way, in which the corn isn't shelled automatically during picking in the field but must be elevated to the top of a pile by belt and then shelled, put up with some monkeying.

Still, cornpicking and plowing is a marvelous time of the year on farms; one of the best autumns I've had recently had a few days of fieldwork in it. We were outside all day, from six in the morning to eight at night—coming in only for noon dinner. We ate our lunches on a messy truck flatbed. (For city people who don't know it: *lunch* isn't a noon meal; it is what you eat out of a black lunch pail at 9 A.M. and 3 P.M. If you offer a farmer a cup of coffee at 3:30 P.M. he or she is likely to say, "No thanks, I've already had lunch.") There were four of us hired to help—a couple to plow, Celia (a skilled farmhand who worked steady for our boss), and me. Lunch was always two sandwiches of white commercial bread with luncheon meat, and one very generous piece of cake-mix cake carefully wrapped in Saran Wrap. (I never found anyone around here self-conscious about using Saran Wrap when the Dow Chemical Company was also making napalm.)

It was very pleasant on the flatbed, squinting out over the yellow picked cornstalks—each time we stopped for lunch, a larger part of the field had been plowed black. We fell into the easy psychic habit of farmworkers: admiration of the boss. "Ja, I see he's buying one of those big 4010s," someone would say. We always perked up at inside information like that. Or "Ja," as the woman hired steady told us, "he's going to plow the home fields first this time, instead of the other way round." We temporary help were impressed by that, too. Then, with real flair, she brushed a crumb of luncheon meat off her jeans, the way you would make sure to flick a gnat off spotless tennis whites. It is the true feminine touch to brush a crumb off pants that are encrusted with Minnesota Profile A heavy loam, many swipes of SAE 40 oil, and grain dust.

All those days, we never tired of exchanging information on how *he* was making out, what *he* was buying, whom *he* was going to let drive the new tractor, and so on. There is always something to talk about with the other hands, because farming is genuinely absorbing. It has the best quality of work: nothing else seems real. And everyone doing it, even the cheapest helpers like me, can see the layout of the whole—from spring work, to cultivating, to small grain harvest, to cornpicking, to fall plowing.

The second day I was promoted from elevating corncobs at the corn pile to actual plowing. Hour after hour I sat up there on the old Alice, as she was called (an Allis-Chalmers WC that looked rusted from the Flood). You have to sit twisted part way around, checking that the plowshares are scouring clean, turning over and dropping the dead crop and soil, not clogging. For the first two hours I was very political. I thought about what would be good for American farming—stronger marketing organizations, or maybe a law like the Norwegian Odal law, preventing the breaking up of small farms or selling them to business interests. Then the sun got high, and each time I reached the headlands area at the field's end I dumped off something else, now my cap, next my jacket, finally my sweater.

Since the headlands are the last to be plowed, they serve as a field road until the very end. There are usually things parked there—a pickup or a corn trailer—and things dumped—my warmer clothing, our afternoon lunch pails, a broken furrow wheel someone picked up.

By noon I'd dropped all political interest, and was thinking only: how unlike this all is to Keats's picture of autumn, a "season of mists and mellow fruitfulness." This gigantic expanse of horizon, with everywhere the easy growl of tractors, was simply teeming with extrovert energy. It wouldn't calm down for another week, when whoever was lowest on the totem pole would be sent out to check a field for dropped parts or to drive away the last machines left around.

The worst hours for all common labor are the hours after noon dinner. Nothing is inspiring then. That is when people wonder how they ever got stuck in the line of work they've chosen for life. Or they wonder where the cool Indian smoke of secrets and messages began to vanish from their marriage. Instead of plugging along like a cheerful beast working for me, the Allis now smelled particularly gassy. To stay awake I froze my eyes onto an indented circle in the hood around the gas cap. Someone had apparently knocked the screw cap fitting down into the hood, so there was a moat around it. In this moat some overflow gas leapt in tiny wives. Sometimes the gas cap was a castle, this was the moat; sometimes it was a nuclear-fission plant, this was the horrible hot-water waste. Sometimes it was just the gas cap on the old Alice with the spilt gas bouncing on the hot metal.

Row after row. I was stupefied. But then around 2:30 the shadows appeared again, and the light, which had been dazing and white, grew fragile. The whole prairie began to gather itself for the cool evening. All of a sudden it was wonderful to be plowing again, and when I came to the field end, the filthy jackets and the busted furrow wheel were just benign mistakes: that is, if it chose to, the jacket could be a church robe, and the old wheel could be something with some pride to it, like a helm. And I felt the same about myself: instead of being someone with a half interest in literature and a half interest in farming doing a half-decent job plowing, I could have been someone desperately needed in Washington or Zurich. I drank my three o'clock coffee joyously, and traded the other plowman a Super-Valu cake-mix lemon cake slice for a Holsum baloney sandwich because it had garlic in it.

By seven at night we had been plowing with headlights for an hour. I tried to make up games to keep going, on my second wind, on my third wind, but labor is labor after the whole day of it; the mind refuses to think of ancestors. It refuses to pretend the stalks marching up to the right wheel in the spooky light are men-at-arms, or to imagine a new generation coming along. It doesn't care. Now the Republicans could have announced a local meeting in which they would propose a new farm program whereby every farmer owning less than five hundred acres must take half price for his crop, and every farmer owning more than a thousand acres shall receive triple price for his crop, and I was so tired I wouldn't have shown up to protest.

A million hours later we sit around in a daze at the dining-room table, and nobody says anything. In low, courteous mutters we ask for the macaroni hotdish down this way, please. Then we get up in ones and twos and go home. Now the farm help are all so tired we *are* a little like the various things left out on the headlands—some tools, a jacket, someone's thermos top—used up for that day. Thoughts won't even stick to us any more.

Such tiredness must be part of farmers' wanting huge machinery like the Deere 6600. That tiredness that feels so good to the occasional laborer and the athlete is disturbing to a man destined to it eight months of every year. But there is a more hidden psychology in the issue of enclosed combines versus open tractors. It is this: one gets too many impressions on the open tractor. A thousand impressions enter as you work up and down the rows: nature's beauty or nature's stubbornness, politics, exhaustion, but mainly the feeling that all this repetition—last year's cornpicking, this year's cornpicking, next year's cornpicking—is taking up your lifetime. The mere repetition reveals your eventual death.

When you sit inside a modern combine, on the other hand, you are so isolated from field, sky, all the real world, that the brain is dulled. You are not sensitized to your own mortality. You aren't sensitive to anything at all.

This must be a common choice of our mechanical era: to hide from life inside our machinery. If we can hide from life in there, some idiotic part of the psyche reasons, we can hide from death in there as well.   [1973]

EDWARD HOAGLAND

The Courage of Turtles

TURTLES ARE A KIND OF BIRD WITH the governor turned low. With the same attitude of removal, they cock a glance at what is going on, as if they need only to fly away. Until recently they were also a case of virtue rewarded, at least in the town where I grew up, because, being humble creatures, there were plenty of them. Even when we still had a few bobcats in the woods the local snapping turtles, growing up to forty pounds, were the largest carnivores. You would see them through the amber water, as big as greeny wash basins at the bottom of the pond, until they faded into the inscrutable mud as if they hadn't existed at all.

When I was ten I went to Dr. Green's Pond, a two-acre pond across the road. When I was twelve I walked a mile or so to Taggart's Pond, which was lusher, had big water snakes and a waterfall; and shortly after that I was bicycling way up to the adventuresome vastness of Mud Pond, a lake-sized body of water in the reservoir system of a Connecticut city, possessed of cat-backed little islands and empty shacks and a forest of pines and hardwoods along the shore. Otters, foxes and mink left their prints on the bank; there were pike and perch. As I got older, the estates and forgotten back lots in town were parceled out and sold for nice prices, yet, though the woods had shrunk, it seemed that fewer people walked in the woods. The new residents didn't know how to find them. Eventually, exploring, they did find them, and it required some ingenuity and doubling around on my part to go for eight miles without meeting someone. I was grown by now, I lived in New York, and that's what I wanted on the occasional weekends when I came out.

Since Mud Pond contained drinking water I had felt confident nothing untoward would happen there. For a long while the developers stayed away, until the drought of the mid-1960s. This event, squeezing the edges in, convinced the local water company that the pond really wasn't a necessity as a catch basin, however; so they bulldozed a hole in the earthen dam, bulldozed the banks to fill in the bottom, and landscaped the flow of water that remained to wind like an English brook and provide a domestic view for the houses which were planned. Most of the painted turtles of Mud Pond, who had been inaccessible as they sunned on their rocks, wound up in boxes in boys' closets within a matter of days. Their footsteps in the dry leaves gave them away as they wandered forlornly. The snappers and the little musk turtles, neither of whom leave the water except once a year to lay their eggs, dug into the drying mud for another siege of hot weather, which they were accustomed to doing whenever the pond got low. But this time it was low for good; the mud baked over them and slowly entombed them. As for the ducks, I couldn't stroll in the woods and not feel guilty, because they were crouched beside every stagnant pothole, or were slinking between the bushes with their heads tucked into their shoulders so that I wouldn't see them. If they decided I had, they beat their way up through the screen of trees, striking their wings dangerously, and wheeled about with that headlong, magnificent velocity to locate another poor puddle.

I used to catch possums and black snakes as well as turtles, and I kept dogs and goats. Some summers I worked in a menagerie with the big personalities of the animal kingdom, like elephants and rhinoceroses. I was twenty before these enthusiasms began to wane, and it was then that I picked turtles as the particular animal I wanted to keep in touch with. I was allergic to fur, for one thing, and turtles need minimal care and not much in the way of quarters. They're personable beasts. They see the same colors we do and they seem to see just as well, as one discovers in trying to sneak up on them. In the laboratory they unravel the twists of a maze with the hot-blooded rapidity of a mammal. Though they can't run as fast as a rat, they improve on their errors just as quickly, pausing at each crossroads to look left and right. And they rock rhythmically in place, as we often do, although they are hatched from eggs, not the womb. (A common explanation psychologists give for our pleasure in rocking quietly is that it recapitulates our mother's heartbeat *in utero*.)

Snakes, by contrast, are dryly silent and priapic. They are smooth movers, legalistic, unblinking, and they afford the humor which the humorless do. But they make challenging captives; sometimes they don't eat for months on a point of order—if the light isn't right, for instance. Alligators are sticklers too. They're like war-horses, or German shepherds, and with their bar-shaped, vertical pupils adding emphasis, they have the *idée fixe* of eating, eating, even when they choose to refuse all food and stubbornly die. They delight in tossing a salamander up towards the sky and grabbing him in their long mouths as he comes down. They're so eager that they get the jitters, and they're too much of a proposition for a casual aquarium like mine. Frogs are depressingly defenseless: that moist, extensive back, with the bones almost sticking through. Hold a frog and you're holding its skeleton. Frogs' tasty legs are the staff of life to many animals—herons, raccoons, ribbon snakes—though they themselves are hard to feed.

It's not an enviable role to be the staff of life, and after frogs you descend down the evolutionary ladder a big step to fish.

Turtles cough, burp, whistle, grunt and hiss, and produce social judgments. They put their heads together amicably enough, but then one drives the other back with the suddenness of two dogs who have been conversing in tones too low for an onlooker to hear. They pee in fear when they're first caught, but exercise both pluck and optimism in trying to escape, walking for hundreds of yards within the confines of their pen, carrying the weight of that cumbersome box on legs which are cruelly positioned for walking. They don't feel that the contest is unfair; they keep plugging, rolling like sailorly souls—a bobbing, infirm gait, a brave, sea-legged momentum— stopping occasionally to study the lay of the land. For me, anyway, they manage to contain the rest of the animal world. They can stretch out their necks like a giraffe, or loom underwater like an apocryphal hippo. They browse on lettuce thrown on the water like a cow moose which is partly submerged. They have a penguin's alertness, combined with a build like a Brontosaurus when they rise up on tiptoe. Then they hunch and ponderously lunge like a grizzly going forward.

Baby turtles in a turtle bowl are a puzzle in geometrics. They're as decorative as pansy petals, but they are also self-directed building blocks, propping themselves on one another in different arrangements, before upending the tower. The timid individuals turn fearless, or vice versa. If one gets a bit arrogant he will push the others off the rock and afterwards climb down into the water and cling to the back of one of those he has bullied, tickling him with his hind feet until he bucks like a bronco. On the other hand, when this same milder-mannered fellow isn't exerting himself, he will stare right into the face of the sun for hours. What could be more lionlike? And he's at home in or out of the water and does lots of metaphysical tilting. He sinks and rises, with an infinity of levels to choose from; or, elongating himself, he climbs out on the land again to perambulate, sits boxed in his box, and finally slides back in the water, submerging into dreams.

I have five of these babies in a kidney-shaped bowl. The hatchling, who is a painted turtle, is not as large as the top joint of my thumb. He eats chicken gladly. Other foods he will attempt to eat but not with sufficient perseverance to succeed because he's so little. The yellow-bellied terrapin is probably a yearling, and he eats salad voraciously, but no meat, fish or fowl. The Cumberland terrapin won't touch salad or chicken but eats fish and all of the meats except for bacon. The little snapper, with a black crenelated shell, feasts on any kind of meat, but rejects greens and fish. The fifth of the turtles is African. I acquired him only recently and don't know him well. A mottled brown, he unnerves the green turtles, dragging their food off to his lairs. He doesn't seem to want to be green—he bites the algae off his shell, hanging meanwhile at daring, steep, head-first angles.

The snapper was a Ferdinand until I provided him with deeper water. Now he snaps at my pencil with his downturned and fearsome mouth, his swollen face like a napalm victim's. The Cumberland has an elliptical red mark on the side of his green-and-yellow head. He is benign by nature and ought to be as elegant as his scientific name *(Pseudemys scripta elegans)*, except he has contracted a disease of the air bladder which has permanently inflated it; he floats high in the water at an undignified slant and can't go under. There may have been internal bleeding, too, because his carapace is stained along its ridge. Unfortunately, like flowers, baby turtles often die. Their mouths fill up with a white fungus and their lungs with pneumonia. Their organs clog up from the rust in the water, or diet troubles, and, like a dying man's, their eyes and heads become too prominent. Toward the end, the edge of the shell becomes flabby as felt and folds around them like a shroud.

While they live they're like puppies. Although they're vivacious, they would be a bore to be with all the time, so I also have an adult wood turtle about six inches long. Her shell is the equal of any seashell for sculpturing, even a Cellini shell; it's like an old, dusty, richly engraved medallion dug out of a hillside. Her legs are salmon-orange bordered with black and protected by canted, heroic scales. Her plastron—the bottom shell—is splotched like a margay cat's coat, with black ocelli on a yellow background. It is convex to make room for the female organs inside, whereas a male's would be concave to help him fit tightly on top of her. Altogether, she exhibits every camouflage color on her limbs and shells. She has a turtleneck neck, a tail like an elephant's, wise old pachydermous hind legs and the face of a turkey—except that when I carry her she gazes at the passing ground with a hawk's eyes and mouth. Her feet fit to the fingers of my hand, one to each one, and she rides looking down. She can walk on the floor in perfect silence, but usually she lets her shell knock portentously, like a footstep, so that she resembles some grand, concise, slow-moving id. But if an earthworm is presented, she jerks swiftly ahead, poises above it and strikes like a mongoose, consuming it with wild vigor. Yet she will climb on my lap to eat bread or boiled eggs.

If put into a creek, she swims like a cutter, nosing forward to intercept a strange turtle and smell him. She drifts with the current to go downstream, maneuvering behind a rock when she wants to take stock, or sinking to the nether levels, while bubbles float up. Getting out, choosing her path, she will proceed a distance and dig into a pile of humus, thrusting herself to the coolest layer at the bottom. The hole closes over her until it's as small as a mouse's hole. She's not as aquatic as a musk turtle, not quite as terrestrial as the box turtles in the same woods, but because of her versatility she's marvelous, she's everywhere. And though she breathes the way we breathe, with scarcely perceptible movements of her chest, sometimes instead she pumps her throat ruminatively, like a pipe smoker sucking and puffing. She waits and blinks, pumping her throat, turning her head, then sets off like a loping tiger in slow motion, hurdling the jungly lumber, the pea vine and twigs. She estimates angles so well that when she rides over the rocks, sliding down a drop-off with her rugged front legs extended, she has the grace of a rodeo mare.

But she's well off to be with me rather than at Mud Pond. The other turtles have fled—those that aren't baked into the bottom. Creeping up the brooks to sad, constricted marshes, burdened as they are with that box on their backs, they're walking into a setup where all their enemies move thirty times faster than they. It's like the nightmare most of us have whimpered through, where we are weighted down disastrously while trying to flee; fleeing our home ground, we try to run.

I've seen turtles in still worse straits. On Broadway, in New York, there is a penny arcade which used to sell baby terrapins that were scrawled with bon mots in enamel paint, such as KISS ME BABY. The manager turned out to be a wholesaler as well, and once I asked him whether he had any larger turtles to sell. He took me upstairs to a loft room devoted to the turtle business. There were desks for the paper work and a series of racks that held shallow tin bins atop one another, each with several hundred babies crawling around in it. He was a smudgy-complexioned, serious fellow and he did have a few adult terrapins, but I was going to school and wasn't actually planning to buy; I'd only wanted to see them. They were aquatic turtles, but here they went without water, presumably for weeks, lurching about in those dry bins like handicapped citizens, living on gumption. An easel where the artist worked stood in the middle of the floor. She had a palette and a clip attachment for fastening the babies in place. She wore a smock and a beret, and was homely, short and eccentric-looking, with funny black hair, like some of the ladies who show their paintings in Washington Square in May. She had a cold, she was smoking, and her hand wasn't very steady, although she worked quickly enough. The smile that she produced for me would have looked giddy if she had been happier, or drunk. Of course the turtles' doom was sealed when she painted them, because their bodies inside would continue to grow but their shells would not. Gradually, invisibly, they would be crushed. Around us their bellies—two thousand belly shells—rubbed on the bins with a mournful, momentous hiss.

Somehow there were so many of them I didn't rescue one. Years later, however, I was walking on First Avenue when I noticed a basket of living turtles in front of a fish store. They were as dry as a heap of old bones in the sun; nevertheless, they were creeping over one another gimpily, doing their best to escape. I looked and was touched to discover that they appeared to be wood turtles, my favorites, so I bought one. In my apartment I looked closer and realized that in fact this was a diamond-back terrapin, which was bad news. Diamond-backs are tidewater turtles from brackish estuaries, and I had no sea water to keep him in. He spent his days thumping interminably against the baseboards, pushing for an opening through the wall. He drank thirstily but would not eat and had none of the hearty, accepting qualities of wood turtles. He was morose, paler in color, sleeker and more Oriental in the carved ridges and rings that formed his shell. Though I felt sorry for him, finally I found his unrelenting presence exasperating. I carried him, struggling in a paper bag, across town to the Morton Street Pier on the Hudson. It was August but gray and windy. He was very surprised when I tossed him in; for the first time in our association, I think, he was afraid. He looked afraid as he bobbed about on top of the water, looking up at me from ten feet below. Though we were both accustomed to his resistance and rigidity, seeing him still pitiful, I recognized that I must have done the wrong thing. At least the river was salty, but it was also bottomless; the waves were too rough for him, and the tide was coming in, bumping him against the pilings underneath the pier. Too late, I realized that he wouldn't be able to swim to a peaceful inlet in New Jersey, even if he could figure out which way to swim. But since, short of diving in after him, there was nothing I could do, I walked away.

[1968]

ACKNOWLEDGMENTS (CONT'D)

Excerpt from "Shakespeare's Sister" and "The Shadow across the Page" from *A Room of One's Own* by Virginia Woolf, copyright 1929 by Harcourt Brace & Company and renewed 1957 by Leonard Woolf, reprinted by permission of the publisher.

Excerpt from "A Sketch of the Past" in *Moments of Being* by Virginia Woolf, copyright © 1976 by Quentin Bell and Angelica Garnett, reprinted by permission of Harcourt Brace & Company, the Executors of the Virginia Woolf Estate, and The Hogarth Press.

"Shooting an Elephant" and "A Hanging" from *Shooting an Elephant and Other Essays* by George Orwell, copyright 1950 by Sonia Brownell Orwell and renewed 1978 by Sonia Pitt-Rivers, reprinted by permission of Harcourt Brace & Company, and the estate of the late Sonia Brownell Orwell and Martin Secker & Warburg Ltd.

"Marrakech" and "Why I Write" from *Such, Such Were the Joys* by George Orwell, copyright 1953 by Sonia Brownell Orwell and renewed 1981 by Mrs. George K. Perutz, Mrs. Miriam Gross, Dr. Michael Dickson, Executors of the Estate of Sonia Brownell Orwell, reprinted by permission of Harcourt Brace & Company, and the estate of the late Sonia Brownell Orwell and Martin Secker & Warburg Ltd.

"Politics and the English Language" by George Orwell, copyright 1946 by Sonia Brownell Orwell and renewed 1974 by Sonia Orwell, reprinted from his volume *Shooting an Elephant and Other Essays* by permission of Harcourt Brace & Company, and the estate of the late Sonia Brownell Orwell and Martin Secker & Warburg Ltd.

All pages from "Once More to the Lake" from *One Man's Meat* by E. B. White. Copyright 1941 by E. B. White. Reprinted by permission of HarperCollins Publishers, Inc.

All pages from "Death of a Pig" from *The Second Tree from the Corner* by E. B. White. Copyright 1947 by E. B. White. Copyright renewed. First appeared in *Atlantic Monthly.* Reprinted by permission of HarperCollins Publishers, Inc.

All pages from "On a Florida Key" from *One Man's Meat* by E. B. White. Copyright 1941 by E. B. White. Copyright renewed. First appeared in *Harper's Magazine.* Reprinted by permission of HarperCollins Publishers, Inc.

All pages from "The Ring of Time" from *The Points of My Compass* by E. B. White. Copyright © 1956 by E. B. White. Originally appeared in *The New Yorker.* Reprinted by permission of HarperCollins Publishers, Inc.

All pages from "Walden" from *One Man's Meat* by E. B. White. Copyright 1939 by E. B. White. Copyright renewed 1967 by E. B. White. Reprinted by permission of HarperCollins Publishers, Inc.

"Notes of a Native Son," "Stranger in the Village," and "Equal in Paris" from *Notes of a Native Son* by James Baldwin. Copyright © 1955, renewed 1983 by James Baldwin. Reprinted by permission of Beacon Press.

"Here Be Dragons" © 1985 by James Baldwin. Originally published as "Freaks and the American Ideal of Manhood" in *Playboy,* January 1985. Collected in *The Price of the Ticket,* published by St. Martin's Press. Reprinted by permission of the James Baldwin Estate.

"Goodbye to All That," "On Going Home," "On Morality," and "John Wayne: A Love Song" from *Slouching Toward Bethlehem* by Joan Didion. Copyright © 1965, 1967, 1968 by Joan Didion. Reprinted by permission of Farrar, Straus & Giroux, Inc.

"Why I Write" by Joan Didion. Copyright © 1976 by Joan Didion. First appeared in the *New York Times Book Review.* Reprinted by permission of Joan Didion.

"A Night Stand," © 1960, 1983, by James McConkey. Originally published in *Perspective.* Published in *Court of Memory,* E. P. Dutton, 1983, David R. Godine, 1993.

"The Bullfrog Pond," © 1979, 1983, by James McConkey. Originally published in *The New Yorker.* Published in *Court of Memory,* E. P. Dutton, 1983, David R. Godine, 1993.

"Passages Early and Late," © 1978, 1983, by James McConkey. Originally published in *The Hudson Review.* Published in *Court of Memory,* E. P. Dutton, 1983, David R. Godine, 1993.

"A Family Record," © 1985, 1993, by James McConkey. Originally published in *The New Yorker.* Published in *Stories from My Life with the Other Animals,* David R. Godine, 1993.

"Washington Square, 1946," "The Seam of the Snail," and "On Permission to Write" from *Metaphor and Memory* by Cynthia Ozick. Copyright © 1989 by Cynthia Ozick. Reprinted by permission of Alfred A. Knopf, Inc.

"A Drugstore in Winter" from *Art & Ardor* by Cynthia Ozick. Copyright © 1983 by Cynthia Ozick. Reprinted by permission of Alfred A. Knopf, Inc.

"Brothers and Sisters" from *In Search of Our Mothers' Gardens: Womanist Prose,* copyright © 1975 by Alice Walker, reprinted by permission of Harcourt Brace & Company.

"Beauty: When the Other Dancer Is the Self" from *In Search of Our Mothers' Gardens: Womanist Prose,* copyright © 1983 by Alice Walker, reprinted by permission of Harcourt Brace & Company.

"In Search of Our Mothers' Gardens" from *In Search of Our Mothers' Gardens: Womanist Prose,* copyright © 1974 by Alice Walker, reprinted by permission of Harcourt Brace & Company.

"Women" from *Revolutionary Petunias & Other Poems,* copyright © 1970 by Alice Walker, reprinted by permission of Harcourt Brace & Company.

"Journey to Nine Miles" from *Living by the Word: Selected Writings 1973–1987,* copyright © 1986 by Alice Walker, reprinted by permission of Harcourt Brace & Company.

"A Relic" from *And Even Now* by Max Beerbohm, copyright 1921, 1949. Reprinted by permission of Mrs. Eva Reichmann.